Rural Tourism and Sustainable Business

D1471899

ASPECTS OF TOURISM

Series Editors: Professor Chris Cooper, *University of Queensland, Australia*
Dr C. Michael Hall, *University of Otago, Dunedin, New Zealand*
Dr Dallen Timothy, *Arizona State University, Tempe, USA*

Aspects of Tourism is an innovative, multifaceted series which will comprise authoritative reference handbooks on global tourism regions, research volumes, texts and monographs. It is designed to provide readers with the latest thinking on tourism world-wide and in so doing will push back the frontiers of tourism knowledge. The series will also introduce a new generation of international tourism authors, writing on leading edge topics. The volumes will be readable and user-friendly, providing accessible sources for further research. The list will be underpinned by an annual authoritative tourism research volume. Books in the series will be commissioned that probe the relationship between tourism and cognate subject areas such as strategy, development, retailing, sport and environmental studies. The publisher and series editors welcome proposals from writers with projects on these topics.

Other Books in the Series
Recreational Tourism: Demand and Impacts
  Chris Ryan
Coastal Mass Tourism: Diversification and Sustainable Development in Southern Europe
  Bill Bramwell (ed.)
Sport Tourism Development
  Thomas Hinch and James Higham
Sport Tourism: Interrelationships, Impact and Issues
  Brent Ritchie and Daryl Adair (eds)
Tourism, Mobility and Second Homes
  C. Michael Hall and Dieter Müller
Strategic Management for Tourism Communities: Bridging the Gaps
  Peter E. Murphy and Ann E. Murphy
Oceania: A Tourism Handbook
  Chris Cooper and C. Michael Hall (eds)
Tourism Marketing: A Collaborative Approach
  Alan Fyall and Brian Garrod
Music and Tourism: On the Road Again
  Chris Gibson and John Connell
Tourism Development: Issues for a Vulnerable Industry
  Julio Aramberri and Richard Butler (eds)
Nature-Based Tourism in Peripheral Areas: Development or Disaster?
  C. Michael Hall and Stephen Boyd (eds)
Tourism, Recreation and Climate Change
  C. Michael Hall and James Higham (eds)
Shopping Tourism, Retailing and Leisure
  Dallen J. Timothy
Wildlife Tourism
  David Newsome, Ross Dowling and Susan Moore
Film-Induced Tourism
  Sue Beeton

For more details of these or any other of our publications, please contact:
Channel View Publications, Frankfurt Lodge, Clevedon Hall,
Victoria Road, Clevedon, BS21 7HH, England
http://www.channelviewpublications.com

ASPECTS OF TOURISM 26
Series Editors: Chris Cooper (*University of Queensland, Australia*),
C. Michael Hall (*University of Otago, New Zealand*)
and Dallen Timothy (*Arizona State University, USA*)

Rural Tourism and Sustainable Business

Edited by
Derek Hall, Irene Kirkpatrick
and Morag Mitchell

CHANNEL VIEW PUBLICATIONS
Clevedon • Buffalo • Toronto

Library of Congress Cataloging in Publication Data
Rural Tourism and Sustainable Business/Edited by Derek Hall, Irene Kirkpatrick and Morag Mitchell.
Aspects of Tourism: 26
Includes bibliographical references and index.
1. Tourism. 2. Rural development. I. Hall, Derek R. II. Kirkpatrick, Irene.
III. Mitchell, Morag. IV. Series.
G155.A1R84 2004
338.4'791'091734–dc22   2004026438

British Library Cataloguing in Publication Data
A catalogue entry for this book is available from the British Library.

ISBN 1-84541-012-2 (hbk)
ISBN 1-84541-011-4 (pbk)

Channel View Publications
An imprint of Multilingual Matters Ltd

UK: Frankfurt Lodge, Clevedon Hall, Victoria Road, Clevedon BS21 7HH.
USA: 2250 Military Road, Tonawanda, NY 14150, USA.
Canada: 5201 Dufferin Street, North York, Ontario, Canada M3H 5T8.

Typeset by Techset Ltd.
Printed and bound in Great Britain by the Cromwell Press.

Contents

Preface

This volume contributes both to a continuing debate on the nature and role of rural tourism, and towards filling a gap in the accessible literature on tourism business and sustainability. The importance of rural tourism and recreation and its role within rural development processes has never been more self-evident, and there is a clear need in many countries for an acknowledgement of this and of appropriate policy integration in order to sustain rural tourism businesses and the environments in which they operate. It is often the case that small-scale rural tourism businesses find it more difficult to sustain themselves than those of other sectors or contexts.

Warmest thanks are therefore extended to all the contributors to this volume for providing a stimulating range and balance of expertise, enthusiasm and reflection upon rural tourism and sustainable business in the chapters that follow. We have been able to draw on experience from Austria, Canada, Finland, Ireland, Jamaica, New Zealand, Spain, Taiwan and the United States, as well as from Britain – from Cornwall in southwest England to western Wales and northeast Scotland. We also thank our editorial and production colleagues at Channel View who have encouraged and supported this publication.

When this book was conceived, all three editors were part of the Scottish Agricultural College's Leisure and Tourism Management Department. The range of contributors to this volume partly reflects the local and global partnerships and networks that the Department had forged. We therefore would like to acknowledge all those who contributed to the Department's development and strength during its eight years' existence: James Adams, Ronnie Ballantyne, Alison Beeho/Mackintosh, Moira Birtwistle, Steven Boyne, Mike Burr, Fiona Carswell, Andrew Copus, Rachel Darling, Chris Doyle, Roger Evans, Isabelle Frochot, Claire Gallagher, Joy Gladstone, Deborah Gourlay, David Grant, Jacqui Greener, David Hume, Jim Kean, Richard Kelly, Lennox Lindsay, Yvonne Loughrey, Marsaili MacLeod, Pamela Marr, Joanne McDowell, Stephen Miles, Linsey O'Hanlon/Hunter, Scott Petrie, Robert Rawlings, Lesley Roberts, Fiona Simpson, Stephen Smith, Nick Tzamarias and Fiona Williams.

Derek Hall, Irene Kirkpatrick and Morag Mitchell
Maidens, Failford and Insch
April 2004

The Contributors

David Botterill, Welsh School of Hospitality, Tourism and Leisure Management, University of Wales Institute Cardiff, Wales, UK (DBotterill@uwic.ac.uk)

Gemma Cánoves, Department of Geography, Autonomous University of Barcelona, Catalonia, Spain (gemma.canoves@uab.es)

Donna Chambers, School of Marketing and Tourism, Napier University, Edinburgh, Scotland, UK (D.Chambers@napier.ac.uk)

Jackie Clarke, The Business School, Oxford Brookes University, Oxford, England, UK (jrclarke@brookes.ac.uk)

Andrew Copus, Research Division, SAC Aberdeen, Scotland, UK (andrew.copus@sac.ac.uk)

Kaja Curry, Tourism Development Manager, Caradon District Council, Cornwall, England, UK (Kcurry@caradon.gov.uk)

Stephen Essex, School of Geography, University of Plymouth, England, UK (sessex@plymouth.ac.uk)

Graeme Evans, Cities Institute, London Metropolitan University, England, UK (g.evans@londonmet.ac.uk)

Catherine Gorman, School of Hospitality and Tourism Management, Dublin Institute of Technology, Dublin, Ireland (catherine.gorman@dit.ie)

Wanda George, Department of Business Administration, Tourism and Hospitality Management, Mount Saint Vincent University, Halifax Nova Scotia, Canada (Wanda.George@msvu.ca)

C. Michael Hall, Department of Tourism, University of Otago, Dunedin, New Zealand (CMHall@business.otago.ac.nz)

Derek Hall, Visiting Professor, Häme Polytechnic, Mustiala, Finland, and Seabank Associates, Maidens, Ayrshire, Scotland, UK (derekhall. seabank@virgin.net)

Irene Kirkpatrick, formerly Administrator, Leisure and Tourism Management Department, SAC Ayr, UK (imkirkpatrick@aol.com)

Ming-Huang Lee, Farmers' Service Department, Council of Agriculture, Taipei, Taiwan (mhlee@mail.coa.gov.tw)

David Leslie, Glasgow Caledonian University, Glasgow, Scotland, UK (D.Leslie@gcal.ac.uk)

Heather Mair, Department of Recreation and Leisure Studies, University of Waterloo, Ontario, Canada (hmair@uwaterloo.ca)

Kim Meyer-Cech, Department of Spatial, Landscape and Infrastructure Sciences, University of Natural Resources and Applied Life Sciences, Vienna, Austria (kim.meyer-cech@boku.ac.at)

Morag Mitchell, Research Division, SAC Aberdeen, Scotland, UK (morag.mitchell@sac.ac.uk)

Cliff Nelson, Town and Resort Manager, Vale of Glamorgan Council, and University of Wales Institute Cardiff, Wales, UK (CNelson@valeofglamorgan.gov.uk)

Mirja Nylander, former Secretary General, Rural Tourism Working Group, Government of Finland (mirja@hinku.com)

Paola Parravicini, International Institute for Culture, Tourism and Development, London Metropolitan University, England, UK (p.parravicini@londonmet.ac.uk)

Gerda K. Priestley, Department of Geography, Autonomous University of Barcelona, Catalonia, Spain (gerda.priestley@campus.uab.es)

Donald G. Reid, School of Environmental Design and Rural Development, University of Guelph, Ontario, Canada (dreid@rpd.uoguelph.ca)

Walter Schiebel, Institute for Marketing and Innovation, University of Natural Resources and Applied Life Sciences, Vienna, Austria (walter.schiebel@boku.ac.at)

Miquel Seguí, Department of Earth Sciences, University of the Balearic Islands, Spain (miquel.segui@uib.es)

Dallen J. Timothy, School of Community Resources and Development, Arizona State University, Tempe, Arizona, USA (Dallen.Timothy@asu.edu)

Jon Vernon, North Devon and Exmoor Regeneration Company, England, UK (jon@ndexreg.co.uk)

Montserrat Villarino, Department of Geography, University of Santiago de Compostela, Spain (xemontse@usc.es)

Fiona Williams, Research Division, SAC Aberdeen, Scotland, UK (fiona.williams@sac.ac.uk)

Roz Wornell, Institute of Rural Sciences, University of Wales, Aberystwyth, UK (rsw@aber.ac.uk)

Ray Youell, Institute of Rural Sciences, University of Wales, Aberystwyth, UK (ray@aber.ac.uk)

Abbreviations

€	Euro
ACP	African, Caribbean and Pacific
AECL	Atomic Energy of Canada Limited
AFHO	Austrian Farm Holidays Organisation
AIRE	Association of Irish Riding Establishments
AONB	Area of Outstanding Natural Beauty
AsPIRE	Aspatial Peripherality, Innovation and the Rural Economy
B&B	bed and breakfast
BMLF	Federal Ministry of Agriculture and Forestry (Austria)
BMLFUW	Federal Ministry of Agriculture, Forestry, Environment and Water Management
bn	billion
BOCAIB	*Boletin Oficial de les Illes Balears*
BTA	British Tourism Authority
CA	Countryside Agency (England and Wales)
CAP	Common Agricultural Policy
CCW	Countryside Council for Wales
CEE	Central and Eastern Europe
CerTWG	Ceredigion Tourism Working Group
CNATA	Canadian National Aboriginal Tourism Association
COA	Council of Agriculture
CRS	computer reservation systems
CTB	Cumbria Tourist Board
CTC	Canadian Tourism Commission
DCMS	Department for Culture, Media and Sport (England)
DEFRA	Department of the Environment, Food and Rural Affairs
DETR	Department of Environment, Transport and the Regions
DFID	Department for International Development
DMS	destination marketing systems
DoE	Department of Environment
DoTI	Department of Trade and Industry
DOGA	*Diario Oficial de Galicia*
DOGC	*Diari Oficial de la Generalitat de Catalunya*

EC	European Commission/European Community
ECEAT	European Centre for Eco-Agro Tourism
EDG	Employment Department Group
EMAS	Eco-Management and Audit Scheme
EMS	environmental management system
ERDF	European Regional Development Fund
ETB	English Tourist Board
ETC	English Tourism Council
EU	European Union
EUCC	European Union for Coastal Conservation
FA	Farmers Association
FEE	Federation for Environmental Education
FEEE	Foundation for Environmental Education in Europe
GCA	Green Coast Award
GDP	gross domestic product
GNP	gross national product
GSI	Green Seas Initiative
ha	hectare
HCIMA	Hotel, Catering & International Management Association
HIE	Highlands and Islands Enterprise (Scotland)
ICH	Irish Country Holidays
ICT	information and communications technology
IFES	Institute for Empirical Social Research
IFH	Irish Farmhouse Holidays
IGRA	Indian Gambling Regulatory Act
IHEI	International Hotels Environment Initiative
INE	Instituto Nacional de Estadística (Spain)
IQM	Integrated Quality Management
IST	information society technologies
IT	information technology
KFS	key factors for success
LAP	local action plan
LEADER	EU funded programme for community-based rural development
LDNP	Lake District National Park
MICE	meetings, incentives, conventions and exhibitions
mn	million
MTA	Malta Tourism Authority

NGO	Non-Governmental Organisation
NRTF	National Rural Tourism Foundation
NTOM	National Tourism Organisation of Montenegro
NTOS	National Tourism Organisation of Serbia
OECD	Organisation for Economic Co-operation and Development
OQFD	Orkney Quality Food and Drink
ÖSTAT	Austrian National Statistical Office
PF	personality factor
PHARE	Pologne Hongarie Assistance à la Reconstruction des Economies
PMG	product marketing grouping
PRC	Policy and Resources Committee, Jersey
PYO	pick-your-own
RDC	Rural Development Commission (England and Wales)
RTC	Rails-to-Trails Conservancy
SAC	The Scottish Agricultural College
SEE	south-eastern Europe
SL	sustainable livelihoods
SME	small- and/or medium-sized enterprise
SMTE	small- and/or medium-sized tourism enterprise
SPICe	Scottish Parliament Information Centre
SSSI	Sites of Special Scientific Interest
TBG	Tidy Britain Group
TCP	Tourism and Conservation Partnership
TGA	tourism growth area
TIA	Travel Industry Association (of America)
TIC	tourist information centre
TIL	Tourism Ireland Limited
TMI	Tourism Management Institute
TPDCo	Tourism Product Development Company
TQM	Total Quality Management
TSV	tourist shopping village
TTWA	travel to work area
UK	United Kingdom (of Great Britain and Northern Ireland)
UNEP/IE	United Nations Environment Programme, Industry and Environment
URL	universal resource locator
USA	United States of America

VFR	visiting friends and relatives
WAG	Welsh Assembly Government
WDA	Welsh Development Agency
WTB	Wales Tourist Board
WTO	World Tourism Organisation
WTTC	World Travel and Tourism Council
WWOOF	Willing Workers on Organic Farms organisation
www	worldwide web

Part 1
Introduction

Chapter 1

Rural Tourism as Sustainable Business: Key Themes and Issues

MORAG MITCHELL and DEREK HALL

Introduction

For this volume, the editors approached specialist contributors who could add to the debate on rural tourism within the context of sustainable business development. For many countries around the world, this is the crucial next step for the rural tourism industries. The industry has been populated with thousands of small- and medium-sized enterprises (SMEs). It is estimated that more than two-and-a-half million SMEs are involved in the tourism industry in Europe (e.g. Middleton, 2001) with 81.5% of these actually falling into the *micro* category. The EU tourism industry is dominated by SMEs employing on average six people. Elsewhere in the world we find that:

- 99% of all tourism-related establishments in rural areas in the USA qualify as small businesses (Galston & Baehler, 1995);
- in New Zealand, the tourism industry is estimated to consist of between 13,500 and 18,000 SMEs (TIA, 2001); and
- in Israel, almost all rural tourism businesses are classified as small and family based, with 95% of those in the accommodation sector employing less than three people (Fleischer *et al.*, 1993).

A positive aspect of this industry structure is that tourism is one of the most labour-intensive industries, so it has the potential to contribute towards job creation and economic development in rural areas, and indeed, is often seen as the linchpin in many rural development strategies (Briedenhann & Wickens, 2004; Fleischer & Felsenstien, 2000; Roberts & Hall, 2001). Negatively, however, there has been a tendency for businesses to develop in an *ad hoc* manner, with little or no meaningful strategy addressing the issue of sustainability, either from an environmental or marketing perspective. This has resulted in the emergence of rural tourism products that have not taken due consideration of environmental impact, demand conditions, competition, or supply side considerations.

Some of the examples presented in this book illustrate these issues and they address many of the structural and product problems facing rural tourism providers. Such problems include:

- lack of concern with and knowledge of demand factors;
- lack of skills with regard to product presentation;
- limited knowledge of the markets they work within; and
- limited development of cooperation and marketing networks (Jenkins & Parrott, 1997).

Key Themes and Issues

If rural tourism is to continue fulfilling expectations that it can contribute to the rural development process and emerge as an industry of sustainable, growing businesses, it must identify and meet the challenges facing it. Four are particularly critical, as given in the following.

Competition

There are signals that the competitive success of some destinations is declining and they are losing what previously had been assumed to be a sustainable market advantage (EC, 2002; Petrić, 2003). 'Some regional environments seem to be more stimulating to economic progress and success than others' (Jenkins & Parrott, 1997: 7) and the continuous emergence of new competitors means that these destinations must monitor their competitive strategies. This needs to be done at a regional planning level as well as by individual providers taking notice of product differentiation, quality, and knowledge of changing markets. It also requires a process of continual restructuring if tourism providers are to maintain any competitive advantage (Vera Rebollo & Ivars Baidal, 2004).

Marketing

Marketing is especially required in a climate where average tourist expenditure is declining and tourism is facing some negative publicity issues including images of environmental degradation and the physical deterioration of some heritage and cultural sites (EC, 2002). Marketing is often viewed as a weak link in rural diversification and development processes, but it can be used to counteract these images, especially in the context of rural tourism.

Many tourism providers seek to develop niche markets for their products, hoping that product differentiation will give them an advantage over their competitors, allowing them to increase their market share (OECD, 1995). However, to be successful, a product differentiation strategy must reach the consumers, and this is where successful marketing is crucial. Market segmentation is another strategy whereby tourism operators may seek to meet particular demands, for example, dance festivals. Several studies have used different forms of conjoint analysis (Green & Srinivasan, 1978; Hong *et al.*, 2003; Wittink *et al.*, 1994) or cluster analysis (Arimond *et al.*, 2003) to identify market segment characteristics, which can then be used to refine a marketing strategy.

Few mainstream marketing texts mention sustainability *per se*, but they do provide insights into such issues as:

- an awareness of customer expectations;
- knowledge of the competition;
- exploitation of any market advantage or opportunity to develop niche/local products;
- market segmentation; and
- advertising and promotion strategies, including the use of internet and communication technologies (ICT),

all of which, if tackled properly, contribute to business sustainability (Middleton, 1989; Middleton & Clarke, 2001; Witt & Moutinho, 1995). Part 2 of this book looks at these issues, and Chapter 5 offers some practical advice on how to capitalise on the marketing process.

Cooperation and networking

The very essence of rural tourism is local cooperation and community involvement through appropriate forms of networking, arguably one of the most important requirements for the sustainability of rural tourism (Caalders, 2002; Petrić, 2003; Tinsley & Lynch, 2001). Community participation and the formation of partnerships that contribute to, and participate in, the development process, are the basic building blocks of this process (Goodwin, 2003; Oliver & Jenkins, 2003). Heritage or cultural aspects of an area may well contribute to its uniqueness and provide the opportunity to attract segmented markets. However, to gain best advantage, local providers, including those supplying accommodation, food and attractions, must work together to gain synergies from complementarity. Part 3 of the book looks at the benefits and problems of creating successful networks, and Chapter 17 includes a discussion of the 'soft factors' that can contribute to this process.

This issue is clearly linked to marketing strategies, and highlights the need for dialogue and training among those involved. Cooperation and building business networks also allows for the organic growth of tourism products in an area, increasing the chances of long-term sustainability and the attraction of investment into the area. Networking can also help to avoid conflicts arising between producers, institutions and local residents. Briedenhann and Wickens (2004) argue that the clustering of activities and attractions and the development of rural tourism routes stimulates cooperation and partnerships between local areas. Meaningful participation, together with public sector support, presents opportunities for the development of small-scale indigenous tourism products.

Globalisation

The impacts and significance of globalisation for rural tourism businesses can be considered from different perspectives (e.g. Teo, 2002). First, there is the increase in global travel and the number of tourists looking for individually tailored products. This growth has suffered some recent setbacks, affected by factors outside the control of the industry, such as wars, epidemics, climatic and political instability, and exchange rate fluctuations (Gonzalez, 2002). Some tourists are turning away from package holidays, and with the increased demand for *à la carte* holidays, opportunities open up for rural tourism products that may be seen – rightly or wrongly – as a more natural, sustainable option, protected to some extent from global contamination (EC, 2002). However, ironically, the tourists looking for and organising these individual packages will mainly expect to be able to do so through linked sites on the Internet, especially for reserving travel and accommodation and gathering information. Responding to this customer demand requires even the smallest provider to enter the global market if it is to continue to maintain its market share, let alone grow. This leaves tourism operators with several dilemmas regarding the best strategy for product development, such as:

- whether to respond to the global consumer, if such an animal exists (Seaton & Alford, 2001);
- how far globalisation is allowed to erode cultural and ethnic diversity (Blench, 2001); and
- whether rural tourism can provide nations with a competitive advantage (Wahab & Cooper, 2001).

This discussion touches on some of the factors facing rural businesses and the need to address seriously such issues as competition, horizontal and vertical linkages, and the need to adopt technological innovations. In addressing these, rural tourism businesses also need to move away from the perception that tourism provides mostly low-waged, low-skilled employment, into an arena where there is recognition of the benefits of attracting skilled entrepreneurs and staff, who can contribute towards the sustainable growth and profitability of the sector and the businesses within it.

Developing a Business Strategy

It may be difficult for SMEs to have access to the resources needed to respond to some of the trends and developments outlined above. They may start from the position that they can offer niche products and specialisms that large producers cannot, but SMEs face the problem of lacking the resources to engage in training, marketing and ICT, all of which are required to compete and maintain customers. Networking and cooperation, linking into promoting local packages and services, and playing a part in the overall development process can help this.

In terms of managing sustainable businesses, managers do not have to reinvent the wheel. Small- and medium-sized enterprises in all sectors have been in existence for a great number of years and have gained valuable experience that can be passed on. Innovation requires investment and a willingness to move on from traditional business practices. The European Commission has recognised that SMEs contribute significantly to the achievement of community objectives in terms of competitiveness, research, innovation, skills, and employment, while facing particular problems (e.g. EC, 2000).

In response to this, the EU has adopted a strategy of integrating sustainable development into its enterprise policy. Similar actions have also been launched within the policy framework of the Organisation for Economic Co-operation and Development (OECD), aimed at improving the financial situation of innovative companies by redirecting finance towards support for new business start-ups, high-tech firms and microenterprises (EC, 2002). Clearly, from a policy perspective there is a commitment to helping small enterprises be part of the sustainable development process, and tourism businesses must take advantage of these opportunities.

The Book that Follows

Part 2 of this book gives examples of how the policy contexts within which tourism businesses operate affect the strategic decisions they make. Chapter 2 provides a useful policy context within which the following chapters based on European research may be placed. It brings out the fragmented nature of EU rural tourism policy, which may be as a result of confusion about the role rural tourism plays within the wider issue of rural development. Mirja Nylander and Derek Hall draw comparisons between what a comprehensive rural policy could include and what is in place in different countries. They argue that, given EU enlargement and the important role it plays in economic development, rural tourism should be more at the forefront of the policy agenda and support mechanisms, so that it is ready to meet the challenges it faces.

In Chapter 3, Dallen Timothy identifies some interesting trends in rural tourism operations in North America. Being forced to diversify because of rising levels of unemployment, rural businesses have turned to tourism and to the service industries, including gambling, festivals, tourist shopping villages, and outdoor and nature-based activities. These developments have management and policy implications, and the challenges faced by operators in achieving sustainable enterprises are identified. These include environmental pressures such as coping with a large influx of numbers; the problems of identifying finance and investment, especially in poorer areas; overcoming a lack of experience and training; and working through a system of fragmented policies at all levels.

Chapter 4 examines the particular strategic decisions accommodation providers in the communities of Navarra in Spain have to make within a legislative process which reflects the immense heterogeneity of types of accommodation available and the cultural and linguistic variations within the region. Rural tourism in the area is growing rapidly and the accommodation sector needs to offer a clearly defined, well-structured, quality product if it is to attract custom, but not at the expense of jeopardising the landscape upon which it relies.

Effective marketing is the subject tackled by Jackie Clarke in Chapter 5. It draws upon her considerable experience in this field to identify the issues influencing marketing in rural tourism, and culminates in a useful checklist of propositions and questions for rural tourism providers. Questions are asked about the context within which rural tourism is marketed, a context hampered by a lack of good information on the rural tourism market. She argues that information and communications technology (ICT) can reduce the effects of remoteness, but stresses that attention must be paid to the depth and quality of linkages among providers and policy makers, a theme pursued later in Part 3 of the volume. To be successful, areas must develop portfolios of attractions, promoting an identifiable brand with which they can generate higher profit margins.

Chapter 6 follows on with a discussion related particularly to ICT and what it offers rural businesses combating the domination of global operators. Rural tourism is seen as a prime sector for economic development in the Aragon region of Spain, but a below average use of ICT, particularly in less developed areas, may limit marketing opportunities. Small- and medium-sized enterprises and micro-enterprises must build up strong interfirm relations before they can realise the full benefits of marketing, and failure to do so may result in widening inequalities between core and peripheral areas in terms of economic development. However, there are encouraging signs of increasing uptake, which can be encouraged by investment, a degree of clustering, and the provision of training.

The specific themes of networks, partnerships and community support beginning to emerge in the first part form the basis of Part 3. In Chapter 7, Catherine Gorman assesses whether cooperation can solve the problems faced by the Irish rural accommodation sector. The Small and Medium Sized Accommodation Marketing Initiative was launched to improve the marketing and competitive capabilities of the smaller accommodation enterprises that operate in a market whose fragmentation is characterised by its part-time nature, irregular profit margins, and a lack of coordination. Three case studies are employed to identify how some of these problems may be alleviated, the primary focus being cooperation. Although there have been mixed outcomes, there is optimism that in the future a vision for rural tourism in Ireland will be developed, based on promoting a quality product.

Similar challenges are facing theme trails in Austria, discussed in Chapter 8. Here the establishment of trails is helping to develop networks of regional attractions, emphasising the importance of marketing, the networking of actors, and the formation of partnerships. Kim Meyer-Cech analyses the organisational structures of some of the trails, and finds that producing a quality product successfully depended on promoting the special features of the region, preserving the cultural landscape, cooperation, self-confidence, the coordination of professional management structures, and a system of quality standards.

In Chapter 9, Michael Hall discusses the importance of wine and food tourism clusters and networks in the economic development of rural areas in New Zealand. He outlines the benefits that may arise from improved economic linkages between tourism and food production and identifies the components that may yield success. It is emphasised, however, that sustained economic development can only be attained by extending beyond tourism networks to encompass broader intersectoral linkages, forming clusters. This development requires the services of a 'local champion', without whom the benefits of increased intellectual capital, innovation capacity, and economic growth will not be realised.

Chapter 10 uses evidence from a three-year research project in rural Canada to study the issue of community power in areas looking to tourism to lead their economic development, within an overarching context of globalisation. It is argued that free-market, international agreements threaten government sovereignty and capacity to support small industries, but a strong community-based tourism development process can resist homogenisation and hold on to its power base. This process is by no means easy, and tourism development can bring its own problems such as overcrowding, pollution and traffic congestion, leading to frustration and a sense of exclusion. However, the authors argue that community participation is part of the product development process, alongside such issues as supply and demand. They have developed a manual that can advise communities looking towards tourism as a means of rural development, resulting in positive participation, which in itself contributes to the long-term sustainability of development.

In an attempt to develop more sustainable tourism activities, the Jamaican government has produced a Master Plan for Sustainable Tourism Development, to promote a viable alternative to traditional mass tourism. Chapter 11 follows one of the themes identified for tourism development, that of promoting the rich culture and heritage of the rural Maroon communities. Donna Chambers poses questions about the quality of participation of the members of these remote settlements in the development process, and indeed whether tourism is a viable option for the development of remote, relatively isolated communities. In areas of economic decline where there are few alternatives, cultural rural tourism may be seen as a lifeline, and in one of the villages studied this was the case. However, the lack of universal support for these developments must be recognised and addressed by planners, and development strategies must be adjusted to local conditions. It is only through the creation of sustainable partnerships of all concerned that cultural tourism can be seen as a viable option, and only then if the cultural heritage upon which the development was based can survive.

Chapter 12 completes this section of the book by applying the Sustainable Livelihoods (SL) approach to an examination of agricultural tourism in Taiwan, using the example of pick-your-own (PYO) farms. Declining farm incomes and falling profit margins have forced Taiwanese farmers, like so many others, to diversify. For some, this has been undertaken by linking agriculture with tourism, making the landscape and rural resources available to tourists on the one hand, and bringing potential customers to producers on the other. The PYO development has encouraged local clusters to form, but maintaining the continued interest of farmers has been a problem except in areas where training courses and communication have led to strong local participation. Ming-Huang Lee also found that success depends upon local community involvement and on cooperation in the planning process, as well as collaboration between all stakeholders.

Part 4 offers a range of discussions on the issue of quality, a critical aspect of sustainable rural development. Ray Youell and Roz Wornell (Chapter 13) argue that Integrated Quality Management (IQM) principles should be adopted by tourism enterprises, impacting positively on how they and tourists perceive the issue of sustainability in relation to tourism. They looked at the introduction of IQM in West Wales and found that it has had beneficial results, both to businesses and visitors, in areas where communication, community participation and understanding of the basic concepts of IQM are present.

In Chapter 14, David Leslie assesses whether the implementation of an environmental management system (EMS) leads to a more balanced and sustainable approach to rural tourism by promoting the inclusion of the environmental performance of enterprises in the policy debate. However, in investigating the businesses within the Lake District National Park in the UK, he found that many were not addressing their environmental performance and that several owners/managers were not aware of the policies designed to do this. This is a worrying trend in light of increased tourist awareness of environmental issues. A heightened awareness of these issues on the part of policy makers at all levels is essential, needing to be followed through by implementation.

David Botterill and Cliff Nelson, in Chapter 15, follow on by analysing the introduction of the Green Coast Award, developed specifically for beaches in Wales. Seaside resorts have seen a marked decline in numbers, except for short-stay holidays in areas where environmental quality rather than entertainment is seen as the attraction. The authors of this chapter investigated whether consumers understood and incorporated beach awards in destination decisions and whether the performance of tourism businesses was linked to the scheme. They developed a methodology of measuring this link but their results are varied. Similar to the previous chapter, there was an absence of comprehensive understanding of the scheme and a lack of awareness of the link between tourist business performance and customer satisfaction in relation to environmental quality.

A period of structural change in Austrian agriculture has forced farmers to become more entrepreneurial in their outlook and to increase their awareness of quality issues. Chapter 16 looks at whether the personality traits necessary for this adjustment can be identified and developed in farmers, and describes a training programme designed to tackle some of these issues.

Chapter 17 discusses the local environmental factors or milieu that characterise the economic vitality of an area and its viability as a rural tourism destination. Using contrasting areas in Scotland, and moving away from a simple comparison of 'hard factors', such as resource availability and location, Fiona Williams and Andrew Copus looked at the so-called 'soft factors' that may explain diversity and sustainability in rural areas. Although such factors are elusive and difficult to quantify, they are recognised as important and act to reduce an area's vulnerability. Broadly, they include training, the pursuit of a coordinated and planned approach to development, the encouragement of cooperation and partnerships, the support of networks, and the presence of proactive development agencies.

The final chapter in Part 4 uses evidence from a study in Cornwall in the UK to investigate how far rural tourism businesses have progressed along the route of adopting sustainable practices. The authors look at how barriers to this are tackled with a view to providing advice on developing a strategy that would encourage the adoption of sustainable business practices. The results again show evidence that there was a general lack of awareness of the link between business operations and the demands of customers and their willingness to pay a premium for positive environmental practices. However, careful scrutiny starts to throw up certain patterns of adoption that can be used to develop a strategy to encourage extended use of environmental practices. This chapter provides a useful insight for anyone wishing to encourage the adoption of environmental practices, as it challenges some of the latent assumptions on this issue.

Chapter 19, as Part 5, rounds off the book with a brief summary and set of conclusions, drawing on previous studies viewing rural tourism development through a business perspective. The meanings of the individual key words in the title of this book may all be contestable. In combination, however, they represent what we hope is a stimulating, interesting and pertinent range of studies that can contribute in both principle and practice to the success of businesses involved in rural tourism and in the pursuit of its sustainability ideals.

References

Arimond, G., Achenreiner, G. and Elfessi, A. (2003) An innovative approach to tourism market segmentation research: an applied study. *Journal of Hospitality and Leisure Marketing* 10 (3/4), 25–56.

Blench, R. (2001) *Globalisation and Policies Towards Cultural Diversity.* London: Overseas Development Institute.

Briedenhann, J. and Wickens, E. (2004) Tourism routes as a tool for the economic development of rural areas – vibrant hope or impossible dream? *Tourism Management* 25, 71–79.

Caalders, J. (2002) *Rural Tourism Development: A Network Perspective.* Leiden, Netherlands: Uitgeverij Eburon.

EC (European Commission) (2000) *Agricultural Policy and Rural Development.* Brussels: European Commission.

EC (European Commission) (2002) *Early Warning System for Identifying Declining Tourist Destinations and Preventive Best Practices.* Brussels: European Commission.

Fleischer, A. and Felsenstein, D. (2000) Support for rural tourism: does it make a difference? *Annals of Tourism Research* 27 (4), 1007–24.

Fleischer, A., Roham, A. and Banin, T. (1993) *New Direction in Recreation and Tourism Activities in the Rural Sector in Israel: Demand and Supply Factors.* Rehovot, Israel: Development Study Centre.

Galston, W.A. and Baehler, K.J. (1995) *Rural Development in the United States: Connecting Theory, Practice and Possibilities.* Washington, DC: Island Press.

Gonzalez, A.L. (2002) The effects of globalisation on the world tourist market. *Estudis de Turisme de Catalunya* 6 (10), 4–10.

Goodwin, H. (2003) Local community involvement in tourism around national parks: opportunities and constraints. In M. Luck and T. Kirstges (eds) *Global Ecotourism Policies and Case Studies: Perspectives and Constraints* (pp. 166–88). Clevedon, UK: Channel View Publications.

Green, P.E. and Srinivasan, V. (1978) Conjoint analysis in consumer research: issues and outlook. *Journal of Consumer Research* 5, 103–23.

Hong, S., Kim, J. and Kim, S. (2003) Implications of potential green tourism development. *Annals of Tourism Research* 30 (2), 323–41.

Jenkins, T. and Parrott, N. (1997) *Regional Images and the Promotion of Quality Products and Services in the Lagging Regions of the European Union*. Aberystwyth, UK: Welsh Institute of Rural Studies, Working Paper 4.

Middleton, V.T.C. (1989) SMEs in European tourism: the context and a proposed framework for European action. *Revue de Tourisme* 4, 29–37.

Middleton, V.T.C. (2001) The importance of micro-businesses in European tourism. In L. Roberts and D. Hall (eds) *Rural Tourism and Recreation: Principles to Practice* (pp. 197–201). Wallingford, UK: CABI Publishing.

Middleton, V.T.C. and Clarke, J. (2001) *Marketing in Travel and Tourism* (3rd edn). Oxford: Butterworth-Heinemann.

OECD (Organisation for Economic Co-operation and Development) (1995) *Niche Markets as a Rural Development Strategy*. Brussels: OECD.

Oliver, T. and Jenkins, T. (2003) Sustaining rural landscapes: the role of integrated tourism. *Landscape Research* 28 (3), 293–307.

Petrić, L. (2003) Constraints and possibilities of the rural tourism development with special emphasis on the case of Croatia. Jyväskyllä, Finland: Paper presented at the European Regional Studies Association Congress, 27–30 August.

Roberts, L. and Hall, D. (2001) *Rural Tourism and Recreation: Principles to Practice*. Wallingford, UK: CABI Publishing.

Seaton, A.V. and Alford, P. (2001) The effects of globalisation on tourism promotion. In S. Wahab and C. Cooper (eds) *Tourism in the Age of Globalisation* (pp. 97–122). London: Routledge.

Teo, P. (2002) Striking a balance for sustainable tourism: implications of the discourse on globalisation. *Journal of Sustainable Tourism* 10 (6), 459–74.

TIA (Travel Industry Association of America) (2001) *Annual Report*. Washington, DC: TIA.

Tinsley, R. and Lynch, P. (2001) Small tourism business networks and destination development. *International Journal of Hospitality Management* 20 (4), 367–78.

Vera Rebollo, J.F. and Ivars Baidal, J.A. (2004) Measuring sustainability in a mass tourist destination. In B. Bramwell (ed.) *Coastal Mass Tourism: Diversification and Sustainable Development in Southern Europe* (pp. 176–99). Clevedon, UK: Channel View Publications.

Wahab, S. and Cooper, C. (2001) *Tourism in the Age of Globalisation*. London: Routledge.

Witt, S. and Moutinho, L. (eds) (1995) *Tourism Marketing and Management Handbook*. London: Prentice Hall.

Wittink, D.R., Vriens, M. and Burhenne, W. (1994) Commercial use of conjoint analysis in Europe: results and critical reflections. *International Journal of Research in Marketing* 11, 41–52.

Part 2

Strategic Considerations

Chapter 2

Rural Tourism Policy: European Perspectives

MIRJA NYLANDER and DEREK HALL

The purpose of this chapter is essentially twofold:

- to provide a generic overview of 'policy' within which to place the debates and case study exemplifications of rural tourism business development in the chapters of subsequent sections of the book; and
- to examine the currently dynamic and somewhat fragmented nature of rural tourism policy and strategy frameworks in different parts of Europe.

Two fundamental issues underpin this perspective chapter:

- *The appropriateness or otherwise of an explicit 'rural' tourism policy or strategy within regional and national tourism development.* This in part reflects the contested nature of the appropriateness of tourism and recreational activities in particular rural places and the form it should take (Bramwell, 1994: 5), which is the result of individual and group-held values and ideologies, which may vary within and between organisations, sectors, local residents, regions and countries.
- *The emphasis, priority and role of policy in stimulating and sustaining tourism business as an integral element of rural development processes.* Until recently, policy for rural tourism has tended to be *ad hoc* and incremental as a result of both a lack of good quality information and the availability of little experience in rural tourism policy formulation and implementation (Hall & Jenkins, 1995: 4).

This chapter does not attempt to define or differentiate between policy and strategy: although the former is usually embedded within the latter, the two are often interchanged and, in a volume emphasising the real-world practicalities of rural tourism business, development and sustainability, the authors are (for once) eschewing academic niceties. Within this chapter, therefore, the term 'policy' is employed in a generic sense to embrace issues of strategy and plan implementation.

The content of tourism strategy aimed at, or including rural areas, whether an explicitly rural policy or not, will normally embrace two broad dimensions, the characteristics of which may well reflect the various values and ideologies held by actors involved in the tourism development process, such as the relationships between private and public interest, business and planning, entrepreneurial profit and visitor well-being, rural and urban, sectoral and spatial approaches. These broad dimensions are:

- structure and function; and
- relationship with place.

Structure and function emphasises the aims, objectives (or often wish-lists), actions and outcomes that relate to the structure and function of the tourism industry itself. These may include:

- products: research into, quality of, changing fashions in, and promotion of them;
- training and professionalism: raising the quality of service and adding value to industry human resources;
- markets: research into, the changing nature and demands of, and ability to respond to them;
- coordination, cooperation and integration: the development, operationalisation and sustaining of collaborative partnerships and networks, both within and between rural tourism organisations themselves, and between rural tourism and other enterprises and bodies, such as food producers or regional planners; and, not least
- the values and ideologies underlying any policy formulation process and the location of power dominant in policy implementation.

Relationship with place, while explicitly intermeshing with the structural and functional elements of the sector, is more concerned with the nature of, relationships with, and promotion of the place context within which the structure of tourism is functioning. Thus concerns here include:

- tourism's role in local and regional economic diversification and rejuvenation;
- the spatial emphasis of tourism activity, for example, an explicit shift from being concentrated along coasts to being focused on interior cultural attractions;
- the importance of local cultures, identity, representation and image; and
- issues of local resource utilisation and environmental management.

The synthesis or integration of these two dimensions – structure and function, and relationship with place – might be seen as embodying the rural tourism development process. Critical factors in the success of such a process, as conditions for successful rural tourism development, have been summarised by Heneghan (2002: 3) as a critical mass, cooperation and group development, a strategic plan, focused marketing, and education and training.

Yet there is something of a paradox here. Rural tourism is employed as a vehicle for place image and identity projection – for example through regional specialist gastronomy (e.g. Boyne *et al.*, 2002, 2003). Yet marketers argue that destination marketing and branding is becoming more difficult because of the growing range of stakeholders and activities within any given destination. Further, as Roberts and Hall (2001), amongst others, have argued, the increasing role of niche segmentation, not least in rural tourism, is focusing promotion and marketing effort on specific activities rather than on place. This reflects both the growth of 'new' more dynamic forms of rural tourism activities compared to more passive traditional ones (Butler, 1998), and the reality that rural tourists have become equally dynamic and fragmented as a definable market, rapidly changing their behaviour patterns, roles and allegiances in relation to any given destination or activity. Additionally, the activity of many tourists in rural areas may be a (relatively minor) adjunct to tourism activities in urban areas.

For rural tourism business therefore, the structure and function of process may be far more important than relationships with place. Yet it is the latter that may be of paramount importance for public sector planners and policy makers, and local residents.

Within this perspective, Roberts and Hall (2001: 70) have pointed to a number of critical factors to be addressed that would appear to shape the effectiveness and sustainability of rural tourism policy. These include:

- the oft-cited paradox of the need for effective management and planning of tourism and recreation in rural areas, but the frequent absence or poorly developed nature of strategy;
- the importance of integration, both vertical and horizontal, between the various stakeholders and strategic bodies with an active interest and role in policy formulation;
- the need for integrated thinking and actions in terms of the way in which tourism and recreation are managed within processes of rural development; and
- the requirement for planning and management to recognise and respond to the fact that much rural tourism activity may be mass rather than niche in character, with consequent impacts.

Taking this further, we offer three simple diagrams to suggest ways in which to conceptualise rural tourism policy in relation to business sustainability, in terms of the relative significance of, and relationships between key components. For this purpose we focus on three pairs of components that can best articulate the relevance of, respectively, the *role*, *nature*, and *impact* of policy for rural tourism business and its sustainability:

- scale of implementation, and level of strategy detail;
- degree of integration of strategy components, and extent of emphasis on product quality; and
- degree of integration of stakeholders, and the temporal dimension.

First, in considering the *role* that policy is to perform for tourism business within the rural space economy, the nature of, and interrelationships between, two key dimensions of policy, are fundamental (Figure 2.1):

- the scale of implementation, which may range from local, through regional to national; and
- the level of strategy detail, ranging from low to high, depending upon strategic objectives.

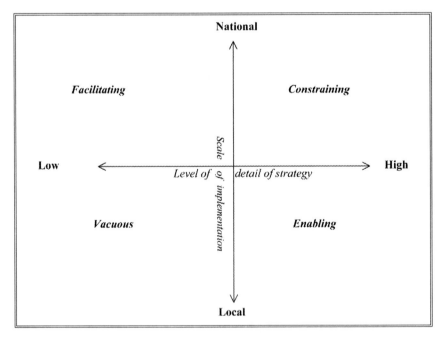

Figure 2.1 Role of rural tourism policy: key dimensions

The range of relationships between these two dimensions suggests the possibility of four types of role for the resulting policy. These can be referred to as:

- *Facilitating*, where policy is focused at the national or higher regional scale. Likely to be focusing on overall strategy, it will generally contain a low level of detail, which by implication, will need to be filled in at a lower level of policy formulation.
- *Constraining*, where policy is still targeted at the higher scale but entails a high level of detail. This can result in a more prescriptive framework approach, which may subsequently be susceptible to the criticism of being insensitive to local area characteristics and needs.
- *Enabling*, where policy has a more local focus with a degree of detail enabling direction and support for local development. It will act to complement and feed into a wider strategic overview, which it is unlikely to be able to provide alone.
- *Vacuous*, where policy is locally focused but it contains little detail to respond to either local or strategic needs.

Next, in Figure 2.2 we suggest that the *nature* of policy in relation to the needs of rural tourism business will relate to two key dimensions:

- the level of integration of the components of the strategy, which may range from low to high; and, similarly,
- the level of emphasis upon product quality.

The relationship between these two dimensions suggests the possibility of four typologies for the nature of policy, which can be referred to as:

- *undifferentiated*, where a high level of integration within the policy is combined with a low emphasis on product quality;
- *sophisticated*, a policy both highly integrated and emphasising product quality;
- *isolated*, referring to a policy emphasising product quality but poorly integrated; and
- *fragmented*, where poor integration within policy is matched by a low emphasis on product quality.

Thirdly, Figure 2.3 suggests that the *impact* or effectiveness of policy for rural tourism business will relate to two key dimensions:

- the level of integration of stakeholders, which may range from high integration of different groups to isolation of groups and individuals; and

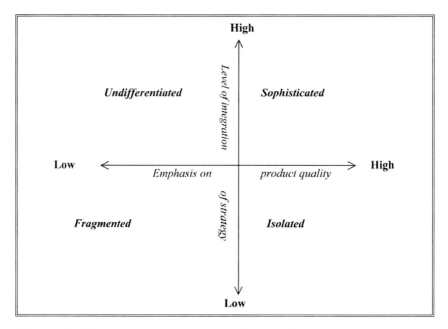

Figure 2.2 Nature of rural tourism policy: key dimensions

- the temporal dimension, extending from the present into the medium- and long-term future.

The relationship between these two important dimensions suggests the possibility of four types of outcomes for the impact and effectiveness of policy. In these circumstances we find no alternative but to use the 'S' word (Roberts & Hall, 2001), and despite believing that tourism sustainability is essentially an absolute quality, we have nonetheless employed a set of relative terms with which to qualify the sustainability of policy (but not of the tourism development that may follow from that policy). The four types of outcomes can be represented as:

- *potential sustainability,* where at the present time there exists a high level of group integration in contributing to and participating in the policy formulation process, but with no guarantee of this continuing into the longer-term future;
- *apparent sustainability,* where a high level of integration can be projected into the future with some degree of confidence (even if conditions may not be appropriate at the present time);
- *limited sustainability,* where the present context for strategy development is one of isolated groups and individuals; and

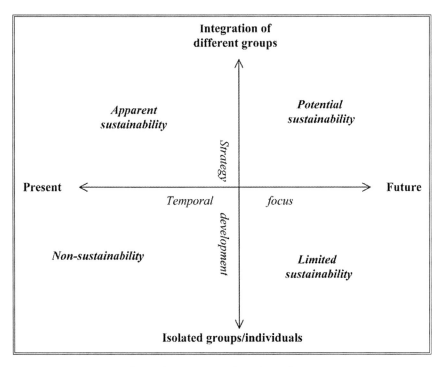

Figure 2.3 Impact of rural tourism policy: key dimensions

- *non-sustainability*, where stakeholder isolation within the strategy development process is likely to be the norm for the foreseeable future.

These attempts to focus on critical elements for rural tourism business sustainability within the policy formulation and implementation process emphasise that policy-makers need to hold a clear conceptual understanding of the role, nature, and impact of their policies. Two major considerations follow from this. First, that strategic planning is fundamental for the efficient use of resources and funds, and requires the involvement in policy formulation of key stakeholders. To this end, a policy for rural tourism should have clearly formulated goals, sustainable development and marketing programmes, and measurable performance criteria. Secondly, the lack of attention paid to the wider policy and planning context within which rural tourism development takes place can result in both business failure and negative local impacts (Butler & Hall, 1998).

Indeed, policy implementation often results in 'winners' and 'losers'. Rural tourism businesses may be too small and fragmented to present a unified voice: the Finnish Rural Tourist Entrepreneurs Association, for example, established in 1995, has just 260 members (Nylander, 2001: 79). And local residents may be unable to muster sufficient 'community' power to exert an influence on development policy decisions. As indicated in relation to Figure 2.3, rural tourism policy should seek the integration of and encourage collaboration between the stakeholders in rural tourism policy outcomes. But the 'implementation gap' between what policy-makers aim to achieve and the reality of policy implementation and outcome may be significant, particularly where subsequent monitoring and evaluation are poorly conducted.

The wish-list ideal for rural tourism strategy frameworks has been well encapsulated by Heneghan (2002), who, from an Irish perspective, has argued the need for a national policy that offers integrated approaches to development in order to optimise the benefits of rural tourism, both for rural people and for tourists to rural areas. Such a policy should:

- define rural tourism, incorporating its various components of natural facilities, activities, and services;
- develop a specific statistical database for rural tourism to help establish product availability, development possibilities, and market information;
- propose a strategic plan, which should set clear objectives and targets for rural tourism development and marketing;
- integrate and coordinate the various agencies involved, and identify clear areas of responsibility;
- overcome any duplication of effort or lack of clarity of message, factors that are often seen as a reason for poor marketing results;
- address key issues of research, training provision, networking, quality product development, innovation and standards, to maintain competitiveness; and
- develop functional links with key players in the marketplace and ensure measurable results from marketing efforts in rural tourism.

An immediate issue is that few European countries actually have an explicit rural tourism policy at national or regional level, although many recognise both the importance of tourism in rural development and a rural component within wider tourism policy. Such an absence may reflect:

- a perceived low importance of the rural sector in terms of income and additional employment generation;
- a perceived unprofessional work force; and/or
- a perceived lack of explicit and separate demand for rural tourism products.

An exception to this is Finland. Here, rural tourism was first recognised as a separate entity for policy purposes in 1995, and a rural tourism policy was published in 2000 (Maaseutumatkailun teemaryhmä, 2000), specifically as part of a wider national rural development policy. Indeed, rural tourism in Finland is recognised as an essential part of the economy, and a key body administering rural tourism policy has been the Rural Policy Committee. This body's membership, representing ministries and NGOs, is appointed by government. The committee's main tasks are to coordinate rural development measures and to promote effective use of resources channelled into rural areas. To help promote the comprehensive development of rural tourism, the Committee established the Rural Tourism Working Group in 1995, with a term of office extending until the end of 2002. It formulated a three-year rural tourism action programme to guide national rural tourism policy as part of the Finnish Government's Rural Areas Programme.

At the time when the country's rural tourism policy programme was being produced, around a hundred organisations were marketing rural tourism and more than half of the entrepreneurs were marketing themselves. This large number of organisations was seen as one of the reasons for poor previous marketing results. Part of the policy programme has been to bring about collaboration and integration, overcome duplication, and achieve a 50% utilisation rate by 2007. Finland, like Scotland or Ireland, has a small population of five million people and therefore has to look to neighbouring countries to supplement its domestic market (Nylander, 2001; Nylander & Hall, 2001).

A rural tourism policy can provide encouragement and incentive to meet the specific education and training needs of entrepreneurs, but it may face a number of challenges:

- Rural tourism entrepreneurial activity may only be one part of a business, or only an active part of the business on a seasonal basis.
- For many small businesses – where profit margins are low – the costs of training and advice – both in terms of money and time – are often perceived to be too great.
- The rapid change in the nature and number of small tourism businesses makes it difficult to monitor business development and target training and other needs.
- In Finland, trainers, teachers, and project managers' skills and knowledge of rural tourism and tourism are in too many cases insufficient and not updated.
- In Finland trainers and teachers who usually train urban hotel or restaurant managers often appear to 'lower' their training message and methods when they are speaking to rural tourism entrepreneurs.

Strategic Considerations

It has become something of a cliché that, because of problems of identification and measurement, rural tourism business in Europe tends to be
pursued within a policy vacuum (Middleton, 1998). It is usually
suggested that, for a range of reasons, including an apparent lack of
tourism development policy direction within the EU, the most important
impacts on the sector are often derived from generic policies and
measures directed at business generally, rather than from tourism-specific
strategy (Heneghan, 2002; Roberts & Hall, 2001; Wanhill, 1997).

European Union enlargement, encompassing further substantial rural
regions, and the growth, increase in number, and sophistication of rural
tourism and recreation activities, should emphasise within Europe the
central importance of tourism development for enhancing the prospects
for rural areas attaining economic, social, and environmental sustainability. Yet, the impression is still often perpetuated that, compared to the
concern and finance expended on agricultural policy, rural tourism is
marginalised as a somewhat secondary adjunct to, and a pursuit
dependent upon, agrarian activity and the unquestioned – implicitly
'safe' – rural 'custodianship' of farmers. This propagandist distortion perpetuated by the politically powerful farming lobby (compared to the fragmented representation of tourism) contrasts sharply with the reality of
rural tourism as a complex of skills, resources, markets, and network
relationships (e.g. Bramwell, 1994). The painful experience, for example,
of UK rural tourism businesses during the foot and mouth disease crisis
of 2001–2002 articulated only too well the folly of this perception of the
rural 'land economy' still apparently perpetuated by government (e.g.
Hall, 2004; Scott *et al.*, 2004; Sharpley, 2003). The persisting sense in a
number of countries of either a lack of policy direction or the marginalisation of tourism reinforces the warnings of earlier authors who pointed to
the almost universal lack of policy and support strategies for rural
tourism at higher levels of administration (e.g. Page & Getz, 1997).

Various reasons have been put forward for this apparent marginalisation, such as the perceived low capital and employment generation
characteristics of the sector, a poor statistical base, or even the spurious
contention that rural tourism is mainly 'domestic' (a notably ambiguous
term in this context), and therefore is considered able to look after itself.
Yet, rural tourism is itself a relatively fragile business, characterised by
a number of potentially vulnerable elements:

- The small scale and dispersed nature of the sector tends to offer low
  returns on investment.
- As a consequence of this, capital availability, inward investment, new
  firm creation, and employment generation may be severely limited.

- Rural tourism business requires a range of diverse skills to be successful: these may not be easy to develop or attain in one person.
- This is particularly significant because rural tourism development is often in the hands of those rural entrepreneurs, such as farmers, small town and village business people, and local officials, who may not have specific training in the appropriate skills.
- The rural tourism sector is comprised of a high proportion of micro-businesses, which may not have the resources – time, labour, finance, and knowledge – for engaging in a strategic planning process or concentrating on longer-term visions.
- There may be a limited number or even absence of entrepreneurs in particular rural areas, such that where activity takes place it may be stimulated by outsiders or incomers who may not share the values, identity of, and attachment to the local rural area held by long-time residents.
- The time scale for success is usually short, perhaps critically depending upon the vagaries of the weather, the dictates of fashion or global events taking place elsewhere, over the period of a single season (Cavaco, 1995; Lane, 1998; Roberts & Hall, 2001; Tuohino & Hynönen, 2001).

Further, inappropriate rural tourism development pursued without professional advice, but based on the false assumption that it is easy to generate markets and thus income and employment, may result in a negative image for the local area, region, or even country. For the development of farm tourism in Central and Eastern Europe, for example, a number of such risk factors have been identified (Brabencová, 1998). These may apply almost anywhere, and point to a number of typical 'implementation gaps':

- mediocre knowledge of agritourism and rural tourism, perhaps reflecting a precipitate sector entry based on false assumptions;
- low-quality farm accommodation, possibly indicating low investment capital and a lack of forward planning;
- lack of information about the requirements of guests, exposing poor market awareness and information flows;
- lack of time to spend with guests, possibly indicating poor time management and a lack of prioritisation and commitment;
- lack of finance to start or adequately sustain a business, perhaps indicating insufficient recognition by, and lack of provision of appropriate investment instruments from the banking and financial sectors;
- low levels of village infrastructure, but this can be turned to an advantage in attracting small-scale ecotourism;

- low levels of information about tourism activities and opportunities in villages, which may reflect both poor networking activities and a lack of support from public bodies; and
- a lack of complementarity with local government and other agency objectives, reflecting poor communication, perhaps an absence of trust, and a lack of common vision.

These and other reasons suggest the inappropriateness of competition between rural tourism businesses within a region and emphasise the conventional wisdom of local cooperation and partnership. In Part 3 of this volume, *'Networks, Partnerships and Community Support'*, this point is elaborated.

Rural Tourism Policy, Regional and National Development

Significantly, many, and perhaps most, European countries' tourism policies do not distinguish 'rural' tourism as a distinct sector for strategic, statistical, and other purposes. Identifying the number of people involved in the specifically 'rural' tourism industry and calculating the income generated is equally not easy. The well-known problems of trying to identify part-time, partial, or indirectly tourism-related employment and those self-employed, are amplified in this context. Thus, in this respect alone, the relationship between rural tourism, rural development, and 'sustainability' is not easy to establish empirically, with the result that claims and counterclaims are neither easy to prove nor disprove.

The crucial factor of attempting to integrate tourism within a wider rural development strategy has been exemplified in relation to rural tourism policy in Finland (Nylander, 2001). As one of the few European countries to pursue a specific rural tourism policy, the experience of Finland, in terms of tourism's role in rural restructuring processes along economic, environmental and cultural dimensions, is instructive. The country's Rural Tourism Working Group has defined rural tourism as "customer-oriented tourism in rural areas ... based on rural areas' natural facilities and resources – culture, nature, landscapes – and on family and small scale entrepreneurship" (Maaseutumatkailun teemaryhmä, 2000: 3). It is this emphasis upon SMEs and entrepreneurship that provides Finnish policy – where rural tourism is a term employed in close conjunction with rural policy – with a sense of direction and immediacy.

Key issues of training provision, networking, and quality product development have been critical. The social construction and re-imaging of the Finnish countryside has been an important theme, and has been set within the Nordic tradition of 'everyman's right' (and responsibilities) of recreational access to rural land.

'The rural' is (still) deeply rooted within Finnish culture and of course in a number of other European societies, and is expressed in rural land ownership patterns. In some other countries, such as the UK and especially England, processes of urbanisation and patterns of rural land ownership have divorced many from their rural roots. Yet, while Finland's rural tourism is strongly rooted in its people, greater cooperation and coordination and a sense of professionalism and product quality are required at all levels if Finland's rural tourism products are to become internationally competitive. Current policy is focusing on these areas.

Indeed, while a wide range of domestically driven factors encourage government intervention in rural tourism and recreation, many of the problems and opportunities associated with its development have an international and likely multicultural dimension (Hall & Jenkins, 1998: 25), and require new policy approaches. This is certainly evident in the tensions expressed in Finland, which probably typify the situation in a number of countries: the largely unprofessionalised, almost hobbyist ('satisficer') approach taken by many rural tourism accommodation providers, reflecting reliance on a hitherto relatively secure domestic market, being confronted increasingly by new and strengthening demands for variety and quality from a range of international markets, in their turn stimulating an increasing sophistication in the domestic market.

Policy and Governance

The balance between representing and embedding bottom–up values and the need for bringing to bear top–down resources, is a delicate one (as expressed in Figures 2.1 to 2.3). Publicly declared strategic actions therefore need to be framed with care and sensitivity, to embrace and represent host communities, business interests, and environmental considerations (see Figure 2.3). This ideal may be less realistic for developing countries, where a top–down approach may be perceived as necessary to kick-start or give an impetus to rural tourism development and to better integrate it into national tourism and development policy.

As the 'hollowing out' of the state places more emphasis at both supranational and local/regional levels, there has evolved a complex structure and set of interrelationships between a variety of public, private, and voluntary associations involved in the administration and management of rural areas. This indicates a shift in emphasis from 'government' to 'governance' (e.g. Sharpley, 2003: 40–41). As part of this process, governing there is increasing emphasis within regional development strategy on the importance of partnerships, networks, and cooperation between institutions. At the local level, a wide range of governmental, para-statal and non-governmental stakeholders have a direct interest in the development of tourism and recreation as an element of integrated rural and regional development. As coastal resorts experience relative decline from tourism, and as agricultural hinterlands face economic reorientation, local agencies have sought a range of strategies for economic regeneration and restructuring such as in southwest England, long a popular holiday destination region for visitors from across the UK (e.g. Meethan, 1998).

For many local authorities and regional development agencies, notions of sustainability, SME support, equal opportunities, community involvement, and partnership working are invoked almost as the mantras of post-industrial economic (re-) development strategy. But in the management of an holistically sustainable development strategy, balancing the interests of, and encouraging complementarity between, local stakeholders, most of these concepts and their operationalisation become far from unproblematic.

Major questions that permeate this volume, and indeed any evaluation of the nature, significance, and integration of tourism activities in rural areas include:

- Is it appropriate to have a separate rural tourism (as opposed to other forms of tourism) policy?
- Is it important to promote a specific rural tourism policy to emphasise and symbolise rural tourism's interface role between tourism and rural and regional development?
- Does the experience of those countries, such as Finland, which have evolved a specific rural tourism policy, provide a model for other European or less developed countries?
- Is it realistic to try to isolate the rural aspects of tourism from their wider tourism context through an explicitly rural tourism policy?
- Similarly, is it realistic to abstract tourism dimensions of the rural from a wider rural and regional development strategy?

Each country, subregion and locality has its own particular set of often intangible characteristics, aspirations and priorities ('milieu' factors – see Chapter 17). More easily recognised are the tangible critical issues that can act to stimulate or constrain the ability to render rural tourism development both financially successful and socially and environmentally sustainable. These may include:

- The role of global development agencies, consultants (Simpson & Roberts, 2000) and the 'transition' goal of incorporation into the global capitalist system, through, for example, such institutions as the European Union (EU) (Coles & Hall, 2004).
- The policy shift to minimise state intervention when in fact there may be a need for governmental intervention and/or public–private partnership ventures to assist the longer-term sustainability of tourism (Hall, 1998). Notable may be the need to improve rural

infrastructures and to support local private sectors confronted by the competition of multinational companies, particularly in encouraging collaboration and networking for overall promotion and marketing.

- The need to manage the spatially separated demands of higher spending market segments and those of apparently diffusing domestic and regional mass market demands from emerging regions such as Central and South Eastern Europe (Jordan, 2000a, 2000b).
- The market and product differentiation consequent upon EU enlargement: for example, development pressures in such important ecological areas as the Carpathian mountains in Romania may intensify as a result of being perceived by a new generation of travellers as part of an exotic non-EU European 'other' (Turnock, 2002).
- The requirement to resolve conflicting perceptions of need, both between outsiders – developers, conservationists, tourists – and locals (Houliat, 1999), and between members of the local 'community' themselves (Verbole & Cottrell, 2002).
- The need for tourism development to be integrated into local economies and social structures through back-linkages, local ownership and control, such as gastronomy (e.g. Boyne *et al.*, 2002, 2003; Kraus, 2000; National Authority for Tourism, 2000), and the recognition of the nature and role of social capital to enable this to be effective (Roberts, 2004).

New policy approaches are therefore required in such circumstances that both stimulate the ability of local human capital and capacity to take advantage of such developments, while finding means to protect and enhance the natural and cultural resources of such areas in a complementary way.

Policy and Regional Development

Within restructuring processes, tourism has the potential to ameliorate uneven regional development, although in practice, it may often help to reinforce the economic dominance of metropolitan regions. In Central and Eastern Europe, for example, where rural tourism is still relatively weakly developed, and where a lack of confidence in rural tourism has relatively deep roots (Hájek, 2002), tourism has tended to reinforce spatial and structural distortions, exacerbating the concentration of activity and consequent congestion in major urban honey pots within already favoured regions. European Union enlargement is likely to intensify such territorial distortions at least in the short term, as new Member States' capital cities re-position themselves as major European cultural destinations.

A useful model, however, can be found in Hungary, where large regional associations overseeing the development of rural tourism have responsibilities for infrastructural development, marketing, and advisory services for small businesses (Czegledi, 1999). This is perhaps influenced by Austrian experience, where, in support of early strategic plans for farm-based rural tourism, an hierarchical organisational structure was developed, focused at federal, provincial, and regional levels. Since 1989, the owners of some 3400 tourist farms have become members of the Austrian Farm Holidays Organisation (AFHO). In all, 8% of all Austrian farmers – some 15,500 – offer one-seventh of the total Austrian supply of tourist beds as rooms or apartments. Significantly, in a strategic appraisal to the year 2010, AFHO is reforming its structure to a more coherent single body rather than nine separate organisations – one federal and eight provincial associations (Embacher, 2003).

Indeed, farm-based tourism can play a crucial role in regional restructuring and revitalisation when small farms have to adjust to depressed agricultural prices and increased competition. European Union policy (such as LEADER, the structural adjustment and accession programmes) is encouraging this, albeit with an often over-optimistic and over-simplistic view of what is required for sustained success. Organic farming and its attractions for visitors has substantial potential (e.g. McIntosh & Campbell, 2001). From a 1992 pilot organic farm holiday programme in the then Czechoslovakia arose the European Centre for Eco-Agro Tourism (ECEAT). This now generates 3500 guests annually, and is considered a valuable partner in tourism development by the Czech government. It produces a rural tourism and heritage trail guidebook (Burian, 2000). On the other hand, surveys undertaken in the Czech Republic have suggested that the development of agritourism had been rather elementary, suffering from a lack of purposeful guidance and formulated strategy. Overshadowed by the enormous growth of urban and cultural tourism in the post-communist years, the rural population's level of interest in entering agritourism business has been generally low, with conditions for development differing significantly between regions (Pourová, 1999).

Policy Challenge for the New Europe: Strategies for National Re-imaging

Notably in Central, Eastern, and parts of Southern Europe, for purposes of escaping from recent or current regional instability and projecting an ethos acceptably 'European', the employment of rural area promotion as an element of or vehicle for national identity, is complementing the re-imaging of rural areas for strategic place promotion (Kotler *et al.*, 1993; Roberts & Hall, 2001). Part of the escape strategy from the communist past in South-Eastern Europe, and from the down-market mass tourism image in the Western and Central Mediterranean, is to diversify away from coastal tourism and to emphasise the uniqueness of cultural and natural resources (Bralić, 1995; Meler & Ruzic, 1999), and more specialised higher value-added activities in the interior (e.g. Bachvarov, 1999; Hall, 2003; Jordan, 2000a, 2000b). For example, in efforts to leave behind the fractious recent past of the former Yugoslavia, Serbia is seeking to identify itself with 'natural' imagery of sustainable and ecotourism (e.g. Popesku & Hall, 2004). The country is attempting to target new markets and promote a new positive national brand image based on the richness of the country's natural and cultural heritage. Montenegro, Serbia's partner in the erstwhile rump Yugoslavia, has declared itself to be 'an ecological state' (Montenet, 1997; NTOM, 2002).

However, there are dangers (e.g. see Stem *et al.*, 2003). 'Ecotourism', for example, has come to be viewed as an 'easy' entry to niche tourism markets drawing on a perceived 'inexhaustible' supply of natural products, while gesturing towards ideals of sustainability and environmental awareness. Bulgarian strategy professes the ambition for the country to become the model European destination for 'eco-tourism' development (Popiordanov, 2003). Yet the specific meaning and implications of the term are less than clearly articulated. Similarly, according to Vajda-Mlinacek and Gradisnik (2001), the whole of continental Croatia has the potential for rural tourism and ecotourism development. They argue that the promotion and sale of services in ecotourism such as bird-watching is well suited to e-commerce and its substantial potential growth.

But generating consistent identities via rural tourism imagery in the European periphery may be constrained by such factors as fragmented and underfunded marketing, and the seeking of short-term results when longer time frames for returns on development investment are required.

By contrast, 2004 EU accession states Slovenia and Malta are much better placed. Slovenia is the only EU member that was a component of the former Yugoslavia and of its mass market 'Mediterranean' product. Rural tourism has been targeted as an important component in Slovenia's economic and political strategy and national image projection. The country has just 47 km of Adriatic coastline, and the development of its interior attractions in many cases dates from Austro-Hungarian times: Lake Bled and the Julian Alps, Postojna and other extensive karstic cave systems, and the Lipica stud farm, famous for supplying Lippizaner horses to the Spanish Riding School in Vienna (Bozic, 1999). A coherent promotion and marketing policy was, at best, ephemeral, until the Slovenia Tourist Board was established in 1996. Its stated mission was:

> to promote Slovenia as a country with a clear and distinctive identity and clearly defined comparative and competitive advantages and thereby assist the Slovene economy by marketing Slovene tourism in a concrete manner (Slovenia Tourist Board, 1998: 1).

The Tourist Board adopted a strategy to promote the country's tourism resources in terms of five sector 'clusters': coast and karst, mountains and lakes, health resorts, cities and towns, and the countryside. This has been supplemented with an emphasis on niche segmentation within an environmentally friendly framework, such as the integration of gastronomy and tourism in promotions for 'wine journeys' (e.g. Intours, 2000). Increasingly the role of activity tourism is being viewed as an important component of the rural product (Konecnik, 2004). This policy approach benefits from an environmental resource diversity within a small, compact country appealing to relatively affluent neighbours Italy, Austria, and Germany.

Further south, 25% of Malta's GNP is derived from tourism, and the industry employs over 9300 people (Micallef Grimaud, 2002). The density of tourist accommodation is the highest in the Mediterranean, with a range of hotels mostly concentrated in northern and eastern coastal areas. Until the mid-1980s, resort-based mass tourism, largely catering to the UK market, reinforced Malta's role as a sun, sand, and sea destination, with the concentration of tourist arrivals in summer and early autumn.

The country's 1989 tourism master plan called for the development of higher quality tourism and for the encouragement of winter and spring attractions to reduce the high level of seasonality of international arrivals. Sports such as diving and golf, alongside cultural and rural tourism, were thus given a higher level of development priority and promotion (Markwick, 1999, 2000). At the same time, poor-quality development was discouraged and the construction of hotels below four-star grading was prohibited (Markwick, 2001).

Such a policy has, however, led to environmental conflicts involving both the natural resources and residents of the island. On the one hand, the promotion of golf requires the diversion of scarce water resources and valuable land-take (Markwick, 2000; Planning Authority, 1997). On the other, both logistic and moral conflicts have arisen as a consequence of foreign tourists visiting the countryside and being intimidated by local hunters and trappers, of which there are some 20,000 (Fenech, 1992), especially where the latter have carried out their pursuits in 'protected' areas (Markwick, 2001).

Restructuring of tourism administration saw establishment of the Malta Tourism Authority in 1999, with the aim of 'advancing the economic and social activity of tourism in the national interest, by working with all stakeholders to develop a sustainable industry for current and future generations' (MTA, 1999). A new brand image was promoted (MTA, 2000), a new strapline was adopted (MTA, 2003) and a strategic plan for 2002–2004 re-emphasised the need to spread the arrival of tourists more evenly throughout the year to reduce pressure in peak months, provide effective product delivery and commitment to service quality, and increase efforts to establish a network of stakeholder alliances, where motivation, coordination, and a sense of common achievement are promoted (MTA, 2002).

These years of transition have seen a major shift in tourism product development. While mass tourism continues, policy focus now emphasises high-value niche tourism. New brand images have been promoted in advertising and other media aimed at both the European market and EU opinion formers, as an outward sign of Malta's modernisation and acceptability within the European family. Yet social and environmental conflicts, exacerbated by the country's political polarisation, have followed (Attard & Hall, 2004; Bramwell, 2003).

Summary and Conclusions

This perspective chapter has sought to take a generic approach to 'policy' in the context of rural tourism development and business sustainability within Europe. In so doing, it has been underpinned by two fundamental issues:

- the appropriateness or otherwise of an explicit 'rural' tourism policy or strategy within regional and national tourism development; and
- the emphasis, priority and role of such policy/strategy in stimulating and sustaining tourism business as an integral element of rural development processes.

Few countries have established an explicit rural tourism policy, and the chapter has debated why this may be the case. Finland is one country that has developed an explicit rural tourism strategy, and the salient features of this have been discussed. The chapter has examined the components, role, and impacts of policy and their implications for rural tourism business and regional development. It has also addressed some of the rural tourism policy challenges facing the 'new' Europe.

The purpose of this chapter has thus been twofold:

- to provide a generic overview of 'policy' within which subsequent debates and case study exemplifications of rural tourism business development can be placed; and
- to examine the currently dynamic and somewhat fragmented nature of rural tourism policy and strategy frameworks in different parts of Europe.

Most authors writing on rural tourism policy have tended to conclude in a generally negative manner, arguing that where explicit policy exists, it is often fragmented, unclear, uncoordinated and lacking integration with other sectors and between spatial scales. These persisting conditions result from a number of factors:

- different attitudes towards the nature, role, and purpose of rural areas;
- varying perceptions and aspirations for the role and nature of tourism development;
- the spasmodic interest in rural tourism as a development tool;
- a too specific spatially based case study approach that may similarly preclude a more holistic approach to issues of sustainability by being unable to draw wider implications from specific situations;
- studies focusing on minor aspects of policy decision making or of tourist motivations that tell us little about policy, values, and behaviour in complex environments;
- an imbalanced concentration on farm-based tourism and the role of farming for rural tourism development; and
- a too specific sectoral focus to policy and development, which may preclude a more holistic approach to issues of sustainability by focusing solely on:
  - economic dimensions (employment generation, spending, income); or
  - physical impacts (on the natural and built environment); or
  - social factors (cultural disparities, crowding and congestion, demonstration effects) (Hall & Jenkins, 1998: 38–39; Opperman, 1996).

It is clear from this brief review that explicit rural tourism policy is rare, and that the strategies impacting upon rural tourism business may emanate from a range of bodies within the framework of rural governance, and may originate from a number of sectors and disciplines such as agriculture, rural land use planning, economic development, environmental management, and social policy. This fragmented and often inchoate context for rural tourism business development is unlikely to change significantly in the foreseeable future.

References

Attard, M. and Hall, D. (2004) Transition for EU accession: the case of Malta's restructuring tourism and transport sectors. In D. Hall (ed.) *Tourism and Transition: Governance, Transformation and Development* (pp. 119–32). Wallingford: CABI Publishing.

Bachvarov, M. (1999) Troubled sustainability: Bulgarian seaside resorts. *Tourism Geographies* 1 (2), 192–203.

Boyne, S., Hall, D. and Williams, F. (2003) Policy, support and promotion for food-related tourism initiatives: a marketing approach to regional development. *Journal of Travel and Tourism Marketing* 14 (3/4), 131–54.

Boyne, S., Williams, F. and Hall, D. (2002) On the trail of regional success: tourism, food production and the Isle of Arran Taste Trail. In A.-M. Hjalager and G. Richards (eds) *Tourism and Gastronomy* (pp. 91–114). London and New York: Routledge.

Bozic, M. (1999) *Lipica 1580*. Lipica: Kobilarna Lipica.

Brabencová, H. (1998) Globální hodnocení regionu z hlediska zavedení a rozvoje agroturistiky a venkovské turistiky. In *Sborník prací z mezinárodní vedecké konference, Agrární perspektivy VII. Evropská integrace a vyuzívání prírodních zdroju, Díl I, Praha, Czech Republic, 17–18. Zárí 1998* (pp. 159–64). Prague: Provozne Ekonomická Fakulta, Ceská Zemedelská Univerzita v Praze.

Bralić, I. (1995) *The National Parks of Croatia* (2nd edn). Zagreb: Skolska Knjiga.

Bramwell, B. (1994) Rural tourism and sustainable rural tourism. *Journal of Sustainable Tourism* 2 (1–2), 1–6.

Bramwell, B. (2003) Maltese responses to tourism. *Annals of Tourism Research* 30 (3), 581–605.

Burian, M. (2000) New markets for sustainable tourism: the way from centrally planned tourism to active local communities. *Tourism* (Zagreb) 48 (4), 341–46.

Butler, R. (1998) Rural recreation and tourism. In B. Ilbery (ed.) *The Geography of Rural Change* (pp. 211–32). Harlow, UK: Addison Wesley Longman.

Butler, R. and Hall, C.M. (1998) Conclusion: the sustainability of tourism and recreation in rural areas. In R. Butler, C.M. Hall and J. Jenkins (eds) *Tourism and Recreation in Rural Areas* (pp. 249–58). Chichester and New York: John Wiley & Sons.

Cavaco, C. (1995) Rural tourism: the creation of new tourit spaces. In A. Montanari and A.M. Williams (eds) *European Tourism: Regions, Spaces and Restructuring* (pp. 127–49). Chichester and New York: John Wiley & Sons.

Coles, T. and Hall, D. (2004) Tourism and EU enlargement. *Journal of International Tourism Research* 6 (2).

Czegledi, J. (1999) Az idegenforgalom területi irányitásának korszerüsitése Magyarországon. *Alma Mater* 2 (3), 85–90.

Embacher, H. (2003) Strategy formulation in rural tourism – an integrated approach. In D. Hall, L. Roberts and M. Mitchell (eds) *New Directions in Rural Tourism* (pp. 137–51). Aldershot, UK and Burlington, VT: Ashgate.

Fenech, N. (1992) *Fatal Flight: The Maltese Obsession with Killing Birds*. London: Quiller Press.

Hájek, T. (2002) The development potential of Czech rural areas and rural tourism. *Zemedelská Ekonomika* 48 (12), 559–62.

Hall, C.M. and Jenkins, J.M. (1995) *Tourism and Public Policy*. London: Routledge.

Hall, C.M. and Jenkins, J.M. (1998) The policy dimensions of rural toursm and recreation. In R. Butler, C.M. Hall and J. Jenkins (eds) *Tourism and Recreation in Rural Areas* (pp. 19–42). Chichester and New York: John Wiley & Sons.

Hall, D. (1998) Tourism development and sustainability issues in Central and South-eastern Europe. *Tourism Management* 19, 423–31.

Hall, D. (2003) Rejuvenation, diversification and imagery: sustainability conflicts for tourism policy in the Eastern Adriatic. *Journal of Sustainable Tourism* 11 (2/3), 280–94.

Hall, D. (2004) Managing rural tourism as education: a critical evaluation of real and putative networks and partnerships. Naples: Paper presented at ATLAS Annual Conference, *Networking and Partnerships in Destination Development and Management*, 4–6 April.

Heneghan, M. (2002) *Structures and Processes in Rural Tourism*. Athenry: Teagasc, Rural Development Centre. On WWW at http://www.teagasc.ie/publications/2002/ruraldev2002/paper08.htm. Accessed 17.1.04.

Houliat, B. (1999) Le tourisme rural au service du développement durable en Roumanie. *Cahiers Espaces* 62, 113–16.

Intours (2000) *Gourmet, Wine and Golf Tours Through Slovenia*. Ljubljana: Intours.

Jordan P. (2000a) Croatian tourism and the challenges of globalisation. *Tourism* (Zagreb) 48 (2), 167–74.

Jordan, P (2000b) Restructuring Croatia's coastal resorts: change, sustainable development and the incorporation of rural hinterlands. *Journal of Sustainable Tourism* 8 (6), 525–39.

Konecnik, M. (2004) Evaluating Slovenia's image as a tourism destination: a self-analysis process towards building a destination brand. *Journal of Brand Management* 11 (4), 307–16.

Kotler, P., Haider, D.H. and Rein, I. (1993) *Marketing Places: Attracting Investment, Industry and Tourism to Cities, States and Nations*. New York: The Free Press.

Kraus, V. (2000) *South Moravian Vineyards and Wine Cellars*. Valtice: Vinarskou Akademii Valtice.

Lane, B. (1998) Rural tourism: global overviews. In *Rural Tourism Management: Sustainable Options Conference Programme* (p. 3). Auchincruive: The Scottish Agricultural College.

Maaseutumatkailun teemaryhmä (2000) *Maaseutumatkailu Strategia ja Kehittämisohjelma Vuoteen 2007*. Helsinki: Maaseutumatkailun teemaryhmä.

Markwick, M. (1999) Malta's tourism industry since 1985: diversification, cultural tourism and issues of sustainability. *Scottish Geographical Journal* 115 (1), 53–72.

Markwick, M. (2000) Golf tourism development, stakeholders, differing discourses and alternative agendas: the case of Malta. *Tourism Management* 21, 515–24.

Markwick, M. (2001) Alternative tourism: change, commodification and contestation of Malta's landscapes. *Geography* 86 (3), 250–55.

McIntosh, A. and Campbell, T. (2001) Willing workers on organic farms (WWOOF): a neglected aspect of farm tourism in New Zealand. *Journal of Sustainable Tourism* 9 (2), 111–27.

Meethan, K. (1998) New tourism for old? Policy developments in Cornwall and Devon. *Tourism Management* 19 (6), 583–93.

Meler, M. and Ruzic, D. (1999) Marketing identity of the tourist product of the Republic of Croatia. *Tourism Management* 20, 635–43.

Micallef Grimaud, J. (2002) *Framing the Future for European Tourism*. Valletta: Malta Ministry for Tourism.

Middleton, V.T.C. (1998) SMEs in European tourism: the context and a proposed framework for European action. *Revue de Tourisme* 4, 29–37.

Montenet (1997) *Ecological State of Montenegro*. Podgorica: Montenet. On WWW at http://www.montenet.org/econ/ecostate.htm. Accessed 13.04.04.

MTA (Malta Tourism Authority) (1999) *A New Brand Image for Malta*. Valletta: MTA. On WWW at http://visitmalta.com/history.htm. Accessed 12.10.99.

MTA (Malta Tourism Authority) (2000) *The Malta Brand Image – Visual and Verbal Language*. Valletta: MTA. On WWW at http://www.maltatourism authority/dev/resources/corporate_man.shtml. Accessed 21.01.01.

MTA (Malta Tourism Authority) (2002) *Malta Tourism Authority Strategic Plan 2002–2004*. Valletta: MTA. On WWW at http://www.maltatourism authority.com. Accessed 14.04.04.

MTA (Malta Tourism Authority) (2003) *Malta: Welcome to the Heart of the Mediterranean*. Valletta: MTA. On WWW at http://www.visitmalta.com. Accessed 14.04.04.

National Authority for Tourism (2000) *Romanian Gastronomy*. Bucharest: National Authority for Tourism.

NTOM (National Tourism Organisation of Montenegro) (2002) *Visit Montenegro*. Podgorica: National Tourism Organisation of Montenegro. On WWW at http://www.visit-montenegro.com/. Accessed 13.04.04.

Nylander, M. (2001) National policy for rural tourism: the case of Finland. In L. Roberts and D. Hall (eds) *Rural Tourism and Recreation: Principles to Practice* (pp. 77–81). Wallingford, UK: CABI Publishing.

Nylander, M. and Hall, D. (2001) Rural tourism policy in comparative perspective: views from the North. In T. Toivonen and A. Honkanen (eds) *North–South: Contrasts and Connections in Global Tourism* (pp. 385–98). Savonlinna: ATLAS and Finnish University Network for Tourism Studies.

Opperman, M. (1996) Rural tourism in Southern Germany. *Annals of Tourism Research* 23 (1), 86–102.

Page, S.J. and Getz, D. (eds) (1997) *The Business of Rural Tourism: International Perspectives*. London: International Thomson Business Press.

Planning Authority (1997) *Golf Course Development in Malta: A Policy Paper*. Planning Authority, Floriana.

Popesku, J. and Hall, D. (2004) Sustainability as the basis for future tourism development in Serbia. In D. Hall (ed.) *Tourism and Transition: Governance, Transformation and Development* (pp. 95–103). Wallingford: CABI Publishing.

Popiordanov, L. (2003) Entre biodiversité et culture: pour un tourisme alternatif en Bulgarie. *Espaces, Tourisme & Loisirs* 202, 50–54.

Pourová, M. (1999) Agritourism business in the Czech Republic. *Acta Universitatis Bohemiae Meridionales* 2 (3), 25–28.

Roberts, L. (2004) Capital accumulation – tourism and development processes in Central and Eastern Europe. In D. Hall (ed.) *Tourism and Transition: Governance, Transformation and Development* (pp. 53–63). Wallingford: CAB International.

Roberts, L. and Hall, D. (2001) *Rural Tourism and Recreation: Principles to Practice*. Wallingford, UK: CABI Publishing.

Scott, A., Christie, M. and Midmore, P. (2004) Impact of the 2001 foot-and-mouth disease outbreak in Britain: implications for rural studies. *Journal of Rural Studies* 20 (1), 1–14.

Sharpley, R. (2003) Rural tourism and sustainability – a critique. In D. Hall, L. Roberts and M. Mitchell (eds) *New Directions in Rural Tourism* (pp. 38–53). Aldershot, UK and Burlington, VT: Ashgate.

Simpson, F. and Roberts, L. (2000) Help or hindrance? Sustainable approaches to tourism consultancy in Central and Eastern Europe. *Journal of Sustainable Tourism* 8 (6), 491–509.

Slovenia Tourist Board (1998) *Marketing of Slovenia's Tourism: Corporate Image*. Ljubljana: Slovenia Tourist Board. On WWW at http://www.tourist-board.si/podoba-eng.html. Accessed 03.02.99.

Stem, C.J., Lassole, J.P., Lee, D.R. and Deshler, D.J. (2003) How 'eco' is ecotourism? A comparative case study of ecotourism in Costa Rica. *Journal of Sustainable Tourism* 11 (4), 322–47.

Tuohino, A. and Hynönen, A. (2001) *Ecotourism – Imagery and Reality. Reflections on Concepts and Practises in Finnish Rural Tourism*. Savonlinna: University of Joensuu. On WWW at http://matkailu.org/jarvimatkailu/pdf/anja_Ecotourism.pdf. Accessed 12.03.04.

Turnock, D. (2002) Ecoregion-based conservation in the Carpathians and the land-use implications. *Land Use Policy* 19 (1), 47–63.

Vajda-Mlinacek, L. and Gradisnik, V. (2001) E-trgovina u ekoturizmu. *Tourism and Hospitality Management* 7 (1/2), 151–58.

Verbole, A. and Cottrell, S. (2002) Rural tourism development: case of a negotiating process in Slovenia. *World Leisure Journal* 44 (2), 21–28.

Wanhill, S. (1997) Peripheral area tourism: a European perspective. *Progress in Tourism and Hospitality Research* 3, 47–70.

Chapter 3

Rural Tourism Business: A North American Overview

DALLEN J. TIMOTHY

Introduction

Only very recently has North America not been a predominantly rural society. While some of the earliest indigenous people lived in communes (e.g. pueblos), the majority of Native Americans lived in small family groups that depended on each other and the land for their survival. Even after the arrival of Europeans in the 15th and 16th centuries, the population remained rural for many years. By 1790, only 5% of Americans lived in cities and towns with populations of 2500 or higher. Today, the figure is over 80% (Jensen, 1995). The process of urbanisation only began to take place in earnest in the mid-19th century with the industrial revolution. Even as recently as the late 19th century, the American and Canadian west were primarily rural, although the arrival of the steam train and the extensive railroad system in the east and the burgeoning western frontier brought about a shift from rural to urban life – a process accelerated by the proliferation of the automobile in the early 1900s.

Traditionally, rural North America was economically dependent upon natural resource extractive activities, such as agriculture, fishing, forestry, petroleum, and mining. However, since the 1970s, there has been a major shift in the rural economy, as industrial restructuring, ongoing farming crises, and over-exploited natural resources have rigorously curtailed rural economic opportunities. Economic restructuring, or the shift from a predominantly natural resource-based, extractive economy, to a more service-based economy, caused a loss of many rural jobs. The farm crisis and changes in agricultural practices in the 1980s also resulted in a decrease of rural jobs and the failure of many large and small farm operations, forcing many families to supplement their agricultural earnings with off-farm work, or to abandon farming, to emigrate to cities, or to declare bankruptcy (Bourke & Luloff, 1995; Edgell & Cartwright, 1990; Luloff et al., 1994; MacDonald & Jolliffe, 2003; Wilson et al., 2001).

As a result of these changes, rural unemployment rates exceeded urban levels and rural income growth languished. Small communities and rural regions throughout all of North America were thus forced to seek non-traditional ways of sustaining themselves, and most turned to tourism and other service-oriented economic activities to utilise their resources and strengths (Botkin *et al.*, 1990; Dahms and McComb, 1999; Henning, 1995; Long & Edgell, 1997; Wilson *et al.*, 2001). This shift in economic focus has taken place rather quickly during the past 25 years, and today only a small handful of the United States' 2300 rural counties are agriculture-dependent (Edgell & Cartwright, 1990; Long & Edgell, 1997). Whereas the majority of Americans and Canadians were, until relatively recently, employed in agriculture, only about 3% of both countries' populations are farmers today (Weaver & Fennell, 1997a).

North America's rural areas have long been of interest to domestic and foreign tourists, for the majority of Canada and the United States is rural in nature and includes bounteous natural and cultural features that appeal to many types of travellers. However, it has only been since the 1970s and 1980s that rural regions, small villages, and county, state/ provincial, and national governments have begun considering the importance of rural tourism development in earnest as a result of declining traditional farming and extractive industries. This chapter examines the appeal of rural North America for tourists and the types of resources and attractions that combine to create one of the most visited mega-regions of the world. It also considers many of the issues and challenges currently involved in rural tourism business in the United States and Canada, and describes some of the management and structural issues that have come to the fore in recent years with the recognition of the importance of tourism in the rural economies of both countries.

The Appeal of Rural North America

North America's position as a leading global destination – the United States and Canada both consistently being included in the World Tourism Organisation's list of most popular destinations – can be attributed in large part to its rural appeal. The continent spans dozens of climatic, topographic, and botanical zones. This expanse bestows significant variations in climate and weather, natural landscapes, landforms, cultures and human settlements, and flora and fauna, forming the foundations for rural tourism (Timothy, in press; Weaver, 2001a). Despite the fact that less than a quarter of the North American population is rural, over 90% of its natural resources are in rural areas (Edgell & Edwards, 1993).

Among Americans and Canadians there is a certain mystique and romanticised representation associated with the countryside. According to Willits (1993: 159), the notion of rurality is seen as wholesome and desirable – an idea perpetuated through various media, such as television, books, and movies. Willits also notes the paradoxical notion that, in spite of the regrettable predicament of rural life today, the mass media and popular culture at large glorify rural people, places, and things. Open spaces, farming, and small town living are portrayed as wholesome, good, and beautiful. In this context, Bunce (1994) speaks of the 'country-side idyll', where there is 'a reservoir of warm feelings and positive images about people, places and things called rural . . . rural is a hallowed element' (Willits, 1993: 170). On the other hand, urban living is represented as unnatural, dangerous, fast-paced, and undesirable. To offset the discrepancies, urbanites migrate *en masse* to the country during weekends and holidays, and many people scramble to purchase a piece of rural solitude in the form of recreational second homes (Jensen, 1995).

Hopkins (1998b: 65) explains that in urban North America, the country-side is a deeply ensconced value in the geographical imagination of society. Rural places are seen as the 'other', distanced temporally, symbolically, and spatially from the everyday and harried life of urban space. This image is fundamental in the consumption of rural tourism in Canada and the United States (Hopkins, 1998a; Park & Coppack, 1994). In the Canadian context, the countryside has been romanticised so much in the minds of Canadians that it has become an integral part of society's iconography (Halseth, 2004).

This romanticised image is felt not just among Canadians and Americans. Overseas tourists have a tendency to equate the countryside as 'real America' or 'real Canada', implying that cities are not representative of North American life, but rural regions are (Edgell & Cartwright, 1990).

According to the Travel Industry Association of America (TIA), 62% of all American adults travelled to a small town or village in the United States between 1998 and 2000 (Dane, 2001). Furthermore, according to a study by English *et al.* (2000), there are 472 rural counties in the United States, or nearly a quarter of the total, where more than 6% of the jobs – double the national average – are based on tourism. In 372 counties, the percentage of income from non-resident visitor expenditures was at least 3% of the total income.

While cities are important gateways and tourist destinations, rural space is a vitally important part of the tourism industries of both countries for domestic and foreign visitors (Murphy, 2003; Murphy & Williams, 1999). The countryside in the United States and Canada is viewed primarily in terms of wilderness areas and nature reserves, such as the national parks of the west (Sharpley & Sharpley, 1997), although agricultural lands, forested regions, mountain zones, and coastal areas are all very important in the realm of rural tourism.

Owing to North America's natural and cultural diversity, there are many different activities and attractions available to rural tourists.

Table 3.1 The most popular activities undertaken by rural tourists in North America

Activity	%
Dining	70
Shopping	58
Visit a beach/lake/riverfront	44
Visit historic sites	41
Fish/hunt/boat	32
Attend a festival or fair	29
Ride a bicycle or hike	24
Attend religious services	23
Camp	21
Attend or participate in a sporting event	18
Visit a winery/working farm/orchard	15
Gamble	12
Visit a Native American community	11

Source: Adapted from Dane, 2001

Table 3.1 demonstrates the most popular activities undertaken by rural tourists in North America based on a study by Dane (2001). The results of Bowling's (1992) study were very similar to those of Dane.

These types of activities and the diverse forms of rural landscapes in North America have influenced significant trends in rural tourism, including Native American reservation tourism, gambling, festivals, shopping, outdoor and nature-based tourism, heritage tourism, trails and corridors, second homes, and farm-based and agritourism (Dane, 2001; Edgell & Dalton, 1993; English *et al.*, 2000; Fennell & Weaver, 1997; Honadle, 1990; Luloff *et al.*, 1994). Each of these is examined in the sections that follow.

Indian reservations

One of the most interesting and uniquely North American trends in the past 15 years is the rapid growth of tourism on Native Canadian and American reservations, the majority of which are completely rural in nature. Indian reservations have long possessed a certain appeal for tourists, especially foreigners, because the natives have come to symbolise much of what makes America different from the Old World (Lew & Van Otten, 1998: ix).

Tourism on Indian reservations has traditionally been based upon natural amenities, special events, native cultures (e.g. dances, architecture, lifestyles), and handicrafts. Adventure tourism is also taking hold as an important sector on aboriginal lands (Getz & Jamieson, 1997). However, since the late 1980s, a new form of tourism has developed – gambling. In 1988, the US Congress passed the Indian Gaming Regulatory Act (IGRA) to govern commercial gambling on Native American reservations. The law also opened the door for reservations to establish casinos with many forms of gaming. Casinos have developed rapidly on native lands in the United States since the IGRA was enacted, and it has become the most notorious and profitable form of tourism on the reservations. The world's largest casino, Foxwoods, opened in 1992 on the small rural Mashantucket Pequot reservation in Connecticut. Foxwoods earns more than a billion dollars a year in gambling, and with that knowledge many other small, rural reservations have followed suit to build profitable casinos (Carmichael *et al.*, 1996; Lew, 1996; Stansfield, 1996).

Canada is undergoing a similar change as many of its 'First Nations' reservations have begun to develop casino gaming legally in provinces where casinos are otherwise prohibited (Smith & Hinch, 1996). In response to the growth of reservation tourism, the Canadian National Aboriginal Tourism Association (CNATA) was established in 1990 with the mandate of protecting the integrity of, and promoting, aboriginal tourism (Getz & Jamieson, 1997). No such organisation exists in the United States, although many reservations have their own tourism development offices and handicraft cooperatives to help market Indian products on and off the reservations. Likewise, collaborative alliances have been created in recent years between various tribes and reservations as a way of strengthening their advertising dollar and building awareness of their tourist potential from a broader regional perspective.

Gambling

While gambling has far surpassed other types of tourism on native lands, other forms of rural gaming have grown elsewhere. By the mid-1990s, 25 states had permitted the development of casinos on riverboats, at dockside facilities, in historic mining towns or Indian reservations (Eadington, 1996). One example is Black Hawk, Colorado, a small town that developed into a major gaming community, where casinos were built as a replacement economy for the now derelict mining industry. While gaming brought in many new jobs, increased visitor spending, and assisted in preserving the community's heritage, there are some significant concerns regarding whether or not the heritage status of the community will be able to withstand the pressures of this new form of tourism (O'Driscoll, 1997; Stokowski, 1992).

Riverboat casinos began to develop in rural and suburban areas in the early 1990s in the state of Iowa. Other states on the banks of navigable rivers, such as the Mississippi and Ohio Rivers, have passed gaming legislation that permits riverboat gambling as well (Eadington, 1996).

Rural festivals

Most small communities, villages, and rural townships have festivals, fairs, or other events. Many of these festivals were designed originally to celebrate various local events, such as autumn harvests, founders days, and so on, primarily to entertain local residents. However, with the knowledge of the potential economic impacts, most rural communities have decided to broaden their scope to include bringing visitors from out of town. Among the most common types of festivals in rural areas are food and farm fêtes, folk life festivals, arts and crafts shows, historical re-enactments, and music festivals.

While rural festivals can be found throughout all of North America, they tend to demonstrate some distinctive regional patterns. This is primarily a result of the fact that many, if not most, festivals developed in celebration of Earth's abundance (i.e. people's livelihoods) and lifestyles. For example, in Canada's Atlantic Provinces and the northeastern United States, many rural festivals celebrate fish and fishing. In the Midwest and Canadian Prairies, agricultural celebrations dominate. Almost every small settlement in the US Midwest, regardless of its size, boasts some sort of festival. Events like peach, strawberry, cherry, pickle, apple butter, turkey, egg, and cheese festivals illustrate the importance of agriculture in socio-economic life. Ethnic festivals, such as FinnFest, Tulip Time, Swedish Fest, Ukrainian Festival, and German Days attest to the settlement of various ethnic groups in parts of the rural Midwest and the Canadian Prairies.

Rural festivals are now an important part of the tourism economy in North America, and more than 10,000 festivals are being held annually in small settlements in the United States alone (Janiskee & Drews, 1998). While the aim of most rural festivals today is financial benefit, they are also important for enriching the quality of small-town life and strengthening rural community identity (Janiskee & Drews, 1998). According to the Travel Industry Association of America (1999), 20% of all American adults attended a festival while travelling in 1998, the most popular being of a rural nature, such as music or arts (33%), folk or heritage (22%), and county or state fairs (20%).

Shopping

Shopping is a universal tourist activity and an important part of rural tourism in the United States and Canada. Two primary themes exist in the realm of rural shopping. The first is the growth and popularity of shopping malls and outlet centres in the countryside. While urban shopping centres developed as early as the late 19th century, multistore retail malls became a standard feature of ex-urban areas only during the mid-20th century in North America, the earliest rural shopping centre being built in Kansas in the 1920s (Jones, 1991). The move from central city locations to rural areas and suburban fringes came about as a result of crowded urban conditions, new zoning regulations, suburbanisation processes, the growth of highway systems, and the proliferation of the automobile, which provided easy access to retail venues for both urban and rural residents (Goss, 1999; Kowinski, 1985; Reynolds, 1993; Timothy, 2005). The same spatial pattern occurred with factory outlet shopping, which began in the 19th century at the textile mills in the northeastern United States, where imperfect products, excess supplies, and damaged goods were sold to clear out floor space (Lowe, 1998). Outlet shops have also become popular attractions in rural destinations, where people can get out of town to enjoy a consumer experience browsing and searching for brand-name items at discount prices. Today, in the United States alone, there are over 300 outlet malls and 14,000 factory stores (Outletbound, 2002).

Shopping malls and outlet centres in rural areas have become popular recreational and tourist attractions not only for shopping, but also for their role as leisure complexes where restaurants, special events, cinemas, bowling alleys, swimming pools, arcades, ice-skating arenas, mini-zoos, fitness clubs, casinos, food courts, and playgrounds abound. From a strictly tourism perspective, rural malls and shopping centres have become major attractions in their own right, transforming many small towns, villages, and suburban areas into significant destinations (Patton, 1986; Ritzer & Liska, 1997), complete with hotels, timeshare accommodation, car rentals, amusement parks, tour operators, banks and currency exchanges, and many other services that cater to the specific needs of tourists.

The well-known rural outlet malls of New York, Pennsylvania, Connecticut, Virginia, and Maryland function as important tourist destinations and often attract more tourists than major national monuments such as George Washington's home, the Empire State Building, and Colonial Williamsburg (Patton, 1986; Timothy, 2005). For many groups, such as Japanese tourists, malls and outlet centres are nearly always included in the basic tour itinerary.

The second theme of rural shopping in the United States and Canada is the growth, development and popularity of small villages that offer retailing opportunities as a primary appeal alongside attractive natural and/or cultural amenities. Getz (1993) identifies these as 'tourist shopping villages' (TSV), and Mitchell *et al.* (1993) call them 'recreational shopping villages'. These villages typically offer tourism-related products, such as souvenirs, and are usually designed thematically and associated with historic structures.

Such TSVs are also identified by a high concentration of speciality shops, eating establishments, and entertainment opportunities, including tea rooms, ice cream parlours, clothing stores, souvenir shops, sweets shops, book stores, antique dealers, potteries, bakeries, handicraft outlets, toy stores, and restaurants (Getz, 1993; Getz *et al.*, 1994; Mitchell *et al.*, 1993).

While TSVs are a rural phenomenon, they are usually situated near enough to larger towns to benefit from a steady flow of visitors and the services offered in larger communities. In most cases, TSVs began as agricultural or mining settlements that possessed cultural and/or natural heritage features that were of interest to outsiders. As part of a natural process, then, tourism began to grow, transforming them into boutique communities where shopping dominates the tourism scene.

Many examples of these exist throughout North America, although several have been highlighted extensively in the literature, including St. Jacobs, Ontario (Dahms, 1991; Mitchell *et al.*, 1998); Elora, Ontario (Getz, 1993); and Holland and Frankenmuth, Michigan (Che, 2004; Timothy, 2005).

Outdoor and nature-based tourism

Natural areas comprise the largest proportion of rural land in North America, and in common with destinations around the world, they have become major attractions for nature/ecotourists and outdoor recreationists. Both countries have large systems of protected areas, including national parks, national forests, and protected coastal zones. The idea of nature conservation in the United States began officially in 1864, when the US government gave land in the Yosemite Valley to the state of California to protect the giant Sequoia trees. Later, in 1872, Yellowstone, the world's first national park, was established. Soon after, Canada established its first national park, Rocky Mountain National Park, which was later named Banff National Park (Ibrahim & Cordes, 2002; Nelson, 2000; Sharpley & Sharpley, 1997). Today Parks Canada operates 35 national parks and several other types of natural areas (see Table 3.2) (Boyd & Butler, 2000). The US National Park Service operates 55 national parks and nearly 300 other conservation areas of mixed cultural and natural value (see Table 3.3).

As noted in Table 3.1, boating, fishing, hunting, hiking, camping, cycling, and sightseeing are among the most popular outdoor tourist pursuits. Despite the continued popularity of hunting and fishing outfitting services, there has been a decline in recent years in the more consumptive activities (e.g. hunting and fishing), one of the most recent and fastest

Table 3.2 Parks Canada properties

Type of property	Number
Federal Heritage Buildings	235
Heritage Places & Exhibits	3
National Parks	35
National Marine Parks	2
National Park Reserves	4
National Historic Sites	105
Total	384

Source: Parks Canada, 2002

growing trends being bird watching (Fennell, 2001; Scott & Thigpen, 2003; Weaver, 2001b). In fact, according to Ibrahim and Cordes (2002), bird watching grew 155% between the mid-1980s and the mid-1990s. Weaver (2001b) suggests that the decline in recreational hunting may be a result of the growing ecotourism movement and the conservation consciousness being promoted by various non-profit organisations.

Table 3.3 US National Park Service properties

Type of property	Number	Type of property	Number
National Battlefields	10	National Parkways	4
National Battlefield Parks	3	National Preserves	8
National Historic Sites	70	National Recreation Areas	17
National Historical Parks	37	National Reserves	1
National Lakeshores	4	National Rivers	4
National Memorials	28	National Seashores	10
National Military Parks	9	National Wild & Scenic Rivers	5
National Monuments	68	Other Parks	11
National Parks	55	Total	344

Source: US National Park Service, 2001

In common with other forms of nature-based tourism and outdoor recreation, ecotourism has grown a great deal in North America in recent years, especially in national parks and other federally protected areas. According to Weaver (2001b), Americans are the world's largest ecotourist market, and the United States supports one of the world's largest ecotourism industries.

While rural tourism in general is now seen as a viable economic option to traditional activities, ecotourism is seen in many peripheral regions as an especially appropriate tool for economic rejuvenation, particularly in remote northern regions and the Atlantic Provinces of Canada (Weaver, 2001b). In Canadian ecotourism, there is an increasing level of involvement of indigenous peoples, especially in the north where they comprise a population majority. There are several concerns, however, related to the northern and other peripheral regions: first is the need to co-exist with powerful extractive industries such as logging and fishing; secondly, there is a need to provide winter opportunities for ecotourists to assuage the effects of seasonality; finally, the far north must retool itself to be able to transfer from consumptive activities to non-consumptive pursuits (Weaver, 2001b: 288).

Heritage tourism

North America has been blessed with an interesting and long history of indigenous cultures and colonial heritage. Rural areas provide the backdrop for much of this patrimony. Some of the most important rural attractions include small villages, mines and quarries, covered bridges, archaeological sites related to Native Americans and Canadians, and battlefields, all of which fit within the definition of heritage (Timothy & Boyd, 2003).

Heritage resources have the potential to assist in regenerating rural areas. Canada has been active in this regard and the Heritage Regions program was developed by Heritage Canada to encourage Canadians to identify, protect, and enhance their cultural, built and natural environments (Brown, 1996). In the United States as well, national-level programmes have been established (discussed later in the chapter) to assist rural areas in preserving and promoting heritage. And, in both countries, the national parks systems protect, manage and promote cultural and built attractions just as they do also for natural features. Parks Canada historic sites (approximately 350) in the east spotlight maritime history and colonial heritage, while the primary attractions in the west focus more on the cultures and lifestyles of Native Canadians and frontier settlement. In the United States, as noted in Table 3.3, hundreds of heritage areas are under the management and protection of the National Park Service, including historic parks, battlefields, and monuments.

Trails and corridors

An important trend today that involves many aspects of natural and cultural heritage is the development of trails and regional corridors. Long-distance trails in North America typically include some urban clusters, but they are developed primarily as a way of creating spatial linkages between places of cultural, historical, and natural importance (Smith *et al.*, 1986).

In 1968, and amended in 1978, the US Congress passed the National Trails System Act, which established the National Trails System and determined that trails should be developed near urban areas and along historic travel routes in more remote areas. The act also defines three main categories of trails that comprise the National Trails System: scenic trails, historic trails, and recreation trails. Scenic trails are long trails that provide opportunities to visit important natural and scenic areas (e.g. the Appalachian Trail and the Pacific Crest Trail). Historic trails are long-distance corridors that follow as closely as possible historically significant routes of travel or migration (e.g. the Mormon Pioneer Trail, the Oregon Trail, the Lewis and Clark Trail, and the Trail of Tears). National historic trails are often paralleled by marked driving routes. Recreation trails provide opportunities for outdoor recreation near cities (e.g. hiking trails, rails-to-trails, and ex-urban nature trails) (Ibrahim & Cordes, 2002; Jensen, 1995; Long & Edgell, 1997).

In the United States, the National Trails System is administered by the National Park Service in cooperation with the National Forest Service to manage the rural environments, hubs, and nodes along the routes. Today there are eight national scenic trails and 14 national historic trails, with many other recreational trails scattered throughout the country (Ibrahim & Cordes, 2002). National recreation trails are administered jointly by the National Park Service and the US Forest Service, with assistance from the Bureau of Land Management, US Fish and Wildlife Service, the Army Corps of Engineers, the Federal Highway Administration, the American Recreation Coalition, American Trails, the National Association of State Trail Administrators, the American Hiking Society, and the Rails-to-Trails Conservancy. In excess of 800 national recreation trails have been designated throughout the United States and are located in every state (Ibrahim & Cordes, 2002).

The Rails-to-Trails Conservancy (RTC) has already been mentioned. Its role involves the development and protection of greenways in the United States. Since its foundation in 1986, the RTC's objective has been to protect railroad corridors that are being abandoned at the rate of some 3280 km each year. With support from individual activists, private organisations, and community conservation groups, over 16,000 km of derelict rail corridor has been converted into rail-trails with thousands more projects under way (Ibrahim & Cordes, 2002).

Second homes

Compared to Europe, second home ownership in North America is a relatively new phenomenon, although it is increasing in popularity in both countries. In most cases, recreational second homes are located in rural areas of high aesthetic beauty, seacoasts, lakefronts, and mountain regions (Clout, 1972; Wolfe, 1952). In the Canadian context, Halseth (2004) notes that the lakeside cottage has assumed a place in the folklore of Canada, along with other elements of the rural-recreation countryside.

In the mid-20th century, developers began to acquire large pieces of land in desirable rural areas. These were subsequently divided into plots whereon individual homes were built in a 'recreational subdivision' or estate (Ragatz, 1977; Stroud, 1995). This trend began to take on some of the characteristics of urban and suburban development, such as paved roads, street signs, owners associations, and small lot sizes. Nevertheless, these subdivisions became popular rural destinations for tourists and recreational home owners.

Despite its popularity, the recreational second home trend has its share of problems. In the United States, developers gained a reputation for being dishonest and fraudulent, selling large areas of raw land without being able to gain title to it or provide utility services (Stroud, 1995). This resulted in many consumers buying land on which they could not build. Developers also chose inappropriate locations where cheap land was available and where building restrictions were relaxed, creating many environmental and structural problems later (Gartner, 1987; Stroud, 1995).

In the 1970s, oil shortages and economic recessions reduced demand for second homes, which resulted in many unfinished structures sitting derelict for years and many developers declaring bankruptcy. The image has changed since those troubled times, however, and public trust was gained again once developers began to alter their sales tactics and improve their building standards (Timothy, 2004).

Farm and agritourism

Declining rural economies and lifestyles, as well as demand for alternative rural forms of tourism, have led many North American farmers either to abandon farming altogether or adapt to changes in demand. One form of adaptation has been the creation of vacation farms in both countries, which incorporate both working farm functions and commercial tourism elements (Weaver & Fennell, 1997a, 1997b). At many ranches and farms in North America, tourist fees are the largest source of revenue. While this pattern is fairly common and well established in much of Europe, it is relatively new in the United States and Canada. Hundreds of farms and ranches provide vacation facilities and holiday opportunities for tourists. According to the *Edmonton Journal* (1999), there are some 360 vacation farms in the provinces of Alberta, Saskatchewan, Manitoba, and Ontario. In the United States thousands more abound in the form of 'dude ranches' in the west and guest farms in the east and midwest.

The appeal of 'dude ranches' and guest farms lies in their role as preservers of the rural, idealised past. They are also popular because they are working entities where the main form of entertainment is closely related to the work of the ranch. For most city dwellers, the main market for farm-based tourism, sampling a different way of life is an enchanting notion. Visitors benefit from the fresh air, freedom to walk and hike wherever they choose, and from the rural scenery (*Edmonton Journal*, 1999; Jensen, 1995).

The most popular activities at guest farms and ranches include horse-back riding, doing farm-related chores, fishing, swimming, hunting, camping, hiking, viewing wildlife, boating, cross-country skiing and snowmobiling, photography, packing trips, trail rides, cattle herding, barn dancing, and picnicking and cooking out. Some farms and ranches have even built golf courses and swimming pools to cater to the desires of visitors (Fennell & Weaver, 1997; Ibrahim & Cordes, 2002; Jensen, 1995).

Aside from farmstays and 'dude ranches', other forms of agritourism have become popular in North America (Dane, 2001). Often rural tours include developments and services that allow visitors to see agricultural products and operations. In Idaho, visitors can observe the planting or harvesting of potatoes. In Arizona, California, and Florida, foreign tourists and visitors from colder climates in North America are intrigued by the millions of acres of farmland devoted to citrus orchards. Visitors to Saskatchewan, Alberta, or Manitoba can witness the thrashing and combining of grain. In Hawaii, tourists typically have opportunities to sample field-ripened pineapple at large pineapple plantations (Goeldner & Ritchie, 2003).

Another form of agritourism that has received considerable academic attention throughout the world is wine tourism. In North America, viticulture-based tourism is becoming a major force in places famous for their wines, such as California, Texas, and Ontario. Many wineries in the Niagara Peninsula and northern California, for instance, have opened their doors to tour busloads of visitors who observe the wine production process, taste samples, and purchase the product. In Canada's Niagara wine region, more than half of the wineries sell 50% of their wine at the place of production; some of the smaller boutique enterprises sell as much as 100% of their wines on site (Telfer, 2001).

Policy and Management Challenges

Despite the popularity and success of these attractions and activities, rural tourism in North America is not without challenges. Observers have identified several issues that raise concerns about the future of rural tourism in the United States and Canada.

Environmental pressures

The pressures placed upon small communities and rural areas by large numbers of tourists and increased traffic can have considerable negative impacts. One of the most widely recognised is the loss of a small town and rural atmosphere (Mitchell *et al.*, 1993). This is a concern where shopping malls and casinos are built in rural areas. Their very existence and functions make rural places urban, thereby diminishing the very qualities being sought by rural visitors. Other effects include increased traffic, greater demands on local services, inadequate parking, longer lines in grocery stores and other service providers, increased crime, inflated property taxes, and potentially, job displacement (Bourke & Luloff, 1995; Tourism Center, 2001).

In the context of protected areas such as national parks, pollution and crowded conditions are major management concerns. In places such as Yosemite, Grand Canyon, and Zion National Parks, the congestion problem became so bad that the Park Service started limiting vehicular access to certain parts of the parks, replacing some sections of roadway with mass transit systems during the busiest parts of the year.

Financial constraints

Limited financial resources are a significant constraint for many rural areas in North America. Most areas have insufficient budgetary resources to enable them to develop the types of tourism they desire or to prepare their communities for the onslaught of tourism. Rural promotional budgets can rarely compare to those being spent by cities and state/provincial-level tourism agencies (Bowling, 1992). This recognition has led to calls by several observers for national and subnational governments to focus more attention on poorer rural areas that need matching grants and other forms of assistance from higher-order administrations (Bourke & Luloff, 1995).

Lack of experience and training

Limited knowledge and education regarding tourism among rural residents is another major obstacle to successful tourism in some North American locations. Often rural people do not understand the importance of service quality in a tourism setting and are unfamiliar with the behaviour and expectations of urbanites. In addition, according to the

Tourism Center (2001), it is not uncommon to find rural tourism businesses not keeping regular hours because the owner has other things to do, or he/she closes shop when an employee is unavailable to work.

In many cases, there is a significant brain drain as the younger generation desires to move to the city in search of work, and research shows that residents of rural communities in the United States lag behind their urban counterparts in formal education (Edgell & Edwards, 1993).

In both countries there are some concerns regarding public awareness and knowledge of tourism on indigenous lands. First, in most cases aboriginal peoples do not understand the full potential of tourism. Secondly, the levels of education lag far behind the national averages in both countries. Likewise, there is a notable scarcity of tourism skills and formal training, although this is beginning to change as more reservation tourism leaders have begun to train residents, who may be able to work in the casinos. Finally, tourism development on most reservations is not fully participatory, and a lack of understanding of tourism and participatory processes excludes many tribal members from taking part in tourism organisations (Getz & Jamieson, 1997: 97).

Fragmented national-level policy and administration in the United States

Perhaps the most obvious challenge is the lack of governance of rural tourism, especially in the United States. After repeated attempts to establish a national-level administration to oversee and develop tourism in the United States, efforts were abandoned. Although the United States is without an official federal-level public tourism organisation, several other agencies have interests in, and responsibilities over, various elements of the industry. For instance, the Tourism Industries Unit of the US Department of Commerce does attempt to promote employment in tourism and strengthen economic development opportunities through tourism, but its role is severely limited. Other interested departments include the US Customs Service, the Secretary of State, the Secretary of Labor, the Department of Homeland Security, the National Park Service, the Department of Agriculture, the Bureau of Land Management, and the Secretary of Transportation, but there is no unifying national body to deal with tourism governance. This fragmented approach to tourism administration has earned considerable criticism from industry leaders (Brewton & Witham, 1998; Fennell, 2001; Goeldner & Ritchie, 2003).

Just as the United States does not have a national tourism organisation, there are also no public organisations that deal specifically with rural tourism or its various components. In the absence of a national association, rural tourism, and in fact all forms of tourism in the

United States can best be described as a loose mosaic of 50 separate state models that differ significantly with regard to level of recognition and institutionalisation (Weaver, 2001b: 286). By way of example, in his analysis of ecotourism, Weaver (2001b) suggests that some states openly recognise ecotourism, while others emphasise more consumptive forms of nature-based tourism, such as hunting and fishing.

This lack of structural support and administration notwithstanding, and in spite of the federal rural focus on agriculture, the US government has shown some interest in rural tourism and a degree of willingness to support it in policy formulation. In 1989, for instance, Congress directed the US Travel and Tourism Administration (now defunct) to undertake studies on the feasibility of using tourism to help grow and diversify rural economies (Edgell & Cartwright, 1990). However, it was not until 1992 that a formal policy was designed regarding tourism development in rural America. The policy created the National Rural Tourism Foundation (NRTF), a non-profit organisation charged with attracting visitors to rural America. The NRTF is comprised of private sector representatives together with delegates from the National Park Service, US Forest Service, Department of Agriculture, Bureau of Indian Affairs, and the Bureau of Land Management (Edgell & Dalton, 1993; Heise, 1994; Long & Edgell, 1997). Despite the fact that there is no true federal agency to deal with tourism policy, and rural tourism in particular, several foundations and programmes have been formulated to assist rural areas in promoting themselves as tourist destinations: the NRTF, the National Historic and Scenic Byway Program, and the National Trust for Historic Preservation's rural conservation program (Brown, 1996).

This national asymmetry is evident in efforts to utilise the countryside as a tourism resource. Luloff *et al.* (1994) and Sharpley & Sharpley (1997) noted that there were 30 US states in the mid-1990s with programmes specifically for rural areas, 14 with some treatment of the countryside embedded within their broader development plans, and six with no rural tourism strategies whatsoever.

In Canada, the situation is different. While there have been some significant changes in tourism administration, there has long been a federal-level agency in charge of tourism policy making, research, and development. Known earlier as Tourism Canada, the agency today is known as the Canadian Tourism Commission (CTC), whose job is to regulate tourism, conduct research, maintain orderly tourism development, market Canada at home and abroad, and develop tourism-related products (Timothy, in press). Additionally, there have been considerable efforts in recent years by the Canadian government in cooperation with the CTC in setting a strong rural tourism agenda at the national level. Despite this national-level action, like the United States, the actual development of various forms of rural tourism typically takes place at the provincial level (Weaver, 2001b: 287).

Conclusion

The diverse cultural and natural landscape features of North America provide the foundations of a large and growing rural tourism sector. The most important elements of rural tourism in Canada and the United States today are Indian reservations, gambling, festivals, shopping, outdoor and nature-based tourism, cultural heritage, trails and corridors, recreational second homes, and agritourism. These facets of rural North America instill nostalgic conceptions of wholesomeness, goodness, and peace among domestic travellers and the 'real', or authentic, America and Canada among overseas visitors.

This notion itself has considerable management and policy implications, particularly in relation to marketing and promotion, conservation, and planning. However, it also raises important concerns and challenges for rural residents and community leaders, including environmental and social pressures, fiscal constraints, lack of education and training, and perhaps most importantly, a dearth of national-level policies and administrations that can guide and encourage rural tourism development. For the most part, there is a lack of communication between the US national government and the state governments regarding tourism development and planning, and each state is left to its own devices regarding how best to promote itself and encourage community cooperation in conservation and planning. The situation is less *ad hoc* in Canada, but the problem exists there as well.

Rural tourism managers in North America are now facing the challenge of an urbanising countryside. While there was a major migration to the cities throughout the 19th and 20th centuries, there is now an urban to rural movement, where people desire to live farther away from the city and its suburbs. In addition to the general migration reversal, the establishment of tourism in the form of shopping centres, casinos, second home estates, and perhaps even large-scale agritourism projects, is contributing to the urbanisation of the countryside and therefore a loss in the rural and small village appeal that residents cherish and tourists crave. This phenomenon needs considerable more attention by scholars and government leaders to address the countless questions that accompany it.

References

Botkin, M.R., McGowan, M.L. and Thistlewaite, P. (1990) *Economic Impacts and Effects of Types of Travel and Tourism Attractions in Rural Illinois.* Macomb, IL: Illinois Institute for Rural Affairs.

Bourke, L. and Luloff, A.E. (1995) Leaders' perspectives on rural tourism: case studies in Pennsylvania. *Journal of the Community Development Society* 26 (2), 224–39.

Bowling, M. (1992) Illinois rural tourism: do rural areas benefit from increases in travel expenditures? *Small Town* 22 (4), 19–26.

Boyd, S.W. and Butler, R.W. (2000) Tourism and national parks: the origin of the concept. In R.W. Butler and S.W. Boyd (eds) *Tourism and National Parks: Issues and Implications* (pp. 13–27). Chichester: John Wiley & Sons.

Brewton, C. and Withiam, G. (1998) United States tourism policy: alive but not well. *Cornell Hotel and Restaurant Administration Quarterly* 39 (1), 50–59.

Brown, V. (1996) Heritage, tourism and rural regeneration: the Heritage Regions Programme in Canada. *Journal of Sustainable Tourism* 4 (3), 174–82.

Bunce, M. (1994) *The Countryside Ideal: Anglo-American Images of Landscape.* London: Routledge.

Carmichael, B.A., Peppard, D.M. and Boudreau, F.A. (1996) Megaresort on my doorstep: local resident attitudes toward Foxwoods Casino and casino gambling on Indian reservation land. *Journal of Travel Research* 34 (3), 9–16.

Che, D. (2004) Reinventing Tulip Time: evolving diasporic Dutch heritage celebration in Holland (Michigan). In T. Coles and D.J. Timothy (eds) *Tourism, Diasporas and Space* (pp. 261–78). London: Routledge.

Clout, H.D. (1972) Second homes in the United States. *Tijdschrift voor Economische en Sociale Geografie* 63, 393–401.

Dahms, F. (1991) Economic revitalisation in St. Jacobs, Ontario: ingredients for transforming a dying village into a thriving tourist destination. *Small Town* 21 (6), 12–18.

Dahms, F. and McComb, J. (1999) 'Counterurbanisation', interaction and functional change in a rural amenity area – a Canadian example. *Journal of Rural Studies* 15 (2), 129–46.

Dane, S. (2001) *Stories Across America: Opportunities for Rural Tourism.* Washington, DC: National Trust for Historic Preservation.

Eadington, W.R. (1996) The legalisation of casinos: policy objectives, regulatory alternatives, and cost/benefit considerations. *Journal of Travel Research* 34 (3), 3–8.

Edgell, D.L. and Cartwright, M.L. (1990) How one Kansas town used tourism to revitalise its economic base. *Business America* 111 (21), 14–17.

Edgell, D.L. and Dalton, S.J. (1993) Home on the road: Exploring rural America is a commanding business asset. *Business America* 114 (24), 18–20.

Edgell, D.L. and Edwards, S. (1993) A new initiative in tourism development: South Dakota's Oyate Trail. *Business America* 114 (7), 8–11.

Edmonton Journal (1999) Agri-tourism: Growth industry in Canada. *Edmonton Journal* 2 February, F1.

English, D.B.K., Marcouiller, D.W. and Cordell, H.K. (2000) Tourism dependence in rural America: Estimates and effects. *Society and Natural Resources* 13 (3), 185–202.

Fennell, D.A. (2001) Anglo-America. In D.B. Weaver (ed.) *The Encyclopedia of Ecotourism* (pp. 107–22). Wallingford: CAB International.

Fennell, D.A. and Weaver, D.B. (1997) Vacation farms and ecotourism in Saskatchewan, Canada. *Journal of Rural Studies* 13 (4), 467–75.

Gartner, W.C. (1987) Environmental impacts of recreational home developments. *Annals of Tourism Research* 14, 38–57.

Getz, D. (1993) Tourist shopping villages: development and planning strategies. *Tourism Management* 14 (1), 15–26.

Getz, D. and Jamieson, W. (1997) Rural tourism in Canada: issues, opportunities and entrepreneurship in aboriginal tourism in Alberta. In S.J. Page and D. Getz (eds) *The Business of Rural Tourism: International Perspectives* (pp. 93–107). London: International Thomson Business Press.

Getz, D., Joncas, D. and Kelly, M. (1994) Tourist shopping villages in the Calgary region. *Journal of Tourism Studies* 5 (1), 2–15.

Goeldner, C.R. and Ritchie, J.R.B. (2003) *Tourism: Principles, Practices, Philosophies* (9th edn). Hoboken, NJ: Wiley.

Goss, J. (1999) Once-upon-a-time in the commodity world: an unofficial guide to Mall of America. *Annals of the Association of American Geographers* 89 (1), 45–75.

Halseth, G. (2004) The 'cottage' privilege: increasingly elite landscapes of second homes in Canada. In C.M. Hall and D. Müller (eds) *Tourism, Mobility and Second Homes: Between Elite Landscape and Common Ground* (pp. 35–54). Clevedon: Channel View.

Heise, D.A. (1994) *Promoting Tourism in Rural America*. Beltsville, MD: Rural Information Center, National Agricultural Library.

Henning, S.A. (1995) Tourism and economic development in rural Louisiana. *Louisiana Agriculture* 38 (2), 7.

Honadle, B.W. (1990) Extension and tourism development. *Journal of Extension* 28 (2), 8–13.

Hopkins, J. (1998a) Commodifying the countryside: marketing myths or rurality. In R. Butler, C.M. Hall and J. Jenkins (eds) *Tourism and Recreation in Rural Areas* (pp. 139–56). Chichester: John Wiley & Sons.

Hopkins, J. (1998b) Signs of the post-rural: marketing myths of a symbolic countryside. *Geografiska Annaler B: Human Geography* 80 (2), 65–81.

Ibrahim, H. and Cordes, K.A. (2002) *Outdoor Recreation: Enrichment for a Lifetime*. Champaign, IL: Sagamore.

Janiskee, R.L. and Drews, P.L. (1998) Rural festivals and community reimaging. In R. Butler, C.M. Hall and J. Jenkins (eds) *Tourism and Recreation in Rural Areas* (pp. 157–75). Chichester: John Wiley & Sons.

Jensen, C.R. (1995) *Outdoor Recreation in America* (5th edn). Champaign, IL: Human Kinetics.

Jones, P. (1991) Regional shopping centres: the planning issues. *Service Industries Journal* 11 (2), 171–78.

Kowinski, W.S. (1985) *The Malling of America: An Inside Look at the Great Consumer Paradise*. New York: William Morrow & Company.

Lew, A.A. (1996) Tourism management on American Indian lands in the USA. *Tourism Management* 17, 355–65.

Lew, A.A. and Van Otten, G. (1998) Preface: the allure of the American Indian. In A.A. Lew and G.A. Van Otten (eds) *Tourism and Gaming on American Indian Lands* (pp. ix–x). New York: Cognizant.

Long, P. and Edgell, D. (1997) Rural tourism in the United States: The Peak to Peak Scenic Byway and KOA. In S.J. Page and D. Getz (eds) *The Business of Rural Tourism: International Perspectives* (pp. 61–76). London: International Thomson Business Press.

Lowe, W. (1998) Bagging a real deal on your next vacation. *New Choices* 38 (4), 98–99.

Luloff, A.E., Bridger, J.C., Graefe, A.R., Saylor, M., Martin, K. and Gitelson, R. (1994) Assessing rural tourism efforts in the United States. *Annals of Tourism Research* 21, 46–64.

MacDonald, R. and Jolliffe, L. (2003) Cultural rural tourism: evidence from Canada. *Annals of Tourism Research* 30 (2), 307–22.

Mitchell, C.J.A., Nolan, R. and Hohol, F. (1993) Tourism and community economic development: a case study of St. Jacobs, Ontario. In D. Bruce and M. Whitla (eds) *Tourism Strategies for Rural Development* (pp. 16–25). Sackville, NB: Mount Allison University, Rural and Small Town Research and Studies Program.

Mitchell, C.J.A., Parkin, T. and Hanley, S. (1998) Are tourists a blessing or bane? Resident attitudes towards tourism in the village of St. Jacobs, Ontario. *Small Town* 28 (6), 18–23.

Murphy, A.E. (2003) Illustrating the utility of a modified gap analysis as a regional tourism planning tool: case study of potential Japanese and German travelers to the Cowichan region. *Journal of Travel Research* 41 (4), 400–409.

Murphy, A.E. and Williams, P.W. (1999) Attracting Japanese tourists into the rural hinterland: implications for rural development and planning. *Tourism Management* 20, 487–99.

Nelson, J.G. (2000) Tourism and national parks in North America: an overview. In R.W. Butler and S.W. Boyd (eds) *Tourism and National Parks: Issues and Implications* (pp. 303–21). Chichester: John Wiley & Sons.

O'Driscoll, P. (1997) Gambling gulch is both bonanza and battleground. *USA Today* 27 October, 17.

Outletbound (2002) *Outletbound: Guide to the Nation's Best Outlets*. On WWW at www.outletbound.com. Accessed 18.11.02.

Park, D.C. and Coppack, P.M. (1994) The role of rural sentiment and vernacular landscapes in contriving sense of place in the city's countryside. *Geografiska Annaler B* 76 (3), 161–72.

Parks Canada (2002) *National Parks of Canada, National Park Reserves of Canada and National Marine Conservation Areas of Canada.* On WWW at www.parkscanada.pch.gc.ca. Accessed 30.10.03.

Patton, S.G. (1986) Factory outlets and travel industry development: the case of Reading, Pennsylvania. *Journal of Travel Research* 25 (1), 10–13.

Ragatz, R.L. (1977) Vacation homes in rural areas: towards a model for predicting their distribution and occupancy patterns. In J.T. Coppock (ed.) *Second Homes: Curse or Blessing?* (pp. 181–93). Oxford: Pergamon.

Reynolds, J. (1993) The proliferation of the planned shopping centre. In R.D.F. Bromley and C.J. Thomas (eds) *Retail Change: Contemporary Issues* (pp. 70–87). London: University College London Press.

Ritzer, G. and Liska, A. (1997) 'McDisneyisation' and 'post-tourism': complementary perspectives on contemporary tourism. In C. Rojek and J. Urry (eds) *Touring Cultures: Transformations of Travel and Theory* (pp. 196–208). London: Routledge.

Scott, D. and Thigpen, J. (2003) Understanding the birder as tourist: Segmenting visitors to the Texas Hummer/Bird Celebration. *Human Dimensions of Wildlife* 8 (3), 199–218.

Sharpley, R. and Sharpley, J. (1997) *Rural Tourism: An Introduction.* London: International Thomson Business Press.

Smith, G.J. and Hinch, T.D. (1996) Canadian casinos as tourist attractions: chasing the pot of gold. *Journal of Travel Research* 34 (3), 37–45.

Smith, V.L., Hetherington, A.Q. and Brumbaugh, M.D.D. (1986) California's Highway 89: a regional tourism model. *Annals of Tourism Research* 13, 415–33.

Stansfield, C. (1996) Reservations and gambling: Native Americans and the diffusion of legalised gaming. In R. Butler and T. Hinch (eds) *Tourism and Indigenous Peoples* (pp. 129–47). London: International Thomson Business Press.

Stokowski, P.A. (1992) The Colorado gambling boom: an experiment in rural community development. *Small Town* 22 (6), 12–19.

Stroud, H.B. (1995) *The Promise of Paradise: Recreational and Retirement Communities in the United States since 1950.* Baltimore: Johns Hopkins University Press.

Telfer, D.J. (2001) Strategic alliances along the Niagara Wine Route. *Tourism Management* 22, 21–30.

Timothy, D.J. (2004) Recreational second homes in the United States: development issues and contemporary patterns. In C.M. Hall and D. Müller (eds) *Tourism, Mobility and Second Homes: Between Elite Landscape and Common Ground* (pp. 133–48). Clevedon: Channel View Publications.

Timothy, D.J. (2005). *Shopping Tourism, Retailing and Leisure.* Clevedon: Channel View Publications.

Timothy, D.J. (in press) Supply and organisation of tourism in North America. In D. Fennell (ed.) *North America: A Tourism Handbook.* Clevedon: Channel View Publications.

Timothy, D.J. and Boyd, S.W. (2003) *Heritage Tourism.* Harlow: Prentice Hall.

Tourism Center (2001) *Community Tourism Development.* St Paul, MN: University of Minnesota Extension Service.

Travel Industry Association of America (1999) Festival attendance. *Leisure Travel News* 16 August, 6.

US National Park Service (2001) *National Parks Guide.* On WWW at www.nps.gov/parks.html. Accessed 10.02.04.

Weaver, D.B. (2001a) Deserts, grasslands and savannahs. In D.B. Weaver (ed.) *The Encyclopedia of Ecotourism* (pp. 251–63). Wallingford: CAB International.

Weaver, D.B. (2001b) *Ecotourism.* Sydney: Wiley.

Weaver, D.B. and Fennell, D.A. (1997a) Rural tourism in Canada: the Saskatchewan vacation farm operator as entrepreneur. In S.J. Page and D. Getz (eds) *The Business of Rural Tourism: International Perspectives* (pp. 77–92). London: International Thomson Business Press.

Weaver, D.B. and Fennell, D.A. (1997b) The vacation farm sector in Saskatchewan: a profile of operations. *Tourism Management* 18 (6), 357–65.

Willits, F.K. (1993) The rural mystique and tourism development: data from Pennsylvania. *Journal of the Community Development Society* 24 (2), 159–74.

Wilson, S., Fesenmaier, D.R., Fesenmaier, J. and Van Es, J.C. (2001) Factors for success in rural tourism development. *Journal of Travel Research* 40 (2), 132–38.

Wolfe, R.I. (1952) Wasaga Beach: the divorce from the geographic environment. *Canadian Geographer* 2, 57–65.

Chapter 4

Legislative Frameworks for Rural Tourism: Comparative Studies from Spain[1]

GERDA K. PRIESTLEY, GEMMA CÁNOVES, MIQUEL SEGUÍ, and MONTSERRAT VILLARINO

Introduction

The development of rural tourism in Spain dates from the mid-1980s, rather later than in much of Western Europe (Ardillier-Carras, 1999; Dehoorne, 1999; Yagüe, 2002). This date is of particular significance as it has brought specific consequences, for by then, tourism legislation had become the responsibility of the individual Autonomous Communities (17 in all) within the Spanish state. In addition, spontaneity was the keynote in the initial stages of the development of rural tourism during the 1980s, as the product was allowed to develop and legislation ensued (Blanco Herranz, 1996; García-Henche, 2003). Moreover, the objectives of the development of tourism in rural areas vary from one Autonomous Community to another. Thus, in the Communities of Navarra, the Basque Country, and Asturias, its development was designed to complement incomes from agriculture and achieve integrated development in which the rural population was the principal actor. On the other hand, in the Communities of Galicia, Castille-León, and Extremadura, it has been encouraged as a means to preserve and enhance the cultural heritage (buildings), and scenery is the main sellable attraction. Meanwhile, in the Communities where tourism has long been established, notably the Balearic Islands and Andalusia, the expansion of tourism into the interior is more a result of the saturation of coastal development, and constitutes the emergence of a new 'elite' tourism product, in which the countryside has become a highly valued attraction for the use of a privileged minority (Cánoves & Villarino, 2002).

As a number of authors have already pointed out (Blanquer, 1999; Cánoves & Villarino, 2000b; Pedreño Muñoz, 1996; Tudela Aranda, 1999; Vera Rebollo, 1997; Villarino & Cánoves, 2000), one of the problems of this tourist product is its heterogeneous nature. An analysis of the corresponding legislation makes it possible to identify the different types of tourism that have emerged in rural areas, and to predict, to a certain extent, the future development of the areas involved. This chapter briefly summarises this legislative process in Spain and draws attention to the resulting heterogeneity of accommodation types and conditions. It also illustrates the consequent variety in greater detail by outlining the situation in three Autonomous Communities: the Balearic Islands, Catalonia, and Galicia, where striking contrasts exist in terms of landscape, socio-economic structure, objectives, and extent of tourism development in rural areas.

Rural Tourism Legislation in Spain

The first official incursion of tourism into rural areas in Spain was the programme called *Vacaciones en casas de labranza* (Holidays in farmhouses), which was introduced in 1967 as a joint initiative of the Ministries of Agriculture and Information and Tourism (García-Henche, 2003). Within this programme, limited financial aid was provided, almost exclusively in the form of interest-free loans,[2] which made little more than minor reforms to farmhouses possible. The increase from 1152 beds in 1967 to 8312 beds in the space of ten years cannot, therefore, be attributed to the success of the programme, which lasted until 1986, when the programme brochure was published for the last time. Widespread growth did not, in fact, arrive until the later 1980s, and, since then, there has been a constant numerical and geographical expansion.

The success of this form of tourism in other European countries, the regional policies of the European Community, and the transfer of responsibilities to the Autonomous Communities in Spain, were all factors in the expansion of the provision of tourism accommodation in rural areas as an increase in this segment of demand in the tourism market became apparent. The process of development followed a series of stages: originally it performed a social function, as it was a family-linked form of tourism; later it became an instrument for regional development; and, finally, the market dimension was incorporated, for, as clients requested the product, so it had to be commodified. As supply continued to increase – albeit with a considerable degree of spontaneity – the administrative authorities began to consider the necessity of regulating and structuring the product, in order to establish an adequate management and commercial structure.

The pioneer region in this regulative process was Catalonia, where legislation was first introduced in 1983. This was soon followed by neighbouring Aragon. It is significant that both regions include large stretches of the Pyrenean mountains bordering France, where the scenery is spectacular but also where rural depopulation was advancing rapidly (see Figure 4.1 and Table 4.1). The northern coast Autonomous Communities of the Basque Country and Cantabria, where picturesque coastal and mountain areas are in close juxtaposition, soon followed suit. Obviously all these areas were attractive destinations. Gradually, all the other Autonomous Communities introduced their own legislation, with the exception of Madrid.

Agritourism[3] was the original form of rural tourism in some regions, such as Catalonia, Basque Country, Navarra, and Extremadura. But as provision expanded, other forms of accommodation were introduced, and regulations were also adjusted to match this reality. As a result, throughout the legislative and regulating process, conditions and rules of compliance for rural accommodation establishments were also laid down. Aspects covered included the making of a distinction between agritourism and other forms of accommodation, location in rural areas or small urban centres (and in this case, the definition of 'rural' and the size of such villages), minimum and maximum number of beds/rooms, the presence or absence of permanent residents on the premises, requirements regarding the dedication of residents to agriculture, architectural value and age of buildings.

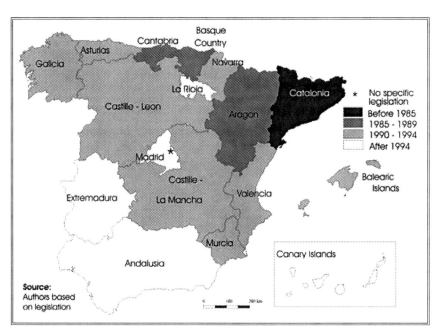

Figure 4.1 Date of introduction of rural tourism legislation in Spanish autonomous communities (*Source*: authors, based on current legislation)

Table 4.1 Legislation and categorisation of rural tourism in Spain's autonomous communities

Autonomous Community	*Legislation*	*Categorisation*
Andalusia	Decree 94/1995, 4th April	*Casa rural* (rural house)
		Edificio o unidad singular completa rural (complete, distinguished rural building or unit)
	Decree 20/2002, 29th January	*Casa rural* (rural house)
		Hotel rural (rural hotel)
		Apartamento turístico rural (rural tourist apartment)
		Complejo turístico rural (rural tourism complex)
Aragon	Decree 113/1986, 14th November	*Vivienda de turismo rural* (rural tourism residence)
	Decree 193/1994 Decree 69/1997	*Vivienda de turismo rural en alojamiento compartido* (rural tourism residence with on-farm lodging)
		Vivienda de turismo rural en alojamiento no compartido (rural tourism residence in independent accommodation)
Asturias	Decree 26/1991, 20th February Resolution of 1993, 26th April Decree 69/1994 Decree 85/1995 Resolution of 2000, 12th May	*Casa de aldea* (village house)
		Casona asturiana (Asturian country house)
Balearic Islands	Decree 30/1991	*Agroturisme* (agritourism)
		Turisme rural (rural tourism)
	Decree 13/10 of 1995 Regulation of 1995, 13th October	*Agroturismo* (agritourism)
		Hotel rural (rural hotel)
		Turisme d'interior (inland tourism)

(continued)

Table 4.1 *Continued*

Autonomous Community	Legislation	Categorisation
Basque Country	Decree of 1988	*Alojamiento turístico agrícola* (agricultural tourism accommodation)
	Decree 128/1996 Decree 210/1997 Decree 191/1997	*Agroturismo* (agritourism)
		Hotel Rural (rural hotel)
		Casa rural (rural house)
		Camping rural (rural campsite)
		Apartamento rural (rural apartment)
Canary Islands	Law 7/1995, 6th April	*Establecimiento de turismo rural* (rural tourism establishment)
	Decree 18/1998, 5th March Decree 39/2000, 5th March	*Casa rural* (rural house)
		Hotel rural (rural hotel)
Cantabria	Decree 50/1989	*Posada en casa de labranza* (farmhouse inn)
		Posada (inn)
		Vivienda vacacional (vacation dwelling)
	Decree 31/1997, 23rd April	*Palacio y casona cántabra* (Cantabrian mansion and country house)
		Posada de Cantabria (Cantabrian inn)
		Casa de labranza (farmhouse)
		Vivienda rural (rural dwelling)
		Albergue turístico (tourist hostel)
Castille–León	Decree 298/93 Decree 84/95, 11th May	*Casa rural* (rural house)
		Posada (inn)
		Centro de turismo rural (rural tourism centre)

(continued)

Table 4.1 *Continued*

Autonomous Community	*Legislation*	*Categorisation*
Castille–La Mancha	Decree 43/1994 Decree 205/2001	*Casa rural de alojamiento compartido* (rural house with on-farm lodging)
		Casa rural de alquiler (rural house to rent)
		Casa de labranza (farmhouse)
Catalonia	Decree 365/1983	*Residència casa de pagès* (farmer's residence)
	Decree 214/1995	*Masia* (farmhouse)
		Casa de poble (village house)
		Allotjament rural independent (independent rural accommodation)
	Law 13/2002, 21st June	*Casa de pagès* (farmer's residence)
		Allotjament Rural (rural accommodation)
Extremadura	Decree 120/1998, 6th October Decree 4/2000, 25th January	*Casa rural* (rural house)
		Agroturismo (agritourism)
		Apartamento turístico rural (rural tourism apartment)
		Hotel rural (rural hotel)
Galicia	Regulation of 1992, 26th February	*Pazo–Hospedería* (mansion–guest house)
		Pazo–Residencia (mansion–accommodation)
		Casa de aldea–Hospedería (village house–guest house)
		Casa de aldea–Residencia (village house–accommodation)
		Casa de labranza (farmhouse)

(*continued*)

Table 4.1 *Continued*

Autonomous Community	Legislation	Categorisation
	Regulation of 1995, 2nd January Regulation of 1996, 7th May	*Pazo, Castillo, Monasterio, Casa grande y Casa rectoral* (mansion, castle, monastery, large house, rectory)
		Casa de aldea (village house)
		Casa de labranza (farmhouse)
Madrid	There is no specific legislation	*Apartamento turístico* (tourist apartment)
Murcia	Decree 79/1992, 10th September Decree 26/2000	*Alojamiento turístico especial en zona de interior* (special tourist accommodation in inland area)
Navarra	'Foral' decree 200/1991 'Foral' decree 105/1993 'Foral' decree 53/1995 'Foral' decree 243/1999	*Casa rural de alojamiento compartido* (rural house with on-farm lodging)
		Casa rural de alquiler (rural house to rent)
La Rioja	Decree 8/1995 Decree 26/2000, 19th May	*Casa rural de alquiler por habitaciones* (rural house to rent rooms)
		Casa rural de alquiler completo (entire rural house to rent)
Valencian Community	Decree 253/1994 Decree 207/1999, 9th November	*Casa rural* (rural house)
		Albergue turístico (tourist hostel)

Source: Authors, based on current legislation

One obvious consequence of the legislative fragmentation of rural tourism is the enormous variety of accommodation types and their characteristics, which is aggravated by the use of the local nomenclature, a reflection not only of historical regional differences but also of the different languages that exist in Spain. Thus, in Catalonia a farmhouse is called a *Casa de pagès* or a *Masia*, while in Galicia and Castille-La Mancha it is known as *Casa de labranza*, and in Asturias as a *Posada en Casa de labranza*.

In the category of *Pazo*, a Galician country mansion, it is known as a *Palacio* in Cantabria, but has no equivalent term in other regions, while further confusion is caused by the use of an intermediate category of *Casona* in Asturias and Cantabria (Cánoves & Villarino, 2003).

The analysis of this legislative process demonstrates a growing interest in the development of tourism in rural areas (Sayadi, 2001), shared with an interest in taking advantage of funds made available for rural development projects, especially through European Union initiatives. In fact, the main declared objectives became to create a high-quality product, to achieve an attractive and competitive image, to decrease seasonal concentration of tourist demand, to restore built heritage and/or complement incomes from agriculture (Cánoves & Villarino, 2000a).

A Comparative Analysis of Legislation in Catalonia, Balearic Islands, and Galicia

A closer examination of the legislative process and regulation of rural tourism in three Autonomous Communities illustrates the fragmentation and considerable regional variations in the product (see Table 4.2[4]).

The necessity of regulating supply

With regard to the three regions analysed, as already stated, it was in Catalonia that legislation was first introduced, in 1983 (Garcia Ramón *et al.*, 1995). This process was not undertaken until 1991 in the Balearic Islands (Seguí *et al.*, 2002), followed one year later, in 1992, by Galicia (see Tables 4.1 and 4.2). There were coinciding motives in Galicia and Catalonia, for development had reached such a stage that regulation was imperative (see Table 4.3). This was not the case in the Balearic Islands, undoubtedly because traditional forms of tourism absorbed all the initiatives, and it is only recently that interest has been shown in this particular form. There is, however, one coincident objective in the encouragement of tourism in rural areas in Galicia and the Balearic Islands, for in both regions it has been seen as a means to recover a heritage in danger of destruction. This is, in fact, a common objective in other countries, such as Portugal, where many country residences – *pazo, quinta* – were restored for use as tourism accommodation. Certainly, in all three regions studied, there was a need to find complementary sources of income to supplement agriculture, coinciding with European policy. In the case of Galicia, however, another factor has also been important in stimulating demand: the increasing attraction of 'natural' areas, and thus the typical Galician landscape became a sellable product (Cánoves & Villarino, 1999).

Initial legislation was modified in 1995, mainly because the considerable growth in supply that had taken place was extremely heterogeneous

Table 4.2 Typology of establishments in Catalonia, the Balearic Islands and Galicia

Catalonia	Balearic Islands	Galicia
1983: one category • *Residencia–Casa de pagès* (accommodation–farmhouse)	**1991**: two categories • *Agroturisme* (agritourism) • *Turismo Rural* (rural tourism)	**1992**: five categories • A–*Pazo–Hospedería* (mansion–guest house) • B–*Pazo–Residencia* (mansion–accommodation) • C–*Casa de aldea–Hospedería* (village house–guest house) • D–*Casa de aldea–Residencia* (village house–accommodation) • E–*Casa de labranza* (agrotourism farmhouse)
1995: updating of previous legislation. *Residencia–Casa de pagès* is subdivided into three groups: • *Masia* (farmhouse) • *Casa de poble* (village house) • *Allotjament rural independent* (independent rural accommodation)	**1995**: modification of previous legislation: • *Agroturisme* • *Hotel Rural* (name replaces *Turisme Rural*) • *Turisme d'interior* (inland tourism – new category) • *Altres ofertes complementaries* (other complementary activities – new category)	**1995**: restructuring of categories: • Group A: *Pazo* and other similar mansions • Group B: *Casa de aldea* • Group C: *Agroturismo* Groups A and B can be either *Hospedería* (proprietor shares residence with guests) or *Residencia* (guests use independent building)
2002: reclassification on basis of presence/absence of farming activities: • *Casa de pagès* (farmer's residence) • *Allotjament rural* (rural accommodation)		

Source: Authors, based on official regional government bulletins: Balearic Islands: BOCAIB (1991, 1995); Galicia: DOGA (1992, 1995); Catalonia: DOGC (1983, 1995, 2002)

Table 4.3 Underlying factors governing legislation and regulation of rural tourism supply

Catalonia	*Balearic Islands*	*Galicia*
1983: • Regulation of a rural product in view of growth expectations	**1991:** • Increase income for farmers • Conservation of existing buildings in the rural environment, then seriously deteriorated	**1992:** • New trends in tourism demand (renewed interest in nature) • Galician landscape as an attraction factor • Recover *pazo* heritage buildings • Complement farmers' incomes • Redistribute tourism demand towards inland areas
1995 (updated previous legislation): • Incorporate understanding of the product acquired through experience • Considerable increase of tourism supply in inland and mountain areas • Need to restructure this form of tourism to improve services and distinguish between different products **2002** (reclassification on basis of presence/absence of farming activities): • Differentiate a true agritourism product from rural tourism without crop farming, animal husbandry or forestry activities	**1995** (modified previous legislation): • Favourable response to product in the tourist markets • Necessity to diversify the tourism product in an attempt to reduce seasonality • Increase market quota • Modify establishments to satisfy the foreign market	**1995** (replaced previous legislation): • Establish a good image for a growth product • Guarantee minimum standards in installations necessary to provide high-quality services in order to satisfy clients • Make use of unique buildings (*pazos,* monasteries, castles, etc.) for tourism purposes in order to make conservation feasible

Source: Authors

in style and quality. The underlying objective of this new regulation was to adjust supply to demand in general, and to fulfil specific additional objectives in each region. Thus, it intended to contribute to a reduction of seasonality in the Balearic Islands, to convey a clear and competitive image in the market in Galicia, take stock and build on past experience in Catalonia, and to widen the range of unique buildings used – attractive farmhouses in Catalonia, castles and monasteries in Galicia. The modifications introduced are indicative of the type of tourism favoured in each region. In the Balearic Islands and Galicia, stress is placed on the restoration of valuable or fine buildings, and on image, which shows that they aim at an upper sector of the market. Renovation grants can reach between 35 and 55% in the former region and 50% in the latter. In fact, in Galicia, this policy has been reinforced, for, since 1996, traditional farmhouses (*Casas de labranza*) have no longer been eligible for subsidies. Subsequent partial modifications introduced in the Balearic Islands and Galicia have aimed to adjust supply to demand. These include exemption from some requisites for unique buildings in the Balearic Islands, or specifications on prices and services in Galicia, while in Catalonia a new product has been introduced, inspired by French experience. It is known as *Gites de Catalunya*, and is the first step to establishing categories based on quality levels.[5] Nevertheless, the use of the term could, in fact, lead to a certain degree of confusion, as the better known French counterpart does not invoke the idea of high quality that is inferred in the Catalan product. Further modifications to legislation were to be introduced in Galicia in 2004. These would include the introduction of additional categories, complicating even further the range of nomenclature employed.

Typology of establishments

In Catalonia, initial legislation made no distinction between accommodation provided in private homes or on independent (non-home) premises (see Table 4.2). Two categories were also established in the Balearic Islands in 1991: *Agroturisme*, to define the provision of tourism services in traditional farmhouses integrated on agricultural properties, and *Turisme Rural*, where tourism services were provided at well-appointed country residences. In contrast, five categories were established in Galicia: *Pazo–Residencia, Pazo–Hospedería, Casa de aldea–Residencia, Casa de aldea–Hospedería*, and *Casa de labranza*. The last category could be considered the equivalent of Balearic agritourism. *Pazos* are buildings of considerable architectural value, *Casas de aldea* are village houses, and the combinations depend upon whether the rural proprietors share their home with the guests (*Hospedería*) or provide independent accommodation units on their properties (*Residencia*).

Subsequent modifications have been more profound and significant in the Balearic Islands than in the other two regions. In Catalonia, where agritourism was the original form of rural tourism, and later expanded to other forms, regulations were adjusted to match reality in 1995. The original name of *Residencia–Casa de pagès* was maintained, but three subdivisions were made in order to distinguish between accommodation in private homes or on independent premises and also to differentiate houses in the countryside from those in villages. Hence, a distinction was made between *Masia* (isolated farmhouse) and *Casa de poble* (house in a small town), corresponding to the two types of population units in rural areas. To this was added the category of *Allotjament rural independent* (independent rural accommodation), the difference being that in this category the proprietor was not required either to share the residence nor to be employed in farming. However, legislation was modified once again in 2002 in order to make a basic distinction between properties where part of the owner's income is obtained from agricultural activities (denominated *Casa de pagès*) and those that had no connection with agriculture (*Allotjament rural*). This would appear to oversimplify the nomenclature, but the law also made provision for the subsequent creation of subcategories to introduce further distinctions, such as those previously made between the different locations (village, countryside).

Meanwhile, new legislation introduced in the Balearic Islands in 1995 maintained the category of *Agroturisme*, but replaced the concept of *Turisme Rural* by that of *Hotel Rural*. A third, new category was introduced, namely *Turisme d'interior* (inland tourism), to group accommodation units in urban areas previously not involved in the tourist industry, obviously endorsing tourism expansion away from the coast. Finally, a category for *Altres ofertes complementaries* (other complementary activities) was created, and this includes leisure, recreation, and catering services. This constitutes an important innovation, because most efforts are directed towards the creation of accommodation, while the necessary (and in many ways, even more important) complementary elements are seldom – if ever – considered. In this respect, it should be remembered that the quality of tourism in rural areas depends not only on accommodation, based on the hotel concept, but on the entire destination, as a long-term guarantee of success.

In Galicia, the names of the categories were simplified without introducing basic structural changes. Thus, the various types have been regrouped to form three categories, and these have been more strictly defined: Group A includes the provision of tourist services in unique well-appointed buildings, Group B comprises rustic Galician buildings, and Group C denotes agritourism activities. Groups A and B are subdivided into the prior categories of *Hospedería* and *Residencia*. A later modification now makes the presence of a named person on the premises a requisite, in those cases in which the proprietor is a company. This new system thus introduces a scale based on the quality of the buildings, somewhat similar to the classification introduced by the TURIHAB Association in Portugal, where the A, B, and C categories denote differences in service provision and consequently prices. In this way, a certain degree of homogeneity is introduced in a product, which, due to its very nature, is inevitably heterogeneous. Nevertheless, there are now 11 different categories to denominate tourism accommodation in rural areas in the three autonomous communities studied, some of which are indeed confusing, as, for example, the term *Hotel Rural*, which mixes conventional terminology with the rural concept.

Rules and conditions governing establishments

As already pointed out, the legislative process involved the establishment of conditions and rules of compliance for all forms of rural accommodation. Antiquity is a basic criterion for establishing categories, and is present in the regulations applied in all three communities, and, although changes have been introduced through time, it remains one of the means of ensuring conformity to certain categories. The key dates lie between 1940 and 1950, as it is in this period that economic development and social modernisation led to a boom in construction in which traditional architecture was often brushed aside. Hence, in the Balearic Islands, all buildings in the top quality categories – *Hotel Rural* and *Turisme d'interior* – must have been built prior to 1940. To qualify for the *Agroturisme* category, buildings can be built as late as 1960, possibly because this type of building had been subjected to fewer modifications. In Galicia, initially the deadline construction date was 1940, but later further restrictions were imposed, and the limit for Group A buildings was fixed at 1900, and at 1940 for Group B, but no limitations were placed on Group C. Evidently, in this respect, Galicia and the Balearic Islands follow similar criteria. On the other hand, the construction limit in Catalonia is 1950 for all categories.

In this way, age became a key criterion for establishing categories, but obviously the restoration of buildings also had to be regulated. No modifications of the original structure can be introduced, and traditional materials typical of each region must be employed. On the other hand, tourism regulations impose standards for accommodation that also have to be complied with, and that may require certain modifications to installations, in which case, exceptions are made. Regulations are especially strict in the case of Galician Group A buildings, as these also belong to the Heritage Catalogue, which has its own set of rules for rehabilitation. Likewise, the regulations applicable for the restoration of unique buildings in the Balearic Islands are extremely strict.

Although the topic in question is 'tourism in rural areas', the term 'rural' is, in itself, ambiguous and variable, as can be seen through examination of the definitions adopted. In the Balearic and Catalan legislation, specific reference is made to location: establishments in the categories of *Hotel Rural* and *Agroturisme* (Balearic Islands) must be situated on land classified as non-urban, and *Turisme d'interior* establishments must be located in urban areas at least 500 m from certain specified tourist zones. The criterion applied in Catalonia is numerical: the maximum size of rural settlements where establishments can be located is 1000 inhabitants. In Galicia, the term used is vague: it simply states that establishments must be located in rural areas. In both these regions, qualitative criteria are also introduced, for one of the requisites is that establishments cannot be near roads or activities that disturb the tranquillity and integration with the countryside that clients expect. In the Balearic Islands, the minimum extension of properties is also specified: 50,000 m² in the case of the *Hotel Rural* and 25,000 m² in the case of *Agroturisme*, which obviously constitute large properties. Such restrictions could not be applied in Galicia, where properties are almost invariably small, and would encounter certain difficulties in Catalonia for the same reason.

The restrictions outlined above have conditioned the provision of accommodation, but it is the regulations referring to services and installations that determine the characteristics of the supply in each area. A universal requisite is a well-preserved building and compliance with local architectural styles. However, regulations in the Balearic Islands and Galicia are more specific. In the former region, a *Hotel Rural* is required to incorporate <u>high</u> quality finishing, furniture, furnishings, table ware, and so on, while in *Turisme d'interior*, the quality must be <u>good</u>. No mention is made of these aspects in *Agroturisme* regulations. In Galicia, installations, furniture, and furnishings must be of <u>excellent</u> quality in Group A and <u>good</u> quality in other categories. In the case of bedrooms and common quarters, instructions and differences are clearly stated for each category. In the first place, a maximum and minimum number of beds is normally stipulated, which is understandable in the case of a type of tourism that cannot, due to its very nature, be large scale. In the Balearic Islands, no minima have been established, and the maxima are relatively high, bearing in mind the non-mass nature of the product. Hence, a *Hotel Rural* can have up to 25 bedrooms, *Turisme d'interior* eight, and *Agroturisme* 12, although the upper limit in this last category was initially six. In Galicia, the maximum was originally 10, but with the introduction of A, B, and C categories, variations were introduced: the Group A limit was raised to 12, and can even increase to 15 if sufficient space is available, while the previous limit of 10 was retained for categories B and C. In any case, the limited size of these types of buildings would make it impossible to increase their capacity beyond the existing limit. Minimum sizes were also established: five, three, and two rooms for Groups A, B, and C, respectively. In Catalonia, a *Masia* or a *Casa de poble* can vary from a minimum of three bedrooms and five beds to a maximum of 15 beds, distributed in single, double, triple, or four-bedded rooms. An *Allotjament rural independent* must provide at least four beds, with the same upper size limit of 15 beds as in the other categories, but the maximum capacity per room in this case is limited to three beds.

These regulations clearly define the type of rural accommodation that is being encouraged by the authorities, but this becomes even more evident on analysis of the requisites for the size of rooms. Minimum sizes are indicated for all cases, varying between 10 and 15 m^2 for a double room. Habitability conditions are added to these restrictions. They are of a general nature for *Agroturisme* in the Balearic Islands, imposing a minimum length and breadth (3.6 m), while in Galicia a minimum circular diameter (2.5 m) is stipulated, to avoid the use of strangely shaped rooms. In Catalonia, a minimum height requisite is applied (2.25 m), to prohibit the use of unsuitable lofts. Habitability requisites are completed with those related to bathrooms. In *Hotel Rural, Turisme d'interior* (Balearic Islands), and Groups A and B (Galicia), each bedroom must have a private bathroom with a minimum size that varies between 3 and 4.5 m^2. In *Agroturisme* and Group C categories, there must be a ratio of 0.5 bathrooms per bedroom and the minimum size is 3 m^2. In Catalonia, there must be one bathroom for every five beds. The bathrooms must have <u>direct</u> ventilation, according to Balearic and Galician regulations, and <u>sufficient</u> ventilation in the case of Catalonia. Suitable furniture is required in Catalonia, while in Galicia, the components are individually specified.

In all cases, communal areas for the exclusive use of the guests must be provided, but, there again, standards vary according to category. In the Balearic Islands, the lounge must provide a minimum space of 3.5 m^2 per bedroom in *Hotels Rurals*, and 3 m^2 in *Turisme d'interior* establishments. In Galicia, the corresponding areas are 2 m^2 per bed and a minimum total size of 30 m^2 for Group A, and 1.5 m^2 per bed for Groups B and C. In Catalonia, no size is specified. Requisites for dining rooms are identical in the case of the Balearic Islands, to which must be added the bare statement that *Agroturisme* premises must make provision for breakfasts. In Galicia, reference is made only to the *Hospedería* categories and Group C, and it is stated, logically, that eating space must be provided for at least the same number of people as the sleeping capacity of the establishment, with an upper limit of 35 table settings. In the B and C categories, if sleeping capacity does not exceed eight persons, the lounge and dining room can be a single room. In Catalonia, regulations on dining facilities are based on the number of beds. In this respect, a proportional relationship between category and size is maintained. Likewise, there is unanimity in the provision of private areas for the exclusive use of guests, especially the dining area, which cannot be used by the general public. Nevertheless, there is an increasing number of rural tourism establishments that are acquiring complementary incomes from catering for day trippers and passers-by.

A miscellany of additional services complete the list of quality standards to be complied with. In Catalonia and Galicia, central heating is an obligatory requisite in bedrooms and communal areas. This is a particularly taxing requisite in the more modest establishments, such as traditional country farms, which are not normally equipped with heating systems, unlike urban houses. Balearic Island regulations on this aspect are even more detailed: a *Hotel Rural* must have central heating in the bedrooms and both heating and air conditioning in areas for communal use. On the other hand, no requirements are stated for *Agroturisme*. It is evident that not only climatic conditions but the high-quality standards intended for this product in the Balearic Islands are reflected in such regulations. All establishments must have a telephone, but it is only in the case of the *Hotel Rural* and Group A that all bedrooms must also have a connection.

The provision of meals can constitute a problem or, at least, a challenge, for not all proprietors have sufficient knowledge of catering. Many are farmers who simply take advantage of the opportunity to renovate their homes or complement their incomes and do not fully understand the eating requirements of guests. The maximum requirements are the provision of breakfast and one main meal in the *Hotel Rural*, in Groups A and B (but only in the *Hospedería* subcategory) and in the *Casas de labranza*. In the other categories in the Balearic Islands, only breakfast service is obligatory, while, in Catalonia, meals may be served, but to guests only. In Galicia, on the contrary, such opposition to providing meals was encountered that proprietors who shared their homes with guests (technically included in the *Hospedería* category) were allowed to transfer to the *Residencia* category, in order not to be obliged to provide meals. A further difference between Galician and Catalan legislation is thus revealed with respect to the provision of meals: in the former region, catering for non-residents is permitted, whereas in the latter, it is prohibited. This situation does not take into consideration the true needs of the clients, for catering should really be considered a necessity in isolated establishments, whereas this would not be so for those close to restaurants and bars. In fact, not only could economic benefits be spread more evenly in a country community if various services were provided by different establishments, but also service could be more professional. Such criteria were not taken into consideration in the regulations. Finally, in the Balearic Islands, and only there, parking facilities are required in a *Hotel Rural* (one space per double bedroom) and there must also be a swimming pool.

Maintenance of agricultural activities

The original underlying rationale for the development of this type of tourism in all three regions was to provide a complementary income for agricultural activities and, hence, it was supposed that it would be developed and run by farmers. However, through time, trends have changed and legislation has, in some cases, been modified in consequence. The most outstanding example is that of Catalonia, where, originally, being a farmer was a basic condition for establishing tourism accommodation on premises; but this is no longer a requisite. In fact, there is now doubt as to the advisability and even viability of mixing agricultural and tourism use. Moreover, as has already been pointed out, since 1996, the *Casas de Labranza* (farmhouses for agritourism) have not been eligible for rehabilitation grants, which is further evidence of the change in policy. Nowadays, in the Balearic Islands, it is only in the *Agroturisme* category that proprietors are obliged to dedicate at least half of one person's annual work load (i.e. 1920 hours) to farming activities in order not only to obtain initial approval, but for tourism activity to continue to exist. In Galicia, agricultural activity is implicit in the *Casa de labranza* category, while in Catalonia, it is considered preferable – but not obligatory – in the *Masia* and *Casa de poble* categories for part of the income to be gained from agricultural practices.

Other conditions

A register of rural tourism activities was introduced in both the Balearic Islands and Galicia. In order to be included in the register, relevant reports demonstrating compliance with regulations must be submitted: a heritage report for listed buildings, an insurance policy for civil responsibility,[6] and, in the case of Galicia, a municipal licence. Registered establishments can then use the official logo. In Galicia there are additional requisites: for the *Hospedería* categories, the proprietor must be domiciled in the corresponding municipality, the establishment must remain open for at least 11 months per year, and those establishments that have received grants must join a centralised regional government booking system. Finally, pricing is the prerogative of the proprietor, who has to communicate rates to the Administration each year for publication in *Turgalicia*'s Official Guide.[7]

Supply and marketing trends

In the Balearic Islands, tourism in rural areas must be viewed within the context of the already established tourism sector. There were only 61 establishments in 1999 (Govern Balear, 1999), but by the beginning of 2004 the number had risen to 192.[8] There are certain imbalances, as the vast majority (73%) belong to the *Agroturisme* category, and most establishments are located on the island of Mallorca (85.4%). In relative terms, this constitutes a limited supply, but, in general, it is a high-quality product, something that is not very abundant in Balearic tourism. The clientele is somewhat different from the rest of Spain, as a result of the well-developed commercial channels, which attract a high percentage of foreign guests in search of a more exclusive product than that available as a general rule along the coast. Prices are high, as corresponds to the type of product that is being developed. Available complementary activities include: golf, tennis, a gym on the premises, as well as a swimming pool. Access to scuba diving, mountaineering, and traditional water sports can also be arranged. An Agritourism Association (*Associació d'Agroturisme Balear*) has been founded, providing a centralised booking system and brochures about the available supply, edited in Spanish, English, and German, which is a clear demonstration of the potential market.

In Galicia, in 2003 there were 383 registered establishments, of which approximately 70% belonged to Group B (Xunta de Galicia, 2003), and by the beginning of 2004, the number had risen to 440.[9] Prices vary considerably according to category and season, but on average, they are about half that of equivalent accommodation in the Balearic Islands. Clients are mostly Spanish. Most establishments have bicycles available for their guests, and are equipped with a games room and a small library. They also offer the possibility of participating in farm activities and provide information on other activities available in the surrounding region. There is clearly a trend towards close cooperation between rural establishments and independent leisure activity providers, in which the former act as a liaison, rather than competing with the latter by providing activities themselves. In most cases, the variety of recreational pursuits within a radius of approximately 20 km is quite considerable: fishing, hunting, hiking, horse riding, and nautical sports. There are a number of local business associations, of which *AGATUR* is the most important, as it covers the entire region and includes almost 75% of all establishments. Some of the smaller local associations have formed a federation in order to be more competitive. In addition, *Turgalicia*, the regional government tourism agency, has a specific rural tourism division that publishes an annual guide in various languages and provides a centralised booking service. In fact, the role of this public agency is fundamental in the development, promotion, and marketing of the product in Galicia.

In Catalonia, there were 926 establishments at the beginning of 2003 (Generalitat de Catalunya, 2003), and by June 2003 the number had risen to 1007.[10] Prices are comparable to those in Galicia. The majority of the clients are from the Barcelona region, although in recent years there has been a significant increase in the number of foreign tourists (mainly from France, Germany, and the Netherlands) and of tourists from the rest of Spain. In collaboration with specialised businesses in the surrounding area, most establishments can provide access to bicycles, nautical sports, horse riding, adventure sports, and hiking. It is noteworthy that an increasing number of houses are incorporating swimming pools, as a means to satisfy the rising demand for family holidays. Promotion and marketing in Catalonia is fragmented and, as a result, private initiative is fundamental in the commercialisation of rural tourism in the region.

Conclusions

There is no doubt that tourism in rural areas is growing rapidly. In the year 2003, there were approximately 35,000 beds available in over 6500 establishments in Spain (see Figure 4.2). It must be recognised, however, that this constitutes only a minor sector in Spanish tourism, amounting to approximately 3% of all registered accommodation.

Nonetheless, greater consensus on the regulation of this emerging sector is an urgent necessity. Agreement must be reached on some degree of standardisation of the regional laws and regulations, a process that is obviously complicated by the cultural and linguistic variations at the root of the differences. As has been demonstrated, the net result so far is the proliferation of types and categories of accommodation and the corresponding local nomenclature.

These circumstances make it difficult to commercialise rural tourism as a clearly defined and well-structured product with guarantees of uniform quality. This is particularly problematic in the international market, but even at domestic level, knowledge of and access to the product is not always satisfactory. Therefore, it is now imperative to introduce

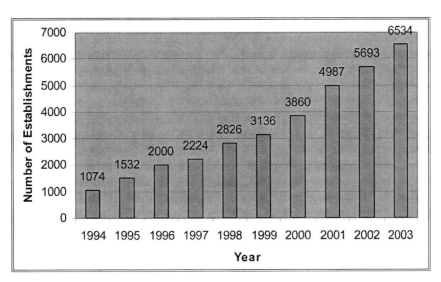

Figure 4.2 Rural tourism establishments in Spain, 1994–2003 (*Source*: INE (2001–2003); El País Aguilar (1994–2000))

new regulations in order to achieve the unification of terminology, with two specific objectives in mind. In the first place, it would enable intermediaries and consumers to identify the product in the market and, second, it would make it possible to establish categories based on quality standards. In spite of these difficulties, the progressive introduction and modification of legislation and regulation on buildings and service provision demonstrates how tourism in rural areas has been drawn into the general tourism market. Nonetheless, the product has gradually evolved towards a niche market, aiming to attract the middle to upper socio-economic groups.

The progressive modification of legislation concerning the relationship between the agricultural component and rural tourism accommodation raises a number of queries. Similarly, the increasing incidence of companies as proprietors, which introduces greater flexibility and more professional management, is proof of the recognition that this form of management and rural tourism are no longer considered incompatible, but rather that a sector-specific professional attitude is required. Nevertheless, there are inherent dangers in this conceptual change, for, taken to its ultimate consequences, the product could become subject to the same process of concentration in the hands of hotel chains, as has happened in mass coastal tourism. Moreover, the increasing provision of sports facilities and other leisure activities in conjunction with rural accommodation is taking the emphasis away from the original objectives of 'agritourism'. On the basis of this evidence, it is worth giving some thought to the kind of 'rural experience' that is, in fact, being offered to visitors.

It is also questionable whether or not this form of tourism will serve as sustenance for agricultural activity. This is especially evident in the case of the Balearic Islands, where 'rural tourism' simply constitutes an up-market niche within the general framework of the tourism sector, and certainly does not contribute to the sustainability of traditional rural life and its economy. Nonetheless, the conservation of agricultural practice is fundamental because, if agriculture is gradually abandoned, part of the attractiveness of the landscape, and the cultural and human environment of the rural area may be lost. It is not unthinkable that this landscape, which is now being abandoned, might have to be reconstructed in the future. For it certainly must be recognised that the real attraction for visitors who venture into the countryside is not its price – for rural tourism cannot by any means be considered family or social tourism – but rather a certain type of rural landscape, one in which society is integrated with its environment.

Likewise, it is fundamental to orient growth towards an integrated development model, in which the rural population plays a leading role.

In these circumstances, the specific role of country women is fundamental, offering them the alternative of performing tasks that are both
remunerated and socially valued, and that can contribute, at the same
time, to the survival and maintenance of agricultural activities and the
farm population (Cánoves & Garcia-Ramón, 1995). It must be recognised,
however, that the diversifications of supply and market segmentation are,
together, leading to an increasingly professional attitude to tourism in
rural areas. On the other hand, seasonality remains a problem, and imaginative solutions for this are required. It is, therefore, evident that in
the future, the development of tourism products in rural areas cannot
be limited to the provision of accommodation, but must widen their
range to include cultural, social and sporting activities, set in the
overall context of the surrounding district or region. In this way, a
diverse product consisting of complementary subproducts will evolve,
and it would appear to be the only solution for the integrated development of tourism in rural areas.

Notes

1. This paper reports on part of a more comprehensive research project currently
   being carried out by *Grupo TER*, a Spanish interuniversity research group,
   with the objective of establishing a classification of tourism in rural areas in
   Spain. The research team is composed as follows: Gemma Cánoves (Director),
   Gerda K Priestley, Asunción Blanco, Luis Herrera and Lucia Cuesta, Department of Geography, Autonomous University of Barcelona (*Universitat Autònoma de Barcelona*); Montserrat Villarino, Department of Geography, University
   of Santiago de Compostela (*Universidad de Santiago de Compostela*); Pedro
   Armas, Department of Geography, University of La Coruña (*Universidad de
   A Coruña*), Miquel Seguí, Department of Earth Sciences, University of the
   Balearic Islands (*Universitat de les Illes Balears*); Lluis Garay, Open University
   of Catalonia (*Universitat Oberta de Catalunya*).
2. It was only in 1984 and 1985 that grants were awarded to a small number of
   integrated projects, which involved lodging and services or leisure facilities.
3. The term agritourism, when used throughout this text, is defined as the
   provision of tourism services in traditional farmhouses integrated on agricultural properties.
4. The abbreviations used to denote sources are: BOCAIB Butlletí oficial de la
   Comunitat Autònoma de ses Illes Balears; DOGA Diario Oficial de Galicia;
   DOGC Diari Oficial de la Generalitat de Catalunya.
5. There are now 45 establishments in this category. They are independent dwell-
   ings that can be rented as an entire unit on a weekly or monthly basis at an
   approximate cost of 150 euros per week.
6. Initially, possession of an Economic Activity Licence, except in the case of
   Agroturisme in the Balearic Islands, had to be demonstrated through

payment of the corresponding tax (*Impuesto de Actividades Económicas*), but this tax – and therefore the requisite – was abolished in 2003.

7. *Turgalicia* is a company set up by the Galician government, the *Xunta*.
8. Statistics dated 31 January 2004, provided by the *Conselleria de Turisme, Govern Balear*. Detailed data are as follows: Mallorca – category *Hotel Rural* 17, *Agroturismo* 116, *Turismo d'interior* 31; Menorca – *HR* 4, *A* 10, *TI* 1; Ibiza/Formentera – *HR* 2, *A* 11, *TI* 0.
9. Statistics dated 31 January 2004, provided by *Turgalicia*, the regional government tourism agency.
10. Statistics provided by the Conselleria de Comerç, Industria i Turisme, Generalitat de Catalunya.

References

Ardillier-Carras, F. (1999) Espace rural et tourisme: mirage ou opportunité? Reflexion autour d'un ensemble regional entre Poitou et Limousin. In P. Violier (ed.) *L'Espace Local et les Acteurs du Tourisme* (pp. 33–39). Rennes: Presses Universitaires de Rennes.

Blanco Herranz, F. (1996) Fundamentos de la política comunitaria y española en materia de turismo rural. Consideraciones sobre la legislación española. *Estudios Turísticos* 131, 25–49.

Blanquer, D. (1999) Régimen jurídico del turismo rural. In J. Tudela Aranda (ed.) *Régimen Jurídico de los Recursos Turísticos, Monografías de la Revista Aragonesa de Administración Pública* (pp. 473–82). Pamplona: Revista Aragonesa de Administración Pública.

BOCAIB (Butlletí oficial de la Comunitat Autònoma de ses Illes Balears) (1991) Decret 30/1991.

BOCAIB (Butlletí oficial de la Comunitat Autònoma de ses Illes Balears) (1995) Decret 62/1995.

Cánoves, G. and Garcia Ramón, M.D. (1995) Mujeres y turismo rural en Cataluña y Galicia: La nueva panacea de la agricultura? *El Campo* (Servicio de Estudios del BBV) 133, 221–38.

Cánoves, G. and Villarino, M. (1999) Rural tourism, gender and landscape conservation: the north of Spain and Portugal. *Proceedings of the Gender and Rural Transformations in Europe Conference*. Wageningen: Agricultural University of Wageningen.

Cánoves, G. and Villarino, M. (2000a) Turismo en espacio rural en España: actrices e imaginario colectivo. *Documents d'Anàlisi Geogràfica* (Barcelona: Universitat Autònoma de Barcelona) 37, 51–77.

Cánoves, G. and Villarino, M. (2000b) Turismo rural en Portugal: las mujeres piezas clave para 'recibir' y 'servir'. In M.D. Garcia Ramón and M. Baylina (eds) *El Nuevo Papel de las Mujeres en el Medio Rural* (pp. 199–216). Barcelona: Oikos-Tau.

Cánoves, G. and Villarino, M. (2002) Rural tourism, gender, and cultural conservation in Spain and Portugal. In M. Swain, B. Henshall and J. Momsen (eds) *Gender/Tourism/Fun* (pp. 90–102). New York: Cognizant.

Cánoves, G. and Villarino, M. (2003) Turismo rural y desarrollo rural: perspectivas y futuro en Cataluña, Baleares y Galicia. *Serie Geográfica* (Alcalá: Departamento de Geografía de la Universidad de Alcalá) 11, 117–40.

Dehoorne, O. (1999) Le tourisme rural en Aveyron: L'affirmation d'une nouvelle activité économique. In P. Violier (ed.) *L'Espace Local et les Acteurs du Tourisme* (pp. 73–80). Rennes: Presses Universitaires de Rennes.

DOGA (Diario oficial de Galicia) (1992) Orden de 26 de febrero de 1992.

DOGA (Diario oficial de Galicia) (1995) Orden de 2 de enero de 1995.

DOGC (Diari oficial de la Generalitat de Catalunya) (1983) Decret 444/1983, de 27 d'octubre, pel qual es fixen els criteris de distribució i el procediment per a la concessió de subvencions a la millora de l'habitatge rural i a l'adequació de cases de pagès com a allotjaments turístics.

DOGC (Diari oficial de la Generalitat de Catalunya) (1995) Decret 214/1995, de 27 de juny, pel qual es regula la modalitat d'allotjament turístic anomenada residència-casa de pagès.

DOGC (Diari oficial de la Generalitat de Catalunya) (2002) Llei 13/2002, de 21 de juny, de turisme de Catalunya.

El País Aguilar (1994–2000) *Guía de Alojamiento en Casas Rurales de España.* Madrid: El País Aguilar (annual publication).

Garcia Ramón, M.D., Cánoves, G. and Valdovinos, N. (1995) Farm tourism, gender and the environment in Spain. *Annals of Tourism Research* 22 (2), 267–82.

García-Henche, B. (2003) *Marketing del Turismo Rural.* Madrid: Pirámide.

Generalitat de Catalunya (2003) *Guia d'Establiments de Turisme Rural.* Barcelona: Generalitat de Catalunya, Departament d'Indústria, Comerç i Turisme.

Govern Balear (1999) *Guia de Turisme Rural.* Palma de Mallorca: Govern Balear.

INE (Instituto Nacional de Estadística) (2001–2003) *INEbase.* Madrid: INE. on WWW at www.ine.es. Accessed 02.02.04.

Pedreño Muñoz, A. (ed.) (1996) *Introducción a la Economía del Turismo en España.* Madrid: Editorial Civitas.

Sayadi, S. (2001) Agroturismo y desarrollo rural. *Cuadernos de Turismo* 7, 131–57.

Seguí, M., Cánoves, G., Villarino, M., Armas, P., Priestley, G. and Garay, L. (2002) Tourisme rural en Espagne. Analyse de l'offre des Baléares, de la Galice et de la Catalogne. *Espaces* 194, 51–55.

Tudela Aranda, J. (ed.) (1999) *Régimen Jurídico de los Recursos Turísticos, Monografías de la Revista Aragonesa de Administración Pública.* Pamplona: Revista Aragonesa de Administración Pública.

Vera Rebollo, J.F. (ed.) (1997) *Análisis Territorial del Turismo.* Barcelona: Editorial Ariel.

Villarino, M. and Cánoves, G. (2000) Turismo rural en Galicia: sin mujeres imposible. In M.D. Garcia Ramón and M. Baylina (eds) *El Nuevo Papel de las Mujeres en el Medio Rural* (pp. 171–98). Barcelona: Oikos-Tau.

Xunta de Galicia (2003) *Guía de Turismo Rural.* A Coruña: Xunta de Galicia.

Yagüe, R.M. (2002) Rural tourism in Spain. *Annals of Tourism Research* 29 (4), 1101–10.

Chapter 5

Effective Marketing for Rural Tourism

JACKIE CLARKE

Introduction

The understanding and practice of marketing might be considered a weakness in the development and management of rural tourism (Gannon, 1995; Lane, 1994; OECD, 1994). Factors such as limited budgets, poor coordination of marketing expertise, the variety of stakeholder interests, and the misconception of marketing as a discipline equating to promotion, all contribute to this generality. This chapter, practical in its outlook and rooted in secondary research, previous rural tourism research (e.g. Clarke, 1995, 1999), and a consultancy project (e.g. Clarke *et al.*, 2001) aims to:

- re-visit the issues influencing the practice of marketing for rural tourism; and
- present a checklist of propositions or questions to guide those responsible for rural tourism towards the more effective use of marketing.

The chapter is not comprehensive in content – the successful application of marketing to rural tourism could fill a book – but it covers a range of ideas and is intended to provoke thought and to trigger fresh insight into the effective use of marketing beyond its current limited (and false) remit as a producer of leaflets.

Setting the Context for Rural Tourism

Before examining the issues and responses of marketing, this chapter outlines some commonly and not so commonly held beliefs about rural tourism with which this author is happy to work. This set of assumptions about rural tourism supports the frame of the chapter, and is presented here as three chains or strands of thought. The author, for ease of reader convenience, has named these linked ideas as the stakeholder chain, the development chain, and the global chain.

The stakeholder chain

Here, the author perceives the following ideas linking into the stakeholder chain:

- there is a multiplicity of disparate stakeholders accompanied by varying degrees of power ...
- ... within the private sector, rural tourism is very much SME, even micro, driven ...
- ... so that competition between providers, rather than cooperation, is the default nature of the game, and the problems of small business are very much the problems of rural tourism ...
- ... nonetheless, integration and partnership between public and private sector and integration between rural tourism and other economic sectors are buzz strategies for rural tourism (see, e.g. English Tourism Council and The Countryside Agency, 2000).

The development chain

A further set of ideas are connected by the author into the development chain:

- responsibility for rural tourism is multilevel, from national to local (where the product is actually experienced), and requires coherence in planning to fit with an overall sense of direction ...
- ... but may work best where strong national or international leadership is given (e.g. government investment in France post-war, the PHARE programme and results in Slovenia) ...
- ... and certainly involves coordination between government departments to ensure that legislation is compatible.

The global chain

The final chain, the author's global chain, is shaped by the following thoughts:

- rural tourism is rooted in the three subsystems of sustainability (environmental, social, and economic), or 'wise growth' (in UK Government 'speak'); clean air, clean water and so forth lie at the heart of any rural offer even more so than for many other types of tourism, so that protection of the natural and socio-cultural environment, and encouraging sustainable practice amongst providers and consumers ...
- ... arguably contributes on a global environmental front as well as at the local level ...
- ... important because rural tourism competes in a global business environment ...

- ... a fact often hidden as spatial dispersion of providers and relative remoteness from potential markets are also characteristics of rural tourism.

The global context of rural tourism is an interesting one. Although commentators have pointed to a tendency in rural tourism for adopting an inward-orientation or product-led perspective, most countries in the world with developed tourism portfolios have a rural tourism offer, and, where targeting international tourists, are locked into the global tourism system. For the international visitor (and to some extent, the domestic), the options for a rural tourism experience are interchangeable both between countries and within, especially when there is no clearly defined proposition to hinder substitution. This may not be well understood by the rural tourism organisers, who see the neighbouring local area as the competitor. Furthermore, rural tourism for the consumer may not have a globally consistent interpretation. We are not talking here of technical definitions, but of consumer perceptions. What is seen as 'green', 'clean', 'spacious', or 'free' in one country may not be so in another. Thus, different nationalities will bring with them culturally determined expectations of 'rural' that may not fit with the host country's rural tourism offer.

Setting the Context for Marketing Rural Tourism

Marketing does not replace planning; it should work in tandem, each discipline through its own lens. But has planning taken over 'product development' and 'auditing', and relegated marketing to the role of promoter of the finished product?

Marketing for rural tourism exists at many destination levels: national, regional, and local. It exists not only for destinations, but also for specific product sectors, such as farm accommodation, cycling, or museums, and then again at the different product sector levels: national, regional, local, and individual. To take the first example, in the United Kingdom, Farm Stay UK, a consortium composed of serviced and self-catering farm accommodation members, practises marketing at a national level through its head office, at a local level through area groups, and individually through members (Clarke, 1999). Marketing efforts for rural tourism will overlap between destination levels and between specific product sectors. Is marketing at so many levels really effective? How should marketing be adapted at each destination/product level to utilise the strengths of each? Where are those decisions taken? And do adequate resources follow the expertise? Marketing in rural tourism is probably under-resourced; conversely, resources that do exist may be wasted on ineffective activities, such as the production of an unmemorable leaflet or flyer.

Examining the Rural Tourism Product with a Marketing Lens

There is variety within rural tourism globally, and not just on the product components. Variety is represented by the balance of tourism in the local economy, by its pulling power or ability to attract visitors (local urban areas, regional, nationally, short-haul internationally, globally – the physical catchment radius refined by travel time), and by its life-cycle stage. The issues, problems, and solutions addressed by marketing will vary by life-cycle stage. A mature rural tourism destination struggling with second home ownership, saturation and over-supply of dubious quality attractions, may need to look at de-marketing and product rejuvenation. By contrast, a developing rural tourism destination battles with creating a distinctive proposition and market awareness in its chosen segments.

As a destination, rural tourism is an amalgam of different components. Schemes such as Middleton's (1994) accommodation, attractions, facilities and services, accessibility, image, and price, Gannon's (1995) accommodation, amenity attractions, access facilities, activities, and available services, and Buhalis' (2000) attractions, accessibility, amenities, available packages, activities, ancillary services, can each be used to map the rural tourism destination. Unpacking each component will reflect instinctively the country or region; this chapter probably has a United Kingdom feel simply by dint of its author's nationality. Seaton and Bennett (1996) also emphasised the destination in the consumer's mind; for that destination marketers should consider what is actually 'there', what is thought to be 'there' by the consumer, and what has been represented as being 'there' in the past. This may have particular relevance for rural tourism destinations that have evolved or emerged slowly through time.

In addition, this author suggests that rural tourism destinations might usefully think about their portfolio of attractions as 'seeing', 'buying', and 'being' from the leisure consumers' perspective.

- *'Seeing' attractions* are primarily passive, 'sightseeing' attractions; traditional perhaps, but not to be underestimated, such as the 12 million visits to English parish churches in 1999 (English Tourism Council, 2000). Attractions and events with a UK bias might include sheepdog trials, castles and historic homes and gardens, museums, religious buildings, steam railways and other forms of transport (horse-drawn, water-based, ballooning), village fetes and festivities. *'Look, see, or think'* is the motto and enters the modern realms of info- and edutainment.
- *'Buying' attractions* provide opportunities for visitors to buy physical goods and perishables. Souvenirs (low-value, mass-produced, high-volume, low-margin, but of great importance to certain segments),

crafts (high-value, skills-orientated, low-volume, higher margin), and food and drink. The latter two categories are important in integrating tourism into the economy, expressing the local identity or sense of place, and in creating and strengthening those vital networks: farmers' markets, markets, farm shops, pick your own, local craft fairs, rural craft exhibitions and centres, open days or permanent sales points and tours of rural food and drink producers, antique and curiosity shops. *'Spend, spend, spend'* is the mantra of Western media, and, as increasing the spend per head per trip in rural areas is a common problem, these buying attractions need sensitive integration into the rural product. It needs to be sensitive because of the very nature of the rural tourism offer (an escape from materialism?), and because of certain segments' need for discovery and exploration.

- *'Being/doing' attractions*, are activities rooted in skill acquisition and special interest, appealing to tourists who wish to spend their leisure time in self-development and even transformation (*being*), and activities that fit with the wellness/fitness trend (*doing*). These doing or being attractions may be rooted in local identity, or they may not be connected at all, but reap the benefits of a rural location. Caving, orienteering competitions, night hiking, horse riding, watersports, hang-gliding may stem from the natural resources of the area itself. Niche products such as creative writing courses, painting and sculpture, sporting tournaments, yoga, may have no links with the rural area that successfully courts its development, using only the rural environment backdrop and qualities provided.

Of the three types of attraction, it is arguably the 'doing/being' category that is overlooked in rural tourism product development, although this represents a growth area in demand. Sufficient thought may not have been given to integrating 'buying' experiences into the rural offer either. For some rural destinations, there may be an over-supply of 'seeing' attractions; this market may be the largest, but is unlikely to be expanding. A recent rural tourism strategy document for England and Wales (English Tourism Council & The Countryside Agency, 2001; see also Chapter 2) argued for better linkage between activity suppliers and other types of rural tourism enterprise. Any rural destination needs a product mix of 'see, buy, and be' attractions.

Building networks

Company does not compete against company. Network competes against network. (Buttle, 2001: 55)

An organisation's network of suppliers, intermediaries, employees, customers, investors, and partners on joint initiatives, and the principle of creating a network with which to compete (Buttle, 2001), is a useful concept for tourism *per se*. Building networks in rural tourism may help to:

- tackle the inherent competitiveness between micro enterprises and foster greater cooperation, and draw together private and public sector interests;
- increase visitor spend while minimising leakage and maximising the multiplier effect in the local economy;
- disperse visitors spatially to aid new attractions or to manage peak demand periods when capacity is stretched;
- increase visitor length of stay by signalling additional activities or attractions;
- strengthen rural area identity as perceived by the tourist and by the local businesses and residents who 'buy into' the network concept;
- strengthen relationships with travel trade intermediaries for product distribution and encourage (if desired) the development of packages by specialist tour operators and other external packagers of leisure products;
- nurture entrepreneurial talent and managerial expertise in the area through support networks and training partners; and
- open up opportunities for funding bids as many government and quasi-governmental bodies favour partnerships and integration.

Included within the rural tourism network should be the individual component providers, goods and service suppliers from other local economic sectors, intermediaries, key customer segments, trade and professional associations from tourism and other rural sectors, training institutions in the area, local government bodies, and so forth. Attention should be paid not only to the linkage, but to the density and quality of the connections, and multilevel connections may prove more enduring.

Spatial networks may be devised by 'packaging' rural tourism components into inclusive and coherent routes through the use of themes and stories (such as folklore, working lives, food and drink routes, religious routes), which help to move the tourist around geographically dispersed attractions. For example, the island of Réunion, close to Madagascar in the Indian Ocean, offers a spice route, linking attractions and producers and opportunities to buy around the spice theme. Routes can be used to develop local forms of transport and for luring tourists from their cars: for example, wine routes in Alsace offer a horse and cart as an option. Typically, the resulting route or theme is communicated to individual tourists by printed map, display board and website. This theming and routing technique is one favoured by Gannon (1994, 1995).

The author of this chapter also suggests that attention be paid to the design of

- attractions of 'height' (e.g. church towers, town hall clock towers, mining watch towers) and
- attractions of 'scope' (e.g. guided walking tours, bus tours, horse-drawn vehicle tours)

so that mental orientation to the area also provides 'clues' for add-on attractions and activities as spied from the visual potential of 'height' and 'scope' attractions, and feeds the visitor's sense of discovery.

The scope of the product portfolio may be specialised, or, quite commonly, may offer a 'pick "n" mix' menu from which, in the words of Sharpley and Sharpley (1997), the consumer 'assembles' their own tailor-made product. For the destination organiser, specialising may increase the exposure to external events and to over-reliance on segmentation, but will allow image focus. Widening the portfolio lines/width/depth may reduce vulnerability to one-off events and serve a range of segments, but at the possible expense of a clear and unique proposition. Cross-fertilising between attractions and activities (e.g. introducing falconry displays into an historic castle, or incorporating parish churches into a cycle route) may open up one attraction to the segment of another, which otherwise might not have been visited. When cross-fertilising, due caution should be paid to the issue of segment compatibility.

Building the brand

Branding is considered complex for destinations (Goodall, 1990). For rural tourism, branding may occur at national, regional, or local level, and for individual product sectors, so that rural tourism is represented by a medley of 'brands'. But many of these are too weak to have emerged as true brands with identifiable propositions, values, and images acknowledged by the market. These local rural tourism brands are simply a collection of definable components (accommodation, attractions, and so forth) with some added atmosphere and landscape, all topped off by a logo and slogan. For the browsing consumer, there is no emotional epicentre and no emotional connection, which are the driving force of a powerful brand.

Some rural areas have used a form of branding franchise, where they have borrowed an existing identity associated with the area (e.g. in the United Kingdom, Tarka country, Catherine Cookson country, or Hardy country). Gilbert (1990) referred to status or commodity areas. Status areas have unique product attributes, either genuine or imagined by the market, and are regarded as irreplaceable, commanding higher prices and a greater willingness to pay. Perhaps rural areas such as Umbria, the Lake District, or Provence have achieved such status in the British market. But the majority of rural tourism fits the commodity description: substitutable, sensitive to price, and low definition and awareness of benefits. Marketing effort should seek to move the rural destination towards a status area. High-volume tourism and cost-leadership are not attractive options for most rural tourism destinations; brands built on product differentiation and associated higher margins make better sense. It therefore follows that rural brands need to accentuate their local identity and sense of place in a manner meaningful to the market, and to think about the emotional heart of the brand as perceived by the visitor.

The capacity/demand link

Capacity, in the physical sense of actual bedspace/attraction throughput, in the environmental sense of sustainability, and in the psychological sense of tourist satisfaction with feelings of 'freedom' and 'spaciousness', needs to be handled carefully. Rural tourism is characterised by

- limited, spatially dispersed physical capacity that is locally owned and controlled, which might vary in its availability by season, and which grows incrementally;
- limited environmental capacity; and
- limited psychological capacity, in that tourist expectations of 'freedom' and 'spaciousness' infer relatively low tolerance of other tourists expressed numerically (or behaviourally) before satisfaction is adversely affected.

Marketing is the management discipline best suited to matching supply with demand. If the gaps between the supply and demand curves for different times of the year are known, then strategies, such as identifying new market segments, joint sales promotions, and themed special events can be developed to plug the gaps where demand falls lower than desired capacity. For rural tourism, the demand issues may also relate to the behavioural characteristics of certain segments, as well as numerical volume.

Examining Rural Tourism Demand with a Marketing Lens

Beyond the hands-on feel of the individual provider, there is little understanding of the rural tourism market. Rooted in poor marketing research and access to data, even traditional visitor statistics such as visitor numbers, length of stay, and expenditure are poorly recorded, and the methodologies from which local statistics derive may be of dubious design. Calculation of market share and comparison is an impossibility. This paucity of data is recognised by the English Tourism Council and The Countryside Agency (2000), who have criticised the monitoring of rural tourism performance. Understanding the market also requires a thorough understanding of visitor motivation, needs and wants, images and perceptions, and purchase/usage/post-usage behaviour. There may be a misplaced emphasis on the importance of numeric information about the market, which can only provide a partial picture of the consumer.

Segmentation in rural tourism is weakly developed; although a destination is open to 'unwanted' segments, decisions on favoured segments and subsequent targeting are needed. Rural tourism destinations should consider the balance of their segment portfolio in terms of the following.

- The leisure purpose/business purpose split: the growth of the MICE (meetings, incentive, conference, and exhibitions) market offers opportunities that should not be ignored by rural tourism providers (e.g. Farm Stay UK actively pursues the business segments).
- The independent/inclusive tour split: the independent segments are characterised by greater flexibility in their experience subdecisions, but within the UK, even domestic short break rural holidays are increasingly available as packaged products.
- The domestic/international visitor split: the domestic visitor can be more reliable in terms of loyalty, have greater product familiarity, and can benefit incremental growth, as well as act as ambassador for VFR travel. Yet the domestic market is sometimes overlooked in favour of the arguably more glamorous international market, even though it may well contain the more robust segments suitable to target for disaster recovery.
- The repeat/first time visitor split: the differences in characteristics and the balance between these two types of visitors need to be appreciated, and marketing campaigns adapted accordingly.
- The demand and capacity patterns, with particular attention to segments who visit during shoulder and trough periods: each segment has its own 'seasonality profile', and these need to be understood and valued appropriately.

In the practical search for new segments, rural tourism providers and destinations might reflect on the following options:

- second (third) generation markets now residing overseas interested in exploring their historical roots;
- conversion of international first-time visitors, who mainly visit gateway cities and honeypot locations, to rural tourism visitors on subsequent trips;
- societies and clubs based on special interests and skills – Web-based searches may be useful in this regard; and

- growth of the 'experience' sector of the gifting market – that is, the purchase of leisure experiences and short breaks as gifts for loved ones – which may be particularly relevant amongst ABC1s in later stages of the family life-cycle and time-crushed yet cash-rich urban professionals.

Examining the seasonality profile and the risk factor in terms of reliability and robustness of short-listed segments, as well as the more accepted growth trends, size, accessibility, and complementarity with the existing segment portfolio, may prove useful in assessing each segment's attractiveness to rural tourism organisers.

Linking into information and communications technology (ICT)

For a product spatially isolated from its markets, such as rural tourism, Website and other ICT reduces remoteness through global electronic distribution and reduces reliance on intermediaries. This may be especially important for rural tourism where independent markets like to pick and choose. Essential to these forms of electronic distribution are systems of quality assurance to support consumer confidence in the decision process. This is particularly so with rural tourism where individual 'brands' are often poorly developed. ICT-based systems offer an alternative to the traditional paper-based literature direct mail practices; 'click and brick' ICT behaviour may mean that potential tourists use the Web for information (the 'click' element), before turning to the traditional telephone/postal systems for purchase (the 'brick' element).

In fact, ICT can be used creatively to support rural tourism initiatives, both as a source for improving business practice, and for reaching the consumer. Take the author's anecdotal example of Herrang, a tiny village two hours north of Stockholm. 'Herrang' is a niche brand, with strong awareness, understanding of values, and emotional pull for around ten to twelve thousand people globally. 'Herrang' is a dancers' brand, where devotees of a particular form of dance gather once a year during a one-month timeframe to take instruction (Zoot Society, 2002). This is an ICT-literate, largely professional middle-class, twenties-to-forties international market, with around 350 coming each week and spending approximately €700 per person per week, with a probable lifetime value span to Herrang of between three and five years. From the rural tourism perspective, it is worthwhile to note the following.

- This is a market that communicates almost entirely through information technology and informal word of mouth; the global spread of the dance form has largely been fuelled by Internet accessibility, so that there is arguably an 'on-line community'.
- This is a tailor-made product with a 'being/doing' attraction focus, that is skills acquisition and development.

- The market leader 'Herrang' brand has no obvious linkage to this one particular village over and above community willingness and a relationship link between the village and one of the organisers; it does not rely on dramatic scenery or outstanding natural features.
- Fascinatingly, the brand bypasses all traditional tourism channels; there is no tourist board, nor TIC, nor travel agent involvement (beyond individual flight purchase in country-of-origin). Essentially, the brand is 'invisible' to the official tourism structure.
- The local community rent out second and vacant houses and have developed add-on 'seeing' attractions, such as boat trips, salmon restaurant trips, and tours of the local quarry and paper mill. Self-catering guests obviously spend money in the village store and at the limited number of food outlets and restaurants. There are, as yet, no 'buying' attractions.

So, here is presented a combination of an 'on-line community' and a powerful niche brand, which just happens to be associated with one remote village with not much to distinguish it from other remote Swedish villages. But it has nurtured a long-standing relationship with the acknowledged world experts of a given skill. For rural areas with suitable assets, an exercise to track down any useful contacts, plus a Website search for special interest 'on-line communities' may be fruitful in any search for a new target segment. Once familiar with the 'on-line community', it is not hard to identify the opinion leaders and experts, nor to approach them with an opening proposal.

Back to Some Marketing Basics

A re-examination of some of the marketing basics merits the attention of rural tourism practitioners. Audits for rural tourism, which tend to focus on the destination and the range of existing and potential products, must also evaluate the market potential for this primarily asset-led development, and assess the competition both locally and internationally with an eye to substitute destinations and possible partner destinations with whom to network. In considering objectives, what is the community trying to achieve through rural tourism? Buhalis (2000) considers the long-term prosperity of residents, visitor satisfaction, the maximisation of enterprise profitability (which is closely related to extending the length of the season in many rural tourism cases), in relation to optimising the positive impacts and minimising the negative. To this list could be added economic objectives with regard to revitalising the economy, integration of economic sectors, stabilisation of employment, and support for or diversification of existing economic structure. At the prosaic level, objectives translate into visitor numbers, increasing spend per head per trip, increasing length of stay, re-balancing the spread of demand both spatially and temporally, and altering visitor consumption behaviour. How well are these objectives understood and bought into by the local community?

Identifying and strengthening distinctive competencies and key factors for success are facets rarely examined in rural tourism marketing. The former is the mainstay of competitive advantage, and the latter are the 'must haves' in order to be able to compete in the market over the medium to longer term. How easy is it for any competitive advantage to be copied? An authentic sense of place and unique identity (preferably as expressed through a brand) are harder for a competitor to steal, as are people-based skills highlighted through investment in training. Price, where too many rural tourism areas compete, is only too easy to mirror. This author would argue that the key factors for success in rural tourism include personal customer care, quality assurance schemes linked to ICT distribution in the electronic age, attention to environmentally sustainable practice, and a unique sense of place locked into natural or socio-cultural resources. Any play-off between the soft aspects of 'space', 'freedom', 'cleanliness', or 'contrast to urban life' must be seen in the context of a thorough understanding of target segments. With regard to customer care, it is tempting to impose Western ideals onto non-Western rural communities, but, as part of its unique identity, the destination must retain its own style of hospitality, requiring an adapted form of customer care training that enhances the providers' understanding of consumer needs and wants while respecting (and, indeed, drawing out) the traditions of local hospitality.

A final word on the marketing mix, in particular, communication and pricing: communication for rural tourism is frequently translated as leaflet production and advertising (coupled with use of direct mail). The Internet opens up possibilities for two-way communication (as opposed to one-way promotion), perhaps with leaflets and brochures as tangible support mechanisms. There is now a myriad of communication associations with informative Websites. As just one example, the evil-named 'viral marketing' might offer effective communication solutions – and the Website of the Interactive Advertising Bureau (www.iabuk.net) provides a starting point. Public relations as a communications tool is often neglected, although it complements advertising effort and may even be a better use of limited financial resources. Networks should be exploited for opportunities for joint communications campaigns, and also for pricing schemes, typically attached to sales promotions or to designed themes and routes, as discussed earlier.

Checklist of Propositions and Questions for More Effective Use of Marketing in Rural Tourism

By way of summary and to give practical expression to this chapter's objectives, Table 5.1 presents a series of propositions and questions that rural tourism organisers responsible for marketing might reflect upon in order to improve the effectiveness of their marketing practice. It is not a comprehensive list, but one that highlights the main points brought out within this chapter.

Table 5.1 Checklist of propositions and questions for rural tourism providers concerned with marketing

Do we appreciate that we operate in a globally competitive market for rural tourism?   – is our rural area of status or commodity standing?
How extensive is our current marketing practice and do we think strategically?   – or is marketing used to produce hard copy literature?
What levels and parties are involved in marketing the rural tourism destination/product sector?   – and are we best coordinating their individual strengths and   expertise?
Are there specific objectives and goals for our rural tourism?   – which are supported by the community?
What are the key factors for success for our type of rural tourism provision?   – where are our weaknesses within these KFS?
What are our distinctive competencies?   – and are they fully exploited in respect of competitive advantage?
Can we develop a true brand with emotion at its core?   – or should we concentrate on developing a clear positioning for our   target markets?
Do we have a network with which we can compete?   – how could this network be further developed in line with   our goals?
Do we use marketing to manage demand against capacity?   – how well do we understand the seasonality patterns by capacity   and by segment?

(continued)

Table 5.1 *Continued*

What is the quality of the market information we use to make decisions? – how might collaboration within our network and IT be used to improve the situation?
How well balanced is our target segment portfolio in respect of our goals? – do we understand each segment's strengths and weaknesses in respect of our goals?
Does our rural tourism offer as a destination contain the best balance of component sectors? – for attractions, in terms of 'seeing, buying, and being' and in terms of 'height' and 'scope'?
Have we assessed the rural tourism offer in terms of product lines, width and depth? – have we explored any opportunities for cross-fertilisation?
Have we themed routes that link tourism components and strengthen our unique identity? – how well do these routes operate spatially and by season?
Have we exploited the opportunities of IT for communication, distribution, and information? – are there undiscovered 'on-line communities' that might be attractive to us?
Have we investigated quality assurance schemes to boost consumer confidence? – and linked these schemes to our IT strategies?
Do we consider the full range of marketing mix tools, particularly for communication? – is our network used to best advantage for communication (including sales promotions), product packaging, and pricing?

Conclusion

By re-visiting the issues influencing marketing practice in rural tourism and through the presentation of a checklist for more effective marketing action, this paper has emphasised the wider role of marketing for rural tourism, and, in particular, the use of marketing at a strategic level. All too often relegated to a producer of leaflets and literature, it is hoped that this paper has provoked wider thought as to the contribution of marketing as a discipline and has stimulated some initial thoughts about marketing through the range of ideas presented. Folklore suggests that successful marketing is about incremental improvements across many fronts, a 'game of inches' (Davidson, 1987). The ideas in this chapter are offered as signposts for appropriate action in rural tourism marketing and to help move all forms of rural tourism towards greater success.

References

Buhalis, D. (2000) Marketing the competitive destination of the future. *Tourism Management* 21 (2), 97–116.

Buttle, F. (2001) The CRM value chain. *Marketing Business* 96, 52–55.

Clarke, J. (1995) The effective marketing of small-scale tourism enterprises through national structures: lessons from a two-way comparative study of farm accommodation in the United Kingdom and New Zealand. *Journal of Vacation Marketing* 1 (2), 137–53.

Clarke, J. (1999) Marketing structures for farm tourism: beyond the individual provider of rural tourism. *Journal of Sustainable Tourism* 7 (1), 26–47.

Clarke, J., Denman, R., Hickman, G. and Slovak, J. (2001) Rural tourism in Roznava Okres: a Slovak case study. *Tourism Management* 22 (2), 193–202.

Davidson, H. (1987) *Offensive Marketing. Or How to Make Your Competitors Followers* (2nd edn). London: Pitman.

English Tourism Council (2000) *Action for Attractions*. London: English Tourism Council.

English Tourism Council and The Countryside Agency (2000) *Rural Tourism: Working for the Countryside. A Joint Consultation Document*. London: English Tourism Council and The Countryside Agency.

English Tourism Council and The Countryside Agency (2001) *Working for the Countryside. A Strategy for Rural Tourism in England 2001–2005*. London: English Tourism Council and The Countryside Agency.

Gannon, A. (1994) Rural tourism as a factor in rural community economic development for economies in transition. *Journal of Sustainable Tourism* 2 (1 & 2), 51–60.

Gannon, A. (1995) Critical issues in the development of rural tourism. Joint ECA–ECE Symposium on Rural Tourism, Galilee, Israel, 2–7 April.

Gilbert, D. (1990) Strategic marketing planning for national tourism. *The Tourist Review* 1, 18–27.

Goodall, B. (1990) The dynamics of tourism place marketing. In G. Ashworth and B. Goodall (eds) *Marketing Tourism Places* (pp. 259–79). London: Routledge.

Lane, B. (1994) Sustainable rural tourism strategies: a tool for development and conservation. *Journal of Sustainable Tourism* 2 (1 & 2), 102–11.

Middleton, V.T.C (1994) *Marketing in Travel and Tourism* (2nd edn). Oxford: Butterworth-Heinemann.

OECD (Organisation for Economic Co-operation and Development) (1994) *Tourism Policy and International Tourism in OECD Countries 1991–1992*. Paris: OECD.

Seaton, A.T. and Bennett, M.M. (1996) *Marketing Tourism Products. Concepts, Issues and Cases*. London: International Thomson Business Press.

Zoot Society (2002) *Herrang 2002*. Leeds: Leeds University. On WWW at http://www.scs.leeds.ac.uk/vincent/herrang_2002.html. Accessed 03.03.04.

Chapter 6

Exploitation of ICT for Rural Tourism Enterprises: The Case of Aragon, Spain

GRAEME EVANS and PAOLA PARRAVICINI

Introduction

Information communications technology (ICT) has been fêted by national, regional, and European governments, and by the 'new media' industry, as a major opportunity for tourism firms, destinations, and information providers. As well as cost efficiencies and more effective market penetration, ICT is seen to offer remote and more peripheral destinations an advantage in gaining greater control over their promotional and destination image and in accessing new customers, particularly in urban and overseas generator markets. This is particularly so where major tour operators and the global travel industry crowd out local, independent firms: 'the Internet as a commercial tool has provided the supply side with an alternative channel for communication, marketing, and distribution, which may prove capable of sidestepping these middlemen' (Vich-I-Martorell, 2002: 91). However, over 90% of tourism enterprises in Europe are small, predominantly micro-enterprises, including seasonal, family-run, and life-style operations. Barriers to take-up and successful development of ICT by SMEs are therefore significant, despite the technological determinism that is driving public policy initiatives and the advantages that are apparent through global computer reservation systems (CRS) and on-line sales. Small tourism and related firms, it is claimed, are therefore 'lost in the electronic marketplace' in contrast to larger operators and transnationals, which dominate *e-commerce* in the visitor economy. A further irony is that while the communication and commercial applications offered by the Internet remove the physical and spatial barriers that traditionally limit remote and rural areas, the new media sector that drives this technological phenomenon itself chooses to cluster in close proximity (Evans, 2004; Pratt, 2000). This suggests that while ICT and e-commerce present technical opportunities, micro-enterprises still require physical clusters and other networks in order to compete and innovate – an admission largely absent in the ICT literature. Inter-firm relations are therefore as important in benefiting from ICT, as a study of tourism SMEs in regional Australia found: 'overcoming the loss of competitive advantage in the digital economy will require community building with connectivity, collaboration, and trust' (Braun, 2002: 20).

Survey

This chapter is based on a comparative survey of ICT usage, plans, and skills of small tourism enterprises in Europe, which has focused on three regions/destination types: London (UK), the Netherlands, and the Aragon autonomous region in northeast Spain. The study was conducted under the EU's LEONARDO survey and analysis programme between 1997 and 2001, with follow-up in 2003. The Aragon region is the subject here of detailed analysis across its three districts, in this largely rural, mountainous and underdeveloped province. In Aragon, tourism is a prime sector for economic development, with an increase in rural accommodation provision during the 1990s and growth in demand for outdoor recreation and heritage tourism activity. Usage of ICT by tourism firms in Aragon, not surprisingly, is lower than northern and urban regions, with poorer telecommunication and transport infrastructure limiting its development. Moreover, engagement with ICT varies widely between tourism activity sectors and between type of firm and their location. Intervention through European and regional programmes has not had a significant impact on ICT usage or skills and possible reasons for this are discussed, in terms of the factors influencing ICT take-up, and the role of intermediaries. Variation within the region itself is also apparent with an urban–rural divide that is exacerbated by the transport infrastructure and the pattern of largely domestic tourist activity.

The expansionist European region is the largest tourist destination in the world, but one whose share has been declining in a growing international tourist market (WTO, 1998). European and national government policy has, since the early 1990s, sought to retain this market share and to spread the seasonal and geographic distribution and diversity of tourism activity, including promoting eco/agrotourism, cultural tourism and routes (Richards, 1996). Quality improvement has also focused attention on customer service, training, and the development of ICT as both a management and marketing tool. In the case of technology-based projects assisted by the EU in this period, the most innovative aspects were their transnational character and the attempt to apply new technology to new areas such as information handling, previously addressed through guidebooks and maps. In all cases, however, projects failed to address post-project sustainability. The evaluation also raised the relevance to the wider tourism system since, as the authors note, 'Technology offers both a barrier and an opportunity to SMEs, and this has not satisfactorily been addressed . . .' (EC, 1996: 21). More recent responses and initiatives within the EU include *Information Society Technology* under the five-year 'Fifth Framework' Research and Development Programme, as well as ERDF and LEADER programme funding (see below), supporting research and advocacy networks, and which together have targeted ICT, SMEs and tourism in rural and post-industrial – manufacturing, extraction, and agricultural – regions.

Small is Beautiful?

While the rapid growth of ICT usage and on-line travel and reservations systems dominate the field of tourism marketing and communication, the tourism 'industry' in practice is both fragmented and represented by, on the one hand, a large number of small enterprises and, on the other, a small but powerful number of global and national operators and intermediaries (Buhalis, 1994; 1998; Evans & Peacock, 1999): 'a diverse and highly fragmented industry, most of which are SMEs, often resulting in less coherent policy formulation and ineffective co-ordination at many levels' (EC, 1996: 2). Small firms are key elements of economic development and employment growth prospects within European and local economies, and policies to support and enhance SMEs are evident at European (EU) and national levels. However, while constituting by far the largest number – an estimated 93% of all firms in the EU – SMEs as a whole represent a tiny proportion of the total sales turnover and produce below-average 'value added per employee', when compared with medium- and larger-sized firms (EC, 1997). The other side of the technological revolution and accompanying determinism also sees a growing divide between those with full access and skills in information society technology (Werthner *et al.*, 1997) and those lacking such access, control, and ownership – a form of socio-economic exclusion creating a group of disempowered employees and disadvantaged, potentially non-competitive businesses. As Downey (1999: 137) predicts, 'While it is likely that the greater use of ICT will have significant benefits in terms of productivity, GDP growth and employment, it is also probable that these benefits will not be equally distributed. Inequalities between core and peripheral [European] regions will grow as core regions increase their grip on the global economy; inequalities will widen. . .'

The poorer quality of telecommunications infrastructure in rural European regions was observed earlier by Williams and Shaw (1989), and the EC itself found that there were clear urban–rural differences in network modernization between southern and northern countries, and the greatest variation between urban–rural regions was in tourism compared with other sectors. Over ten years on, divergence is still apparent within EU member states (Table 6.1), with Spanish SMEs having an extremely low level of Website ownership, over-reliance on external sites, and, crucially, very low access to e-commerce. Subregional variations are of course apparent in a highly skewed tourism distribution market. For instance, in the Balearics, one of Spain's three main destination regions, e-commerce capability was 43% (Vich-I-Martorell, 2002: 103). Good practice and support policies are therefore not being effectively promoted and transferred nationally, undermining both national and European redistributive policies in general.

In practice, small firms may traditionally lack capital, research and development resources, and the scale of operation required to justify investment in ICT. As Werthner and Klein (1999: 44) note, 'Their size is their main disadvantage. Small suppliers have normally little know how about marketing and technology . . . and limited access to distribution channels'. They also cite the fact that over 85% of European accommodation suppliers are not listed on airline CRS that serve travel agents

Table 6.1 SME e-business adoption rates in 2001

% of SMEs	*Using ICT*	*Having Web access*	*Having a presence on Web via own Website*	*Having a presence on Web via third party Website*	*Making e-commerce purchases*	*Making e-commerce sales*
Austria	92	83	53	26	14	11
Denmark	95	86	62	N/A	36	27
Spain	91	66	6	28	9	6
Finland	98	91	58	N/A	34	13
Greece	84	54	28	8	5	6
Sweden	96	90	67	N/A	31	11
UK	92	62	49	11	32	16
Germany	96	82	65	21	35	29
Luxembourg	90	54	39	13	18	9
Netherlands	87	62	31	N/A	23	22
Italy	86	71	9	26	10	3
Norway	93	73	47	N/A	43	10

Source: EC (2002)

worldwide (Werthner *et al.*, 1997). From an earlier study of UK hotels, it was evident that smaller hotels with less than 20 rooms were far less likely than larger ones to use ICT (Main, 1995), and smaller establishments tended to employ older and less qualified staff; low ICT usage and skills were also confirmed in a similar study of letting agencies (Mutch, 1995). Other barriers may include an antipathy to new technology itself where personal service and contact is a key comparative advantage of the owner-operator and niche supplier (Evans, 1999). Small enterprises may also represent a 'life-style choice' by owners, which may dictate their attitudes to ICT and their management styles and rationales in general. In some cases this may embrace new technology, a concern for image and design (e.g. Website, customer relations), while others may positively reject the notion of marketing and organisational development altogether, which computing and ICT infers (Bennett & McCoshan, 1993; Webster, 1999). From a study of tourism micro-enterprises in rural New Zealand for instance, ICT usage was not uniform across the sector nor even among those serving common market groups, whereas, 'The education and professional background of operators appeared as the most significant influence on IT uptake and its successful utilization' (Ateljevic *et al.*, 1999: 16). The most cited barriers to IT adoption were 'time', 'lack of knowledge', and 'money', and operators were found to be intimidated by hidden costs associated with the adoption of IT such as training and software upgrades. Other southern European regions cited barriers in terms of security and reliability/speed of Internet systems, as well as a lack of skills (Deimezi, 2002). Risk of fraud is also cited in a survey of tourism SMEs in Scotland (SPICe, 2002). This is a growing concern as bad experience and publicity accumulates on this downside of the Internet. From our survey of European tourism SMEs it was also found that independent micro-firms were some of the most creative users of ICT in presenting a unique image, in relationship marketing, and within speciality networks, in contrast to larger SMEs, which had a more standardised and static approach and Web presence.

Aragon Region

Aragon is a landlocked province south of the Pyrenees (Figure 6.1). The region has suffered from de-population (40% during the 20th century), both as a result of its poor infrastructure and declining agricultural base, and due to a lack of regional assistance by the Spanish government during the Franco regime. The resident population is low relative to the land area, with 25 people per square km (Teruel, the poorest of the three districts, has only 10 people, some local areas as low as 5), compared with 75 for Spain as a whole, itself half the EU average density. With migration to urban areas and other regions (e.g. Catalonia), the

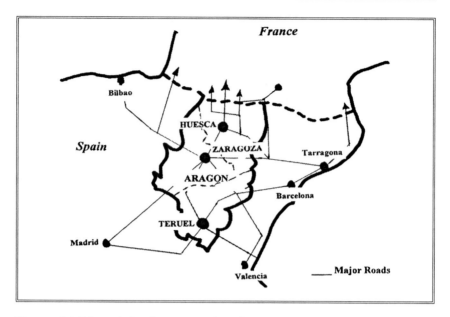

Figure 6.1 Map of the Aragon region, Spain

residual population includes a high over-60 age group, a high proportion working in agriculture – 83% of the land is designated as
'productive' – but with a recorded unemployment rate of 15%, below
the national average of 20%.

As a tourist destination, Aragon is typified by outdoor recreation
(skiing, mountaineering), historic towns, and an upland topography,
with high seasonality between the extremes of the summer and winter climates. The Ordesa National Park adjoins an equivalent park in the French
Pyrenees, and with growing regionalism within both countries (e.g. the
attraction of direct European regional aid), joint initiatives on both sides
of the mountain border have included transport, cultural, and tourism
development and promotion. With a high proportion of domestic tourists,
with its mountain resorts and support activities such as guides, it also
attracts international, first-time visitors, notably from near-neighbour
France, as well as from Belgium, Italy, and the UK. The region supports
over 600 hotels/bed and breakfasts (B&Bs) and a similar number of
rural tourist accommodation establishments. These are highly concentrated in the Pyrenees region (35%) and the provincial capital of Zaragoza
(20%), which has the only international airport serving the region. Air
access from other countries is, however, better and more cheaply served
(e.g. by low-cost airlines) by the more popular airports of Barcelona
and Madrid (a two-to-three hour drive to Zaragoza). This rural and

mountainous region has a radial transport network that therefore relies on road rather than rail or internal air links: rail connections are sparse – 35% of towns have no rail link. Overnight visitors comprise 90% Spanish and 10% from other countries, staying an average of 2.04 nights, but tourists from overseas stay an average of only 1.7 nights (see Table 6.2).

In the national context, Aragon represents only 3% of the total number of visitors to Spain, whereas 78% of all tourists (measured by bed nights) are based in the resort regions of Andalusia, the Balearic islands, Catalonia, and the capital, Madrid. Aragon is therefore a relatively undeveloped region within Spain, but one in which tourism is a prime sector for economic and rural growth (Molina, 1998). Accommodation provision increased by 30% between 1993 and 1999, with an 85% increase in rural accommodation premises, which are primarily micro and family-run enterprises.

Survey of Aragon tourism SMEs

The comparative survey methodology and analysis is discussed at greater length by Evans *et al.* (2001a, 2001b), based on the three country survey. This employed a standard questionnaire that profiled tourism SMEs by main activity: status (public, private, not-for-profit), service provided, and number of employees. It then detailed their current and planned ICT usage, training expertise held in each ICT application, current on-line reservation/booking and payment facilities, and details of any presence on a Website, whether owned or leased/rented (via an external server, Destination Marketing System, or TIC). The questionnaire was translated into Spanish for initial piloting to a small sample in each area after which some refinements were made, mainly around technological terms and accommodation type and measurement, and the final coded questionnaires were circulated to 750 tourism SMEs in Aragon. Using a

Table 6.2 Profile of visitors to Aragon region by provincial district

Aragon province	Visitors		Overnight stays		Average stay/nights
	Domestic	Overseas	Domestic	Overseas	
Prov. Huesca	369,306	42,033	1,002,070	94,855	2.67
Prov. Teruel	178,523	12,821	303,406	15,856	1.67
Prov. Zaragoza	565,870	91,345	1,022,925	135,803	1.76
Zaragoza City	397,795	63,011	674,400	97,997	1.68
Total Aragon	1,113,699	146,199	232,840	6,514	2.04

Source: Arnaiz (1998)

standard questionnaire for comparative purposes naturally meant some simplification in terms of the depth and number of questions asked in each country, not least in the emerging and technical field of ICT. Striking a balance between likely response rates, particularly among SMEs without designated marketing or technical/IT staff, and a larger, more detailed survey, therefore limited the range of questions. This was in part compensated by follow-up and analysis of non-respondents and face-to-face interviews carried out with a sample of SMEs who indicated their willingness to participate in a case study review.

In total, 230 completed questionnaires were received from Aragon, a net response rate of 33%. The district returning the largest number was Huesca (54%), followed by Zaragoza (30%) and the lowest Teruel (16%). This reflects the tourism economy and relative activity levels in this region between the touristic Huesca, the provincial capital Zaragoza, and the poorer and less active (but aspirational) district of Teruel. In order to determine reasons for non-responses, a telephone follow-up of 10% of firms was undertaken, with the common reply that they were 'not interested in ICT', it was 'not for them', or they had 'no time to reply'. Non-respondents therefore include a large proportion of non-ICT-aware or disinterested firms, which in itself is significant, given the industry predictions of ICT take-up. This suggests a further avenue for research and policy intervention. A follow-up of Websites cited by respondents revealed that a third of the URL addresses given were no longer 'live' a year later, with no link to any new site. A survey of hotels in London, for example, found that they were neither using sites for discounting nor updating room availability (Buhalis & Main, 1998), rendering Websites ineffective as an e-commerce opportunity and quality service. This suggests maintenance and continuation problems, the effects of rapid change in Web technology/systems, and perhaps a lack of robustness in ICT involvement at this stage.

Profile of tourism firms

Not surprisingly, the majority of respondents were small enterprises employing fewer than 50 staff members. In fact nearly 90% employed 25 or less and 67% fewer than 10 people, in line with the European tourism and hospitality sector in general. A small number of larger, 'medium-sized' firms were part of public sector networks (museums, tourist information centres). The majority were private companies (76%) with 16% operating as sole traders, although less so in the more urban district of Zaragoza where private companies predominate. The range of tourism-related services represented in the region reflects the tourism supply chain, and in this rural area, the high reliance on accommodation and hospitality sectors, and to a lesser extent tour organisers/guides. This is particularly pronounced in the Huesca district where outdoor recreation, historic towns and skiing activity is most concentrated, and in Teruel where 86% of respondent SMEs were accommodation based. In the capital district, Zaragoza, cafes/restaurants represented a higher proportion of tourism SMEs, although 34% were hotels (business-oriented) and a higher proportion of travel agencies were located here than in the more rural districts, again serving a more urban catchment.

Usage of ICT

The extent to which tourism SMEs were currently using new technology as part of e-business and e-commerce was assessed – from the more traditional teletext and fax, to the full use of e-mail, Internet and even virtual reality (e.g. museums, tour guides and hotels). Focusing on ICT (e-mail/Web) as the key tools required for e-commerce and on-line reservations, the results in this region revealed a low take-up, particularly compared with northern European destinations, where over 50% of tourism SMEs were using such applications and nearly 25% more were planning to do so in the near future. In Aragon, however, only a third of firms were using e-mail/Web, the lowest proportion in the Teruel district and highest in Huesca, although even here only 40% used e-mail and the Web. An even smaller number used on-line reservation systems, indicating that of those with a Web presence, far fewer actually controlled their own site and reservation system, instead using intermediaries, for example, TICs/tourist boards, tour operators, and agencies. Significantly 29% of these firms indicated that they planned to acquire a Web facility (and 23% e-mail), suggesting that awareness was high, at least among about half the firms, leaving the other half either unaware of the benefits of ICT, or seriously turned off due to particular entry barriers or the lack of justification for doing so. The most latent demand was evident from the least developed district of Teruel where 46% planned to use the Web in the future. This region has been the recipient of European Regional Development (ERDF) and LEADER funding programmes, including training support in new technology and practical management skills. It is clear, however, that take-up by SMEs in this sector has been poor and that such interventions have not met either the needs of firms themselves, or presented a convincing case for the adoption of ICT and related skills. While EU and national programmes promote such projects as ICT and rural development, sustainability at a local level is therefore less robust. In the case of the LEADER-funded project that was established in the Maestrazgo district of Teruel, Aragon, in the mid-1990s, to improve networks and cooperatives through ICT, the project Website is no longer active or redirected. This reflects a political and structural divide between European regional programme policy and funding (EU, national, and regional government), and the aspirations and needs of local areas and communities, with projects and intervention too often of the wrong type and in the wrong place, and where 'form has followed funding' (Evans and Foord, 2000). Moreover, the beneficiaries of such investment programmes have tended to be larger and intermediary organisations (including universities and professional urban elites), and not the SMEs who have ostensibly been the prime target group.

Websites and links on tourist board and area destination sites are important ways in which more remote destinations and peripheral areas can gain attention and generate consumer interest and access new markets. Information – even well presented and user-friendly – is, however, largely ineffective unless a full booking/reservation facility is available at the same time to on-line users and intermediaries. The low penetration of ICT obviously limits the extent to which SMEs can access such marketing opportunities. However, the survey also revealed that an even lower proportion of SMEs used e-mail (24%) and Web (17%) to take bookings directly; most relied on the phone and, to a lesser extent, fax. When it came to actually receiving payment, very few of these firms used an on-line facility: only about 10% used phone/fax, despite the fact that over 80% accepted credit cards for payment. Even where firms had e-mail/Web (a third of respondents), less than 10% could offer an on-line payment method. This confirms that where ICT applications were used, they were neither integrated nor e-commerce-based, and relied on external agencies to collect payment and maintain Websites. When asked what training and skills SME staff had in ICT applications, a lower percentage than those actually claiming to use e-mail/Web revealed a skills gap, suggesting under-utilisation and under-capacity of ICT systems within SMEs. Again this indicates that micro-enterprises have only partial access to the Internet (e.g. shared or networked system, local area Website or destination marketing system), but no reliable payment facility. This is a lost opportunity for marketing and reservations (including pre-payment facilities), and a potential loss of income where commission and credit payments are made by SMEs to intermediaries. This is one reason cited by SMEs and local area TICs for the low membership of destination marketing systems (DMS) that incorporate reservation and payment arrangements on their behalf.

Barriers to ICT take-up

The survey results offer an insight into the variations between activity and destination area in terms of ICT usage and the determinants and likely barriers to ICT take-up. A general conclusion is that size measured by employees tends to indicate likely ICT take-up, but this is not consistently so across each sector, destination, or organisation type. There was little observable correlation for instance between organisation type/ status and ICT usage, while not surprisingly, those with e-mail were more likely to use the Internet than those without. The influence of the owner, key staff and network membership, as well as tourist market and location, also contributed to the likely propensity to use ICT applications, as Table 6.3 summarises. Location, transport, and poor tourism infrastructure in Aragon are important determinants, while SMEs are either largely absent from tourist board and local area TIC systems, or are not fully on-line or networked with central DMS and accommodation reservation operators.

While the survey provides a useful insight and summary of ICT usage and related determining factors across a range of activity and SME types, this does not adequately reflect the depth of either the impacts or the 'quality' of ICT applications used. In order to conduct a more qualitative assessment, respondents who expressed both a willingness to be interviewed and indicated involvement in ICT applications were selected across a range of the activity types using a semi-structured interview. This was designed to collect more detailed profiling information of the SME in terms of its market, service and client base, its operation and organisational structure, and in particular to map its development of ICT systems alongside other business applications and marketing, including an assessment of the effectiveness and rationales behind such usage. Eleven SMEs (5% of the total sample) were interviewed as case study examples across the region. This was therefore not a representative sample in any sense, and concentrated on those already involved in ICT applications, thereby providing an insight as to how ICT was being used rather than barriers to those not yet involved.

Table 6.3 Determinants of ICT take-up by tourism SMEs in Aragon

Key factor	*Prime*	*Secondary*
Size by number of employees	✓	
Owner interest/Skills/Education	✓	
Sector/Activity	✓	
ICT usage by sector: Activity and tour organiser Café/restaurant; hotel	✓	✓
Local destination marketing system (DMS)	✓	
Tourist market/Origin		✓
Destination infrastructure	✓	
Location, transport	✓	

Source: Evans *et al.* (2001a, 2001b)

In terms of the rationales for ICT development and investment by SMEs, while not homogenous given the range of activities and destination areas represented, these tended to fall into one of three main types:

(1) Larger SMEs where ICT (e.g. Website) was imposed centrally by head office, including local authorities/town halls, for example, museum, tourist information centre.

(2) Those where ICT was developed organically, 'bottom-up' albeit with external expertise, for example, web design, server choice, content management system.

(3) Micro-enterprises – 'self-help' or afficionados for whom ICT was as much a social, networking and/or image and promotional tool, as an e-commerce opportunity.

In the case of (1) and (2), supplier-led developments were felt to be key factors in the timing and nature of ICT application, and in both cases, Internet/Web applications were less developed and tended to rest with a key member of staff (or consultant *webmaster*), whereas e-mail was more widely accessed and appreciated by employees. The latter point is perhaps underestimated given the attention given to Web-based promotion of on-line reservations, since e-mail was seen to benefit even smaller organisations where staff communications were fragmented due to shift and evening working (e.g. venues, hospitality), and with the use of part-time and volunteer staff (e.g. not-for-profit organisations). Here organisations were using e-mail both for traditional mailing list/database functions, as well as to capture and disseminate market research and customer/usage data to staff, network members, and customers them-selves. Where external advisers/consultants were used, particularly if SMEs lacked in-house expertise and capacity, quality rather than cost was the prime issue; however, for smaller organisations cost remains a key constraint (Soriano *et al.*, 2002).

Conclusions

This study has presented a profile of the penetration and distribution of ICT applications among a range of tourism SMEs in this rural Spanish region. With two-thirds of all respondents surveyed indicating usage of one or more ICT applications, and one-third already using the Internet, this shows the rapid uptake of ICT within this sector, although the position of non-respondents must caution against any over-optimism for ICT adoption by SMEs. For example, the regional *Turismo Verde y Rural* organisation, which promotes the accommodation provision of over 350 residencies, operates both Website and computerised enquiry systems. However, since suppliers are generally not on-line, actual booking relies on phone/fax and traditional payment methods. Spain's weaker position in the penetration of CRS is also evident in relation to other European countries; for instance in Britain and the Netherlands Global Distribution Systems (GDS) measured by the number of terminals per travel agency outlet was between 3.8 and 4.2, respectively, compared with a below-average (=2.4) of 1.57 in Spain (Buhalis, 1998: 413). Teruel was the least developed of the three districts of Aragon. Some 25% of its 40 villages (with 150 to 2000 inhabitants) surveyed, operated computerised networks to promote local area tourism – an important consideration for its largely domestic market. Although not fully networked, this suggests that even at the very local level, this IT infrastructure may form the basis for ICT and related DMS development in the future, linking small accommodation providers in this rural area. But this is likely to require investment assistance and/or a clear cost–benefit analysis for small accommodation owners, and, as has been noted, even greater cooperative 'clustering'.

The relationship that tourism SMEs have with their own trade sectors and within both local areas/destinations and national/regional tourism systems is varied, with clear opportunities for the development of networking, joint marketing, and collaboration between and across activity sectors. The role of DMS and intranet systems is still undeveloped, with insufficient appreciation of, or means of evaluating the costs and benefits by SMEs themselves, and there is little evidence of DMS and joint Web-based reservation systems being sustained beyond the set-up stage. The leap from benign use of the Internet for information (as a secondary marketing outlet), to full, interactive e-commerce is a major one for most firms. To quote an SME interviewed: 'If someone visits a site, they are already looking for something, they already have a question. They have already made their choice', and this reflects the browsing culture experienced by established e-commerce sectors and the dominance of direct sales to airlines and hotel chains, rather than searches via independent portals and sites (TIAA, 2000). The practical problems of Website design, maintenance/updating, staff training, and access to on-line information and booking systems are, from this survey, still fundamental barriers to sustained SME involvement in ICT. Moreover, the lack of access/ skills in the design, operation, and maintenance of sites and in management and supplier control (rather than capital equipment and finance), and a lack of information on the quantitative benefits of ICT compared with the global hype and pressure from commercial suppliers/servers experienced by SMEs, are persistent concerns revealed in the study. A case for customised advice (less so training), good practice guides, and independent business support in ICT applications, and greater attention to destination marketing and the design and maintenance of Websites, are key requisites cited by SMEs. This is echoed Europe-wide: 'The Commission should support the development and widespread dissemination of digital information, awareness raising and training tools and materials directly applicable to the business processes undertaken by SMEs' (Werthner *et al.*, 1997: 26).

A major risk is that many rural tourism SMEs remain marginalised in e-commerce, or receive inappropriate advice and 'support' for applications that they are not able to fully exploit and from which they are unable to derive sustained benefit. Their more remote location exacerbates this with restricted choice and access to alternative suppliers, sources of advice and expertise. Meanwhile the urban core areas with highly concentrated clusters of ICT knowledge and networking further advance their control and competitive advantage. Policy implications are therefore raised that may inform EU, national, and regional initiatives, and that in part explain the limited success and impact of previous programmes in this field (Buhalis & Main, 1998; EC, 1996; Evans *et al.*, 2001a; Evans & Peacock, 1999; Wanhill, 1997) – as the Strategic Advisory Group on IST for Tourism concluded, 'SMEs may be lost in the electronic marketplace unless they are shown how and assisted in the usage of the tools and in learning skills necessary to participate in the Digital Economy' (Werthner *et al.*, 1997: 27).

References

Arnaiz, R. (1998) Alojamiento turistico en Aragon. *Heraldo de Aragon*, 24 May, 5.

Ateljevic, J., Milne, S., Doorne, S. and Ateljevic, I. (1999) *Tourism Micro-Firms in Rural New Zealand: Key Issues for the Coming Millennium*. Munich: ATLAS Annual Conference.

Bennett, R.J. and McCoshan, A. (1993) *Enterprise and Human Resource Development*. London: Paul Chapman.

Braun, P. (2002) Networking tourism SMEs: e-commerce and e-marketing issues in regional Australia. *Information Technology & Tourism* 5, 13–23.

Buhalis, D. (1994) *ICT as a strategic tool for small and medium tourism enterprises*. In A.V. Seaton (ed.) *Tourism: The State of the Art* (pp. 254–74). Chichester: John Wiley & Sons.

Buhalis, D. (1998) Strategic use of information technologies in the tourism industry. *Tourism Management* 19 (5), 409–21.

Buhalis, D. and Main, H. (1998) IT in small and medium hospitality enterprises. *International Journal of Contemporary Hospitality Management* 10 (5), 198–202.

Deimezi, R. (2002) *ICT use by Greek SMEs*. On WWW at http://www.hella sob.com/bt/articles.php?Artid=4. Accessed 14.03.03.

Downey, J. (1999) XS 4 all? 'Information society' policy and practice in the European Union. In J. Downey and J. McGuigan (eds) *Technocities* (pp. 121–38). London: Routledge.

EC (European Commission) (1996) *Report on the Evaluation of the Community Action Plan to Assist Tourism 1993–95.* Brussels: European Commission.

EC (European Commission) (1997) *The European Observatory for SMEs, 5th Annual Report.* Brussels: European Commission.

EC (European Commission) (2002) *ICT & SMEs Benchmarking Project.* Brussels: European Commission.

Evans, G.L. (1999) Networking for growth and digital business. In W. Schertler (ed.) *Information and Communication Technologies in Tourism 1999* (pp. 376–87). Vienna: Springer-Verlag.

Evans, G.L. (2004) Cultural industry quarters – from pre-industrial to post-industrial production. In D. Bell and M. Jayne (eds) *City of Quarters: Urban Villages in the Contemporary City.* Aldershot: Ashgate Press.

Evans, G.L., Bohrer, J. and Richards, G. (2001a) Small is beautiful? ICT and tourism SMEs – a European comparative. *Information Technology & Tourism* 2 (3/4), 1–15.

Evans, G.L., Bohrer, J. and Richards, G. (2001b) ICT development and small tourism enterprises in Europe. *Anatolia: An International Journal of Tourism and Hospitality Research* 11 (1), 22–40.

Evans, G.L. and Foord, J. (2000) European funding of culture: promoting common culture or regional growth? *Cultural Trends* 36, 53–87.

Evans, G.L. and Peacock, M. (1999) ICT in tourism: a comparative European survey. In W. Schertler (ed.) *Information and Communication Technologies in Tourism 1999* (pp. 247–58). Vienna: Springer-Verlag.

Main, H. (1995) IT and the independent hotel – failing to make the connection. *International Journal of Contemporary Hospitality Management* 7 (6), 30–32.

Molina, P. (1998) *Rural Tourism in the Province of Teruel: Contribution to the Stabilisation of its Population and Sustainable Development.* Unpublished MA dissertation, University of North London.

Mutch, A. (1995) IT and small tourism enterprises: a case study of cottage-letting agencies. *Tourism Management* 16 (7), 533–39.

Pratt, A. (2000) New media, the new economy and new spaces. *Geoforum* 31 (4), 425–36.

Richards, G. (ed.) (1996) *Cultural Tourism in Europe.* Wallingford: CAB International.

Soriano, D.R., Roig, S., Sanchis, J. and Torcal, R. (2002) The role of consultants in SMEs: the use of services by Spanish industry. *International Small Business Journal* 20 (1), 95.

SPICe (Scottish Parliament Information Centre) (2002) *Tourism E-Business* (Research Paper 02/03). Edinburgh: SPICe.

TIAA (2000) *Traveler's Use of the Internet.* Washington DC: Travel Industry Association of America.

Vich-I-Martorell, G.A. (2002) The internet as a marketing tool for tourism in the Balearic Islands. *Information Technology and Tourism* 5, 91–104.

Wanhill, S. (1997) Peripheral area tourism: a European perspective. *Progress in Tourism and Hospitality Research* 3, 47–70.

Webster, F. (1999) Information and communications technologies: Luddism revisited. In J. Downey and J. McGuigan (eds) *Technocities* (pp. 61–89). London: Routledge.

Werthner, H. and Klein, S. (1999) *Information Technology and Tourism – A Challenging Relationship.* Vienna: Springer-Verlag.

Werthner, H., Nachira, F., Orests, S. and Pollock, A. (1997) *Information Society Technology for Tourism. Report of the Strategic Advisory Group on the 5th Framework Program on Information Society,* 8 December, Brussels.

Williams, A.M. and Shaw, G. (1989) *Small Firms and Information Technology: The Rural Areas of the European Community.* Exeter: University of Exeter, Exeter European Studies.

WTO (1998) *Tourism 2020 Vision: A New Forecast.* Madrid: World Tourism Organization.

Part 3

Networks, Partnerships and Community Support

Chapter 7

Cooperative Marketing Structures in Rural Tourism: The Irish Case

CATHERINE GORMAN

Cooperation as a Competitive Advantage

People have formed cooperative groupings in both an informal and formal capacity since man has inhabited the Earth. Cooperation is also common between many other living organisms, in some cases culminating in symbiosis and partnership such as that between the egret and water buffalo in the animal kingdom and between lichens and algae in the plant kingdom. However, in all cases the benefit of cooperation must provide a value that is recognised by each cooperative member.

Cooperation can be thought of as exemplified by groups of independent businesses that recognise the advantage of developing markets jointly rather than in isolation, who are tied in a loose way (Palmer *et al.*, 2000; Palmer, 2002). Morrison (1998: 194) identified the importance of cooperation in the tourism sector, particularly for those who are located in a peripheral region or area. She defined cooperation as that which is 'between one or more tourist product providers, whereby each partner seeks to add to its marketing competencies by combining some, but not all of their resources with those of its partners for mutual benefit'. Gray (1985) identified five critical characteristics of collaboration necessary to ensure that working together is successful. These include:

- interdependency of the stakeholder whereby an incentive is required to induce participation;
- joint ownership of decisions;
- solutions emerging by dealing constructively with differences;
- collective responsibility for future direction; and
- the recognition that collaboration is a dynamic, emergent process.

Cooperation can lead to networking opportunities such as economies of scale, access to professional marketing expertise, the development of technology and distribution networks, educational and training support, and pooled financial resources (Morrison, 1998). Development of cohesiveness over time within a cooperative can be helped by several factors. Palmer *et al.* (2000) found that similarity of work, group size, threats from outside, leadership style, and common social factors such as age, race, and social structure could contribute to cohesiveness.

The aim of this chapter is to illustrate the different structures through which rural tourism product providers cooperate. Two of the case studies focus on the same type of product provision, although the structural approach of the cooperatives is different. Case 1 considers the individual product provider, and in the second case a number of area-based product providers constitutes membership. Case 3 focuses on individual provider membership, although it reflects the diversity of rural tourism provision within a county-delineated geographical area. Supports and inhibitors for successful cooperation are explored.

Tourism in Ireland

The tourism sector in Ireland (a country with a population of 4 million) has had a substantial impact on the national economy over the past 15 years. The sector has seen unprecedented growth in both visitor numbers and revenue, with over 6 million overseas visitors generating revenue of €3.2 billion in 2002 (or almost €4 billion taking into account carrier receipts) (Table 7.1). In 2002 it supported 140,000 jobs and contributed 4.4% to GNP, making it the country's most successful ever 'indigenous' industry (Bord Failte, 2002).

However, the publication of *New Horizons for Irish Tourism – An Agenda for Action* (DAST, 2003) acknowledged that the industry was at a cross-roads. Although there was still significant satisfaction with the Irish rural tourism product expressed by visitors, there had been a decline, particularly in relation to their perception of value for money, with Ireland considered by some to be an expensive destination. The *Agenda* document set out a strategy to regain competitiveness and to continue to emphasise the importance of 'People, Place and Pace' – elements that have been identified as the main attractors for the country. On the supply side, both under-utilised capacity and falling margins have been problems,

Table 7.1 Republic of Ireland: Overseas visitor numbers and revenue generated, 1990 and 2002

	1990	*2002*
Total overseas visitors (million)	3.096	5.919
Total foreign revenue (billion €)	1.446	3.985

Source: DAST (2003)

and a number of key drivers, including marketing and promotion, were identified to combat these.

Structural changes in the administration, management, and marketing of tourism have been put in place. The Northern Ireland peace process has acted as a catalyst for change whereby Ireland is now marketed as an all-Ireland destination incorporating Northern Ireland, which is under the governance of the UK.

Tourism in Ireland grew through the 1960s and 1970s, but it was in the mid-1980s, after the publication of the first White Paper for tourism in 1985, that the industry took a more strategic approach to both its development and marketing. The rural tourism industry in Ireland is dominated by small and medium enterprises as well as by sole traders, with many of them operating as part-time tourism providers. Entering into cooperative networks can enable small- and medium-size firms to pool their resources in order to increase their competitiveness, draw up strategic management and marketing plans, reduce operating costs and increase know-how (Buhalis & Cooper, 1998). With over 80% of tourism enterprises in Ireland being SMEs, many located in isolated areas, the focus moved from individual marketing to the development of same product and destination marketing cooperatives.

Rural Tourism in Ireland

Rural tourism is defined in Ireland specifically as 'rural areas/towns with less than 1500 people'. The EU definition of rural tourism is 'a holiday that is primarily motivated by the desire to closely experience the countryside, its people, heritage and way of life. The holiday should be primarily based in a rural setting, as opposed to being general touring/sightseeing holiday' (Fāilte Ireland, 2004). It is this definition that is used by the National Tourist Board. 'Agritourism', however, is quite specific and in terms of the Irish situation it tends to be linked directly to on-farm activities or accommodation. Grant aid in relation to agritourism was allocated to farmers or in the case of a group application, farmers were required to be part of the applicant group. Owing to the fragmented nature of the rural tourism product, it is difficult to ascertain its worth to the economy. Estimates have suggested 30% of the total value of tourism, or about €1 billion in 2002 (Henaghan, 2004). *Teagasc* is the country's farm advisory body and is involved in providing advice and training to the rural and farming community. It cites four important factors that need to be addressed in order that growth is sustained: quality, uniqueness, the adoption of an innovative approach, and the importance of training. *Teagasc* provides information on its Website for the setting up of alternative enterprises including rural tourism, self-catering, B&B, angling, walking, and visitor attractions (Teagasc, 2004).

In the 1960s, owing to the decreasing viability of agriculture and the increasing number of tourists to Ireland, farmers were urged to look at developing alternative enterprises to support farm incomes. Tourism bodies encouraged the opening of farmhouse accommodation. From the early 1970s until the mid-1980s, agriculture and agro-industry did well. The state did not need to involve itself with land ownership structures or reform within agriculture as it was a reasonably viable sector. Private investment took place and there was no real integration between agriculture and other sectors. From the mid-1980s to the early 1990s, reform of the Common Agricultural Policy and the introduction of milk quotas caused a fall in incomes for some farmers. Rural tourism development now looked more attractive. The mid-1980s saw a drive to develop and invest in tourism in Ireland and to increase visitor numbers. Grant aid from different sources, primarily from the EU – such as the Operational Programme for Tourism, Operational Programme for Agritourism grant and LEADER programme – encouraged development and marketing in a diverse range of rural tourism products such as equestrian facilities, open visitor farms, golf facilities, and accommodation.

The revitalisation of rural areas well complements present tourism objectives, which include a more equitable regional distribution of visitors throughout the country. Scenic rural areas in Ireland also tend to be areas of agricultural disadvantage, and hence the farming community now often looks towards rural tourism as a source of supplementing income. Rural tourism has helped to sustain agriculture and boost local related industries. It has also been a catalyst in the creation of jobs through direct and related enterprises.

The Development of Rural Tourism

There are a number of bodies involved in the development and marketing of rural tourism in Ireland. *Teagasc*, the farm advisory board, employs a rural tourism specialist based in County Galway. County council and county tourism committees are involved in the development and marketing of rural tourism at county level and they contribute to the work undertaken by the regional tourism authorities. The six regional tourism authorities develop, service, and promote tourism in a regional context. Shannon Development operates in this capacity in the mid-west of the country. There are at present 38 LEADER+ companies in the Republic of Ireland that are involved in support, marketing, and training in all sectors of rural development. Under LEADER 2, 22.6% of funds were allocated to rural tourism, which was significantly more than from any other measure (Brendan Kearney & Associates, 2000). LEADER+ presently allocates funding to projects where there is a proven market demand. In a national capacity, *Fáilte Ireland* (the national tourism board and tourism training authority) employs a product development officer whose remit it is to help develop, market, and give advice to the rural tourism sector.

The Marketing of Rural Tourism

The marketing of rural tourism is undertaken by a number of bodies. County tourism committees and regional tourism authorities focus on destination marketing within a county and regional context. Irish Farm-house Holidays (IFH) and Irish Country Holidays (ICH) cooperatively market the farm accommodation sector: both offer bed and breakfast, and ICH additionally offers self-catering accommodation. Product marketing groupings (PMGs) have emerged at county, regional, and national levels, and many of these contribute to the rural tourism experience. Operating criteria for these groupings are mainly linked to quality standards. The accommodation sector has strict criteria that lead to approval by the national tourist board. In this sector, marketing cooperatives have been in existence for many years and criteria focus on the tangible aspects of accommodation delivery. Within the other activities and attractions sectors, criteria are not as clear. If there is a regulatory body, such as AIRE (Association of Irish Riding Establishments) in the case of the equestrian product, those that participate in the product marketing group have to adhere to the agreed regulations. In the case of other activities, such as gardens/heritage houses, there are no regulatory bodies, criteria are vague, and products are diverse. Time in operation, standard of product, capability of attracting visitors, and availability of facilities for visitor use are mentioned, although those members that are part of the groups may sometimes not fulfil all the criteria.

At a national level, *Fáilte Ireland* advocates that cooperative marketing opportunities are the most effective means of accessing overseas markets in a cost-effective manner. With this in mind, product marketing groups have been developed in many different products, and include Horse Riding Ireland, Health Farms of Ireland, the Great Fishing Houses of Ireland, Rural Tourism, Heritage Island, and Sailing.

In 1999, the Small- and Medium-Sized Accommodation Marketing Initiative was launched to improve the marketing and competitive capabilities of the smaller accommodation enterprises. Administered by the National Tourist Board, this initially focused on the bed and breakfast sector but has since been extended to all sectors of SME accommodation. Its main objectives include the following:

- provision of support for the smaller accommodation sector;
- creation of greater cohesion within the sector;
- creation of awareness and knowledge of individual and cooperative marketing efforts; and

- encouragement of more marketing activity by both associations and groups with industry and the regional tourism authorities.

Tourism Ireland Limited focuses on international marketing and is involved with marketing Ireland abroad as an all-Ireland destination. Product quality and cost competitiveness are emphasised as an essential element of the attractiveness of Ireland as a tourism destination.

Barriers and Problems in Relation to Rural Tourism in Ireland

One of the main problems of rural tourism in Ireland is the fragmented nature of the product. Many of those involved in providing a rural tourism experience to the visitor are part-time, either in terms of working hours or in terms of the focus of the enterprise. A wide range of different organisations deliver different elements of the product, and at times organisations that are involved within the sector are accused of lacking coordination. The need for a common ground to facilitate consensus and implement collaborative results requires a more integrated approach based on regular communication and shared values (Jamal & Getz, 1995). Seasonality factors such as climate, lack of daylight hours, and traditional holiday-taking patterns, result in irregular profit margins. This is exacerbated by the fact that employment may only be seasonal and part-time and thus seen as supplemental rather than central to the business or income stream.

The fragmented nature of the business also contributes to the overall lack of vision, direction, and image of the sector as perceived by those working in the industry. Changes in perception have been noted over the past 14 years during periods of close contact while working with product providers in the rural tourism sector. Gradually, with the advent of greater cooperation, it is hoped that this will change. Rural tourism has gone through a cycle over the past ten years. During the 1990s a vision had been identified for the product, yet those delivering focused mainly on the accommodation provision element of the experience. Open farms, walking, cycling, and other such rural attractions and activities were developed, although there was a lack of integration between the accommodation element and these activities in many cases.

The tourism strategy document, *Developing Sustainable Tourism 1993– 97* (Bord Fáilte, 1993), had identified 25 different rural tourism areas, whose criteria were based on natural and built resources of the area, commitment of the local community organisation, variety and distinctiveness of centres, and geographic balance. The National Tourist Board was aware that unrealistic expectations of rural tourism as an identified product had occurred in other countries, and it therefore identified these areas in order to provide a framework within which to concentrate activity.

There is an identified lack of training. Many of those who are involved in the business do not have business experience or formal training in skills such as management, customer service, and marketing. *Teagasc*, LEADER+ companies, *Fáilte Ireland*, and some destination groups have striven to combat this situation and provide advice and courses, encouraging participation through the provision of subsidies and certification.

Infrastructural shortcomings are recognised throughout rural Ireland. Internal transport is limited, impacting on both visitor and rural dweller and contributing to difficulty in gaining access to certain areas and for rural tourism practitioners attending meetings. These constraints need to be considered when both developing and marketing the rural tourism product.

The next section outlines three case studies demonstrating the cooperative marketing approach used within the rural tourism sector in Ireland.

Case Studies of the Cooperating Marketing Approach

Case 1: Marketing farmhouse accommodation

 Irish Farmhouse Holidays

In the early 1960s, farmhouse accommodation units were encouraged by *Bord Fáilte* to form a cooperative whose main objective would be to market the farmhouse accommodation sector. Thus Irish Farmhouse Holidays (IFH) was established, and has been in operation for almost 40 years. The organisation is limited by guarantee and its offices are situated in Limerick in the southwest of Ireland. The organisation also depends greatly on voluntary contribution from its members as well as from paid staff. All accommodation is approved and fulfils minimum criteria for visitor accommodation.

Since the regulation involved in the inspection of premises and standards was devolved from *Bord Fáilte* in the late 1990s, a new body, *Farm and Country Standards*, has undertaken inspections of premises throughout the year. This regulating body is located in the same offices as Irish Farmhouse Holidays, and a link is maintained between both the marketing and the standards element of provision. This is important to ensure the quality of the accommodation offered to the visitor.

The main objectives of Irish Farmhouse Holidays are:

- to expand the tourism base so that the rural economy can enjoy a greater spread of benefits rather than just in the honey-pot areas;
- to increase market share for farm holidays; and

- to attract year-round tourism by promoting off-season and weekend breaks.

The IFH is now viewed more as a network particularly since the organisation's portfolio has been extended from accommodation to all products involved in the delivery of the rural tourism experience. The organisation offers accommodation in both the Republic and Northern Ireland. Other rural tourism providers such as farm hostels and restaurants will be invited to participate in the organisation from 2005.

Irish Farmhouse Holidays consists of a board that is made up of members of the farmhouse accommodation sector. This board meets several times a year. The board of directors tends to make most of the decisions based on contributions from members, and strong leadership is seen as being important. There is a keen sense to retain and increase the membership each year. Group identification is important to the members and they embrace the importance of having a strong brand. Newsletters are circulated five times a year with content being discussed by those members who have developed a social as well as a business bond. There are county groups and a county chairperson that meet independently of the national group. Issues of a local/county nature are discussed and these may be brought to the national forum if applicable. Local groupings have also emerged with geographical proximity creating strong links between members.

The marketing of the organisation and subsequent promotion is strategic. The organisation annually produces a booklet detailing information and prices on bed and breakfasts located on farms throughout Ireland. Each year 3000–4000 brochures/booklets are distributed to potential customers through trade and consumer shows, tourist offices at home and abroad, tour operators, and to service enquiries. The organisation also has a Website (Irish Farmhouse Holidays, 2002).

Members attend tradeshows and fairs and are involved with joint advertising. The IFH provides a central reservation system for members and there is representation in Irish Tourist offices worldwide through Tourism Ireland Limited.

Initially farm families became involved in rural tourism due to the decline in income derived from farming. Farms under a certain acreage had to look to alternative enterprises in order to survive. There are a number of issues that are presently being addressed within the organisation. In the past many of the members of the IFH would say that it was the farm tourism business that carried the farm business. However, the fact that the number of farms is decreasing and there is a trend towards part-time farming has impacted on the IFH. In a review of the organisation undertaken in 2000, it was found that 55% of the members were over the age of 70, and fewer younger people were becoming involved.

There are also fewer women staying at home, with increased numbers entering the workforce outside the home.

The lack of continuous funding is seen as a problem. At present, the organisation is partially funded through LEADER+, although a large percentage of the organisation's funds does come from its membership.

Factors that have contributed to cooperation include the availability of expertise from the Irish Tourist Board, particularly in the form of the SMA (Small and Medium Accommodation Marketing Initiative), which has been administered by the Irish Tourist Board since 1999.

The organisation is optimistic about its future. There is a strong bond between members and this is enhanced by county groups who have meetings on a regular basis and contribute ideas to the national cooperative. The main aim of the IFH is to extend its product offering and this in turn will provide the visitor with a one-stop shop in relation to rural tourism holidays in Ireland.

Case 2: Rural tourism as a national product

Irish Country Holidays

Irish Country Holidays (ICH) was founded in 1990 as the national rural tourism society. In 2004, there were 18 groups of self-catering product providers and some bed and breakfast providers, located in both the Republic and part of Northern Ireland (Figure 7.1). They represent a total of 200 different properties. A central reservations office is located in County Tipperary and a reservations officer takes phone calls and enquiries about the properties. Managers/facilitators from each of the groups around the country are involved in cooperative marketing activities. These include attendance at trade and consumer fairs, the operation of familiarisation trips, and the production of a common brochure that is used for both consumer and trade. A new Website was developed in 2003 (Irish Country Holidays, 2003b), and this became the fastest growing medium used by prospective visitors for both information and reservations. The stated main aim of the organisation as indicated on the Website is to offer the visitor 'a rural experience at a relaxed pace of life and the traditional heritage of rural Ireland'. To be included, the product provider must fulfil specific criteria and agree to incorporate certain practices as part of their delivery of the visitor experience. All accommodation must be approved by the National Tourism Board. A welcome pack that contains information on the area, events, and a welcome letter is provided for visitors on arrival. A voucher is also provided for a guided tour of a

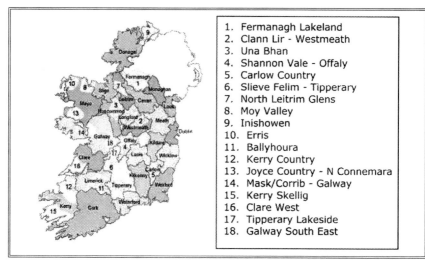

1. Fermanagh Lakeland
2. Clann Lir - Westmeath
3. Una Bhan
4. Shannon Vale - Offaly
5. Carlow Country
6. Slieve Felim - Tipperary
7. North Leitrim Glens
8. Moy Valley
9. Inishowen
10. Erris
11. Ballyhoura
12. Kerry Country
13. Joyce Country - N Connemara
14. Mask/Corrib - Galway
15. Kerry Skellig
16. Clare West
17. Tipperary Lakeside
18. Galway South East

Figure 7.1 Location map of Irish Country Holiday member groups 2004 (*Source*: Irish Country Holidays (2003a))

working farm with refreshments for all guests. Complimentary Irish coffees with the hosts and personal assistance from the group coordinator are all part of the package. The emphasis is on hospitality and the delivery of an experience which will be remembered by the visitor. A customised approach to groups focuses on tailor-made packages that can incorporate a wide range of rural features.

As with many rural cooperatives, there is an issue in relation to the retention of personnel. Many of the 18 membership groups have facilitators or coordinators. Because they are dependent upon funding, some may be semi-voluntary in nature. Frequent changes in personnel lead to a lack of continuity and difficulty in strengthening the links and relationships required to maintain an effective cooperative structure.

The cooperative approach undertaken by ICH is portrayed as a group of people with the same interests, marketing their own products in a collective way for financial gain. There is, however, a variable level of members' activity, which leads to an unbalanced sense to the organisation's functioning. Where once tour operators were considered a major source of business, it is the independent traveller, who seeks information and who books on-line that now constitutes much of the business. In response, the marketing focus has changed.

Increased commitment can lead to a perceived improved effectiveness of the organisation, as has been shown by Coffey (2003). As in most organisations, group identification is important. A willingness to connect will help to develop a common vision leading to specific group objectives. A vision for the product is presently being developed by Irish Country

Holidays and it is hoped that this will strengthen both the sense of identity for its members and deliver a recognised brand for the organisation.

Issues in Relation to Cooperative Marketing in Rural Tourism

Communication and frequency of communication is considered an essential component of cooperative marketing by both Irish Farmhouse Holidays and Irish Country Holidays. The geographical distance between groups can be seen as one of the barriers and can constrain efficient operation of a cooperative. Increased use of the Internet and e-mail as communication tools can help ameliorate such situations, although personal face-to-face contact through meetings/seminars is important in helping to strengthen the links that exist between members. Ireland's low population density results in a widespread dispersal of providers, and poor access can lead to problems, particularly in relation to face-to-face personal communication. Planned and frequent communication is necessary in order to sustain and strengthen the bonds between members, giving the group a stronger sense of identity.

The size of the group can be an issue: critical mass in membership numbers is required in order that the group is viable. In the case of Irish Country Holidays, each group pays an annual subscription that goes towards the salary of an employee who deals with the reservation system and towards marketing activities. Funding for Irish Country Holidays has come mainly from LEADER+, though similar to Irish Farmhouse Holiday, membership also contributes to both the operational and marketing functions of the organisation.

During the late 1990s rural tourism became better integrated with other tourism provision. However, varying definitions and interpretations of 'rural tourism' do not assist development of a clear and focused image for the sector. Amalgamation between the IFH and ICH due to their product similarity has been considered and may occur in the future. Closer cooperation between the two bodies, which basically target the same market, might be a more cost-efficient approach in such a small country.

Case 3: County destination marketing

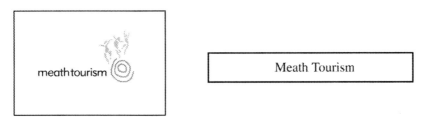

County Meath is located in a rural hinterland, northwest of Dublin. It has a population of 134,000 and over the past ten years has seen an increase in the number of Dublin City inhabitants moving out of the city and commuting due to the increasing cost of land and accommodation in the capital. Meath is known as the 'Royal County' as its main resource is its history and heritage, which spans 5000 years and contains some of the most important historic sites in Ireland. These include the internationally recognised site of Newgrange, which is a 4000-year-old megalithic tomb and attracts over 200,000 visitors each year. Meath is a fertile agricultural county well known for its interest in the equestrian industry.

The tourism industry in Meath is dominated by small, independent business operators. Meath Tourism was set up in 1994 as a collaborative county tourism network. It is operated through the county council and has an appointed board of directors and chairperson. It has at present over 260 members contributing to a diverse product portfolio. Its strategic objective is to develop marketable products based on the strengths and resources of the county and compatible with the goal of environmental protection and enhancement in a sustainable manner (Meath Tourism, 2003, 2004). It advocates that new product development should be consistent with the marketing objectives of expanding tourism inflows, increasing the average length of stay and revenue yield, extending the season, and spreading tourism activity throughout the county. The success and effectiveness of the network in realising these objectives is dependent on the willingness of its members to change from a traditional competitive approach to business to one of networking and collaboration with other cooperative members.

The 2004 *Development and Marketing Plan* for Meath Tourism focuses on a cooperative approach, particularly in the area of promotion. Recent research by the company has indicated that the accommodation sector in the county performs well and that there has been an increase in business in the catering, garden, equestrian, crafts, and golf sectors. The county attracts mainly overseas visitors (79%), with the majority opting to use bed and breakfast accommodation. The marketing of these sectors is primarily undertaken through cooperative marketing groups set up by each of the specific sectors. These groups are involved in the attendance at trade and consumer shows, the production of a cooperative brochure, and organisation of familiarisation trips.

A study focusing on Meath tourism to evaluate the concept of county tourism cooperatives and to explore the effectiveness of such associations (Coffey, 2003) identified four elements as essential to the success of cooperative networks: reciprocity, interdependence, power, and loose coupling (Barringer & Harrison, 2000; Hall, 2000).

The vast majority of the members of Meath Tourism claimed a belief in the concept of working together and coordinating efforts, as well as in the direct benefits that their company could realise as a result of their membership. The majority of members said they were willing to share information in relation to marketing activities, yet fewer than 50% of the respondents actually participated in joint marketing activities. This clearly reduces the interdependence and potential collective power of the members of the cooperative. Some respondents did stress the need to become allies rather than competitors, echoing the strategy for SMEs advocated by Zineldin (1998), amongst others. Zineldin considers the *co-opetive* perspective whereby an organisation seeks to be more competitive through cooperation and competing at the same time with similar organisations to itself.

A number of barriers to cooperation were identified. Group identity, communication among members, group size, and the distribution of power within the cooperative network were explored. Group identification and communication frequency (Stoel, 2002) are often seen as two elements essential to the development of effective network relationships. Within Meath Tourism, 28% of the respondents replied that the frequency of formal communication with other sector members was rare or non-existent. Frequency of informal communication was more positive with 23% saying that they had regular informal communication with other members of Meath Tourism. It was found that the subgroups who offer similar products, such as gardens and food, maintained much more regular contact, particularly on an informal basis. It is on these structures that Meath Tourism's strength of cooperation built. Some 37.5% of the respondents claimed they joined the network in order to benefit from a wider range of resources, and 25% cited access to the Internet site as a reason for their membership.

The need to continually motivate interaction and participation once a member becomes part of a network or cooperative group is common throughout all businesses. To maintain an interest and create a recognised value for active participation is essential to the strengthening of the cooperative approach for County Meath.

Conclusion and Future

In these three examples of cooperative marketing groups operating within the rural tourism sector in Ireland, the benefits of cooperation have been seen to contribute considerably to the sector's development, and can only be considered in a positive light despite the many issues and problems that surround the cooperative structure. The alternative would be for the individual businesses to 'go it alone', but with an identified lack of training and expertise, this would probably result in casualties. Tremblay (2000) recognises that neither networks or partnerships can be imposed on a community, particularly if that community is not suitably integrated. The total fabric of the community requires a degree of integration, within acknowledged diversity, and of agreement particularly with overall tourism development objectives, before the network approach to marketing can be undertaken. In all cases outlined above there is agreement on objectives, although degrees of involvement and commitment to the longer term are issues that still need to be addressed.

As this chapter was being completed, recognition of the need for a vision for rural tourism and an overcoming of the fragmentation of the industry had stimulated a joint initiative between *Teagasc* and Offaly LEADER+ company for the development of a rural tourism federation. This aimed to bring together representatives of all of those involved in delivering rural tourism, including *Teagasc*, Irish Country Holidays, Irish Farmhouse Holidays, and the providers of activities such as equestrianism, angling, golf, walking, and cycling. The main aim of the federation would be to act as an umbrella group and to provide a common voice for the sector. It would act as a lobby group but not be a marketing entity. It is hoped that such a federation will provide greater direction and vision to a promising sector, and, as Gray (1985) recognised as being an essential factor for successful cooperation, for it to hold a collective responsibility for future direction.

Addendum

Since 29 September 2003, *Bord Fáilte* has been divided into two different organisations. It has been partially amalgamated with CERT, the national tourism training authority, to form *Fáilte* Ireland. *Fáilte* Ireland is responsible for product development, domestic marketing and training within the sector. It has also been partially amalgamated with the Northern Ireland Tourism Board to form Tourism Ireland Limited (TIL). The responsibility of TIL is to market Ireland abroad as an all-Ireland destination.

Acknowledgements

The author wishes to thank Irish Farmhouse Holidays (Kathryn Delany), Irish Country Holidays (Michael Wilkinson), Jennifer Coffey, Alison Condra (Meath Tourism), Orla Woods (*Fáilte* Ireland), and Maria Henaghan (*Teagasc*).

References

Barringer, B.R. and Harrison, J.S. (2000) Walking a tightrope: creating value through interorganisational relationships. *Journal of Management* 26 (3), 367–403.

Bord Fáilte (1993) *Developing Sustainable Tourism 1993–97*. Dublin: Bord Fáilte.

Bord Fáilte (2002) *Statistics – Domestic Tourism 2002*. Dublin: Bord Fáilte, Market Research and Planning.

Brendan Kearney and Associates (2000) *Ex-Post Evaluation Final Report.* Dublin: LINN Service. On WWW at http://www.leaderii.ie. Last accessed 13.03.04.

Buhalis, D. and Cooper, C. (1998) Competition or co-operation: small and medium sized tourism enterprises at the destination. In E. Laws, B. Faulkner and G. Moscardo (eds) *Embracing and Managing Change in Tourism* (pp. 324–46). London: Routledge.

Coffey, J. (2003) A study of the effectiveness of county tourism co-operatives within Ireland: Case Study: Meath Tourism. Unpublished MSc dissertation, Dublin Institute of Technology.

DAST (Department of Art, Sport and Tourism) (2003) *New Horizons for Irish Tourism – An Agenda for Action.* Dublin: Tourism Policy Review Group.

Fáilte Ireland (2003) *The National Tourism Development Authority.* Dublin: Fáilte Ireland. On WWW at http://www.failteireland.ie. Last accessed 13.03.04.

Fáilte Ireland (2004) Personal communication, February 2004.

Gray, B. (1985) Conditions facilitating interorganisational collaborations. *Human Relations* 38 (10), 911–36.

Hall, C.M. (2000) *Tourism Planning, Policies and Processes and Relationships.* Harlow: Prentice Hall.

Henaghan, M. (2004) *Teagasc.* Personal communication, February 2004.

Irish Country Holidays (2003a) *Ireland Map.* Rear Cross, Co. Tipperary: Irish Country Holidays. On WWW at http://www.country-holidays. ie/page10.html. Last accessed 13.03.04.

Irish Country Holidays (2003b) *Welcome to the Warmth of Rural Ireland and the Experience of Irish Country Holidays.* Rear Cross, Co. Tipperary: Irish Country Holidays. On WWW at http://www.country-holidays.ie. Last accessed 13.03.04.

Irish Farmhouse Holidays (2002) *Irish Farmhouse Holidays Farmhouse Bed and Breakfast.* Limerick: Irish Farmhouse Holidays. On WWW at http://www.irishfarmholidays.com. Last accessed 13.03.04.

Jamal, T.B. and Getz, D. (1995) Collaborative theory and community tourism planning. *Annals of Tourism Research* 22 (1), 186–204.

Meath Tourism (2003) *Meath: Always a Treasure to Visit.* Navan, Co. Meath: Meath Tourism. On WWW at http://www.meathtourism.ie. Last accessed 13.03.04.

Meath Tourism (2004) *Tourism Development and Marketing Plan for County Meath.* Navan, Co. Meath: Meath Tourism.

Morrison, A. (1998) Small firm co-operative marketing in a peripheral tourism region. *International Journal of Contemporary Hospitality Management* 10 (5), 191–97.

Palmer, A. (2002) Co-operative marketing associations: an investigation into the causes of effectiveness. *Journal of Strategic Marketing* 10, 135–56.

Palmer, A., Barrett, S. and Ponsonby, S. (2000) Behavioural analysis of co-operative marketing organisations. *Journal of Marketing Management* 16, 273–90.

Stoel, L. (2002) Retail co-operatives: group size, identification, communication, frequency and relationship effectiveness. *International Journal of Retail and Distribution Management* 30 (1), 51–60.

Teagasc (2004) *Irish Agricultural Food Development Authority.* Dublin: Teagasc. On WWW at http://www.teagasc.ie. Last accessed 13.03.04.

Tremblay, P. (2000) An evolutionary interpretation of the role of collaborative partnerships. In B. Bramwell and B. Lane (eds) *Tourism Collaboration and Partnerships* (pp. 314–31). Clevedon: Channel View Publications.

Zineldin, M.A. (1998) Towards an ecological collaborative relationship management – a 'co-opetive' perspective. *European Journal of Marketing* 32 (11/2), 1138–64.

Chapter 8

Regional Cooperation in Rural Theme Trails

KIM MEYER-CECH

Introduction

Since the end of the 1980s about three theme trails per year have been established in Austria. Today there are about 70 theme trails in Austria – be it heritage trails like the Iron Trail, or trails based on products of the region like the famous Austrian wine trails – and still their number keeps on growing. Theme trails are networks of regional attractions that are marketed under a mutual theme in order to bring potential visitors into a region. At the same time they are networks of actors – municipalities, associations, and institutions with either economic or cultural backgrounds – trying to cooperate effectively. The theme should help to create an umbrella identity for the whole region and facilitate a concerted market performance (Mielke, 2000).

Theme trails are mostly established in economically weak rural areas where it is hoped that they will have a positive impact on the regional economy. The fact that theme trails are carried by partnerships between several different actors brings opportunities as well as challenges for the socio-economic development of rural areas. It is the goal of this chapter to analyse and assess the organisational structure of theme trails in Austria as well as the qualities and difficulties of the underlying partnership relationships, which to a large extent are responsible for the success or failure of a theme trail.

Methodology

An overview of theme trail networks in Austria was sought through undertaking telephone interviews with tourist boards and regional development corporations. To gain insights into the functioning of theme trails, five trails were chosen for a deeper examination, both because they appeared to be the most economically promising, and also according to the following criteria: being of average size for an Austrian theme trail (i.e. covering an area of approximately 25 municipalities), having different themes, and presenting intersectoral networks (i.e. stakeholders come from different economic branches and the cultural sector) (Meyer-Cech, 2003). Two of them will be exemplified in this chapter: the Cheese Trail Bregenzerwald and the Austrian Iron Trail.

The main sources of information for the analysis of the theme trail networks were explorative interviews based on structured questions posed to managers or project leaders of five Austrian theme trails. A constraint on this empirical study lies in the fact that people were more willing to talk about achievements and successful processes than about failures and things going wrong. In addition to scientific literature on regional cooperation, regional marketing, as well as sustainable regional and tourism development, a further source of information was statistical data on the socio-economic situation of the regions where the theme trail networks operate.

In this chapter, first, a short overview of two theme trails is given in terms of their underlying concept, the economic situation of the region, and the evolution of the initiative. Then the examples are compared within the context of the overall situation of theme trails in Austria, focusing on goals the networks pursue and their organisational structure. Finally, four crucial factors concerning success or failure of regional cooperation in the examined trails are dealt with in more detail: these are motivation, management, long-term funding, and quality.

Cheese Trail Bregenzerwald

Bregenzerwald is the name of a region in the most western province of Austria. Alpine pastures, valleys, and woods are the typical elements of the cultural landscape of this region, which has a long history in cheese production. The project Cheese Trail Bregenzerwald aims at branding the region as a cheese region, which means making cheese – from the pitchfork to the dinner fork – the central focus of regional and tourist development activities. The project is supported by a loose network consisting of 24 municipalities, almost 50 restaurants, over 50 alpine dairies and cheese makers, as well as supermarkets and handicraft businesses.

Tourism, in winter (55% of overnight stays) as well as summer, contributes most to the region's added value, followed by agriculture and trade. The agricultural sector plays an important role in the region. Some 9.5% of the workforce are employed in agriculture, which is above the provincial average of 2.4%. Farm businesses in the region are small, the average number of cows per farm being 20.

When tourist nights were declining in the early 1990s and imminent accession to the European Union led to financial and structural problems in agriculture, the Bregenzerwald region faced an economic crisis.

The crisis led to the formation of an initiative to promote partnerships around farm products. It consisted of a wide range of actors, such as farmers and municipalities, tourist, gastronomic and regional planning associations, as well as the chamber of agriculture. This forerunner organisation led to the founding of the Cheese Trail association and the festive opening of the Cheese Trail Bregenzerwald in 1998. The Cheese Trail association consists of 200 members from such economic sectors as agriculture and food processing, tourism, handicrafts, and retailing.

In a broader sense the theme trail encompasses more than one organisation. It is an intricate network of parallel or even intertwined initiatives. In the theme trail network an important role is played by the regional planning congregation, an informal organisation similar to a voluntary regional parliament consisting of the mayors and other political leaders of the region. Another relevant actor in the network is the regional tourist board, which acts as the go-between for accommodation in the region and cooperates with the Cheese Trail association in terms of marketing activities.

Austrian Iron Trail

In the region of the Austrian Iron Trail, ore was extracted and iron processed for many centuries. The goal of the Austrian Iron Trail project is to conserve and revive the rich cultural heritage that is related to the days when iron was the focus of the region's economy and society and at the same time to promote the development of tourism in the region.

The Austrian Iron Trail is on the one hand a network of tourist attractions along an old trade route that started at the Styrian Erzberg (Ore Mountain) in the South and led up to the trading towns on the Danube in the North. On the other hand the Austrian Iron Trail is a working group of three associations representing the provinces of Styria, Lower Austria, and Upper Austria, consisting of approximately 25 municipalities each and several museums.

The proportion of the workforce that is employed in industry and trade in the region is above average. This number was even higher before industrialisation. Industrialisation meant that the location of coalfields and steam engines drew iron away from where ore sources were located, thereby weakening the benefits of the region and forcing most forges to shut down. Only very large enterprises were able to survive. Today's regional economy is characterised by a high percentage of commuters and a lack of skilled workers.

Except for a few skiing resorts tourism is not very distinct in the region. Day trip and weekend break tourism dominate. There are still more tourist nights in summer than in winter, but overnight stays in summer continue to decline. It is hoped that the Austrian Iron Trail will help to improve the situation of tourism as well as the general regional economy.

The origin of the three Iron Trail associations – until the year 2001 they operated as three separate entities – lies at the beginning of the 1990s when historians and other culturally interested people began efforts to preserve the region's iron-related cultural heritage, and were financially supported by several municipalities. In the three provinces of the Iron Trail region, municipalities joined the respective associations. At that time it was their main goal to improve the regional quality of life by preserving the cultural heritage and by helping to maintain a few jobs.

In 2001 the three Iron Trail associations joined forces in a working group. Other partners in the network of the Austrian Iron Trail in addition to the regional tourist boards are the 'Iron Trail Restaurants', a group of restaurants that fulfil special quality criteria and offer regional foods, and the 'Houses with History', a group of museums that specialise in the iron history of the region.

Comparison of the Examples

The two above examples both represent and promote a special feature of their region: an aspect all Austrian theme trails share. Thematically, theme trails in Austria can be divided into two groups. Almost two-thirds are culinary trails that market an agricultural product of the region, like the Cheese Trail Bregenzerwald. The remaining third are cultural trails like the Austrian Iron Trail.

The two theme trails were established as a reaction to an economic crisis and are situated in economically weak rural areas – like most Austrian theme trails – where it is hoped that the establishment of the trail will contribute to the added value of the region. Aside from positive effects for the tourism industry, an increase of the value of other economic sectors and a stabilisation of employment prospects is anticipated.

It is not just economic goals that theme trails aim at: preserving the regionally specific cultural landscape is an important objective of many culinary trails. The Cheese Trail is a good example, because it helps guarantee the continuous farming of alpine pastures. A goal of the Austrian Iron Trail and most other cultural trails is to preserve the cultural heritage and to increase the appreciation for it among inhabitants and visitors. A further objective that both case studies and many other Austrian theme trails have in common is to contribute to an atmosphere of renewal and to help create a regional identity. In the initial phase of theme trail development often the special regional feature that later becomes the centre of marketing activities is viewed as something quite normal or even of minor value by the inhabitants. The attention regional assets receive through increased tourist activities can enormously improve their public image and thereby foster the self-confidence of the inhabitants of the region. For example, the inhabitants of the Bregenzerwald did not have a high opinion of their cheese before the Cheese Trail was established. When the first cheese-related public events were held, and when the region was awarded a prize in the 'to do!' international contest on socially responsible tourism in 1997, their self-assurance grew. (The 'to do!' contest awards tourism-related projects whose planning and realisation measures ensure a high degree of public involvement. The award ceremony takes place annually during the International Tourism Exchange in Berlin, Germany.)

The core organisational structure of the examined theme trail networks is usually a voluntary association. This is also true for most other Austrian theme trails with the exception of those that lack an underlying organisational structure, because they are just a route description in a map or in a travel guide.

The members of the voluntary organisations can be cultural initiatives, museums, enterprises (e.g. farmers and cheese makers in the Cheese Trail), or public and semi-public institutions (e.g. associations of municipalities in the Austrian Iron Trail). The theme trail associations cooperate with other regional organisations and institutions and in doing so become part of a greater regional network. In the network the intensity of cooperation of the members of the network is graded. There is a core team whose members cooperate very intensively, then there is an extended circle and finally there are associated partners (Scheff, 1999). The intensity of cooperation especially depends on the level of active personal involvement and on the kind of goals that are targeted.

Fuerst *et al.* (1999) differentiate between 'networks based on projects' and 'networks based on regions'. Whereas in the first case a concrete project is the starting point for cooperation, the latter is focused on the development perspectives of a whole region. In another source (European LEADER Observatory/AEIDL, 1997) the terms 'project partnership' and 'mobilising partnership' are used. The examined theme trails can be viewed as a hybrid of these two models, where the network based on a region or mobilising a partnership is a sort of project in itself, and although this is supported by a wide array of projects, it does not lose sight of the overall vision.

The following section provides insights into the qualities and difficulties of collaboration in the examined theme trail networks, based on an analysis of the interviews undertaken.

Motivation

The aim and benefits of the theme trail have to be completely clear for the involved stakeholders. Most difficulties in motivating people or institutions to enter or even to remain in a partnership relationship come, on the one hand, from a diffuse perception of the benefits, for example, when the expectations concerning the membership in a theme trail associ- ation are too high or wrong. Some farmers that became members of the Cheese Trail Bregenzerwald for instance, thought that the price for milk would rise again; others thought that after the trail signs had been put up the number of tourists would increase automatically. On the other hand, the lack of motivation to join a network often comes from the feeling that there are no benefits to be gained. The benefits that are sought by joining a theme trail network are most often of a financial nature.

Financial benefits

If financial benefits can obviously be derived from participating in the theme trail network there will be hardly any motivational problem. However, for the most part, especially in the very beginning, numbers cannot be named and benefits cannot be explicitly pinned to certain stakeholders.

Different stakeholders in the theme trail network expect different benefits from their involvement in the theme trail network. Farmers, for example, want to sell more produce, upmarket restaurants want more individual tourists, whereas middle-rate restaurants want more coach parties. Meanwhile, municipalities hope for new jobs in the region and higher tax revenues. Concerning tax benefits, a difficult situation was created for theme trails that are based on a local beverage – such as the famous Austrian wine roads – by the elimination of taxes on alcoholic beverages in the year 2000. This meant that municipalities did not gain extra income when more wine was sold.

Social and emotional benefits

The reasons for participating in a network of partnership relationships include social and emotional benefits, such as gaining honour and pres- tige (Zechner, 1998). It takes hard work and lots of personal effort to com- municate these values, for example taking part in city council meetings throughout the region and talking to the public as well as influential key persons. If influential representatives of the region (e.g. the mayors of the municipalities) can be actively involved, that is a great incentive for others to participate as well (Harper, 1997). In the Bregenzerwald, the fact that the regional planning congregation – a network of decision makers and opinion leaders – was in favour of and supported the Cheese Trail, was a great advantage for establishing it so quickly and effectively.

The existence of a regional identity and a feeling of togetherness are important prerequisites for wanting to join and stay in a partnership relationship. As it is most difficult to create a feeling of togetherness, regions that share specific regional characteristics and already have a strong regional cohesion are at an advantage when it comes to networking. The region of the Austrian Iron Trail, which in many places still clearly shows the signs of a branch of the economy that typified the region for such a long time, is an example.

Obstacles to the willingness to participate in a network include:

- if the number of partners in a theme trail cooperation is too large;
- if their interests are too heterogeneous; and
- if the partners are still too much tied to the institutions they come from and therefore only pursue particular interests rather than a common goal.

Tangible results

Results of collaboration need to be presented to all stakeholders who already participate in the regional cooperation and to encourage those who have yet to join. Tangible results are important for those paying yearly membership fees (they want to see what happened to their money) as well as for the region as a whole (projects need not always be of high economic value; sometimes the process is more relevant than the product). The implementation of projects, even if they are quite small, such as putting up a sign or establishing signposted walking paths, can be signals that something is being done (Kistenmacher & Mangels, 2000). Promoting and staging events involving the public and media can also be an important signal for the success of regional cooperation.

Internal communication also contributes to making results visible and tangible. Most theme trails publish a newsletter, in which among other information ongoing projects are documented. These newsletters are a means of keeping the wide basis of members up to date on what is being done and what has been achieved already. Internal communication also takes place in person during meetings, where it is necessary that the gatherings are well structured and that results of previous meetings are clearly referred to so that appropriate procedures are made visible, too. This type of motivation by internal communication is less effective in the very beginning of a project when there is only a loosely organised working group. Neither does it work when the people attending the meeting lack commitment or authority in the organisation or municipality they come from (Fuerst & Schubert, 1998).

Management

Theme trail networks need professional management structures. They need a coordinator who has an overall view over the expectations and interests of the participating stakeholders and who tries to reconcile these expectations and interests. Collaboration in a theme trail network carries the danger of potential conflict because of economic, personal, political, administrational, or institutional reasons.

Economic conflicts

Economic conflicts are mainly found among enterprises of the same economic sector for fear of fierce or unjust competition. This occurred in the Cheese Trail Bregenzerwald between alpine dairies themselves, because they sell cheese directly to the consumer, and between alpine dairies and creameries.

If problems occur in economic cooperation between different sectors, such as between gastronomy and agriculture, they are mainly of an organisational nature. For instance, many farms are too small and therefore not able to deliver their products on a regular basis with the security the gastronomic enterprise would need. But this fact often triggers off further cooperation, such as leading to the formation of direct marketing initiatives, which can provide assured amounts more easily.

Economic conflicts among municipalities participating in a theme trail network may arise in the initial phase of establishing the trail when the geographical position of the trail is discussed. Some networks overcome this problem by doing without a trail in the geographical sense; that is, they are a network of tourist attractions that do not strictly follow a linear route.

Personal conflicts

Personal conflicts are mainly about power and influence, in the theme trail association as well as in the broader regional network. Envy, which often goes hand in hand with economic competition, is another obstacle concerning partnership relationships. Yet a certain amount of personal competition can also have positive effects as it means constant innovation, which, for example, could lead to an increase in the range of products offered in the region.

A significant task of the theme trail management is to facilitate dialogue between the members of the theme trail in a sensible and thoughtful way. All partners interviewed agreed on the fact that the informal level of the theme trail network is at least as important as the management level. Many decisions are made and many conflicts resolved during coincidental meetings in everyday situations.

Long-Term Funding

The continuity of a theme trail network calls for funding on a long-term basis. Certain projects, such as erecting signs or developing a restaurant guide, can be financed by national programmes and institutions and also by EU programmes, such as LEADER. Several Austrian theme trails haven taken part in or are still taking part in the LEADER programme. Danger lies in the time after the support programme ends. Many theme trails only exist for the time span of a promotional period or for the duration of a funded project. One of the three Iron Trail associations is an example for this phenomenon: the Upper Austrian Iron Trail worked well in the time before and during the staging of the provincial exhibition on the history of iron in 1998, during which time the provincial government provided the Upper Austrian Iron Trail association with financial and organisational aid. But when the financial support came to an end after the exhibition, the possibilities for action of the Upper Austrian Iron Trail association and its management structures were badly impaired.

In addition to public financial support, important sources of income for theme trails include revenues from membership fees, entrance fees, royalties, and merchandising. Another source includes in-kind contributions from the network partners, such as voluntary unpaid work.

In most cases the revenues are barely enough to cover running costs, such as office infrastructure or work done by the project coordinator. Financial independence from short-term public funding means that personnel and management costs of the theme trail can be covered on a long-term basis, and that about two-thirds of the stakeholders involved in the theme trail network are on an economically firm footing.

The transition into financial independence opens up an area of conflict between profit-oriented and non-commercial activities. Stalder (2001), who deals with regional strategic networks as learning organisations, speaks of two possibilities for the development of networks: development towards a competitive enterprise on the one hand, and establishment as a non-profit organisation on the other hand. Theme trails usually include both of these components. Municipalities and cultural initiatives, for example, belong to the non-profit group, and enterprises and licensees are part of the commercial group.

In order to improve the economic viability of theme trails it would be necessary to embrace more elements of the core of the tourism industry such as accommodation, gastronomy, and transport. Accommodation facilities are not especially well integrated in theme trail networks, and do not share the financial burden of the network.

Quality

Most theme trails manage to agree on a set of strict quality standards concerning the products offered to ensure a high quality. Standards concerning the core product such as cheese or wine are reached easily enough, but there is a lack of understanding concerning additional criteria that should help to ensure a high quality for the theme trail as a whole. Many components contribute to the quality of a theme trail: the quality of the equipment and service of gastronomy and accommodation, of regional agricultural products, of the surrounding landscape, and also the quality of the tourist's experience concerning the products and activities related to the trail theme.

The number of theme trails that have established a set of minimum quality standards that potential members have to fulfil is small. In order to become a member of the Cheese Trail Brezenzerwald, restaurants, for example, have to offer a certain range of cheese dishes and have to indicate from which farmer in the region the cheese was purchased. There is only one example where a theme trail quality guideline was issued at the provincial level, namely a set of standards issued by the working group Wine Road Lower Austria, which potential members of wine roads have to fulfil in order to join a wine road association.

An aspect that contributes much to the quality of a theme trail from a visitor's perspective, but which is dealt with in very few cases, is the way the theme can be experienced and sensed – for example, how curiosity is awakened or how an atmosphere of adventure is created. One of the rare examples of a theme trail that has defined standards on the quality of the thematic experience is the Cider Trail Lower Austria. It states that the trail must lead through landscapes where the orchards are clearly visible, and that cider must be clearly visible in participating cider restaurants, for example by providing a cider bar and literature on cider.

In addition to the need to continuously instruct theme trail members, efforts in public participation and education have to be made as well. Notably, strong involvement of the public is necessary for an authentic tourist product, because it helps the people who live and work in the region to identify with the trail theme.

Conclusions

The cooperation of different stakeholders in the theme trail network brings opportunities as well as challenges for the enterprises and institutions involved and for the region as a whole.

Opportunities

- Collaboration can help to overcome economic disadvantages resulting from the small size of (tourist) enterprises. The fact that several actors join forces makes them reach the critical mass that is necessary for the potential guest to be made aware of the theme trail and plan a longer stay in the region.

- Theme trails contribute to the branding of a region and to establishing a regional corporate identity. The overall theme on the one hand, and the trail as symbolic union on the other, contribute to creating a regional identity for the inhabitants as well as a regional image for the potential guests.
- The fact that actors from various sectors work together in theme trail networks creates the necessary framework for regional development. Successful regional development is based on intersectoral cooperation.

Challenges

- Owing to tension and conflict, personal and financial resources may be used inefficiently in theme trail networks. Several reasons for such conflict were discussed in the chapter: they include administrational barriers, economic competition, as well as personal conflicts.
- Poor management and coordination at the regional as well as the national level may also be wasteful of resources.
- At the national level, the lack of a coordinating institution means that there is no overall strategy or goal for theme trails in Austria. As a result, energy is lost due to different theme trail networks tackling similar difficulties alone rather than sharing their experience. As a further result some subsidies flow to groups within a regional theme trail network that work on contradicting goals.
- The term 'theme trail' stands for a wide range of tourist products. For example, almost a quarter of all Austrian theme trails are only route descriptions; some are insufficiently signposted. The quality of Austrian theme trails varies to a great degree, many lack coherent tourist products and activities that can be called professional and that can be experienced with all the senses.

Recommendations

In order to help those involved in theme trail networks to work together more efficiently, thereby contributing to their own economic success as well as to the socio-economic development of a whole region, the following points should be taken into consideration and implemented:

- The financial, social, and emotional benefits that come from joining the theme trail network must be made clear for its members. The results of the activities of the theme trail network have to be made visible.
- Long-term financial planning must be an obligatory requirement for receiving and granting funding. All institutions should seek to ensure long-term funding of the theme trail.

- Theme trails call for professional management structures in the region, especially a permanently operating and adequately staffed head office.
- A national strategy and general guidelines for theme trails must be developed by a coordinating board on the national level.
- The term 'theme trail' must become a seal of approval, which will only be awarded to those regional initiatives that fulfil a minimum set of quality standards.

References

European LEADER Observatory/AEIDL (1997) *Aufbau und Organisation Lokaler Partnerschaften.* Innovation im Laendlichen Raum Heft Nr.2. On WWW at http://www.rural-europe.aeidl.be/rural-de/biblio/Rural Europe. Accessed 03.01.

Fuerst, D., Baumheier, R., Jung, U., Kegel, U., Kummerer, K., Thormähler, L., Rohr, G. and Zeck, H. (1999) Auswertung von Erfahrungen zur Kooperation in Regionen. *Raumforschung und Raumordnung* 57 (1), 53–58.

Fuerst, D. and Schubert, H. (1998) Regionale Akteursnetzwerke – Zur Rolle von Netzwerken in regionalen Umstrukturierungsprozessen. *Raumforschung und Raumordnung* 56 (5/6), 352–61.

Harper, P. (1997) The importance of community involvement in sustainable tourism development. In M.J. Stabler (ed.) *Tourism and Sustainability – Principles to Practice* (pp. 143–49). Wallingford: CAB International.

Kistenmacher, H. and Mangels, K. (2000) Regionalmanagement als Motor fuer eine nachhaltige Raumentwicklung? *Raumforschung und Raumordnung* 58 (2–3), 89–102.

Meyer-Cech, K. (2003) Themenstrassen als regionale Kooperationen und Mittel zur touristischen Entwicklung – fuenf oesterreichische Beispiele. Unpublished Doctoral thesis, University of Natural Resources and Applied Life Sciences, Vienna.

Mielke, B. (2000) Regionenmarketing im Kontext regionaler Entwicklungskonzepte. *Raumforschung und Raumordnung* 58 (4), 317–25.

Scheff, J. (1999) *Lernende Regionen – Regionale Netzwerke als Antwort auf Globale Herausforderungen.* Vienna: Linde.

Stalder, U. (2001) *Regionale Strategische Netzwerke als Lernende Organisationen – Regionalfoerderung aus Sicht der Theorie sozialer Systeme.* Bern: Geographisches Institut der Universität.

Zechner, G. (1998) *Projekte auf Kommunaler Ebene Erfolgreich Managen – Praxishandbuch fuer Erfolgreiche Regionalinitiativen.* Vienna: Manz.

Chapter 9

Rural Wine and Food Tourism Cluster and Network Development

C. MICHAEL HALL

Introduction

Food and wine tourism has emerged as a major area of interest for tourism studies, particularly in rural regions (Hall & Mitchell, 2001; Hjalager & Richards, 2002). While some of this interest is undoubtedly related to an increased awareness of the cultural significance of food in everyday life, much of the growth of writing on wine and food tourism parallels the extent to which rural areas have sought to innovate and diversify their agricultural bases through tourism-related consumption and production. Since the early 1970s rural regions in industrialised countries have been substantially affected by successive rounds of economic restructuring within a new globalised economy and society. In response to the abolition or privatisation of government-provided services, changed access regimes to 'traditional' markets, and the removal of tariffs and regional support mechanisms, rural areas have sought to diversify their economic base, with new agricultural products and tourism being two such responses. Food tourism strategies are therefore a significant instrument of regional development particularly because of the potential leverage between products from the two sectors (Telfer, 2001a, 2001b; Hall, 2002; Hall *et al.*, 2003). For example, the Government of South Africa (1996) noted that tourism had the potential to influence visitor tastes and create export markets.

Through tourism, South Africa becomes the supermarket or boutique to which visitors are drawn. Apart from the normal consumption of sun, sand, and sea, wildlife, wine, and water sports, tourism allows its clients to inspect other goods and services for sale in South Africa. Tourists to South Africa have the opportunity to sample the local fare (e.g. wine, beer, food, craft, entertainment, etc.). Moreover, they have the leisure, time, usually the money as well as the convenience (plastic cards) to pay for local goods and services. The potential for South

Africa to influence visitor tastes and create permanent export markets is very real (Government of South Africa, 1996: sec.3.2xiii).

Nevertheless, despite much enthusiasm by many governments, consultants, and academics regarding wine and food tourism, there is often a propensity to overestimate the numbers of those who travel specifically to seek out local food and restaurants. For example, to state the seemingly obvious, everyone has to eat, yet it would not be appropriate to describe everyone who eats when they travel as a food tourist. Despite this, food tourism, which may be defined as visitation to primary and secondary food producers, food festivals, restaurants, and specific locations for which food tasting and/or experiencing the attributes of specialist food production region are the primary motivating factor for travel (Hall & Mitchell, 2001: 308), and of which wine tourism is a subset, may be of significance for income generation and tourism generation for a number of rural regions.

This chapter is divided into three main sections: first, a brief review of the role of food, wine and tourism in regional development; secondly, a discussion of the significance of networks as a particular mechanism for regional development; and thirdly, the results of the study of a wine tourism in New Zealand. The chapter then concludes with a brief discussion of the difficulties of network activation.

Role of Food, Wine, and Tourism in Regional Development

Long seen as only a 'minor' industry, tourism has now assumed centre stage as a major source of foreign income and overseas investment for many countries and as a key component in regional development strategies (Butler *et al.*, 1998). Several reasons can be given for this change of perception. First, most rural areas in western countries have undergone major economic and social restructuring with subsequent job losses due to technological innovation and changed agricultural practices as well as broader population loss from such areas due to perceived better opportunities elsewhere. Tourism is therefore seen as a 'sunrise' industry that is labour intensive and therefore offers the potential to be a substantial source of employment. Secondly, the impact of crises such as 'foot and mouth' in the United Kingdom in 2001 and the subsequent war on terrorism on the mobility of people have made many politicians aware of just how economically and socially significant tourism is in locations in which few other development alternatives exist. Thirdly, in policy terms tourism is perceived as a relatively easy and visible means of government intervention in encouraging regional development. Fourthly, the more urbanised society has become, the more socially significant rural areas, and the rural–urban fringe in particular, become for leisure and recreation activities.

Much of the focus of wine and food tourism is on the development of new product at both the level of the firm and of the region. For example, specialised products offer the opportunity for the development of visitor product through rural tours, direct purchasing from the farm, specialised restaurant menus with an emphasis on local food, and home stays on such properties (Bessière, 1998). Indeed, in these circumstances, outsider interest in local produce may serve to stimulate local awareness and interest, and assist not only in diversification, and the maintenance of plant and animal variety, but may also encourage community pride and reinforcement of local identity and culture. Therefore, some agencies and stakeholders see wine and food tourism as an important element in local economic development strategies because of the potential relationships between different industrial sectors thereby not only providing for longer circulation of money within local economies but also the development of new value-added production (e.g. OECD, 1995; Policy Commission on the Future of Farming and Food, 2002; Scottish Food Strategy Group, 1993). Local economic development strategies that seek to encourage food and wine tourism tend to have a number of similar components (Centre for Environment and Society, 1999):

- reduction of economic leakage by using local renewable resources rather than external sources, for example use local materials for packaging, 'buy local' campaigns;
- recycling of financial resources within the system by buying local goods and services, for example hoteliers and restauranteurs need to purchase and promote local foods, produce, and wine or other beverages, use local banks and credit unions;
- addition of value to local produce before it is exported; for example bottle and package food locally, consider using distinctive local packaging in order to reinforce local brand identity, use local food as an attraction to tourists thereby increasing the circulation of tourist expenditure through the local economy;
- connecting up of local stakeholders, people, and institutions to create trust, new linkages, and more efficient exchanges; for example local farmers and producers' cooperatives, development of local marketing networks, a 'buy local' campaign;
- attraction of external resources, especially finance, skills, and technology where appropriate, for example use the Internet to connect to customers outside the region;
- emphasising of local identity and authenticity in branding and promotional strategies, for example list the place of origin on the label and encourage consistent use of place of origin by producers;

- selling directly to consumers via farm shops, direct mailing, farmers' and produce markets, local events, and food and wine festivals; and
- creation of a relationship between the consumer and the producer, for example using cellar door or farm door sales, utilising news-letters, Websites and the Internet to create an ongoing relationship with consumers.

For example, the 'Eat the View' project, which was set up by the UK Countryside Agency in 2001 with the eventual aim to 'Create improved market conditions for products that originate from systems of land management which enhance or protect the countryside's landscape and character' (Countryside Agency, 2001), has a number of target outcomes that may arise from improved local economic linkages between tourism and food production:

- to inform consumers about the impact of their decisions on the rural environment and economy and how they can take positive action to benefit the countryside;
- the development of systems for marketing/distributing/selling produce, which will enable consumers to show support for local/ sustainable production methods;
- the development of quality standards/accreditation systems to underpin markets for local/sustainable products;
- the development of local marketing/branding initiatives that will utilise unique features, for example rare animal breeds, local customs, and so on;
- the development of new supply chain partnerships between retailers/producers, which will increase the proportion of locally sourced/sustainable products;
- to increase the proportion of produce sold through alternative markets to large retailers and bulk caterers, for example local collaborative arrangements;
- to increase the number of local/community-led food initiatives, creating stronger local markets for produce and strengthening links between producers and consumers (adapted from Countryside Agency, 2001).

Often underlying the above strategy components is a tacit awareness of new economic and social practices of consumption and production in which new sets of relationships are being formed between and among producers and consumers at different scales. At its most transparent this involved the development of new sets of direct relations between food producers and consumers that bypass wholesalers and retailers. For the producer, such relationships lead to greater economic return.

For the consumers it may provide access to fresher and better quality foods, and greater knowledge of the elements of the food chain as well as certain cultural capital. However, new relationships may also develop between producers in terms of supplying the various elements of the visitor experience as well as the exporting of local foodstuffs outside the immediate region. The present chapter does not seek to focus on the consumptive dimension of food and wine tourism (Mitchell & Hall, 2003), yet it is important to note that relationships between consumers may arise because of the cultural positioning of food in contemporary society and the role of food and food consumption as a reflection of lifestyle.

In terms of production Hall (2002) argued that critical to the success of regional food tourism business strategies is the development of intangible capital: intellectual property, networks, brand, and talent. Intellectual property and brand are closely entwined. To a large extent, wine, food, and tourism are products that can be differentiated on the basis of regional identity. For example, wine is often identified by its geographical origin, for example Burgundy, Champagne, Rioja, which, in many cases, have been formalised through a series of appelation controls in turn founded on certain geographical characteristics of a place. It should therefore be of little surprise that the relationship between wine, food, and tourism is extremely significant at a regional level through the contribution that regionality provides for product branding, place promotion, and, through these mechanisms, economic development (Hall, 2002; Ilbery & Kneafsey, 2000a, 2000b). For example, according to Henchion and McIntyre (2000) in a study of consumer preferences in Ireland, region of origin was an important consideration for two out of three consumers when deciding to purchase quality products. Appelation controls and geographically designated origins have long served to act as a form of intellectual property in terms of rural space as well as product (Moran, 1993). Regional speciality food and drink products have also come to be registered as intellectual property as designated quality labels within EU and national law (Ilbery & Kneafsey, 2000a), a process that Ilbery and Kneafsey (2000b) appropriately described within the context of globalisation as 'cultural relocalisation' and which is having substantial ramifications for international trade agreements.

Talent and the management of appropriate knowledge bases are also important for wine and food tourism. In the knowledge economy it becomes vital that regions, as much as individual firms, attract, retain and develop the best of their people. One way that knowledge resources may be maximised in rural areas is through the development of networks in which best practices, market knowledge, and other forms of information may be shared. However, knowledge is only one dimension of networks and it is to this broader issue of network development that the chapter will now turn.

Networks

Networks and cluster relationships are a significant part of the development of intangible capital. Networking refers to a wide range of cooperative behaviours between otherwise competing organisations and between organisations linked through economic and social relationships and transactions. Often the term is synonymous with interfirm cooperation. Industry clusters exist where there is loose geographical concentration or association of firms and organisations involved in a value chain producing goods and services and which is relatively innovative. The suggestion that business clusters add value to a region implies a new set of public policies, one that shifts the focus of attention from an individual place or individual firm to a region and clusters of businesses and the interaction between them (Nordin, 2003; Rosenfeld, 1997). A cluster may be defined as a concentration of companies and industries in a geographic region that are interconnected by the markets they serve and the products they produce, as well as by the suppliers, trade associations, and educational institutions with which they interact (Porter, 1990). Many commentators argue that such chains of firms are the primary 'drivers' of a region's economy, on whose success other businesses, such as construction firms, for example, depend on in terms of their own financial viability. However, objective criteria for clusters have proven exceedingly difficult to pin down, and there are arguably as many definitions as there are types of organisations using the term (Rosenfeld, 1997: 8). For example, Rosenfeld (1997: 9) argues that, to all intents and purposes, networks are a result of mature and animated clusters, not the source of a local production system, whereas clusters are systems in which membership is simply based on interdependence and making a contribution to the functioning of the system. In attempting to clarify the differences between clusters and networks, Nordin (2003), in her examination of the cluster concept in tourism, quotes from the OECD:

> Clusters differ from other forms of co-operation and networks in that the actors involved in a cluster are linked in a value chain. The cluster concept goes beyond 'simple' horizontal networks in which firms, operating on the same end-product market and belonging to the same industry group, co-operate on aspects such as R&D, demonstration programmes, collective marketing or purchasing policy. Clusters are often cross-sectoral (vertical and/or lateral) networks, made up of dissimilar and complementary firms specialising

around a specific link or knowledge base in the value chain. (OECD, 1999: 12)

However, in trying to operationalise this approach, three substantial problems occur. First, how does one measure the density of networks so that the shift from a network to a cluster can be observed? Secondly, and perhaps more significantly, for rural tourism development, how might the value chain of tourism be described? From the perspective of the producers or, perhaps more importantly, given the destination-bound nature of most tourism activity, from the perspective of the consumer, who consumes tourism products from different firms across time and space during a trip? Thirdly, what role does the geography of a place or destination play in clustering?

An industry cluster includes companies that sell inside as well as outside the region, and also supports firms that supply raw materials, components, and business services to them. These clusters form 'value chains' that are the fundamental units of competition in the modern, globalised world economy. Clusters in a region form over time and stem from the region's economic foundations, its existing companies, and local demand for products and services (Waits, 2000). Firms and organisations involved in clusters are able to achieve synergies and leverage economic advantage from shared access to information and knowledge networks, supplier and distribution chains, markets and marketing intelligence, competencies, and resources in a specific locality. The cluster concept therefore focuses on the linkages and interdependencies among actors in value chains (Enright & Roberts, 2001).

Wine has been recognised as one industry in which clustering may be a significant competitive factor (Marsh & Shaw, 2000; Nordin, 2003). Indeed, Porter (1990) himself used the California wine industry as an example of successful cluster development. Similarly, Blandy (2000: 21) cites the example of the South Australian wine industry as 'the classic example of a successful industry cluster in South Australia ... a group of competing, complementary and interdependent firms that have given strong economic drive to the State through the cluster's success in exporting its products and know how nationally and internationally'.

Cluster formation is regarded as a significant component in the formation of positive external economies for firms, including those of the wine industry, with tourism being recognised as an important component (Porter, 1990). Telfer (2001a, 2001b) argued that cluster development has been a significant component of wine and food tourism network development in the Niagara region of Canada. Although one of the lessons of cluster development programmes around the world 'is that there is no precise, "right" (one size fits all) formula for developing industry clusters' (Blandy, 2000: 80), a number of factors have been recognised as significant in the development of clusters and the associated external economy that serves to reinforce the clustering process. These include:

- the life-cycle stage of innovative clusters;
- government financing and policies;
- the skills of the region's human resources;
- the technological capabilities of the region's R&D activities;
- the quality of the region's physical, transport, information, and communication infrastructure;
- the availability and expertise of capital financing in the region;
- the cost and quality of the region's tax and regulatory environment; and
- the appeal of the region's lifestyle to people that can provide world class resources and processes.

What is remarkable in many of the accounts of cluster development, with Blandy's (2000) review being typical, is that few of the models or accounts of clusters adequately capture and describe the underlying dynamics of clusters. They do not explain how they actually 'work' or answer questions of whether and how firms interact and produce synergistically. Scale is only part of reason that clusters and their regions prosper. Equally important to the circuitry of the system is the 'current', or the flow of information, knowledge, technological advances, innovations, skills, people, and capital into, out of, and within the cluster, from point to point (Rosenfeld, 1997). Conventional data often cannot distinguish between a simple industry concentration and a working cluster. However, in a cluster, the social ecology is as important as the agglomeration economies. As Rosenfeld (1997: 10) comments, 'The "current" of a working production system is even less easily detected, often embedded in professional, trade and civic associations, and in informal socialisation patterns . . . The "current" depends on norms of reciprocity and sufficient levels of trust to encourage professional interaction and collaborative behaviour'.

For Rosenfeld (1997: 10) clusters are 'A geographically bounded concentration of interdependent businesses with active channels for business transactions, dialogue, and communications . . . that collectively shares common opportunities and threats'. Importantly, this definition asserts that 'active channels' are as important as 'concentration', and without active channels even a critical mass of related firms is not a local production or social system and therefore does not operate as a cluster. Therefore, in seeking to understand the processes of cluster development, recognition of social capital and the relative efficiency of channels of social exchange becomes vital. Indeed, the co-location of firms may at times lead as much to a lack of social exchange as it does to a positive sharing of knowledge and ideas!

Such a situation may well be critical with respect to maximising the contribution of clusters to regional economy. In the case of Porter's (1990) example of a Californian wine cluster, and Blandy's (2000) reference to the South Australian wine industry cluster, both authors failed to recognise that the wine industry had been in those locations for well over a hundred years with the economic and social relationships of wine firms reinforced by the family networks established over that period. Tourism had been a late arrival in both cases as a component of the cluster. Furthermore, given that the areas had been wine regions for such a long period and that wine is an environmentally dependent resource, it is therefore not surprising that certain elements of a cluster formation had developed in this time. Moreover, certain 'traditional' economic location factors that relate to accessibility and closeness to market may still be recognised as important. Perhaps a more significant question is, what understanding does existing work on clusters provide us for identifying the factors in developing new clusters, particularly in rural areas that have undergone fundamental economic restructuring? Unfortunately, unless research indicates how firms interact and clusters work, the answer is likely to be very little. It is critical to recognise that networks undergo path-dependent evolutionary change, that is, 'the degree to which networks constructed in particular contexts for particular purposes are consolidated over time' (Amin and Thrift, 1997: 153), paying attention to:

- the thickness and degree of openness or closure of networks;
- the asymmetry of power between networks of interdependencies;
- the learning abilities of networks;
- the role of information in networks; and
- the set of institutionalised obligations that exist in networks.

The following case discusses the development of wine and food tourism clusters in New Zealand. It details three regions and their relative success and posits reasons as to why this success has been achieved.

Wine and food tourism in New Zealand

The wine industry has been one of New Zealand's rural success stories in recent years (Hall *et al.*, 2000). Although other traditional rural industries have struggled to maintain growth since the 1970s, wine has grown rapidly from being a minor agricultural industry to dominating the landscape in a number of rural areas. This growth can be charted not only in terms of number of wineries and the area under vine but also in the substantial export returns that have developed.

Three leading New Zealand wine regions, Central Otago, Hawkes Bay, and Marlborough – which exhibit cluster characteristics – have been studied by the author since 1996 in terms of the development of wine and food tourism and associated networks (see also Hall *et al.*, 1997; Hall, 2004). Although Hawkes Bay is the longest established wine region it has recently witnessed a substantial growth in the number of wineries in the area, with Marlborough becoming established in the late 1980s and Central Otago in the 1990s as recognised wine-producing areas. Nevertheless, although having similar numbers of wineries, substantial differences exist in their capacity to establish interfirm cooperation, particularly with respect to wine and food tourism. Moreover, participant observation in the wine regions has been important for separating the images of interrelationships between firms conveyed in promotion and media stories (e.g. Thomson, 2003) versus the reality of interfirm and interpersonal networks in specific settings.

Several barriers to creating effective links between wine producers and the tourism industry may be recognised:

- the often perceived secondary or tertiary nature of tourism as an activity in the wine industry, accompanied by a perception that there is an imbalance of benefits from wine and tourism relationships with the greater advantage accruing to tourism firms;
- a dominant product focus of wine makers and wine marketers that neglects the benefit and service dimensions of their product;
- a general lack of experience and understanding within the wine industry of tourism, and a subsequent lack of entrepreneurial skills and abilities with respect to marketing and service product development; and
- the relative absence of effective intersectoral economic and social linkages, including appropriate institutional structures, which leads to a lack of inter- and intra-organisational cohesion within the wine industry, and between the wine industry and the tourism industry.

Hall (2001) identified several other factors that may affect cluster and network success:

- spatial separation – the existence of substantial spatial separation of vineyards and wineries within a wine region due to physical resource factors;
- administrative separation – the existence of multiple public administrative agencies and units within a region;
- the existence of a 'champion' to promote the development of a network; and
- the hosting of meetings to develop relationships.

Of these, the role of champions as well as the involvement of the local state were regarded as especially important in the creation of wine and food tourism networks and associated new product development in the

New Zealand situation. Such an observation is significant as Audretsch and Feldman (1997) noted that the generation of new economic knowledge tends to result in a greater propensity for innovative activity to cluster during the early stages of the industry life-cycle, and to be more highly dispersed during the mature and declining stages of the life-cycle. Arguably, a further factor may well be a relative lack of social innovation capital in certain regions, possibly related to difficulties in attracting or retaining intellectual capital, external network knowledge, and entrepreneurial skills that influence path dependency.

In the case of Hawkes Bay, such developments have occurred primarily because several local champions emerged convinced of the need to promote Hawkes Bay collectively, as they saw that their own individual businesses would be more successful if there was a strong brand and producer network. In tourism terms they recognised that their individual business may not be sufficient to generate the required volumes of visitors, but that if there was a critical and connected mass of visitor attractors then their own business would benefit because the overall marker for their business would have increased. Just as importantly, the champions recognised the development of networks needed to be undertaken on a multifirm level and not just in relation to their own firms. In many cases the social capital of the champions was converted into the social and economic capital of others. Following their formation at a public seminar in July 2000, the Hawkes Bay Wine and Food Group have developed a food and wine trail, brochures, and improved signage, and have engaged in more effective joint promotion strategies, including the development of a wine- and food-oriented Hawke's Bay regional brand – 'Hawkes Bay Wine Country' (http://www.hawkesbaynz.com/). Indeed, such has been the success of the group that local government is having to respond to their initiative. In November 2001 Hawkes Bay hosted the second New Zealand wine and food tourism conference as part of the development of a national food and wine tourism strategy. However, unlike other jurisdictions noted for government intervention in network development, such as the European Union and Australia, such initiatives have primarily come out of the private sector and from the goodwill of certain individuals, rather than having occurred because of government involvement. Indeed, local government has tended to come on board after the initial initiatives from the private sector, which sought greater cooperation not only between themselves and local agencies but between local agencies. Critical to the development of the Food and Wine Group was the involvement of 'experts' or 'knowledge brokers' at the initial public meeting. They could provide what was perceived as 'independent' advice, separate to that of local stakeholders, which created a climate of trust between potential members of the cluster and, just as importantly, allowed the work of champions to be perceived as wider than self-interest in the creation of the group.

In the case of the Hawkes Bay wine and food tourism network appropriate collaborative arrangements (Forde, 2000; Hall, 2000) have been put in place through:

- *Organisational and institutional arrangements* between cluster members that give the cluster an identity and profile the industry sector, for example Hawkes Bay Food and Wine Tourism Group under the brand of Hawke's Bay Wine Country. They create the framework for development of the cluster and implementation of initiatives.
- *Standard operating procedures* agreed by members for transferring information, communicating with each other, and organizing around market opportunities, for example through regular group meetings.
- *Administrative support services* that are developed to give effect to the above.

Marlborough held meetings to establish a farmers' market in early 2001, with the first market being held in late 2001, although no distinct food and wine tourism brand has been established. Interestingly, attempts to bring the food and wine sectors together within a regional context had been occurring since 1996, although the champions tended to come from the local tourist organisation. As individuals left the organisation so interest was lost, only for it to be 'rediscovered' when another person committed to wine and food tourism joined the local tourism body. Although Marlborough has a strong food and wine tourism profile, the development of industry relationships and public–private sector partnerships is not as well institutionalised as in Hawkes Bay.

Little multifirm wine and tourism development occurred in Otago over the same period although many individual firms were established. However, the arrival of a new local tourism organisation head for one of the towns in the region in late 2002 with an interest in wine and food tourism has provided a champion for cooperative action between the wine and food sectors that have often seen themselves in intraregional competition for scarce public resources.

From fieldwork conducted in the three regions since 1996 it is apparent that at an individual level many firms and public agencies are seeking the creation of networks and the benefits of clustering in both regions. Nevertheless, the pre-existence of wine and tourism organisations is not necessarily a forerunner to cluster development. Indeed, interorganisational rivalry may work against new intersectoral networks being established. Instead, two factors, the role of a champion to initiate cluster development, and the associated holding of regular stakeholder meetings to facilitate cooperation and effective communication, appear to be far more significant in facilitating stakeholder collaboration than other factors. The role of cluster champions who initiate such meetings is to create new forms of social capital by encouraging the development of webs of relationships where none previously existed. Therefore, the lack of continued leadership in terms of cluster development becomes a significant issue. For example, in the case of Marlborough a number of champions emerged seeking to encourage collaboration. However, they were not consistently in place long enough in their positions within local government to lead to the creation of long-term collaborative relationships, in part because of the stakeholders they were directly answerable to. While stakeholder meetings provide part of the basis for the development of trust within a cluster, it is readily apparent that someone has to organise. In some areas such a single act as this can prove difficult because of community politics and sectoral network closure.

Moreover, at the national level cooperation between the various networks, firms, and regions has been extremely hard to achieve, partly because of interregional rivalry, but also because the region is seen as the appropriate level for wine and food tourism promotion rather than the national level. Unfortunately, it is often harder for network champions to operate at a national level because of the time required to visit and persuade key network partners to follow certain courses of action. Therefore, it is not surprising that this role is usually undertaken or sponsored by government. At the time of writing, although a national wine and food tourism strategy has been written, considerable debate continues over who pays for implementation and the institutional structures that should be established. However, the possible granting of a small amount of seed money (NZ$10,000) from Tourism New Zealand may provide for the establishment of a relevant marketing network.

Conclusions

Network creation and development is an important dimension of rural tourism development. However, for rural regions the greatest benefits in the establishment of networks are not to be found within the tourism sector, but by encouraging the development of intersectoral linkages and networks between firms that had previously seen themselves as having little in common. By encouraging such relations, new product and service innovations are developed as well as the generation of new social economic and intangible capital that can lead to improved regional competitive advantage and resilience.

Fundamental to such network developments is the establishment of communicative relationships between partners. In other words, encourage people and firms to talk to each other to see where they have mutual interests and where cooperation may be beneficial. Without an appropriate champion such development may be difficult, and it must also be acknowledged that the development of networks, trust, and relationships take time, often considerably longer than many rural development programmes allow. The availability of local champions with a long-term commitment to cluster and network development provides for path-dependent change leading to network development. Without appropriate champions and institutions, sustainable dense networks of relationships may not be maintained, with a consequent loss of intellectual capital and innovation capacity as well as a lessening of the rate of economic return from wine and food tourism to the region.

Acknowledgement

Earlier versions and components of this chapter were previously presented as conference papers at the Scottish Agricultural College, Auchincruive; Leeds Metropolitan University, UK; and Jyväskylä, Finland. The author is grateful for the feedback and comments received at these symposia.

References

Amin, A. and Thrift, N. (1997) Globalization, socio-economics, territoriality. In R. Lee and J. Wills (eds) *Geographies of Economies* (pp. 147–57). London: Arnold.

Audretsch, D.B. and Feldman, M.P. (1997) *Innovative Clusters and the Industry Life Cycle*, Discussion Paper 1161. London: Centre for Economic Policy Research.

Bessière, J. (1998). Local development and heritage: traditional food and cuisine as tourist attractions in rural areas. *Sociologia Ruralis* 38 (1), 21–34.

Blandy, R. (2000) *Industry Clusters Program: A Review, South Australian Business Vision 2010*. Adelaide: Government of South Australia.

Butler, R., Hall, C.M. and Jenkins, J. (eds) (1998) *Tourism and Recreation in Rural Areas*. Chichester: John Wiley and Sons.

Centre for Environment and Society (1999) *Local Food Systems: Lessons for Local Economies Conference Proceedings*. Colchester: University of Essex.

Countryside Agency, The (2001) *Eat the View – Promoting Sustainable, Local Products*. Cheltenham: The Countryside Agency. On WWW at http://www.countryside.gov.uk. Accessed 25.01.02.

Enright, M. and Roberts, B. (2001) Regional clustering in Australia. *Australian Journal of Management* 26, 65–86.

Forde, H. (2000) *Industry Clusters and Collaboration*, Occasional Paper SABV2010 Industry Cluster Project. Adelaide: Government of South Australia.

Government of South Africa (1996) *White Paper: The Development and Promotion of Tourism in South Africa*. Pretoria: Department of Environmental Affairs and Tourism.

Hall, C.M. (2000) *Tourism Planning*. Harlow: Prentice Hall.

Hall, C.M. (2001) The development of rural wine and food tourism networks: factors and issues. In M. Mitchell and I. Kirkpatrick (eds) *New Directions in Managing Rural Tourism and Leisure: Local Impacts, Global Trends*. Ayr: Scottish Agricultural College, Auchincruive, CD-ROM.

Hall, C.M. (2002) Local initiatives for local regional development: the role of food, wine and tourism. In E. Arola, J. Kärkkäinen and M. Siitari (eds) *The 2nd Tourism Industry & Education Symposium, 'Tourism and Well-Being'*, May 16–18, 2002 (pp. 47–63). Jyväskylä: Jyväskylä Polytechnic.

Hall, C.M. (2004) Small firms and wine and food tourism in New Zealand: issues of clusters, collaboration and lifestyles. In R. Thomas (ed.) *Small Firms in Tourism: International Perspectives* (pp. 167–81). Oxford: Elsevier.

Hall, C.M., Cambourne, B., Macionis, N. and Johnson, G. (1997) Wine tourism and network development in Australia and New Zealand: review, establishment and prospects. *International Journal of Wine Marketing* 9 (2/3), 5–31.

Hall, C.M., Longo, A.M., Mitchell, R. and Johnson, G. (2000) Wine tourism in New Zealand. In C.M. Hall, E. Sharples, B. Cambourne and N. Macionis (eds) *Wine Tourism Around the World: Development, Management and Markets* (pp. 150–74), Oxford: Butterworth-Heinemann.

Hall, C.M. and Mitchell, R. (2001) Wine and food tourism. In N. Douglas, N. Douglas, and R. Derrett (eds) *Special Interest Tourism: Context and Cases* (pp. 307–29). Brisbane, Australia: John Wiley & Sons.

Hall, C.M., Sharples, E. and Mitchell, R. (2003) Consuming places: the role of food, wine and tourism in regional development. In C.M. Hall, E. Sharples, R. Mitchell, B. Cambourne and N. Macionis (eds) *Food Tourism Around the World: Development, Management and Markets* (pp. 22–59), Oxford: Butterworth-Heinemann.

Henchion, M. and McIntyre, B. (2000) Regional imagery and quality products: the Irish experience. *British Food Journal* 102 (8), 630–44.

Hjalager, A. and Richards, G. (eds) (2002) *Tourism and Gastronomy*. London: Routledge.

Ilbery, B. and Kneafsey, M. (2000a) Registering regional specialty food and drink products in the United Kingdom: the case of PDOs and PGIs. *Area* 32 (3), 317–25.

Ilbery, B. and Kneafsey, M. (2000b) Producer constructions of quality in regional speciality food production: a case study from south west England. *Journal of Rural Studies* 16, 217–30.

Marsh, I. and Shaw, I. (2000) *Australia's Wine Industry: Collaboration & Learning as Causes of Competitive Success*. Sydney: Austrialian Business Foundation.

Mitchell, R. and Hall, C.M. (2003) Consuming tourists: food tourism consumer behaviour. In C.M. Hall, E. Sharples, R. Mitchell, B. Cambourne and N. Macionis (eds) *Food Tourism Around the World: Development, Management and Markets* (pp. 60–80). Oxford: Butterworth-Heinemann.

Moran, W. (1993) Rural space as intellectual property. *Political Geography* 12 (3), 263–77.

Nordin, S. (2003) *Tourism Clustering and Innovation: Paths to Economic Growth and Development*. Östersund: European Tourism Research Institute, Mid-Sweden University, ETOUR Utredningsserien Analys och Statistik 2003: 14.

OECD (Organisation for Economic Co-operation and Development) (1995) *Niche Markets as a Rural Development Strategy*. Paris: OECD.

OECD (Organisation for Economic Co-operation and Development) (1999) *Proceedings, Boosting Innovation: The Cluster Approach*. Paris: OECD.

Policy Commission on the Future of Farming and Food (2002) *Farming & Food – A Sustainable Future*. London: Policy Commission on the Future of Farming and Food.

Porter, M. (1990) *The Competitive Advantage of Nations*. London: Macmillan.

Rosenfeld, S.A. (1997) Bringing business clusters into the mainstream of economic development. *European Planning Studies* 5 (1), 3–23.

Scottish Food Strategy Group (SFSG) (1993) *Scotland Means Quality*. Edinburgh: SFSG.

Telfer, D.J. (2001a) Strategic alliances along the Niagara Wine Route. *Tourism Management* 22, 21–30.

Telfer, D.J. (2001b) From a wine tourism village to a regional wine route: An investigation of the competitive advantage of embedded clusters in Niagara, Canada. *Tourism Recreation Research* 26, 23–33.

Thomson, J. (2003) Toasting trails. *Air New Zealand* November, 64–73.

Waits, M.J. (2000) The added value of the industry cluster approach to economic analysis, strategy development, and service delivery. *Economic Development Quarterly* 14, 35–50.

Chapter 10

Globalisation, Rural Tourism and Community Power

HEATHER MAIR, DONALD G. REID and WANDA GEORGE

Introduction

Tourism planning and development in rural areas might be viewed as one way of responding to globalisation as it works to influence the structure of change and growth in rural areas. Indeed, there can be no doubt that tourism has become a powerful force in rural economic development and its importance has grown since Blank (1989: 1) labelled it the 'Cinderella stepchild of economic development' as it has become a primary mechanism for stimulating rural rejuvenation and growth. Understanding the role of tourism planning in rural communities requires an investigation into its place in the overall approach to rural development. As more rural communities undertake the journey to rural growth through enhanced tourism development, conceptions of community identity and power are essential. Moreover, researchers and practitioners must ask a number of critical questions. What is the impact of a tourism-led approach to stimulating growth in rural communities? Are there ways by which members of rural communities can embark on this path and still maintain control over the places where they live?

This chapter is based on the results of a three-year research project involving seven rural communities in Ontario, Canada. It is intended to alert those involved in tourism studies, planning, and development to be wary of the issues and impacts that stem from tourism-led growth, while drawing attention to the potential for empowerment and control at the local level. This chapter first traces the relationship between the increasing acceptance of tourism as a mechanism for rural development and the overarching context of globalisation. Locating tourism within this context is important as it draws attention to underlying assumptions about options for rural communities and frames the ways in which tourism is planned and encouraged.

The second section briefly outlines the results from the first stage of our research in four Ontario rural communities in order to draw attention to the issues and problems that emerged. Not surprisingly, there are reports of frustration and dissatisfaction with the consequences of increased tourism in these areas. More fundamentally, our research uncovered a feeling of alienation from the overall approach to tourism development and the decision-making processes. This point is discussed in some depth.

The third section presents the research team's response to these concerns as we developed a manual or handbook, designed to provide a step-by-step guide outlining a planning process for communities undertaking or considering tourism. The manual incorporates a number of exercises and activities to be used by communities as they work their way towards developing a vision for tourism and product development. We hypothesised that a comprehensive community-based planning approach could assist newly emerging tourism communities, as well as those experiencing tourism-related problems, to avoid some of the pitfalls uncovered by our earlier research. The main purpose was to address the underlying challenges of tourism planning and to develop a grassroots, participatory process that could enhance community power and create a wider basis for decision making. After taking a critical look at the manual and describing pitfalls and stumbling blocks encountered during the initial stages of implementation, the fourth section of the chapter highlights one case community, Deep River, Ontario, in order to exemplify the implementation of the manual at the local level. Finally, a concluding section highlights the potential of this approach for sustainable tourism development.

A small and select group of interested people, often entrepreneurs, who possess a business perspective and, generally, only a vague understanding of the community's ultimate tourism development goals, drive most planning models. Too often, a common and comprehensive vision for tourism development is not constructed before individual businesses or attractions begin to appear. As a result, the tourism product is constructed incrementally and not as a result of a well thought out, comprehensive strategy. This approach to development has the potential to spark discontent in the larger community as the product continues to grow incrementally, without direction and control. There may also be concerns regarding the nature and type of tourism development. This chapter is a reflection upon an ongoing attempt to create an inclusive planning and identity-building process that could lay the groundwork for a community-wide approach able to counter some of the disempowering tendencies of economic globalisation and tourism development.

Globalisation and the Changing Options for Rural Development

Corporate or economic globalisation is having a major impact on rural communities around the world. Dramatic advances in communication and travel technologies have allowed corporations to conduct worldwide business instantaneously as distance is no longer a barrier to trade and commerce. While definitions of economic globalisation abound, the fundamental tendencies towards individualisation, homogenisation and commodification are commonly cited as important trends (Beck, 2000; Cox, 1991). As their relationship to the national and global economy shifts through globalisation, rural communities are undergoing profound socio-economic changes as they experience threats to the predominantly natural resources upon which their economies are based. Authors such as Jenkins, Hall and Troughton (1998) have identified the need to connect broad-based transformations in the production system to changes in rural areas as economic endeavours (at least in the Western world) shift from manufacturing to primarily service-based industries. The literature addressing rural change, growth, and development suggests that as local planners and decision makers in rural communities are pressed to generate economic growth in the face of global restructuring and subsequent decreased government funding (the so-called hollowing out of the state), tourism is becoming attractive as a mechanism for rural development (Aronsson, 2000; Blank, 1989; Bouquet & Winter, 1987; Britton, 1991; Butler *et al.*, 1998; Hopkins, 1998; Ilbery, 1998; Keane, 1992; Luloff *et al.*, 1993; Ramaswamy & Kuentzel, 1998; Reid, Mair & Taylor, 2000; Roberts & Hall, 2001). Associated with this need to generate new forms of economic growth are improved transportation technologies, the institutionalisation of leisure time, and the growth of the service economy, all of which have led to an explosion in demand for travel to rural areas worldwide. Indeed, rural tourism is increasing rapidly and a growing number of communities are becoming retreats, representations of an idyllic past, and places to consume (Urry, 1990, 1995).

The proliferation of tourism-led approaches to economic development is remarkably common. For example, in a 1994 report on rural tourism and development, the Organisation for Economic Co-operation and Development determined the following:

> For many years a number of rural areas have been beset by population loss and declining services. These problems are now exacerbated by changes that have brought job losses and falling income to the farm sector. In contrast to this downturn, tourism has blossomed into a prosperous, fast-growing activity, and has indeed turned out to be a significant factor for economic growth in the countries in which it has

developed. It was therefore important to determine whether tourism's growth potential could be harnessed as a strategy for rural development, in particular by drawing upon resurgent interest in the countryside, its traditional way of life and landscapes and the architectural heritage ... [Tourism] has proved to be a powerful engine for economic growth – transferring capital, income and employment from industrial, urban and developed areas to non-industrial regions. (OECD, 1994: 5–7)

It is important to locate this consideration of tourism in rural communities within the overarching, market-driven logic that pervades community development planning in general. Indeed, the question of why tourism has become an attractive mechanism for rural development is presented within this context as it helps to illuminate a nexus where economic globalisation and community power relations meet. Hopkins identifies this trend:

Post-industrial restructuring has compelled [sites] to exploit and promote local tourist attractions ... in an attempt to minimise, halt or reverse economic decline induced by collapse or contraction in more conventional, manufacture-based sectors. In Canada, funding cuts, the lessening of the welfare state and the prevailing market-driven policy stance of the governing bodies have also encouraged local townships, counties and municipalities to market themselves to investors and consumers alike. (Hopkins, 1998: 66)

Thus, this form of globalisation has fundamentally altered the historic relationship between capital and labour, with capital having more power to set the conditions for development. Moreover, it has also changed the way in which production is organised spatially. This is important for any consideration of rural areas. The proliferation of international trade agreements like the World Trade Organisation (WTO), the North American Free Trade Agreement (NAFTA), and the European Union (EU) has meant that, in an effort to meet neo-liberal standards and expectations about government activity, sovereignty has been sacrificed. Government's ability to set conditions that could protect fledgling local industries, including tourism businesses, against well-financed transnational corporations has been weakened. While this form of globalisation is undoubtedly a powerful force, there are ways to counter these tendencies and much of this can take place at the local level. Indeed, underscoring our research is the assumption that if rural communities do follow a tourism-led path to development, ways must be created to ensure that community power is enhanced, not sacrificed. Power to resist the homogenising and commodifying tendencies of economic globalisation rests in the local community and, in particular with regard to tourism, the local culture, as this is the distinctive environment that makes the area attractive for tourists.

The role of the local community in influencing the tourism product is becoming clear. For instance, while the tourism industry has often seen itself as the attraction on which the tourism enterprise is constructed, upon closer examination it is evident that, in most circumstances, the resort or hotel is only one facilitator among many. In Kenya, for example, the five-star hotels that are placed strategically throughout the Amboselli National Park at the base of Mt. Kilimanjaro exist to support the magnificent environment including the majestic animals and the rich Masai culture prevalent in the area. Without these natural and cultural features there would be no demand for the resort hotels. Thus, it is in this realm that communities find their negotiating strength in dealing with corporate powers (Reid, 2003).

However, there are two reasons why communities have generally not been able to stem these developments. First, many of the affected communities may not realise their inherent power; and secondly, they are often not sufficiently organised to negotiate from a position of strength. The following section highlights our efforts to address these challenges.

Participatory Approach to Tourism Planning in Rural Communities

In Ontario, rural tourism comprises activities ranging from festivals and cultural events to farm tours, 'pick-your-own' produce operations, and back country camping. Tourist travel to rural areas in Ontario has grown in the recent past, and it has become an important topic for both academic and government attention. For instance, a recent business plan released by the Ontario Ministry of Tourism, Culture and Recreation (2001) includes a commitment to build on rural tourism activities, primarily agritourism, in order to stimulate economic growth. Parts of the research project described in this chapter were funded by the Ontario Ministry of Agriculture, Food and Rural Affairs, thus reflecting a growing interest in capturing the rural travel market.

Our research in four rural communities in Ontario began in 1999. The purpose was to trace the effects of significant tourism development in each community. In-depth, qualitative interviews were completed with over 100 respondents representing businesses, concerned citizens' groups, local government officials, economic development officers, local community leaders, and others who told the research team about the issues, concerns, and implications of tourism growth in their communities (Reid, Taylor & Mair, 2000). These research findings support those of other studies assessing the impacts of tourism development in rural communities (Bourke & Luloff, 1995; Mitchell, 1998; Smith & Krannich, 1998).

When asked what they thought was the appeal of travel to rural areas, respondents offered descriptors including 'peacefulness', 'tranquillity', 'friendliness', and 'that small town atmosphere'. The responses describing the adverse effects of tourism development most often incorporated ideas about the lack of initial community organisation for, and control of, tourism development. Specifically, respondents reported planning and management issues such as crowding, pollution, and traffic congestion.

The research suggests that the negative impacts of tourism development were quite severe in these places (Mair *et al.*, 2000). For instance, there was much competition and such limited cooperation among the business community that many were generally reluctant to even consider having consistent operating hours, coordinating events and festivals, or even using similar monetary exchange rates. Businesses oriented to tourism development in each of these communities sprang up and began to attract visitors in an unplanned fashion, leaving the community to grapple with issues such as traffic congestion, crowds, pollution, and resident frustration as visitor numbers increased. More importantly, many respondents reported feeling alienated, being unable to control the unwanted effects of heavy visitation, feeling a loss of access to the community in the high tourism season, and sensing a change in the overall tone and shape of the community (Reid, Taylor & Mair, 2000; Mair *et al.*, 2000). Some respondents acknowledged the irony in attempting to put forward an image of their community built on friendliness while some in the town did not speak to one another due to conflict over tourism issues.

At this stage, the research team concluded that one of the main reasons for this growing frustration and alienation within the community was that many respondents (especially those outside of the business community, but also some who owned tourism-oriented businesses) did not feel part of any overall process for tourism planning. Nearly all respondents expressed deep concern at not being able to discuss the impact of tourism in their communities and a number felt fearful about the repercussions of suggesting that they were not pleased with the nature and scale of tourism in their area (Reid, Taylor & Mair, 2000). Most respondents noted feeling powerless to change the nature of tourism in their communities and openly admitted to having considered moving or at least spending parts of the high tourism season in other places. These results indicate an underlying dissatisfaction with the tourism planning process and point to the need for meaningful participation opportunities.

The importance of bringing people into the planning process for tourism, and any other community activity, is not new. However, the problem remains as to how to create this process in such a way that the members of the community, especially those who have been left out, can become involved. A community-based tourism plan is only part of the answer. Our research concluded that before this planning process could take place, work needed to be undertaken in these communities to build trust, encourage open and equitable dialogue, and build capacity in the community to develop and maintain this process over time.

Planning for tourism development has traditionally embraced the business model with its emphasis on supply and demand, marketing, and product creation. Recently, some authors (Murphy, 1985, 1988; Reid *et al.*, 1993; Ritchie, 1999) have developed models emphasising the community and its values rather than product development and marketing. What has been missing in those earlier models is the identification of the entry point to community discussion and participation; a point critical to building a solid base for these activities.

Developing the Manual

In an effort to address some of the underlying issues regarding access to tourism planning in rural communities, the research team developed a manual based on various components of community studies, community-based rural tourism planning, and environmental management (Daniels & Walker, 1996; Emery & Purser, 1996; Jamal & Getz, 1999; Reed, 1999; Ritchie, 1999). The manual *Visiting Your Future: A Community's Guide to Planning Rural Tourism* was tested in three communities in Ontario in 2000–2001. The manual was developed in two parts. The first part presents an adapted version of a search conference (Emery & Purser, 1996), which we called a 'community visioning conference', and was designed to bring various participants (business and non-business owners, local leaders, interested residents, local politicians) together to share their knowledge of, and personal reflections about, their community in general and the role of tourism development therein. The conferences involved a time commitment ranging from eight hours to a full weekend and were designed to encourage open dialogue, to build trust, and to create an atmosphere where different perspectives within the community about tourism could be discussed openly. Participants began by drawing reflections of their community's past, present, and future on sheets of blank paper posted around the conference room. After extensive discussion, participants voted on what they would like to 'preserve', 'drop', or 'build upon' in the community by using large, coloured dots to indicate their choices. Participants then spent the rest of the session working from the ideas and strategies that came from this community-created collage and, in a collective effort, began to develop a shared vision of their community and tourism.

The second part of the manual includes exercises to help with actual tourism planning and was developed with the assumption that a variety of tourism development strategies had resulted from the preceding visioning exercise. The exercises range from developing an inventory of tourism assets to providing guidance for building and maintaining a tourism development process, including long-term monitoring. While the ultimate goal of the steps outlined in the manual is the creation of a conceptual tourism plan for the community, the emphasis is on building networks to enhance trust and dialogue: a foundation upon which any successful plan must be constructed.

Shortly after beginning the project, however, it became clear that there had been some oversights in the manual's development. One primary oversight was a lack of sensitivity to the differences between the communities and their particular needs. The manual was designed from the results of the first phase of the research project, which was undertaken in rural communities where tourism development had been intense and feelings of frustration and alienation were easily identifiable. The 'trial' communities where the manual was implemented, however, were newly emerging tourism destinations. Thus, a major stumbling block to this approach was the lack of experience and expectation on the part of the communities. While those we spoke to were initially excited and supportive of the manual, they had difficulties gathering many participants for the visioning conference. This was due primarily to a lack of prior experience with the externalities produced by tourism development and as well as a reluctance to appreciate that the problems we had uncovered could also occur in their community.

It would seem that unless tourism has a major presence, and people have felt the tensions and stresses that accompany incremental development, motivation for undertaking the inclusive process is low. This made it difficult for our team to draw out participation, and initial attempts at pulling visioning conferences together were met with limited success. In response, we re-examined the manual and created a number of additional mechanisms to help generate more interest and discussion about tourism and community life. We were also concerned with determining whether a particular community had the leadership and organisation levels necessary to undertake such a process. For instance, we devised a questionnaire, a community tourism assessment instrument (Reid *et al.*, 2004), which encouraged discussion about the problems that can stem from unplanned tourism growth. In addition, this instrument allowed the research team to gauge the community's situation in regard to the level of organisation and preparation for planning activities.

Thus, one main lesson learned from initial experience with the manual was that tourism planners must identify the critical interests of the community and start the discussion of tourism development from there rather than from some other, more generic point. While this may not be a new idea, it is one that often eludes planning consultants and researchers. As this approach consumes time and energy, it is difficult to implement and see immediate results. Notwithstanding this challenge, our experience suggests that to start elsewhere would be futile, and that eventually, through stresses and tensions, the community will demand recognition in later stages of the development process. Following Belsky (1999), it is useful to view the community as a political arena, which is grounded in particular history and constituted through multiple scales and networks of social relations entailing contexts of unequal power. These multiple scales and networks are generally glossed over in the course of tourism development, especially in tourism marketing, but this need not be the case. Further, that a wider notion of community needs to be incorporated into the development of tourism in rural areas is supported by Mitchell's (1998) work in the Southern Ontario community of St Jacobs. The author highlights the importance of bringing as many voices into the tourism planning process as possible. She argues that early and widespread consultation must be coupled with the ability and foresight to control tourism so that it may not be driven solely by entrepreneurial and financial desires. Only these actions can help to prevent a rural tourism destination, and by extension the community, from damaging itself. She writes:

> If left uncontrolled, the inevitable result will be the partial (or in some cases, the total) destruction of the image upon which the initial development was based; one which can only be regained after considerable conflict among stakeholders. (Mitchell, 1998: 285)

Despite the pitfalls, we revised the manual and have continued to engage in planning sessions with a number of communities since the conclusion of the project. The next section outlines the results of using the updated manual in one particular community in 2002.

The Case Community: Deep River, Ontario, Canada

Approximately a two-hour drive from Canada's capital, Ottawa, the Town of Deep River is widely known as the home of Atomic Energy of Canada Limited (AECL). Deep River is a community of 4135 people (Statistics Canada, 2001) and it has had a long history of employment in the atomic energy industry. However, it became clear that the town and surrounding area could no longer rest on what is called by some locals as 'Mother AECL' to take care of them and that other opportunities for development needed to be considered (Rose, 2002). AECL provides Deep River and the surrounding area with high technology, scientific, and engineering spin-off businesses and related economic opportunities. The community, due to its particular industrial heritage and economic development history, was blessed with a number of amenities including athletics centres, a symphony orchestra, a world-class research facility, a golf course, yacht and tennis club, a 100-slip marina, beaches, and trail networks. In addition, due to its economic base, the Deep River area has a highly educated population, including scientists and engineers.

The economic development officer for the Deep River area approached our team at the University of Guelph in October 2002 to help the community undertake a tourism planning strategy session in mid-November. Twenty-four community members attended our two-day visioning conference and most stayed for the full session. Among the participants were current and retired employees of AECL, educators, local council members including the mayor, artists, the economic development officer, business owners, and other interested community members.

The community tourism assessment instrument was used to introduce the planning session. It generated much discussion about the economic situation in Deep River, the results of which have been published elsewhere (Reid *et al.*, 2004). Moreover, the results of the assessment instrument indicated that the community had a good level of readiness and leadership and could move forward with some plans for tourism development. In the next stage, participants were invited to reflect and draw images of their community's past, present, and future on paper placed around the room. This exercise generated extensive, free-flowing discussions about the history of the community, important assets, events and achievements, present concerns and opportunities for future development. For instance, the presence of a symphony orchestra with a professional conductor was considered an important asset. The natural endowments of the area including trails and the local beaches were also noted repeatedly. Among the points raised regarding future challenges and threats was the fear that the community's economic base would deteriorate as AECL down-sized. Participants were concerned with creating other economic development opportunities in order to diversify their economy and lessen impending impacts.

After a lengthy discussion about the drawings, participants 'voted' on these images using the coloured dots voting process. Blue coloured dots were used to represent items that the community wanted to preserve, red dots indicated a desire to halt development, and green dots suggested moving forward on particular projects. This voting process led to the creation of a list of items or ideas that formed the basis for the creation of a vision for tourism development and strategies to reach it. After much discussion, the participants reached consensus on the following vision of tourism development for their community:

> The Deep River area is a place where visitors and residents will learn, enjoy and share recreational and cultural activities in a natural setting providing economic benefits to the community.

Five main strategies were identified as being necessary to realise this vision: fostering partnership and community support; identification of community resources and image; coordination of community and economic activity; coordination of marketing and communication activity; and long- and short-term infrastructure planning.

Each of these five strategies was discussed further in small groups and then operationalised by developing short- and long-term action plans. For example, under the marketing and communication strategy, the group identified a local clock museum as a potential asset and brand for the community. The group developed two potential brands/themes, 'Time for a Change' and 'Get Wound Up'. As a short-term action, they proposed evaluating existing signage. As a longer-term action, they proposed developing a consistent branding message and marketing it through Website improvement.

From this vision planning session, an eight-person tourism task force was created to take the process forward. In addition, one of the participants agreed to share the outcomes of the conference with the community at large and an article was published in the local newspaper. This participant's comments reflect the tone of the session:

> Like it or not, the days of 'Mother AECL' are gone forever and one thing arose loud and clear from this workshop: the tax base in this area is declining and the expenses are rising. Consequently, we have to do something now before more empty storefronts appear and boards replace show windows. Many tentative starts have been made over the years that have fizzled out to nothing. This one is not going to fizzle out, so pay attention because the whole community is going to have to pull up its collective socks to start climbing out of the hole before it gets too deep. (Rose, 2002)

The task force met three weeks later and used the vision statement as the basis for a concrete mission statement and overall goal for tourism development in the community. The mission statement is as follows:

> We will protect, enhance, develop, and share our natural and cultural assets in the Deep River area.

The goal:

> To develop tourism in the area in order to increase community prosperity and vitality, resulting in job retention and creation, business retention, growth, and increased property value.

Our experiences in Deep River allowed us, as researchers, to garner a sense of the newly revised manual and to work with a community determined to use tourism in a proactive way to stem the tide of economic change affecting many rural communities. Subsequent contact with the Director of the Deep River Economic Development Department suggests that while progress is slow, the strategies devised during our time with the community are moving forward (personal communication, 16 January 2004).

Conclusion: Opportunities, Challenges, and Options for Community Power

As with any research project that involves communities, there are lessons to be learned. It should be noted that this particular community was one of the first that we had encountered that was determined to take a proactive approach to addressing economic downturn. As is suggested above, generally, communities are nearing a crisis situation before planning and action take place. In this instance, the community's stance allowed for a more relaxed approach to tourism planning than we had experienced in other communities where the 'pressure' was on to deal with problems or generate economic development. While each community and planning experience is undoubtedly unique, it is useful to provide a few general reflections.

First, the orientation of tourism as part of the community's solution to economic problems, although not the only possible solution, puts power in the community's hands to use tourism in a proactive way. Secondly, by using a participatory approach to tourism planning, we provided a supportive setting where people can relax, reflect, and reveal personal thoughts and feelings about their community. Moreover, group learning and the sharing of ideas became a focus of the exercises and allowed us to move from being 'experts' to 'facilitators'. From our point of view, not only was this fascinating as it provided a first-hand view of community dynamics, but it was a collaboration between the 'researcher' and 'the researched' and brought the academic and practitioner closer together. In a sense, the community became the 'working lab' and the ideas were their own, thus giving them the opportunity to take ownership of, and a leadership role in, tourism development. Thus, the project had more meaning and value for both the community and researchers.

The third and last lesson is perhaps the most intangible. A great deal of time was spent at each of the visioning conferences encouraging participants to dream about their ideal community and to see whether and how tourism might be used to accomplish that dream. Thus, we attempted to shift the focus of tourism development from a tool to meet an economic need to a mechanism for building communities that are liveable and worth celebrating. The community must see the subsequent development of tourism opportunities that spring from this process as fitting into that overall vision. The sense of community control and participation plays an important role in fostering support for tourism development, and may enhance its long-term sustainability as a broad basis for tourism planning and management is created. Moreover, parts of the process may be used as communities experience successful tourism development in order to address inevitable impacts and evaluate the direction that tourism is taking over time.

Undoubtedly, some challenges to this approach remain. The question of participation daunts many who are involved in community-based activities, and a critical view of who is and who is not involved in these endeavours must be maintained. We approached this project with a commitment to evaluation and improvement and have struggled with the issue of participation. Future research, as well as efforts to foster dialogue and reflection within the tourism studies community about the inherent challenges of this approach will certainly continue.

References

Aronsson, L. (2000) *The Development of Sustainable Tourism.* London: Continuum.

Beck, U. (2000) *What is Globalization?* Cambridge: Polity Press.

Belsky, J.M. (1999) Misrepresenting communities: the politics of community-based rural ecotourism in Gales Point Manatee, Belize. *Rural Sociology* 64 (4), 641–66.

Blank, U. (1989) *The Community Tourism Industry Imperative.* State College, PA: Venture Publishing.

Bourke, L. and Luloff. A.E. (1995) Leaders' perspectives on rural tourism: case studies in Pennsylvania. *Journal of the Community Development Society* 26 (2), 224–39.

Bouquet, M. and Winter, M. (eds) (1987) *Who From Their Labours Rest? Conflict and Practice in Rural Tourism.* Aldershot: Avebury.

Britton, S. (1991) Tourism, capital and place: towards a critical geography of tourism. *Environment and Planning D: Society and Space* 9, 451–78.

Butler, R., Hall, C.M. and Jenkins, J.M. (eds) (1998) *Tourism and Recreation in Rural Areas.* Chichester and New York: John Wiley & Sons.

Cox, R. (1991) The global political economy and social choice. In D. Drache and M.S. Gertler (eds) *The New Era of Global Competition: State Policy and Market Power* (pp. 335–50). Montreal: McGill-Queen's University Press.

Daniels, S.E. and Walker, G.B. (1996) Collaborative learning: improving public deliberation in ecosystems-based management. *Environmental Impact Assessment Review* 16, 71–102.

Emery, M. and Purser, R.E. (1996) *The Search Conference: A Powerful Method for Planning Organizational Change and Community Action.* San Francisco: Jossey-Bass.

Hopkins, J. (1998) Signs of the post-rural: marketing myths of a symbolic countryside. *Geografiska Annaler B* 80 (2), 65–81.

Ilbery, B. (ed.) (1998) *The Geography of Rural Change.* Harlow: Addison Wesley Longman.

Jamal, T. and Getz, D. (1999) Community roundtables for tourism-related conflicts: the dialectics of consensus and process structures. *Journal of Sustainable Tourism* 7 (3&4), 290–313.

Jenkins, J.M., Hall, C.M. and Troughton, M. (1998) The restructuring of rural economies: rural tourism and recreation as a government response. In R. Butler, C.M. Hall and J. Jenkins (eds) *Tourism and Recreation in Rural Areas* (pp. 43–67). Chichester and New York: John Wiley & Sons.

Keane, M. (1992) Rural tourism and rural development. In H. Briassoulis and Jan van der Straaten (eds) *Tourism and the Environment: Regional, Economic and Policy Issues* (pp. 43–56). London: Kluwer.

Luloff, A.E., Bridger, J.C., Graefe, A.R., Saylor, M., Martin, K. and Gitelson, R. (1993) Assessing rural tourism efforts in the United States. *Annals of Tourism Research* 21, 46–64.

Mair, H., Reid, D.G. and Taylor, J.T. (2000) Raw material, neutral party or pivotal player? Assessing community in rural tourism development and planning. *Environment Papers Series* 3 (3), 68–74.

Mitchell, C.J.A. (1998) Entrepreneurialism, commodification and creative destruction: a model of post-modern community development. *Journal of Rural Studies* 14 (3), 273–86.

Murphy, P.E. (1985) *Tourism: A Community Approach.* New York: Methuen.

Murphy, P.E. (1988) Community driven tourism planning. *Tourism Management* 9 (2), 96–104.

OECD (Organisation for Economic Co-operation and Development) (1994) *Tourism Strategies and Rural Development.* Paris: OECD.

Ontario Ministry of Tourism, Culture and Recreation (2001) *2001–2002 Business Plan.* Toronto: Ontario Ministry of Tourism and Recreation. On WWW at http://www.tourism.gov.on.ca/english/about/bp2001_e.pdf. Accessed 03.03.04.

Ramaswamy, V.M. and Kuentzel, W.F. (1998) Rural restructuring and the transition of a tourism dependent community. *Tourism Analysis* 3, 63–76.

Reed, M. (1999) Collaborative tourism planning as adaptive experiments in emergent tourism settings. *Journal of Sustainable Tourism* 7 (3 & 4), 334–78.

Reid, D.G. (2003) *Tourism, Globalization and Development: Responsible Tourism Planning.* London: Pluto Press.

Reid, D.G., Fuller, A.M., Haywood, K.M. and Bryden, J. (1993) *The Integration of Tourism, Culture and Recreation in Rural Ontario: A Rural Visitation Program*, Report prepared for The Ontario Ministry of Culture, Tourism and Recreation. Toronto: Queen's Printer, The Ontario Ministry of Culture, Tourism and Recreation.

Reid, D.G., Mair, H. and George, E.W. (2004) Community tourism planning: a self-assessment instrument. *Annals of Tourism Research* 31 (3), 623–39.

Reid, D.G., Mair, H. and Taylor, J. (2000) Community participation in rural tourism development. *World Leisure Journal* 42 (2), 20–27.

Reid, D.G., Taylor, J. and Mair, H. (2000) *Rural Tourism Development: Research Report.* Guelph: School of Rural Planning and Development, University of Guelph.

Ritchie, B. (1999) Interest-based formulation of tourism policy for environmentally sensitive destinations. *Journal of Sustainable Tourism* 7 (3 & 4), 206–39.

Roberts, L. and Hall, D. (2001) *Rural Tourism and Recreation: Principles to Practice.* Wallingford: CABI Publishing.

Rose, A. (2002) We're all in this together. *The North Renfrew Times* 19 November.

Smith, M.D. and Krannich, R.S. (1998) Tourism dependence and resident attitudes. *Annals of Tourism Research* 25, 783–802.

Statistics Canada (2001) *Canada.* Ottowa: Statistics Canada. On WWW at http://www.statscan.ca. Accessed 16.01.04.

Urry, J. (1990) *The Tourist Gaze.* London: Sage.

Urry, J. (1995) *Consuming Places.* London: Routledge.

Chapter 11

The Development of Tourism Businesses in Rural Communities: The Case of the Maroons of Jamaica

DONNA CHAMBERS

Introduction

The concept of rural tourism is by no means well defined and is subject to a number of interpretations. Fleischer and Pizam (1997) associate rural tourism with the 'country vacation' where the tourist spends the vast proportion of his vacation period engaging in recreational activities in a rural environment on a farm, ranch, country home, or the surrounding areas. Oppermann (1996), borrowing from Dernoi (1991), suggests that while rural tourism necessarily takes place in non-urban environments, not all non-urban tourism is rural tourism. For example, recreational activities in wilderness areas, national parks, and national forests, while often taking place in non-urban environments, are not strictly speaking rural tourism. For what distinguishes rural tourism from these other non-urban activities is the existence of a permanent human presence. So that, according to Dernoi (1991: 4), rural tourism might be conceived as tourism activity in a 'non-urban territory where human (land related economic) activity is going on, primarily agriculture: a permanent human presence seems a qualifying requirement'.

Sharpley (2002: 234), in a study on rural tourism in Cyprus, indicates that the term is synonymous in that country with 'agrotourism', which refers to 'the development of tourism based on traditional accommodation facilities in villages in the rural and mountainous Troodos regions'. For their part, Page and Getz (1997) undertook an exegesis of the various interpretations and academic positions on rural tourism since the 1960s and suggest that understandings of rural tourism differ from country to country largely because of the difficulties inherent in defining what is 'rural'. They cite Robinson (1990) as indicating that rural areas have distinct problems that make them unique:

> depopulation, and deprivation in areas remote from major metropoli-
> tan centres; a reliance upon primary activity; conflicts between presen-
> tation of certain landscapes and development of a variety of economic
> activities; and conflicts between local needs and legislation emanating
> from urban based legislators. (Page & Getz, 1997: 4)

While accepting Robinson's (1990) understanding of 'rural', Page and Getz (1997) were nevertheless perplexed as to what might distinguish rural tourism from other forms of alternative tourism. They indicated that such a distinction might be located in a demand side interpretation of rural tourism that focused on the visitors' 'social representations and images of the countryside' (Page & Getz, 1997: 4). In other words the visitors' perception and image of rurality should be an important consideration in any definition of rural tourism. This understanding of rural tourism represented a departure from extant definitions of the concept, which tended to focus on the supply side including such characteristics as types of accommodation, land use, activities, *inter alia*. Still other authors, while maintaining a focus on supply side understandings, have expanded the interpretation of rural tourism to include aspects of culture and heritage such as oral history, folklore, and local and family traditions (see e.g. MacDonald & Jolliffe, 2003). However, it is submitted that while there exist these variations in interpretations of rural tourism, seemingly acceptable to most conceptualisations are the ideas that rural tourism occurs in non-urban, primarily agricultural areas, involves small-scale accommodation facilities (such as bed and breakfasts), and involves close interaction between local residents and visitors (the human element). Importantly, rural tourism is ostensibly seen as more sensitive to the environment (note the inclusion by Dewailly (1998) of 'green tourism' under the rubric of rural tourism) and is thus antithetical to mass tourism, which is environmentally exploitative and which has dominated tourism development, particularly in the 1970s and 1980s.

In the mainstream tourism literature, studies of rural tourism have largely been concentrated in Europe, North America, and Australasia (see Bramwell & Lane, 1994; Butler *et al.*, 1998; MacDonald & Jolliffe, 2003; Oppermann, 1996) with a concomitant dearth of such studies in the developing world and particularly in the Caribbean region. Yet, rural tourism is perceived by some Caribbean governments as a viable alternative to the traditional mass, sun, sea, sand, packaged holiday on which their tourism industries have been built but which have proven to be destructive to the environment, unsustainable, and unreflective of changing consumer tastes. Indeed, according to Sharpley (2002: 234):

> A number of popular sun–sea–sand tourist destinations have, in recent years, attempted to diversify into rural tourism – tourism that is both locationally and experientially rural/traditional, as opposed to coastal/modern – in order to achieve a more balanced, sustainable approach to tourism development.

This is further supported by Morgan (1994) and Scott (2000: 59), who claims that:

> Increasingly, mature and declining tourist centres within the 'pleasure periphery' are promoting their own peripheral regions as an alternative to sun, sea and sand tourism.

In Jamaica, which is arguably one of the oldest mass tourism destinations in the Caribbean, the government has recognised that the traditional sun, sea, sand, tourism product cannot provide long-term benefits for the country and that there is a need to engage in more sustainable tourism activities. Thus, in a Master Plan for Sustainable Tourism Development commissioned by the Jamaican government and completed in 2002 (Government of Jamaica, 2002), a number of alternative tourism activities were identified as vital for the rejuvenation of a mature tourism industry in decline and facing increasing competitive pressures from the newer destinations of Cuba, the Dominican Republic, and Cancun in Mexico. Consequently, an inventory of the island's resources was undertaken and ten key themes identified for future tourism development. One of these themes relates to the involvement of rural Maroon communities, which are deemed to have unique cultural and heritage assets that can be developed to serve the tourism industry. In this sense then rural tourism is interpreted in a wider context incorporating important aspects of culture and heritage. MacDonald and Jolliffe (2003) coined the term 'cultural rural tourism' to refer to this broader understanding of the rural tourism phenomenon. They note that cultural rural tourism can be used to refer to:

> a distinct rural community with its own traditions, heritage, arts, lifestyles, places and values as preserved between generations. Tourists visit these areas to be informed about the culture and to experience folklore, customs, natural landscapes, and historical landmarks. They might also enjoy other activities in a rural setting such as nature, adventure, sports, festivals, crafts and general sightseeing (MacDonald & Jolliffe, 2003: 308).

This hybrid term is clearly derived from the concept of cultural tourism, which although defined in myriad ways, is generally understood as a kind of alternative form of tourism that is based on experience, under-standing, and interacting with distinct local communities (McKercher & DuCross, 2002; Prentice, 2001; Reizinger, 1994; Stebbins, 1997). Indeed, Prentice (2001: 8) suggests that cultural tourism is 'arguably *the* new Romanticism, consumed as emotions and spirituality rather than for more utilitarian purposes'. The concept of cultural rural tourism reflects the experiential basis of cultural tourism, and one can suggest that it is this expanded notion of rural tourism, in the form of cultural rural tourism, that is being considered for development in the Maroon communities. Indeed, the author believes that these rural societies possess a unique cultural heritage that sets them apart from the rest of the Jamaican society and that provides the raw material for the cultural experiences that the modern tourist demands.

However, while the Master Plan aimed at providing a 'comprehensive framework for the future development of Jamaica's tourism industry' (Government of Jamaica, 2002: 1) it did not provide a detailed blueprint for action nor did it issue directives on the 'correct' way in which the tourism industry should be developed. As such it did not provide any indication of the way in which Maroon heritage and culture might be developed for tourism purposes.

Further, while the planning process involved in the development of the Master Plan was said to have included 'broad-based industry and com-munity consultations . . . at all the important stages of the development of the plan' (Government of Jamaica, 2002: 1), it is likely that the con-clusions arrived at reflected the power relationships between the different stakeholders involved in the collaborative process. Indeed, it has been suggested that the 'resource allocations, policy ideas, and institutional practices embedded within society may often restrict the influence of par-ticular stakeholders on the collaborative arrangements' (Bramwell & Sharman, 1999: 393). In this context, a pertinent question is the extent to which the Jamaican Maroons, who live in isolated rural settlements far removed from the urban centres, have participated in the decisions to develop their own communities for tourism purposes. Specifically, what are the views and reactions of the Maroons towards tourism devel-opment opportunities in their communities?

This chapter presents the results of research conducted in three Maroon villages in Jamaica during the summer of 2003, which sought to investi-gate this issue. A second question with which this chapter is concerned is the scope for the development of tourism businesses in the Maroon communities. According to Page and Getz (1997), in assessing the scope for rural tourism business development, several operational issues should be considered, including: accessibility and other spatial factors, degree of integration of tourism business with other businesses in the locale, seasonality, infrastructure and technology, finance, sustainability, marketing, standards, and organization and community integration. In light of these operational challenges and the mentioned issue of collaboration, the overriding consideration in this chapter is whether tourism can indeed be a viable option for the development of rural communities like those of the Maroons of Jamaica.

Historical Overview of the Maroons

Although the etymology of the word 'Maroon' is unclear, it is normally believed to have been derived from the Spanish word Cimarron, which originally referred to domestic cattle that had escaped into the wild. However, over time the word has become used to refer almost exclusively to slaves who escaped from plantation servitude in the New World (Campbell, 1988; Carey, 1997; Price, 1979). Indeed, Maroon communities were ubiquitous in plantation societies, but most have not managed to survive to the present day as distinct communities with the exception of the Maroons in the Caribbean island of Jamaica and Suriname in South America.

While the early Maroons in Jamaica were predominantly African, they were by no means homogenous groupings and were instead ethnically plural with members originating from a diverse range of African societies and ethnicities. However, it has been suggested that most of the Maroon leaders in Jamaica were of the Coromantie group from the Gold Coast in West Africa (now Ghana), although the ethnic origin of the membership is less clear (Campbell, 1988; Kopytoff, 1976a). Still, despite the differences within and between Maroon communities with regard to ethnic origins, many of these communities shared common socio-political, religious and military traditions, which were no doubt African in origin although in later periods these were often suitably adapted to meet the colonial conditions. Religion was key to the Maroon existence and often served as a rallying point to mobilise these groups to action against the colonial regime. Maroon leaders were even expected to have knowledge and power bearing on the supernatural, and in Jamaica the sole known female Maroon leader, Nanny, was considered to be a powerful sorceress. According to popular folklore, so powerful was Nanny's magic that in battles with the colonial authorities she was able to catch bullets between her buttocks, thus escaping death by gunfire.

In Jamaica there were several Maroon communities dispersed throughout the island with the two largest and most well known being the Leeward and Windward Maroons. These communities were able to exist on the outskirts of plantation societies carrying out raids for supplies they could not make or produce themselves. These constant Maroon raids resulted in serious deprivations for the plantation economy and this was a key consideration for the British in their quest to destroy these communities. Given the animosity between the British and the Maroons, the latter existing as 'islands of freedom in a sea of slavery' (Sheridan, 1986: 154), formation of Maroon communities was based on important security considerations. Many were thus located in inaccessible mountainous regions in the rural hinterland with poor agricultural soil. However, the high elevations of the towns provided good vantage points from whence could be observed the approach of British colonial troops. The Leeward town of Accompong to the west is located in an area of Jamaica known as the Cockpit Country, which is comprised of deep canyons and limestone sinkholes where water is scarce and good soil is almost non-existent. The Windward town of Moore Town to the east of the island is located in the high elevations of the Blue Mountains, the highest mountain range on the island, approximately 2256 metres above sea level.

Realising that both were fighting a war in which neither side could be victorious, in 1739 two peace treaties were negotiated between the Maroons and the British, events that had no historical precedence during the period of slavery. The first of the two treaties was signed by the leader of the Leeward Maroons, Cudjoe (or Kojo) on 1 March 1739 and the second a few months later by the leader of the Windward Maroons, Quao. Both treaties had similar provisions whereby the Maroons were granted freedom, large tracts of land, and jurisdiction over their own affairs except for the administering of the death penalty, which authority remained with the colonial government. However, in return for these concessions they agreed to return any future runaway slaves to the British and to assist the British with the defence of the island. They also agreed to allow a representative of the colonial government to reside in their communities in order to foster good relations between Maroons and British. As such, the Treaties have been considered to represent more of a triumph for British diplomacy than a tribute to the Maroons' excellent skills in guerrilla warfare, and many have pondered why it is that the Maroons consented to these seemingly unequal terms (Campbell, 1988).

Importantly, the treaties are seen to represent a turning point for the Maroon communities in Jamaica (Kopytoff, 1976b; Price, 1979), because by agreeing to capture and return runaway slaves the Maroons created hostility between themselves and the slave society, as they were seen more as 'restorationist and isolationist rather than revolutionary' (Campbell, 1988: 13). The granting of land also encouraged their 'perpetuation as a separate group with their own quasi-government free to act out their own cultural imperatives' (Campbell, 1988: 132). Further, given that the Maroons could no longer accept new members into their communities, they came to depend on natural reproduction to augment their numbers.

With the demise of slavery, the importance of the Maroons as a separate and distinct cultural grouping has lessened significantly, and Price (1979) has noted that the Maroons' increasing participation in economic activities outside of their villages has led to the rapid creolisation of Maroon culture. Indeed, according to Campbell (1988: 260) 'that some of the Maroon communities exist today ... is due to atavistic stubbornness'. Walk into any Maroon community today and one is unable to distinguish it from the host of other rural communities that exist on the island. Indeed, Maroon communities have become significantly integrated into wider Jamaican society, and one of the issues for this author is the extent of cultural heritage retention, as this will have implications for tourism development in these rural communities.

Research Method

The author visited three key Maroon communities in Jamaica during the summer months of July and August 2003 in order to ascertain the views of the Maroons towards the development of tourism businesses in their communities and the extent to which there is indeed scope for this type of development. The three communities visited were Accompong, located in the area of the Cockpit Country, which lies to the north of the southwestern parish of St. Elizabeth; Moore Town and Charles Town, which are both located in the eastern parish of Portland in the vicinity of the Blue Mountains. The roads leading up to Accompong and Moore Town are quite treacherous and in a state of disrepair (although compared with Moore Town, the road to Accompong is in a much better state). As indicated previously, the location of these villages is a reflection of the security considerations that obtained during the Maroons' historical conflicts with British colonial governments. The eastern villages are especially susceptible to high levels of precipitation, located as they are in the parish that receives the highest levels of rainfall on the island, approximately 3000 to 5000 mm per year (Jones & Spence, 2003). The constant wet conditions make it very difficult to maintain the good state of the roads, particularly leading up to Moore Town, and the Herculean task of travelling there is not for the faint-hearted.

While the Maroons are a part of Jamaican society and subject to the laws of the land, they still maintain some degree of autonomy over their internal affairs and are governed locally by their own Councils, each of which is led by a Colonel. The leaders or Colonels historically possessed life tenure, but today they are elected by the Maroon citizens, normally every five years. The Colonels then nominate the Council members. The number of Council members and the duties and responsibilities of the Council vary among the different Maroon communities, each of which exists independently of the others. While there have been plans to establish a formal federation of all the Maroon villages in the island (Turner, 1989), this has never become a workable reality. In each of the three Maroon communities, unstructured in-depth interviews were conducted with the Maroon Colonels and other significant individuals. A total of seven persons were interviewed across the three communities.

Given the limited time frame during which the interviews were to be conducted, and in order to ensure that all the key persons would be available, the interviews were set up several months prior to the author's arrival in Jamaica through the use of a contact in the Ministry of Tourism. While it would have been ideal to obtain verbatim responses from the interviewees through the use of a tape recorder, this was considered inappropriate because all of the interviews were conducted in a very informal setting, primarily while walking through the hills and rugged terrain of the Maroon villages. This qualitative method of data collection was considered apposite due to the remote location of the Maroon villages, the small numbers of individuals to be interviewed, and the nature of the information required. Indeed, the in-depth interview, according to Veal (1997: 132):

> seeks to probe more deeply than is possible with a questionnaire-based interview. Rather than just asking a question, recording a simple answer and moving on, the in depth interviewer encourages respondents to talk, asks supplementary questions and asks respondents to explain their answers.

Two additional interviews were conducted with key personnel employed by the Tourism Product Development Company (TPDCo), a statutory body created to deal with all aspects of tourism product development in Jamaica. These latter two interviews were deemed necessary in order to obtain the perspective of the government on the way in which Maroon societies could be developed for tourism purposes. The information received from all these interviews was supplemented with documentary data obtained from the island's national library, The Institute of Jamaica, as well as books and journals. Further, as a Jamaican, the author's own personal knowledge of these communities and the wider Jamaican society also proved of tremendous value. While the fact that the author is a national of Jamaica necessarily creates some bias both in terms of the interaction between interviewer and interviewees and in terms of the reporting of the information, it also meant that access to these remote communities, where secrecy and suspicion of foreigners is a common fact of life, was made easier. It also meant that respondents felt more comfortable and were thus more open in their answers. Still, in research, whether quantitative or qualitative, objectivity is a chimera. In every piece of research, there are varying degrees of subjectivity. The important point is 'to recognise that subjectivity is an issue and that researchers should take appropriate measures to minimise its intrusion into their analyses' (Strauss & Corbin, 1998: 43).

Research Findings

Community comparisons

It was evident that while there were some similarities between the Maroon communities visited, there were also some important differences, especially between East and West. With regard to similarities, the representatives of all the Maroon communities visited agreed on two basic points. The first point on which there is agreement is that the development of tourism is important for the economic survival of these communities. However, as will be explained later, the degree of support for tourism varies between the Maroon communities and especially between Accompong and the eastern villages. In all the communities, the key economic activities are small-scale agriculture (e.g. banana, plantain, and coffee cultivation) and microscopic village grocery shops (selling small items such as beer, cigarettes, biscuits, sweets, soft drinks), which generate little revenue. There is a lack of any major industries and the opportunities for economic activities, as in much of rural Jamaica, are limited. In the eastern parishes, the banana industry, which used to be the primary agricultural activity, has been in decline especially since the 1990s due to increased competition from 'dollar banana' producers in Central America and the gradual removal by key European markets of trade preferences for Africa, Caribbean and Pacific (ACP) countries established under the Lomé Convention. The poverty and lack of opportunity in these villages has meant that many have migrated to the urban centres or have gone overseas in search of a better life. It is within this context of economic decline and the lack of economic opportunities that the development of cultural rural tourism business is being contemplated by the government.

The second point of convergence between the Maroon representatives interviewed is that the Maroons have a rich cultural heritage that distinguishes them from the rest of Jamaican society and which would be the key driver for their involvement in tourism. Elements of this rich cultural heritage include dance, craft, language, and food. Indeed, the popular method of cooking meat, known as 'jerking', which has been exported to international markets in the form of seasonings, is said to have originated with the Maroons. However, the Maroon communities as a whole do not appear to have gained any acclaim or economic benefits from its worldwide success.

Accompong

Yet, despite these areas of convergence, as intimated, important differences were evident between the communities with regard to the degree of tourism awareness and acceptance, and the extent of tourism business development. The village of Accompong represents the most developed community in terms of tourism, with tours conducted to such key sites in the village as the Peace Cave (the alleged location of the signing of the treaty between the Accompong Maroon leader, Cudjoe, and the British) (see Figure 11.1), Old Town (where Cudjoe and Nanny are said to be buried), and Kindah Tree (a mango tree over a century old where all the military plans were said to have been made) (see Figure 11.2). These tours cost US$20 per person and are seen as an important source of income for the Accompong Maroons. The most important event and highpoint for touristic activity in Accompong is the annual January 6th Celebration, which commemorates the signing of the Peace Treaty between the British and the Accompong Maroons. Music, food, and dance (especially the Coromanti dance, which involves the possession of dancers by ancestral Maroon spirits), are important components of the festivities and both local people and tourists alike make the trek through the treacherous terrain to witness these festivities on an annual basis.

The January 6th Celebration has traditionally been run by the Accompong Maroons themselves with little help from the Jamaican government, a situation which was possibly a reflection of the Maroons' fierce independence and the traditional distrust between the Maroons and the government. However, the situation changed in 1997 when the Maroon Colonel at the time approached TPDCo for assistance with tourism development in the community. Five years later, in 2002, a letter of agreement was negotiated between TPDCo and the Council of the Accompong Maroons in which TPDCo 'committed to undertaking human resource

Figure 11.1 Peace Cave, Accompong

Figure 11.2 Kindah Tree, Accompong

development and infrastructural improvements as well as identifying and developing products and services related to tourism' (Anon, 2002). This was the first time any such agreement was signed between the Jamaican government and the Maroons. TPDCo has assisted with the painting of the community centre, the layout of the tourist trail, which incorporates the sites mentioned previously, erection of sign posts, upgrading of sanitary conveniences for visitors, and the refurbishment of the development centre, which is used as a library and computer laboratory. In addition, approximately 10–15 homes within the village are used as bed and breakfast establishments and TPDCo has provided some training for the owners of these accommodation facilities. This partnership with TPDCo represents a pivotal turning point in the Maroons' relationship with government and seems to indicate a willingness on the part of the Accompong Maroons to compromise their fiercely guarded independence for the sake of tourism development. However, the leaders interviewed insisted that it was they who had taken the initiative in creating the partnership with TPDCo, thus intimating that their independence had not in any way been compromised.

Wherever the truth might lie, it seems to this author that the important point is that the partnership created between the Accompong Maroons and the government (through TPDCo) reflects pragmatic thinking on the side of both parties. On the one hand, the Accompong Maroons perceive tourism development as a panacea for the economic advancement of the community, and, in order to drive the industry forward, they acknowledge the need for government financial and technical support to assist with those things they cannot do themselves. Indeed, the Maroon Council in Accompong appeared to be well organised with strong leadership and this, coupled with the establishment of strategic partnerships with the Jamaican government, has contributed to the relative success of tourism business development in the community. On the other hand, the Jamaican government sees tourism development in Accompong as important to the achievement of its policy objective of developing more alternative forms of tourism, such as cultural rural tourism.

Moore Town and Charles Town

In contrast to Accompong, in Moore Town and Charles Town there seemed to be an absence of any sort of organized tourism activity or of established tourism businesses. Nor did there appear to be any significant collaboration between these communities and the Jamaican government with regard to tourism development. Especially with regard to Moore Town this was surprising given that it is the largest Maroon community in the island with a population of about 10,000, while Accompong has a population of between 500 and 1500. A possible explanation for this could be that the Accompong community is better organised because it is more compact and more easily defined geographically, while the Maroons of Moore Town are dispersed over the several smaller villages of Cornwall Barracks, Comfort Castle, Ginger House, Kent and Simmonds Valley. Further, a somewhat antagonistic relationship exists between Moore Town and these smaller villages because Moore Town is seen as the dominant partner. This lack of cohesion, it is suggested, has militated against community organisation and integration in the area, which, it will be recalled, was cited by Page and Getz (1997) as a necessary ingredient for the operation of rural tourism businesses.

Moore Town, despite being the largest Maroon community on the island, appears to have retained many more cultural heritage traditions than the other smaller Maroon villages, and interestingly, tourism is less well developed here. Like most of rural Jamaica, economic activity outside of agriculture is rare and tourism is again seen as a means of stimulating economic development. However, according to the Colonel of the Moore Town Maroons, he does not see tourism as a panacea but as only one of the industries that could be exploited. Indeed, he indicated that tourism was a fickle industry and could not be relied on to achieve long-term sustainability. Of more importance for him is the development of fruit canneries and bottled spring water, as there is an abundance of fruits and pure water in the area. He lamented the fact that in Moore Town, fruits like mangoes were rotting on the trees because there were no avenues for them to be sold for economic benefit. While he expressed general support for the tourism industry, he indicated that any plans for tourism development should emanate from the members of the Moore Town community itself and should involve that community in all aspects of decision making (a bottom–up approach). Although he admitted that community members needed some tourism training and that TPDCo could help in this area, he emphasised that tourism development should reflect the cultural heritage of the Moore Town community.

This view seemed to be shared by other leaders in the Moore Town community, and in an interview with a member of the Maroon Council, he indicated that there were some proposals for the establishment of a working museum to display Maroon cultural artefacts like the drums and the *abeng*, an instrument made from the horn of the cow that was used by the Maroons to warn of impending British enemy attacks and to send intricate messages between villages, as its sound can penetrate across several miles (see Figure 11.3). The *abeng* is now only used occasionally to summon people to community meetings or on ceremonial occasions.

Figure 11.3 A Maroon blowing the *abeng*

During the period of slavery, the Maroons, who prior to the signing of the 1739 peace treaties existed as fugitives, were forced to adapt to their environment and this meant that they developed knowledge about the different types of herbs that existed and the ways they could be used to treat a variety of ailments. Today, the Maroons have continued this tradition and are well known for their herbal remedies. There is a proposal for the development of a herbal garden to display the variety of herbs available in the area and the ways in which they can be put to use for medicinal purposes. However, these proposals have not yet been implemented, possibly because of a combination of factors including lack of commitment and strong leadership, lack of access to financing, the absence of any real partnership with government and other key stakeholders, and the problems of community integration already identified.

Nevertheless, each year on 19th October there is a celebration for the life of Nanny held at *Bump Grave*, which was built with funding from the Jamaican government as a memorial in commemoration of Nanny's life. This celebration is on a much smaller scale than the 6th January Celebration in Accompong and attracts fewer visitors. The monument represents the only tangible manifestation of government involvement in tourism development in Moore Town. Still, Moore Town is not totally devoid of any tourism activity, although this is undertaken by private tour companies whose owners and employees do not live in Moore Town. In this regard, the main private sector tourism activity has been the development of a hiking trail, which takes visitors from Barry Hill to Nanny Falls in the community.

Charles Town is one of the smaller Maroon communities and again there is little economic activity outside of agriculture and small grocery shops. There is also little tourism activity, although, according to the Council member interviewed, there is much potential for tourism development. The main event in Charles Town is the celebration of Quao Day on 23rd June annually. This is a four-day event, which celebrates the life of Quao, the Maroon leader who signed the treaty with the British, and involves a cultural display of song and dance at the main community entertainment venue known as the *Safrey Yard*. In discussions with the Charles Town Maroons it was revealed that they have developed a draft project plan in collaboration with the local Member of Parliament, which seeks to develop the tourism potential of the area through the construction of tourist shops, which would sell craft items, herbs, food, and drink. However, it was suggested by the Council member that this proposal has not yet got off the ground due to a lack of wider government interest and funding. Still, the Charles Town Maroons interviewed expressed optimism for the future of this proposal in light of the increased interest that the 2003 23rd June celebration had generated due to a visit from representatives of its sister village, Quao, in Ghana.

Problems facing cultural rural tourism business development

The government representatives interviewed also agreed that the Maroons have a rich cultural heritage, which can be developed for tourism purposes, but suggested that there are a number of problems in these communities that have so far militated against this development. The first is the absence of documentation about the exact parameters of Maroon lands, which represents a challenge in terms of the spatial definition of these communities. This absence of defined boundaries has led to constant conflicts with the government about appropriation of land. For example, with regard to Accompong, under the terms of the 1739 Treaty there is some confusion as to whether the land given over to the Maroons was 1500, 15,000 or even 150,000 acres, as the boundaries of the land were not defined by the treaty. Successive governments have no doubt encroached upon and appropriated Maroon lands, and more recently there has been conflict between the Accompong Maroons and the government over land. Specifically, the government decision to build a multimillion dollar highway (the *Highway 2000* project) passing through sections of the Cockpit Country alleged to be owned by the Maroons, has led to conflict between the Maroon community and the government. According to Morais (2000), in a newspaper article published in *The Jamaica Gleaner*:

> The Maroons of Accompong have vowed to arrest and prosecute anyone caught trespassing on their ancestral lands, a move it [sic] stands ready to implement if the Government continues to ignore its [sic] calls for dialogue on the Highway 2000 Project . . . The Accompong Maroons and Government agencies, specifically the Forestry Department have had a long-standing debate going on [as to] who has authority over certain sections of the Cockpit, with the Maroons claiming exclusive rights and charging that the state has carved off several thousands of their 150,000 acre property over time.

Disputes between the Jamaican government and Accompong Maroons over the boundaries of their ancestral lands have proven intractable over the years and have served as continual fodder for distrust between both parties. In this context, the strength and sustainability of the partnerships created between the Accompong Maroons and the Jamaican government with regard to tourism business development is brought into question.

The second problem concerns the involvement of Maroons in the general tribal politics of Jamaica, which, it is suggested, has helped to weaken the unity within and between Maroon communities and which has helped to undermine their rich cultural heritage. Jamaican politics is notorious for the hostility that exists between the supporters of the two main political parties, the People's National Party (PNP) and the

Jamaica Labour Party (JLP). Indeed, over the past thirty years, hundreds of Jamaicans have been persecuted and or killed in the name of politics and the Maroons have not been exempt from this civil warfare.

Thirdly, it is the opinion of one of the government representatives interviewed that the acceptance by many Maroons of fundamentalist Christian doctrines has weakened a key pillar of Maroon cultural heritage, that is, their religious beliefs (this was also the opinion of Carey, 1997). As indicated previously, religion played a pivotal role in Maroon life, and many leaders, like Nanny, were believed to have great military prowess, which was acquired through supernatural means. Indeed, a key cultural activity, the *Kromanti* dance, is religiously inspired. According to Bilby (1980: 20–21), the *Kromanti* dance traditionally:

> involves the possession of participants by ancestral Maroon spirits [and] was held most commonly on occasions of crisis, when supernatural aid was desired; it was considered too serious a thing to be used for mere entertainment. Usually in the course of the dance, one or more ritual specialists (known as *fete-men*) would become possessed and would dominate the ceremony from then on. Very often, *Kromanti* dances were held for the purpose of healing a person whose sickness was attributed to supernatural causes.

Belief in the supernatural and in the power of ancestors is seen in Christianity to be demonic, and the conversion of many Maroons to fundamentalist Christian doctrines has meant a concomitant rejection of belief in the supernatural. Hence, it is argued, a key pillar of Maroon cultural heritage has been demonised.

Fourthly, a fact bemoaned by the Maroon leaders interviewed and supported by one of the government representatives, is the lack of respect by the young for the cultural heritage of the Maroons. This has led to disinterest on the part of youngsters in learning about their heritage and many of them have rejected their culture (even to the point of ridicule), and have instead adapted the *mores* of the young in the wider Jamaican society. Indeed, in Moore Town it was suggested that it was difficult to find any young person who knew how to blow the *abeng* or how to speak the traditional Maroon language known as *Kramante*. Yet, this decline of the traditional Maroon language was recognised as far back as 1958 when a leader of the Moore Town Maroons, Colonel Harris (1958), commented that two things conspired to keep the *Kramante* language 'cloistered and inactive':

> One is the jealous care with which it was guarded by the older folk from 'outsiders'. Perhaps they reasoned that their secrets could be better kept if their language were unknown to others. The other is the amalgam of

aloofness and lethargy that kept members of the younger generation from learning it.

The fifth and final problem identified is the geographic dispersal of the Maroon communities at opposite ends of the island and with regard to Moore Town, the dispersal of this community over a wide area. This, it is believed, has prevented a unified stance, which would have served to strengthen these communities and to have facilitated their economic, social, cultural and political development. It will be recalled that a Maroon federation, which had been considered, never became a reality.

Conclusions

Undoubtedly, tourism is perceived by Maroon leaders and government alike as a suitable and viable option for the development of the Maroon villages, which, like most rural communities in Jamaica, are lacking in economic activities. Indeed, the economic plight of the Maroons is not unique, but is symptomatic of the general impoverishment that exists in most rural communities in Jamaica. That tourism development is seen as a lucrative option is therefore not surprising, especially given that tourism is today Jamaica's chief foreign exchange earner. However, the type of tourism development that is seen as most appropriate for these communities is not the traditional sun, sea, sand mass tourism product, which has proven to be unsustainable, but rather, cultural rural tourism, which would utilise the unique culture and heritage of these rural societies.

Yet, despite the general support for tourism, it seems apparent that the strength of this support is not universal among the Maroon leaders interviewed. In Accompong it appears that tourism is embraced as a panacea for the economic survival of the community, and there are already established tourism businesses that have been set up partly through collaboration with the Jamaican government. In this community then, the process of cultural heritage commodification is already well under way and this puts the Accompong Maroons in a more powerful position than the other Maroon communities in terms of any discussions on the future of tourism development.

In the case of Moore Town, however, it seems that tourism is seen as merely one option among a range of other possible economic options such as the development of fruit canneries and the sale of bottled water. Indeed, the organisation of the Accompong Maroons in terms of tourism business development is in stark contrast to the lack of any significant tourism businesses in the other Maroon communities. Reasons for this might be, in the case of Moore Town, the dispersal of the communities over several villages and the lack of cohesion and strong leadership. It is evident that the Colonel in Moore Town did not entirely support the perception of tourism as a 'cure all' solution for economic development in the village. So that, in terms of achieving the policy objectives of the *Master Plan*, which include the development of cultural rural tourism in Maroon villages as part of a wider tourism diversification strategy, the government of Jamaica must take into account the differences between the Maroon communities in terms of support for tourism. No doubt the incorporation of the Maroon communities into the alternative tourism strategy of the Jamaican government represents the higher concentration of power in the Accompong community. It is a mistake to perceive the Maroon communities as homogenous, and the issue of integration of tourism into the wider community of Moore Town is therefore an operational challenge for the development of cultural rural tourism, which needs to be addressed.

It is evident that there is a shortage of skills and finance in the Maroon communities and these represent key operational challenges. It is suggested that the acquisition of skills and finance requires the creation of partnerships between the Maroons and other key stakeholders including the government. The development of partnerships with the government has proved fairly successful for the Accompong Maroons, but in Charles Town and especially in Moore Town, there needs to be a stronger commitment to tourism development in order for these communities to seek out and develop the necessary partnerships and collaborative relationships. Even where partnerships have been created, as in the case of that between the Accompong Maroons and the Jamaican government, it is doubtful whether this can survive the traditional distrust between both parties as demonstrated in the constant disputes over rights to ancestral lands. The point is that not only are partnerships necessary in the creation of viable rural tourism businesses, but in addition, an important consideration must necessarily be whether the partnerships created are sustainable in the long term. Without the creation of sustainable partnerships it is doubtful whether cultural rural tourism can be a viable, long-term, alternative for these communities.

It is submitted that the issue of seasonality represents another operational challenge, which, though a feature of tourism throughout the island, is more pronounced in the Maroon villages largely because of their remoteness and poor road infrastructure. Indeed, in all the Maroon communities, the high point for touristic activity is the 6th January Celebration, the 23rd June Celebration, and the 19th October Celebration in Accompong, Charles Town, and Moore Town, respectively. Outside of these periods, tourism activities are, at best, sporadic. Possible solutions to this problem of seasonality might be to stage other events throughout the year, to establish tourism businesses such as working museums (as suggested by the Moore Town Maroons), and craft centres for the sale and display of items such as the drums and the *abeng*.

The craft centres could also be utilized for the sale of herbal remedies. However, even if these businesses are established it is doubtful whether they could be marketed on their own in the absence of any wider touristic activities. It might be necessary to market these as part of a shopping list of attractions that would include visits to other sites in the closest resort centres such as Port Antonio in the east and Negril and Montego Bay in the West.

However, for this author, the most important factor that can militate against the development of cultural rural tourism businesses in the Maroon communities is not necessarily community integration, infrastructure, marketing, skills or finance, but the disappearing cultural heritage of the Maroons. It is suggested that while the Maroons undoubtedly have inherited a rich cultural heritage, this is fast becoming extinct due to a combination of factors that include the almost total integration of Maroon communities into the rest of Jamaican society. This is taking place through involvement in politics and out-migration, the disappearance of religious beliefs through the widespread adoption of Christian fundamentalist doctrines, which has demonised the Maroon's traditional beliefs in the supernatural, and the disinterest of the young in Maroon cultural heritage traditions. In this light, it is difficult to market a distinct 'Maroon cultural heritage' for tourism purposes.

Indeed, to conclude, it is suggested that a pivotal operational challenge to the development of cultural rural tourism business is how to rejuvenate the unique cultural heritage on which these businesses must necessarily be based. An important consideration in the development of cultural rural tourism in these communities should be not so much to prevent economic decline, but more importantly to ensure the revival of the Maroons' culture and heritage. Indeed, Kirshenblatt-Gimblett (1998: 150) has claimed that heritage can be perceived as a 'new mode of cultural production' that gives a second life to dying ways of life. The Maroon cultural heritage sorely needs a revival at this time if it is not to become extinct, and development of the tourism industry seems to be the most suitable means by which this can be achieved. The scope for the development of cultural rural tourism businesses in these communities must therefore be seen to be inextricably linked with the revival of the Maroon cultural heritage on which the tourism industry is to be founded.

References

Anon (2002) Rift over timing clouds Maroon celebrations. *The Jamaica Gleaner*, 5 January.

Bilby, K. (1980) Jamaica's Maroons at the crossroads: losing touch with tradition. *Caribbean Review* 9 (4), 18–21.

Bramwell, B. and Lane, B. (eds) (1994) *Rural Tourism and Sustainable Rural Development*. Clevedon: Channel View Publications.

Bramwell, B. and Sharman, A. (1999) Collaboration in local tourism policymaking. *Annals of Tourism Research* 26 (2), 392–415.

Butler, R., Hall, C.M. and Jenkins, J. (eds) (1998) *Tourism and Recreation in Rural Areas*. Chichester: John Wiley & Sons.

Campbell, M. (1988) *The Maroons of Jamaica 1655–1796: A History of Resistance, Collaboration and Betrayal*. Massachusetts: Bergin and Garvey.

Carey, B. (1997) *The Maroon Story*. St Andrew: Agouti Press.

Dernoi, L. (1991) About rural and farm tourism. *Tourism Recreation Research* 16 (1), 3–6.

Dewailly, J.M. (1998) Images of heritage in rural regions. In R. Butler, C.M. Hall and J. Jenkins (eds) *Tourism and Recreation in Rural Areas* (pp. 123–37). Chichester: John Wiley & Sons.

Fleischer, A. and Pizam, A. (1997) Rural tourism in Israel. *Tourism Management* 18 (6), 367–72.

Government of Jamaica (2002) *Master Plan for Sustainable Tourism Development*. Kingston: Ministry of Tourism and Sport.

Harris, C.L.G. (1958) The Maroons. *Daily Gleaner*, 3 October.

Jones, E. and Spence, B. (2003) *The Potential Impacts of Climate Change and Severe Weather Events on Urban Water Resources in Jamaica: A Case Study*. Kingston: Caribbean Disaster and Emergency Response Agency (CDERA).

Kirshenblatt-Gimblett, B. (1998) *Destination Culture: Tourism, Museums and Heritage*. Berkeley: University of California Press.

Kopytoff, B. (1976a) The development of Jamaican maroon ethnicity. *Caribbean Quarterly* 22 (2/3), 33–50.

Kopytoff, B. (1976b) Jamaican Maroon political organization: the effects of the treaties. *Social and Economic Studies* 25 (2), 87–104.

MacDonald, R. and Jolliffe, L. (2003) Cultural rural tourism: evidence from Canada. *Annals of Tourism Research* 30 (2), 307–22.

McKercher, B. and du Cross, H. (2002) *Cultural Tourism: The Partnership Between Tourism and Cultural Heritage Management*. New York: The Haworth Hospitality Press.

Morais, R. (2000) Maroons threaten action. *The Jamaica Gleaner*, 16 March.

Morgan, D. (1994) Homogenous products: the future of established resorts. In W.F. Theobald (ed.) *Global Tourism: The Next Decade* (pp. 378–95). Oxford: Butterworth-Heinemann.

Oppermann, M. (1996) Rural tourism in Southern Germany. *Annals of Tourism Research* 23 (1), 86–102.

Page, S. and Getz, D. (eds) (1997) *The Business of Rural Tourism: International Perspectives*. London: International Thomson Business Press.

Prentice, R. (2001) Experimental cultural tourism: museums and the marketing of the new romanticism of evoked authenticity. *Museum Management and Curatorship* 19 (1), 5–26.

Price, R. (ed.) (1979) *Maroon Societies: Rebel Slave Communities in the Americas*. Baltimore: Johns Hopkins University Press.

Reizinger, Y. (1994) Tourist–host contact as a part of cultural tourism. *World Leisure and Recreation* 36, 24–28.

Robinson, G.M. (1990) *Conflict and Change in the Countryside*. London: Belhaven Press.

Scott, J. (2000) Peripheries, artificial peripheries and centres. In F. Brown and D. Hall (eds) *Tourism in Peripheral Areas* (pp. 58–73). Clevedon: Channel View Publications.

Sharpley, R. (2002) Rural tourism and the challenge of tourism diversification: the case of Cyprus. *Tourism Management* 23, 233–44.

Sheridan, R.B. (1986) The Maroons of Jamaica, 1730–1830: livelihood, demography and health. In G. Heuman (ed.) *Out of the House of Bondage: Runaways, Resistance and Marronage in Africa and the New World* (pp. 152–71). London: Frank Cass.

Stebbins, R. (1997) Identity and cultural tourism. *Annals of Tourism Research* 24 (2), 450–52.

Strauss, A. and Corbin, J. (1998) *Basics of Qualitative Research*. London: Sage.

Turner, V. (1989) Maroons celebrate 250th anniversary this year. *The Jamaica Record*, 3 January.

Veal, A.J. (1997) *Research Methods for Leisure and Tourism* (2nd edn). London: Financial Times/Prentice Hall.

Chapter 12
Farm Tourism Cooperation in Taiwan

MING-HUANG LEE

Introduction: Aims and Objectives

Agricultural tourism aims to generate additional income from the use of agricultural resources for recreational purposes so as to promote agricultural development and improve farmers' livelihoods. Under-used agricultural production factors, such as labour, can be used by farm households to produce additional products, such as catering, accommodation services and other tourism activities, and by so doing generate additional income (Goodall, 1987).

This chapter aims to gain an understanding of the impacts of the development of agricultural tourism enterprises, as elements of farmers' livelihood strategies, within the context of Taiwan, through an assessment of the policies, institutions and processes involved. The Sustainable Livelihoods (SL) approach has been adopted by many development organisations as a new way to explore the complexity of people's livelihoods and development impacts (Ashley & Carney, 1999). This chapter seeks to apply the SL approach as a means to explore the wide range of livelihood priorities of local farmers who engage in agricultural tourism, and to explore the effects of tourism business on their livelihoods.

Based on recent research undertaken for a PhD, this chapter first examines the Taiwan context for rural tourism development. It next briefly describes the development of Pick-Your-Own (PYO) farms, as one type of rural tourism in Taiwan. Within this context the chapter specifically focuses on the development and roles of PYO organisations through application of the sustainable livelihoods (SL) framework. Finally the chapter draws some conclusions on the development of rural tourism and the sustainability of PYO farms.

The Taiwan context for rural tourism development

Pearce (1999: 1) has indicated that improving standards of living means domestic travel is 'becoming more accessible to a wider cross-section of society'. One consequence of national economic development in Taiwan has been an increase in people's average income and consumption, and, consequently, travelling for leisure has become more accessible and affordable (Hsiau, 1984; National Statistics Bureau, 2000). The average monthly working hours for non-agricultural employees in Taiwan fell from 219.2 hours in 1976 to 190.4 hours in 1999 (National Statistics Bureau, 2000), rendering more leisure time available for people to travel (Hsiau, 1984). Improvement of transportation also made it easier for people to travel to destinations both near and far. The length of highway in Taiwan increased from 17,101 km in 1976 to 20,319 km in 1999. The number of cars per 10,000 population also increased dramatically from 205 in 1976 to 2426 in 1999 (National Statistics Bureau, 2000).

The development of service businesses, especially travel agents, has created more opportunities for tourists to fulfill their wishes in travelling. The number of travel agents increased dramatically from 766 in 1989 to 1742 in 1999. However, the main focus of travel agents' business in Taiwan remains the selling of overseas holiday tour packages to Taiwanese tourists and providing services for international tourists to visit Taiwan. Generally speaking, they pay little attention to the domestic tourism market because of its lower profits (Tourism Bureau, 2000).

Taiwan was largely an agricultural society until the 1950s, at which time the whole nation struggled to recover from the damage of the Second World War. Citizens were encouraged by government to engage in agricultural production to ensure sufficient food supply, and gradually, to improve the national economic condition. For many, the only period for break or leisure was the gap between harvest and next cultivation. Since the mid-1960s, Taiwan has been transformed through the process of industrialisation. The first obvious change during this period was the influx of population to urban or industrial areas either for residence or for employment. This led to the expansion of urban areas and the increase in population density in these environments. People living in urban areas were increasingly keen to make use of open space while they were not working (Chen, 1989; Hsiau, 1984).

Another change associated with industrialisation was the intensification of working time because of the efficient characteristics of industrial production. This resulted in workers concentrating on their work all the time and, as a result, suffering from stress. Workers anticipated a different space and more relaxed activity for when they had time off from work. All of these stimulated their motivation for travel (Yu, 1989).

In 1998, the government shortened the statutory working week. According to subsequent research by the Ministry of Transportation and Communication (1999), more than 80% of tourists and 50% of travel agents agreed that the above scheme stimulated the motivation of urban workers to travel. Since 2001, the government has promulgated the regulation of the five-day working week in Taiwan. Under such circumstances, it is believed that the demand of tourists for travel activities will continue to increase in the future. The future challenge will be how the tourism enterprises can respond to this changing situation.

Taiwan's agricultural industry has adjusted its roles over time, and according to the changing challenges faced. Importantly, there has been a constant decline in the number of workers engaged in agriculture since the mid-1960s. There are a number of explanations for this change. First, traditional cultivation practices that relied on human and animal power were partially replaced by machinery because of industrialisation, with spare labour gradually transferred to industry and service sectors. Secondly, income from farming was, and remains, generally lower and the working hours longer than in the industrial sectors. The average annual income of the farm household was about 77% of non-farmers' in 1998. This has led to further transfer of labour from the agricultural to non-agricultural sectors: 49.8% of the population were employed in the agricultural sector in 1961, but only 8.3% were thus occupied in 1999 (COA, 1999).

The improvement of technology in agricultural production has encouraged greater utilisation of pesticides and fertilisers, which, in turn, has increased the cost of farming by more than 30% during the last decade (COA, 1999). On the other hand, profits from agricultural production have not matched increasing costs, largely because the government has controlled market prices so as to ensure the stability of food supply. Following national development trends, the income of rural people has mostly increased year by year. However, this has been generated mainly by non-farm enterprises. The proportion of income from farming to farmers' total income is estimated to have declined from 39% in 1976 to 17% in 1998 (COA, 1999). Obviously, this has influenced farmers' motivation to continue in farming.

Joining the World Trade Organisation (WTO) has been a significant goal of Taiwan's government since 1990, entry being seen as an important tool to promote Taiwan's economic development. However, under WTO's regulations, Taiwan needs to open its agricultural markets, and thus needs to confront strenuous competition from overseas products. The challenge for the government and farmers is how agriculture in a small island can compete with those countries with a large labour force and low labour costs reducing their overall cost of production.

In an effort to meet the above challenges, the government has implemented a series of agricultural and rural development projects. Some of these have sought to modify internal mechanisms to enhance production and competitiveness in the market. Other projects have sought solutions through linking agriculture with other sectors, such as tourism.

According to an investigation undertaken during December 1998 and January 1999 by the Tourism Bureau (2000), the main and traditional recreational destinations for Taiwan's tourists included national parks, public scenic areas (in national, provincial and county levels), coastal areas and 'artificial' recreational areas. The policies for tourism development were initially focused on development of these latter recreational areas, which took time and much investment. By contrast, agricultural and rural areas with abundant resources offered natural elements for tourism development. Traditional agriculture creates the landscape and sustains the rural way of life. Rural areas contain scattered settlements with farms and farmhouses, but are characterised by low population densities. Tourists are attracted into these areas by their climate, natural features, landscape quality and rural life-styles. There is a very delicate relationship between tourism and agriculture.

In view of its significant contribution to economic growth, tourism has long been recognised as an important area of activity through which broader rural development objectives might be achieved (de Kadt, 1979; Pearce, 1989, 1999). Through the development of agricultural tourism, additional income from tourism for farmers and local people can be generated. Further, tourism businesses may also provide more employment opportunities for farm families so that they can stay in farming. The prosperity of tourism-related enterprises can contribute greatly to tax revenue for government and local development (Glasson *et al.*, 1995; Healy, 1994; Pearce, 1989).

The development of tourism improves the accessibility to remote rural areas. This provides opportunities for direct contact and communication between tourists and farmers, who play the roles of consumers, and agricultural producers. In this way, it is more likely that farmers can sell their products to customers directly and make an increased profit. The competitiveness of agricultural products has been enhanced to confront the challenge of imported products (Jeng, 1992). It can be argued that agricultural tourism, as the interface of two industries – agriculture and tourism – creates the possibility for a win–win scenario and provides a strong position for the government to support its development.

Rural tourism can broadly support businesses utilising the resources of rural areas for tourism purposes. Such resources include the materials for and outputs from agricultural production such as crops, forests, fisheries and livestock. The processes of production, rural ways of life, rural landscape and open space can all be involved in tourism activities. While tourism has long played an important role in rural development within the developed world (Hall, 2000a, 2000b; Shaw & Williams, 1994), the practice of agricultural tourism in Taiwan has developed step by step, and is related to the ongoing change in the use of rural resources. There have been various official projects implemented to encourage the development of agricultural tourism enterprises in Taiwan, including forestry recreational areas (since 1965), PYO farms (since 1982), holiday farms (since 1990) and allotment gardens (since 1995). These agricultural tourism enterprises have been financially supported through government programmes. Of these, the PYO farm programme is of particular significance as it was the first to establish agricultural tourism enterprises that were managed by farmers.

Assessments of agricultural tourism businesses, whether operated in the public or private sectors, often focus on their economic contribution. Lu (1981), for example, analysed the effects of strawberry PYO farms in Dahu Village of Miauli County through comparing the costs and benefits among different types of farm, and found that managing a PYO farm was more profitable than non-PYO farm and rice production. According to a study of PYO farms producing various fruits in the Chualan area of Miauli County, citrus farms increased farmers' income by 5%, and pear and grape farms both increased farmers' income by 10% (Hsiau, 1984). Taichung County Government (1985) adopted similar 'before and after' approaches to assess the benefits of PYO to farmers. This focused on analysing the cost of production and marketing, and the prices of products in PYO farms and non-PYO farms. Such criteria were also used to judge the value of PYO businesses in the county. The total benefit to farmers from managing PYO farms was estimated to be up to 129,000 NT$ (c. €3000) per hectare. Tsai (1986) similarly evaluated the PYO farm project in Taipei City by comparing the changes in cost and benefits in farms before and after involvement in PYO businesses. He used questionnaires to survey 100 PYO farm households and found that more than 50% had increased their income (by up to 30%) through managing PYO businesses. The PYO farmers and tourists interviewed confirmed that the strategy of developing PYO farms had brought positive outcomes. Jeng (1992) was funded by the Council of Agriculture to evaluate the contributions of agricultural tourism to farmers' income and domestic tourism. Comparing the changes in farmers' income, Jeng found that the benefit to farmers increased further when a PYO farm was expanded to a holiday farm business.

The main objectives of developing agricultural tourism, in addition to its contribution to the tourist industry, relate to how agricultural resources can best be used to promote and sustain agricultural and rural development in the future. The underlying purpose of establishing a forestry recreational area, managed by the government, is to conserve forest and its natural resources, which are taken as public assets. Similarly, PYO farms operated by farmers are expected to reduce the cost of agricultural production and marketing and to increase farmers' income. Holiday farms, operated by farmers, are expected to expand the businesses of agricultural tourism and to serve as an incentive for farmers to cooperate with each other to enlarge the scale of their farm. Allotment gardens have been established in urban areas to promote the involvement and support of citizens in food production.

Brief Development of PYO Farms

Pick-your-own (PYO) farms are working farms open for tourists to pick, taste and purchase agricultural products in season. Traditionally, farmers picked their own products, and transported them to the wholesale markets where they were sold to traders. The traders distributed the products to local retail markets for customer purchase. The concept of the PYO farm encourages customers to visit the farm and, often through the payment of a fee, enter the field where they can taste and harvest for themselves the products they want. These are weighed and customers are charged accordingly. By this arrangement, the cost of picking and marketing in traditional agricultural production is reduced. Moreover, farmers and their families, as operators of a tourism enterprise, gain greater opportunities to earn additional income from tourists (Doorn *et al.*, 1998; Huang, 1986).

Following growth of the national economy and changing patterns of food consumption, a surplus of rice production became significant in the late 1970s. From 1978, in order to reduce this, farmers have been encouraged to cultivate other crops, such as fruit (Chen, 1996). Initially, farmers hesitated to change because of their long involvement in rice production and the absence of subsidy incentives from government. Only a few farmers accepted and tried to change, and at first the increase of fruit production was small. However, due to the growing consumption of fruit in urban areas, the profit from fruit began to prove more lucrative than rice production. As a consequence, more farmers became involved in cultivating fruit. Fruit production increased rapidly, although this had the effect of reducing prices and thus profits. More recently, the increasing importation of agricultural products has resulted in unstable prices for indigenous products in the domestic markets, in some cases falling below production costs. In response, some farmers in northern Taiwan started to search for alternative marketing approaches for their products. Instead of using traditional markets, they tried to sell their products themselves.

The first step was the decision by farmers to display their products along the main roads that tourists might pass along. This meant that tourists could easily buy the products from the farmers directly. In this way, farmers could meet the customers as well. Further, farmers whose farms were located near the main roads would often invite tourists, on an informal basis, to visit their farms and to pick the products by themselves. Thus the development of PYO farms was, in the first instance, a local response to changing market circumstances and opportunities. This development came to the notice of the Taiwanese government, and as a result government officers were sent to visit Europe to learn more about whether the establishment of further PYO farms could be encouraged and supported. The potential of PYO farms was thus recognised both by the government and farmers.

Subsequently, the government took a supporting role in facilitating development of the enterprises. In 1982, the government implemented a PYO Farm Project to encourage and support farmers to establish accredited PYO farms. The accreditation of PYO farms was based upon a minimum farm size and the organisation of a PYO team. In order to overcome expected constraints in dealing with small-scale farms and to ensure the future development of PYO farms as viable businesses, the government decreed that the minimum farm size for each PYO enterprise should be five hectares. Small farmers were therefore advised to combine their adjacent farmland as a 'PYO cluster' so as to meet the minimum size requirement. Further, they were instructed to organise a PYO team to manage the PYO cluster. In order to distinguish similar terms used in this chapter, it is important to note that a 'PYO farm' refers to the farm managed by an individual farm household and 'PYO cluster' refers to the collective PYO enterprise managed by a PYO team organised by various farm households.

According to official procedures, farmers first have to organise a PYO team and then submit an application to manage a PYO enterprise to the local council or farmers' association (FA). The application is reviewed by local council or farmers' association, and then evaluated by county and provincial government. There are a number of criteria, as shown in Table 12.1, used by the government to evaluate any application to join the PYO Farm Project (TPDAF, 1997).

Although PYO farms have been seen as a way of bringing farmers additional income, there do exist constraints to the development of PYO enterprises. The period of harvest of agricultural products is limited, and the harvest season dictates when PYO farms are open (see Table 12.2). This presents a significant constraint on PYO enterprises. For example, the harvest period for lychees is about 20 days a year. This means that tourists who usually visit PYO farms on weekends might only come to lychee PYO farms four times a year. This has both constrained the visiting options open to tourists and the development of PYO enterprises themselves.

Seasonality causes many problems for the tourism industry, and for organisers, travel agents, the labour force, and local residents, as well as for the tourists themselves. In economic terms, seasonality may cause inefficient utilisation of fixed capacity, which can severely reduce the economic profitability of the tourism sector. In a case study of German

Table 12.1 Evaluation criteria for establishing a PYO farm

1. Constraints in land use: slope or sensitive areas unsuitable for tourism are not allowed to be used to establish PYO farms.
2. Accessibility: transport facilities to a PYO farm should allow ease of access for tourists to visit the farms.
3. Parking areas for tourists coming by car or coach should be provided.
4. Crops should be mature, and correspond with the known character of the local area in order to attract tourists' visits during the harvest period.
5. Farm size: there should be enough space to establish additional facilities and offer recreational activities for visitors.
6. There should be an active farmers' organisation and sufficient manpower to support the PYO business.
7. Farmers should show strong willingness and enthusiasm to manage PYO farms.
8. Support from local government and farmers' associations should be forthcoming.

Source: TPDAF (1997)

holidays on the farm, Oppermann (1995: 66) indicated that 'seasonal variation in tourist demand is often the cause of unprofitability or low profits for tourist enterprises'.

In the early 1980s, the idea of visiting PYO farms was novel and initially attracted many tourists to PYO farms. According to the statements of many PYO farmers, the serious traffic jam in the weekends represented the popularity and prosperity of PYO enterprises. However, they also pointed out that such a prosperous situation did not last for very long. From the late 1980s, the number of tourists visiting PYO farms has gradually declined. Since 1982, many PYO farms have been established in many areas. However, tourists now have a number of alternative recreational choices. Various artificial theme parks have been established and proven highly popular with tourists. In PYO farms, tourists can only

Table 12.2 Harvest period of different crops in PYO farms (per year)

	Crop				
	Grape	*Starfruit*	*Grapefruit*	*Lychee*	*Citrus*
Harvest period	4 months	8 months	2 months	20 days	4 months

pick and taste fruit. Such activities are thought by many tourists to be monotonous, especially in mono-crop farms. Moreover, the time for which tourists stay in PYO farms is short, between two and three hours. This implies that PYO tourists are urban day-trippers. It is difficult for tourists to drive a long way to visit PYO farms just for a short stay. While there was no other activity on PYO farms in which tourists could engage, the interests of tourists declined.

The emergence of the preliminary impacts of managing PYO enterprises pushed many farmers to adopt various strategies for further development. For example, a number of PYO farmers have sought to diversify the variety of crops they produce so as to extend the opening period. Since farmers have diversified to various crops, the PYO enterprise has become an all year activity (see Table 12.3).

In addition to the original PYO activity, a barbecue service has been added to some farms in order to provide tourists with a further choice of recreation. Family and other groups are attracted by this in that they can enjoy their meals outdoors rather than in restaurants. Farmers agreed that the barbecue service has also promoted PYO activity. As a result, more than 80% of products are consumed by tourists in PYO farms.

In some other cases, more services, such as a restaurant or accommodation, are now offered to attract more tourists. The most significant characteristic of such PYO enterprises is that the profit from these diversification activities is higher than that of the PYO activity itself, and in some cases these have become the main income source for farm households. Compared with simpler PYO, diversified businesses are more profitable. It was found that managing a restaurant was one of the most popular enterprises among the non-farming diversification activities. A farmer describes the lower entry threshold and high profit of managing a restaurant in Box 12.1.

Table 12.3 Diversification of crops and opening periods of PYO farms of Taichung County

Crops	Jan	Feb	Mar	April	May	June	July	Aug	Sep	Oct	Nov	Dec
Citrus	•	•	•							•	•	•
Plum			•	•	•	•						
Peach				•	•	•	•	•				
Lychee						•	•					
Longan								•	•			
Persimmon							•	•	•			
Starfruit	•	•	•	•					•	•	•	•

Box 12.1   Case study of a PYO farmer managing a restaurant

PYO farmer, Mrs. Yang-Huang; main crop, lychee, 1 ha; livestock, chicken.

The price of lychees in the market is too low to be profitable. Although PYO has the potential to make profit from tourists, the low price of lychees has made this possibility very unlikely. In addition, the harvest period of lychees is too short. It is difficult to sustain PYO business in such circumstances. I think managing a restaurant is a good idea because everyone needs to eat anyway. People coming to my restaurant are not necessarily visitors to my PYO farm. This will expand the sources of customers and income. I decided to invest in a new building for the restaurant. I can offer the chickens as the material of meals. Actually, chicken meals are the main dish in my restaurant. Now I am managing a restaurant with 150 seats all year round. Normally, the turnover from managing the restaurant can reach 500,000 NT$ per month, whereas my total annual income from farming is about 300,000 NT$.

Tourists involved in agricultural tourism may include those who stay away from their residential areas over 24 hours, and the provision of accommodation for tourists has become an essential element of agricultural tourism businesses. The main purpose for PYO farmers to provide accommodation has been to extend the duration of tourists' stay and increase their expenditure on the farms. While many farmers might be familiar with preparing food for customers, providing accommodation is considered more complicated (see Box 12.2). In addition, farmers have claimed that it is difficult to decide priorities for the farm business, the family and the guests while providing accommodation.

Although accommodation management is not an easy task for farmers, some have still decided to make use of their larger farm size and to adopt such a strategy of diversification to sustain their livelihoods and maintain the life-style. This characteristic was consistent with those family-owned enterprises reported from New Zealand who had strongly indicated that 'the risks and responsibility of operating a B&B business were worth the gains in lifestyle' (Hall & Rusher, 2002: 205).

It was admitted by farmers that the income from providing accommodation was more significant than that gained from managing the PYO activity and a restaurant. In this study, the average expenditure on PYO activity or catering was about 100–200 NT$ per person, whereas it took about 600–1000 NT$ for each person to stay overnight in the farms. However, the revenue from accommodation was not as stable as catering

Box 12.2 Case study of a PYO farmer managing an accommodation service

---

PYO farmer, Mr Lin

- Family: wife (female farmer), two sons (studying in primary school), uncle (employed male farmer, 66 years old), mother-in-law (part-time in restaurant).
- Farm: 10 ha, lychees and other fruits, fishing pond, BBQ, restaurant, conference room, accommodation.

Before investing in accommodation, I thought that it would not be difficult for us to diversify our business to provide such a service. However, reality was totally different from what I thought. The problem was how to meet tourists' needs in different situations. Tourists might need various supports at different times. Sometimes, something in the room broke down in the night. We had to fix it as soon as possible. One time, tourists came as family with a baby. The baby was ill in the middle of the night. We had to drive them to the nearest hospital. Even though only one room was occupied, we had to offer the same service as if fully occupied. My family members were responsible for the farming and all services. We needed to prepare for every possible eventuality. I thought this was not easy.

---

services. It was mentioned by farmers that the average occupancy rate of weekends was nearly 100% whereas this fell to only 10% during the weekdays. Tourists were more likely to book a table in the restaurant than book a room for staying overnight. In addition, tourists might elect to stay in accommodation away from the farms. In this circumstance, the profitability and rates of return from the farm accommodation business were uncertain. The result is supported by the study conducted by Gladstone and Morris (1998), who evaluated the income role of providing farm accommodation in rural Scotland.

The reasons for tourists staying in the accommodation provided by PYO farms varied in each case. Most tourists who elected to stay on PYO farms belonged to the same groups or companies who participated in a package tour or conferences held on the farms. It was believed that the various activities arranged by PYO farms would have the additional bonus of providing the visitors with a real-life farming experience and attract tourists to spend more time and/or stay overnight on the farm. Furthermore, PYO farms offered tourists a discount when they selected the package tour. On the other hand, tourists stayed overnight on PYO farms because they simply intended to enjoy the rural life and tranquil environment on the farm. The motivations that surround choice of lodging in New Zealand suggest that B&B guests place far more emphasis on social interaction than do hotel guests, while aesthetics, setting and friendly staff are also regarded as extremely important (Hall & Rusher, 2002: 199). Therefore, tourists might have visited the nearby city or other attractions as 'transit trippers' before registering in PYO accommodation. This is also found in Iwai and Taguchi's (1998) case study of Japanese farm-inns. They pointed out that 'most guests stay at farm-inns for only one or two nights, while en route on sightseeing vacations' (Iwai & Taguchi, 1998: 277).

The Nature, Development and Roles of PYO Organisations

Within the development of PYO farms in Taiwan, there are two different types of PYO business organisation: the family/household farm, and the PYO team. It is important to understand the development of such organisations in PYO management, and what impacts they might have on the performance of PYO farmers.

It is widely identified in the literature that the rural tourism sector has been dominated by small family businesses (Getz & Carlsen, 2000). This characteristic was also found in PYO management in Taiwan. Compared with those farm households in PYO teams, family business farmers were often middle-aged, within the range 41–55 years. Most of them had received secondary school education. With these human capital characteristics, it seemed that farmers in this group were more eager to acquire new concepts of farm management and more willing to adopt diversification options than most in PYO teams. The average farm size (5–10 ha) was bigger than those of farm families in PYO teams. Therefore, more family members were likely to be involved in PYO businesses, but still followed the pattern of a small enterprise that employed five or fewer full-time employees (Hall & Rusher, 2002: 197).

The family-based PYO clusters could be located in different categories according to their different involvement in the process of diversification. Farmers in this group had strong motivation to live and work on their own farmland, and to enjoy a good lifestyle. However, there was also recognition that the business had to be profitable. Some of them acted more like satisficers in that living in a rural environment, together with family and life-style considerations, was more significant for them than business growth. In the tourism industry there are a great number of entrepreneurs who are not motivated by a desire to maximise economic gain, operating businesses often with low levels of employment and in which managerial decisions are often based on highly personalised criteria (Komppula, 2002: 67). On the other hand, farmers of the other PYO clusters, who had diversified into more non-agricultural activities, appeared to be motivated more by profit-making goals, although they still preferred to work on their farms. The analysis from Taiwan confirms the presence of family-oriented businesses and business-oriented families (Getz & Carlsen, 2000: 558).

The characteristics of the family/household farm type of PYO organisation and emphasis on life-style and family-related goals found in this study are thus in broad agreement with research undertaken in other contexts. According to several studies, quality of life and a certain life-style are more important for many small tourism entrepreneurs. In a Cornish study (Shaw & Williams, 1990: 77–78), it was estimated that 55% of entrepreneurs were motivated by the desire for a better way of life. Similar results have been reported in New Zealand (Ateljevic & Doorne, 2000). A growing number of small-firm owners selected to 'stay within the fence' in order to preserve both their quality of life as well as their niche market position. A study of small firm growth in Finland also suggested that the small- and micro-sized rural tourism entrepreneurs emphasise more the quality of life, the emotional and social well-being of the family, than financial growth (Komppula, 2002: 64, 67). Hall and Rusher (2002: 205), examining B&B entrepreneurs' attitudes concerning balance between risk of business and life-style, concluded that 'fulfilling the life-style goals of the owners is more important than meeting business goals and objectives'.

One of the important definitional considerations of family business is 'generational transfer', by which family members of the next generation take over the business to keep ownership remaining within the family (Getz & Carlsen, 2000). Although most PYO farmers interviewed by the author were uncertain about the ultimate disposition of their business, some of them have already arranged for family members (in addition to their spouse) or their children to be involved in PYO management.

The original purpose of organising PYO teams was to combine small-scale farm households to manage a PYO enterprise together. However, PYO teams have often not functioned as intended. The management of a PYO enterprise is usually carried out independently by each farm household in the same PYO team. Regular meetings for team members were found to be no longer being held. The exception was for the purpose of negotiation of official subsidies. In this case, only team leaders are invited by local councils and FAs to participate in the negotiation. As subsidies have shrunk, the interest of farmers to participate in team meetings and team operation seems to have fallen commensurately. Subsidy from the government seems the most important impetus for the maintenance of PYO teams. The biggest factor affecting the operation of PYO teams is the division of subsidy among team members. This is believed to be an obstacle for farmers to work together.

While many PYO farms have been gradually established in many counties since 1982, most PYO farmers have had limited opportunity to communicate with each other. An exception has been through the training courses organised by the former Taiwan Provincial Government, where PYO farmers from different areas meet at the venue of the training course. In the late 1980s, some leaders of PYO teams in different counties started to meet together occasionally. These informal meetings were continued to establish a platform of communication among PYO farmers in different counties. Gradually, the meetings became a regular activity among these participants. An Allied Organisation of PYO Team Leaders was organised by the team leaders in 1992. Through this organisation, PYO team leaders met together annually to exchange their experiences and discuss relevant issues in PYO management. As Tremblay (2000) has pointed out, interorganisational contact between stakeholders can help them to learn from each other's knowledge, understand each other's needs, and to work together to learn about their environment. However, the allied PYO organisation was an informal farmers' organisation that had no clear institutional structure. While some conclusions would be arrived at from the participants' discussion, no further action would be taken on the basis of these conclusions.

In 1996, there were 15 PYO clusters established in Taichung County, which was the largest number of PYO enterprises in one county. Those PYO team leaders who were involved in the allied meetings considered the necessity of a formal PYO organisation within this county. They decided to combine all PYO farmers to push for the establishment of the Taichung County PYO Association. The members were expected to be drawn from all farm households. Consequently, Changhua County and Miauli County PYO Associations were established in 1999 and 2000, both being transformed from the previous alliance meetings. In 1998, the Taiwan Provincial PYO Association was established. Its members comprise PYO farmers from different counties.

The collapse of PYO teams and the establishment of PYO associations indicates the important role of participation in the development of PYO enterprise. People's participation is an essential factor in development. To promote this participation, it is important to establish a rapport among stakeholders: local people who are the main actors in development, experts who have professional knowledge, and government officials who have the responsibility for managing development resources.

One of the most important factors for successful agritourism is whether or not the farm entrepreneur has the support of the local community (Rilla, 2000). The recognition that communities can influence the development of tourism has generated a growing concern regarding community-based tourism and community development in tourism. Literature in the field of tourism planning has stressed the need for local community involvement and cooperation in the planning process. Murphy (1985), for example, emphasised the necessity for each community to relate tourism development to local needs. Building on this basic principle, later studies of community-based tourism have gradually broadened the scope of the term to include a wide range of issues, including ecological factors and local participation and democracy (Richards & Hall, 2000: 4–5). Community-based tourism development should strengthen institutions that enhance local participation and promote the economic, social and cultural well-being of the popular majority (Telfer, 2000: 244). As tourism becomes increasingly important to communities, the need to develop tourism sustainably for communities also becomes a primary concern. It is believed that participation can raise awareness of tourism impacts on communities, and this highlighted awareness should lead to policies that are fairer in their outcomes (Bramwell & Lane, 2000). An important underlying assumption of these studies is that tourism can generate community development through participation of local people.

The PYO associations provide opportunities for members to meet together and share experiences with each other. With its legitimate status, the PYO association has become a representative body of PYO farmers, which can negotiate on relevant issues with external organisations. It can integrate the opinions of its members and reflect them to the government. For its part, the government invites delegates of the PYO associations to join discussions on PYO policies. In this way, the PYO association creates a formal communicating channel between PYO farmers and the government. It also increases the opportunity for farmers to participate in the process of policy-making. Moreover, the government subsidises the associations to implement some elements of the PYO Farm Programme, which were formerly implemented by county governments, local councils or FAs.

Another purpose of the PYO association is to combine PYO farms in different locations to promote their competitiveness in the tourism market. Considering the government policy of reduced working hours in existence since 2000, the demands of tourism are expected to increase significantly. Meanwhile, competition among different tourism businesses will increase. Certainly, PYO enterprises need to consider this trend and face the future challenge. The scale of most PYO farms is currently rather small, compared with other capital-oriented artificial tourism businesses. It is necessary to combine individual PYO farmers into an allied organisation so as to enhance the competitiveness of PYO enterprises in the market. For example, Taichung County PYO Association has set up a Website on the Internet to promote all the PYO clusters in Taichung County. Moreover, the Taiwan Provincial PYO Association supports a national allied development scheme that recommends qualified PYO farms to the public and provides a series of PYO tour options for tourists. For example, tourists can obtain advice from PYO associations. When they decide to spend their holidays in one district or region comprising more than one county, PYO associations design the tour schedule for tourists who are interested in PYO farms. The association now plays the role of tour agent for PYO farmers and tourists. On this point Clarke (1999: 26) suggested that 'better use of the marketing process in rural tourism could help create more sustainable forms of development by reducing provider isolation, utilising resources more effectively, and allowing rural tourism to connect with international flows of tourists'.

The importance of involving diverse stakeholders in tourism planning and management is increasingly recognised (see also Chapters 7 to 9). Collaboration and partnerships that bring together a range of interests in order to develop and sometimes also implement tourism policies are essential ways of achieving this (Bramwell & Lane, 2000). In this study, the active role of PYO associations in PYO development, even though this was not part of the original 'vision' of government, has supported such a viewpoint.

The potential for partnerships involved in tourism planning to contribute to the wider objectives of sustainable development has been widely recognised. Owing to the considerable complexity of the tourism industry, the sustainable development of both tourism and the community resources upon which it depends should involve a collaborative learning process that strikes a balance between different visions and has the flexibility to adapt and generate new ideas and follow them through (Bramwell & Lane, 2000: 16). Clarke (1999) has stressed that the marketing of rural tourism must move beyond the activities of the individual provider to investigate collaborative practice. In addition, M. Hall (2000) has argued that the growing interest in partnerships that engage in policy-making reflects the changing role of the state, which involves a shift from hierarchical control to governance that is dispersed through networks of non-government agencies and collaborative arrangement. He further recognises that collaborative approaches to tourism planning have the potential to involve a wide set of stakeholders and hence to increase potential participation and social equality, and that such consequences may contribute to more sustainable forms of tourism.

Application of the Sustainable Livelihoods Framework

Since development thinking has become more diverse and complex, it is necessary to apply a more holistic approach to study the impact of development interventions. The sustainable livelihoods (SL) framework (Figure 12.1) was developed by the UK's Department for International Development (DfID) and has been adopted subsequently by many development organisations to help understand and analyse the complex livelihoods of rural people. Further, the SL framework has also proved useful

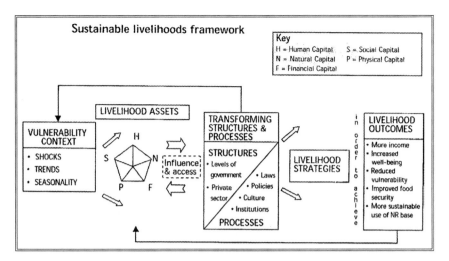

Figure 12.1 Sustainable livelihoods (SL) framework (*Source*: DfID (1999: Section 2.1))

in assessing the effectiveness of existing development interventions (Ashley & Carney, 1999; DfID, 1999). The livelihoods approach provides a way of thinking about the objectives, scope and priorities for development. Livelihoods thinking dates back to the work of Robert Chambers (1987), which was further developed by Chambers and Conway (1992) and others in the early 1990s. Based on the evolution of development studies, the theoretical framework of sustainable livelihoods (SL) has been advocated to emphasise the importance of exploring people's livelihoods through a holistic perspective so as to see the complex reality of their lives (DfID, 1999).

In the SL framework, people's livelihoods are considered to comprise of five key components, including vulnerability context, livelihood assets, transforming structures and processes, livelihood strategies, and livelihood outcomes. The notion of livelihood strategies is one of the essential components used to indicate the activities that farmers undertake in order to achieve their livelihood goals (DfID, 1999). Therefore, the SL framework is considered here as an appropriate framework through which to analyse the process of farmers' decision making on livelihood, in the case of managing PYO farms.

The SL framework further recognises that farmers' decisions on livelihood strategies are influenced by a range of important factors. Ellis (2000: 37) pointed out that 'the translation of a set assets into a livelihood strategy is mediated by a great number of considerations'. These considerations are divided into two broad categories including 'the vulnerability context' and 'transforming processes'. The vulnerability context comprises such elements as history, economic trends and demography. Transforming processes include policies, institutions, laws and incentives. All these factors are recognised to affect farmers' decisions on their livelihood strategies. From the evidence of the case studies on Taiwan's PYO enterprises, it was found that transforming processes (i.e. government policies and institutions) have been among the most significant factors influencing farmers' livelihood strategies. Accordingly, this element of the SL framework is applied to guide the discussion focusing on the interactions between transforming processes (i.e. government policies and institutions) and farmers' livelihood strategies on organisations and cooperation.

One notable element of the PYO organisations is that farmers did not manage PYO enterprises in teams, which was one of the official criteria for establishing accredited PYO farms. Instead, farmers preferred to manage their own farms as individual or family enterprises rather than cooperate with neighbours in a team basis. Nevertheless, the importance of organisation in developing PYO enterprise was still stressed by farmers. They started to organise themselves in creating farmer-based PYO associations. Such organisations seem to provide an appropriate forum through which farmers have been willing to get involved in sharing with others their experiences and expertise.

The character of the small-scale farm has long been considered by the government as a constraint not only to the efficiency of agricultural production, but also to the development of PYO enterprise. The government therefore encouraged small-farm households cultivating the same crops in adjacent areas to combine their farmland and organise PYO teams to cooperate in managing PYO enterprises. Such mode of cooperation among farmers was seen by the government as an important strategy in developing PYO enterprises. However, PYO teams have proven to be less functionally effective, largely as a result of a culture of being independent in cultivation, lack of clear rules for PYO team members, limited communication with the government, and restricted social networks.

Although farmers did not operate the functions of PYO teams, this does not mean that they ignored the importance of organisation in PYO development. Farmers still recognised the need for meeting together to discuss and learn from each other in order, for example, to improve cultivating technology and promote the quality of their products. Farmers also recognised that it is difficult for individual farm households to survive in the market. Moreover, the government had declared that official support such as subsidies would be focused on farmers' organisations rather than on individual farm households. In order to make use of the potential of organisation and follow the government's policies, PYO associations were established as new forms of PYO organisation at county and provincial level. Consequently, farmers have been able to play a more active role in developing PYO enterprise. The emergence and development of PYO associations is attributed to clear rules for members, better communication with government, expanded social networks, and a legitimate status and active role.

Conclusions: Rural Tourism and the Sustainability of PYO Farms

'Tourism is widely regarded as a tool in rural development' (Hall & Jenkins, 1998: 28). Agriculture is the main economic activity in many rural areas. All the elements in agriculture can be utilised as tourism resources: agricultural tourism is often considered as a form of rural development intervention. The emergence of agricultural tourism in Taiwan has a close relationship with agricultural development. Although agriculture has contributed considerably to the national economy, there have been different forms of agricultural tourism (e.g. PYO farms) implemented to tackle the challenges such as falling farming incomes and increased competition from the international market.

Reviewing the development of PYO farms, it is possible to identify a number of lessons that may be learnt from the Taiwanese experience. It is important for farmers to cooperate so as to enhance their cohesion and increase their competitiveness in the market. Therefore, farmers' organisations play a key role in the development of PYO enterprise. The attempt by government to improve farmers' livelihoods by creating farmers' organisations based on product cooperation failed because the PYO farm was actually run as an individual family enterprise. Although farmers were combined in the same PYO team according to government criteria, they often did this just for the purpose of obtaining subsidies. However, even the distribution of subsidy was not undertaken on an equal basis because of the lack of clear rules among members. On the other hand, the establishment and operation of PYO associations by farmers themselves demonstrates that institutions are an important basis for farmers' cooperation. Farmers prefer a transparent system with rules that can ensure their equal opportunities in decision making, and that clearly regulate rights and responsibilities.

Such PYO enterprises are new to farmers who are used to agricultural production. It has been found that new businesses may affect farmers' livelihoods in a number of ways. It is important to establish channels of communication so that farmers can reflect their problems to the government and the government can respond to farmers' needs and help to mitigate the negative impacts. With the established institutions (i.e. PYO associations), farmers have an alternative communication channel with the government. This will ensure the needs of farmers will be recognised in policy formulation.

Moreover, the evidence also demonstrates that farmers have the ability to manage many aspects of development interventions. In the past, the government was responsible for the marketing of PYO enterprises. Through the establishment of PYO associations, farmers are enthusiastic in forward planning, can participate in policy-making, and play an active role in the process of livelihood diversification.

Built on the above findings, a number of recommendations to various stakeholders are offered that relate to the policy and practice of support- ing the sustainability of PYO farm tourism. First, the government should recognise that PYO associations are the appropriate form of organisation for farmers to work together. Such organisations are created by farmers themselves and based on clear institutional arrangements, rather than imposed by government policies. Secondly, government should help farmers to enhance the functions of such organisations by supervising their operation according to law, maintaining communication channels with farmers and increasing their participation in policy-making and implementation. Thirdly, it is necessary for government to adopt a more holistic perspective and framework, such as the sustainable livelihoods framework, to look at the development of agricultural tourism, as the new farm enterprise or diversification. In this way, relevant management issues, including those beyond the narrow confines of economic benefit, can be explored and seen more widely and clearly.

As the cooperation of small farmers is important for developing PYO businesses, farmers should support the development of PYO associations and actively participate in their operation. Most obviously, PYO associations may help the government to implement aspects of related programmes (e.g. infrastructure construction, establishment of accredita- tion or certification scheme), although such collaboration needs to be better structured, and to help farmers strengthen their ability to undertake livelihood diversification (e.g. through access and the provision of train- ing courses). In addition, PYO associations should act as a communication channel between farmers and the government, participating in the shaping of policies, and reflecting farmers' needs at different stages of development. Furthermore, PYO associations should promote mutually beneficial cooperation between PYO farms, and act as representatives of farmers to promote the marketing of PYO enterprise in order to pursue a viable livelihood.

References

Ashley, C. and Carney, D. (1999) *Sustainable Livelihoods: Lessons from Early Experience.* London: Department for International Development (DfID).

Ateljevic, I. and Doorne, S. (2000) 'Stay within the fence': life style entre-preneurship in tourism. *Journal of Sustainable Tourism* 8 (5), 378–92.

Bramwell, B. and Lane, B. (2000) Collaboration and partnerships in tourism planning. In B. Bramwell and B. Lane (eds) *Tourism Collaboration and Partnerships: Politics, Practice and Sustainability* (pp. 1–18). Clevedon: Channel View Publications.

Chambers, R. (1987) *Sustainable Livelihoods, Environment and Development: Putting Poor Rural People First.* Brighton: Institute of Development Studies (IDS), University of Sussex, IDS Discussion Paper 240.

Chambers, R. and Conway, G.R. (1992) *Sustainable Rural Livelihoods: Practical Concepts for the 21st Century.* Brighton: Institute of Development Studies (IDS), University of Sussex, IDS Document Paper 296.

Chen, C.M. (1989) Developing recreational use of agricultural land: experiences and direction. In National Taiwan University (ed.) *The Proceedings of Conference on Developing Agricultural Tourism* (pp. 85–89). Taipei: NTU (in Chinese).

Chen, W.T. (1996) Joining WTO and adjustment of food policies. *Journal of Scientific Agriculture* 44 (7–8), 161–72 (in Chinese).

Clarke, J. (1999) Marketing structures for farm tourism: beyond the individual provider of rural tourism. *Journal of Sustainable Tourism* 7(1), 26–47.

COA (Council of Agriculture) (1999) *Basic Agricultural Statistics.* Taipei: COA.

de Kadt, E. (1979) *Tourism: Passport to Development? Perspectives on the Social and Cultural Effects of Tourism in Developing Countries.* London: Oxford University Press.

DfID (Department for International Development) (1999) *Sustainable Livelihoods Guidance Sheets.* London: DfID.

Doorn, A., Gerrits, L., Jalloh, A., Keijzer, B., Keijzer, H., Kruska, A. and Schattevoet, A. (1998) *'Pick-Your-Own' Farmers and Clients: Are They Aware of Each Other?* Reading: Agricultural Extension and Rural Development Department, University of Reading.

Ellis, F. (2000) *Rural Livelihoods and Diversity in Developing Countries.* Oxford: Oxford University Press.

Getz, D. and Carlsen, J. (2000) Characteristics and goals of family and owner-operated businesses in the rural tourism and hospitality sectors. *Tourism Management* 21, 547–60.

Gladstone, J. and Morris, A. (1998) The role of farm tourism in the regeneration of rural Scotland. In D. Hall and L. O'Hanlon (eds) *Rural Tourism Management: Sustainable Options* (pp. 207–21). Auchincruive: The Scottish Agricultural College.

Glasson, J., Godfrey, K. and Goodey, B. (1995) *Towards Visitor Impact Management: Visitor Impacts, Carrying Capacity and Management Responses in Europe's Historic Towns and Cities.* Aldershot: Avebury.

Goodall, B. (1987) *Dictionary of Human Geography.* London: Penguin Books.

Hall, C.M. and Jenkins, J.M. (1998) The policy dimensions of rural tourism and recreation. In R. Butler, C.M. Hall and J.M. Jenkins (eds) *Tourism and Recreation in Rural Areas* (pp. 28–42). Chichester: John Wiley & Sons.

Hall, D. (2000a) Tourism as sustainable development? The Albanian experience of 'transition'. *International Journal of Tourism Research* 2 (1), 31–46.

Hall, D. (2000b) Identity, community and sustainability: prospects for rural tourism in Albania. In G. Richards and D. Hall (eds) *Tourism and Sustainable Community Development* (pp. 48–60). London and New York: Routledge.

Hall, M. (2000) Rethinking collaboration and partnership: a public policy perspective. In B. Bramwell and B. Lane (eds) *Tourism Collaboration and Partnerships: Politics, Practice and Sustainability* (pp. 143–56). Clevedon: Channel View Publications.

Hall, M. and Rusher, K. (2002) A risky business? Entrepreneurial and lifestyle dimensions of the homestay and bed and breakfast accommodation sector in New Zealand. In E. Arola, J. Karkkainnen and M.-L. Siitari (eds) *Tourism and Well-Being. The 2nd Tourism Industry and Education Symposium, May 16–18, 2002* (pp. 197–210). Jyväskylä: Jyväskylä Polytechnic.

Healy, R.G. (1994) 'Tourist merchandise' as a means of generating local benefits from ecotourism. *Journal of Sustainable Tourism* 2 (3), 137–51.

Hsiau, S.Y. (1984) *Study on the Development and Problems of Pick-Your-Own Farms in Central and Northern Taiwan.* Unpublished MSc Dissertation, Department of Horticulture, National Taiwan University (in Chinese).

Huang, T.P. (1986) The current situation and future development of pick-your-own (PYO) farms. *Journal of Training and Development* 3 (4), 42–47 (in Chinese).

Iwai, Y. and Taguchi, K. (1998) Rural tourism in Japan: a case study from Hokkaido farm-inns. In D. Hall and L. O'Hanlon (eds) *Rural Tourism Management: Sustainable Options* (pp. 277–85). Auchincruive: The Scottish Agricultural College.

Jeng, H.Y. (1992) *Contributions of Agricultural Tourism to Farmers' Income and Domestic Tourism.* Taichung, Taiwan: NCHU (in Chinese).

Komppula, R. (2002) Firm growth or entrepreneurs' well-being? Aspects on small firm growth in tourism industry. In E. Arola, J. Karkkainnen and M.-L. Siitari (eds) *Tourism and Well-being. The 2nd Tourism Industry and Education Symposium, May 16–18, 2002* (pp. 64–73). Jyväskylä: Jyväskylä Polytechnic.

Lu, W.P. (1981) *Study on the Possibility of Agricultural Tourism Development: A Case Study of Strawberry Pick-Your-Own Farms in Dahu Village,*

Miauli County. Unpublished MSc Dissertation, Department of Land Management, National Chengchi University, Taipei, Taiwan (in Chinese).

Ministry of Transportation and Communication (MOTC) (1999) *Study on the Effects of Less Working Days on Domestic Tourism Activities*. Taipei: Statistics Bureau, MOTC (in Chinese).

Murphy, P.E. (1985) *Tourism: A Community Approach*. London: Methuen.

National Statistics Bureau (2000) *Statistics of Social Development in R.O.C.* Taipei: National Statistics Bureau. On WWW at http://www.stat.gov.tw. Accessed 15.03.01.

Oppermann, M. (1995) Holidays on the farm: A case study of German hosts and guests. *Journal of Travel Research* 34 (1), 63–67.

Pearce, D. (1989) *Tourist Development* (2nd edn). Harlow: Longman.

Pearce, D. (1999) Introduction: issues and approaches. In D. Pearce and R. Butler (eds) *Contemporary Issues of Tourism Development* (pp. 1–12). London: Routledge.

Richards, G. and Hall, D. (2000) The community: a sustainable concept in tourism development? In G. Richards and D. Hall (eds) *Tourism and Sustainable Community Development* (pp. 1–14). London and New York: Routledge.

Rilla, E. (2000) *Unique Niches: Agritourism in Britain and New England*. Davis: Small Farm Center, University of California at Davis. On WWW at http://www.sfc.ucdavis.edu/agritourism. Accessed 31.08.02.

Shaw, G. and Williams, A.M. (1990) Tourism, economic development and the role of entrepreneurial activity. In C.P. Cooper (ed.) *Progress in Tourism, Recreation and Hospitality Management* (pp. 67–81). London: Belhaven Press.

Shaw, G. and Williams, A. M. (1994) *Critical Issues in Tourism: A Geographical Perspective*. Oxford: Blackwell.

Taichung County Government (1985) *Introduction of Pick-Your-Own Farms in Taichung County*. Taichung, Taiwan: Taichung County Government (in Chinese).

Telfer, D.J. (2000) Agritourism – a path to community development? The case of Bangunkerto, Indonesia. In G. Richards and D. Hall (eds) *Tourism and Sustainable Community Development* (pp. 242–57). London and New York: Routledge.

Tourism Bureau (2000) *Travel Agents in Taiwan Areas* (in Chinese). On WWW at http://www.motc.gov.tw/service/year-c/ycmain. Accessed 07.04.01.

TPDAF (Taiwan Provincial Department of Agriculture and Forestry) (1997) *The Planning and Establishing Principles for Pick-Your-Own (PYO) Farms, Official Document Issued by TPDAF on 1st November 1997*. Nantou, Taiwan: TPDAF (in Chinese).

Tremblay, P. (2000) An evolutionary interpretation of the role of collaborative partnerships. In B. Bramwell and B. Lane (eds) *Tourism*

Collaboration and Partnerships (pp. 314–31). Clevedon: Channel View Publications.

Tsai, H.J. (1986) Evaluation of Pick-Your-Own Farm Development in Taipei City. *Research Report of City Administration* No. 147. Taipei, Taiwan: Taipei City Government (in Chinese).

Yu, Y.S. (1989) Future development of agricultural tourism. In COA (ed.) *The Proceedings of Conference on Developing Agricultural Tourism* (pp. 3–7). Taipei: COA (in Chinese).

Part 4

Quality Sustainable Business

Chapter 13

Quality as a Key Driver in Sustainable Rural Tourism Businesses

RAY YOUELL and ROZ WORNELL

Introduction

Although there is much debate about the precise meaning of 'quality' in the context of sustainable rural tourism, there is general agreement among its key stakeholders that delivering quality is a key requirement for achieving success in rural tourism businesses. However, the establishment of a practical methodology for increased and sustainable quality tourism product 'on the ground' is something that has not been easily, or consistently, achieved across tourism destinations to date. This apparent inability to satisfy the needs of an increasingly demanding tourism market is perhaps not wholly the fault of tourism businesses and professionals. As expounded by Lane and cited in Jurowski (2002), the underlying difficulty of transferring the theory of sustainable, quality tourism development into reality is that of closing the very real gap that exists between the theoretical concepts of academic practitioners and the role of business practitioners.

This chapter argues that this gap can be bridged, in part, by the adoption of Integrated Quality Management (IQM) principles in rural tourism development at both the micro (enterprise and community) and macro (national) level. Further, it is advanced that individual rural tourism businesses are most likely to prosper if they are within a destination that adopts IQM, rather than working in isolation. The concept of IQM, initially introduced in the late 1990s by the European Commission (1999a, 1999b, 1999c), is an extension of the theory and principles of the Total Quality Management (TQM) industry tool, focusing on a common sense, integrated approach to product quality, delivery and consumption. It is suggested that the transference of the academic theory of IQM into tourism development within rural destinations can have a profound effect upon the ways in which tourism businesses and tourists perceive and act upon issues of sustainability in tourism terms; without attention to integrating quality into all aspects of planning, managing and evaluating tourism products, the visitors' experience is unlikely to be optimised (Youell, 2003).

Concentrating specifically on the issues surrounding sustainable rural tourism at enterprise, community and state level, this research discusses the introduction and implementation of IQM principles within three geographic areas of West Wales over a period of one year, using an analysis of visitor satisfaction data to measure IQM effectiveness.

The Reality of Sustainable Tourism

> ... [tourism] is recognised, perhaps more than any other area of human activity, as having significant social and cultural impacts additional to the economic and physical ones. (Leslie, 1999: 176)

The concepts of sustainable tourism have their origins in the 1970s, where they arose as an academic reaction to criticisms of the seemingly unchecked spread of 'mass' European tourism. However, despite concerns over the growth of unprincipled tourism development, the aforementioned gap between tourism theorist and practitioner has meant that sustainability issues have been slow to appear on the agenda of the tourism industry in general. This is perhaps due, in part, to the fact that there exists no universally accepted definition of sustainable tourism on which practitioners can base their development criteria or evaluate their performance. Indeed, as Aronsson (2000: 15) determines, the very term 'sustainable development' is relative; there *is* no absolute sustainable development, but rather it should be accepted as a *process* through which that which is being developed becomes more sustainable than that which is current. The difficulties surrounding a definitive description of sustainable development are due to its multidimensional nature, encompassing as it does community, environment, economy and culture (for definitions, see English Tourism Council, 2001: 37). Adding to the paradoxes surrounding the actual definitions of 'sustainability' is the fact that the subjectivity of those actors engaging in tourism development will of necessity influence the different emphases placed on aspects of sustainability at any given point in time.

Despite being subject to a multitude of definitions, the wider mass of literature concerning sustainability concentrates, in the main, as Garrod and Fyall (1998: 202) rightly state, on the use, or rather misuse, of natural resources. In addition to this focus on the natural environment, we would argue, in agreement with Robinson (1999), that in tourism terms, the focus of the sustainability debate has tended to lie in the direction of improving the management and regulation of the interface between the tourist and the destination in terms of both the use of resources and the physical enhancement of the destination for the consumer. Indeed, like many other industries, tourism has a tendency to base its actions on relatively short-term economic thinking. However, these tendencies result in 'sustainable' tourism being interpreted in a narrow sense, that is:

> In the case of the tourism industry, sustainable development has a fairly specific meaning – the industry's challenge is to develop tourism's capacity and the quality of its products without adversely affecting the physical and human environment ... (Hunter & Green, 1995: 70)

This understanding that sustainable tourism is solely related to the functionality of the environment and to the long-term viability of tourism businesses and the tourism economy, places the working definition of 'sustainability' close to Turner's (1992) identification of product-centric 'weak sustainability'. That is, a position in which the thrust of tourism initiatives is undertaken within a top–down, state-led approach relating to the refocusing of tourism-related products to appeal to the 'green' consumer, and the promotion of codes of practice relating to energy and resource efficiency, coupled to the notion that the environment is a substitutable capital.

An approach such as this is one that requires tourism to exist in isolation from the everyday rather than as a phenomenon that exists in a social and cultural context. Indeed, as Potts and Harrill (1998) assert, sustainable tourism development should be approached as both a social and political issue very much grounded within a community. Nonetheless, despite this acceptance in theoretical terms that sustainable tourism initiatives are those that draw their strengths from, and show respect for, distinctive community heritage, culture, sociality *and* the environment and tourism product, in practice tourism policies emanating from the dominant centralised state bodies are largely inadequate in addressing the varying socio-cultural values at community level. Indeed, the World Commission on Culture and Development (1995) sees the state policies of economic growth and environmental protection as politically safe, whereas the cultural and social dimensions of tourism policy at state level are seen as inevitably controversial, being as they are a top–down imposition rather than rooted *in* the communities they affect. It is because of this economically focused, centralised state stand, that sustainable tourism is often criticised for implying a weak and parochial approach with an emphasis firmly on business viability (e.g. Hunter, 1997; Wall, 1997).

For those involved in rural tourism management and development, the issues surrounding sustainability are perhaps more visible than most. The impact of tourism development on often fragile rural communities, is not one that is limited to the natural environment. Serious debates surrounding sustainable tourism, rural or otherwise, should recognise that within each instance of tourism, or tourists, interfacing with the natural environment of a destination, a cultural, social, linguistic and economic environment is also impacted upon. Krippendorf (1989), one of the original proponents of sustainable tourism theory, puts forward the notion that tourism gradually destroys, to a lesser or greater degree, all it touches, including the economy, environment, culture and community of a destination. However, if tourism is considered from a truly sustainable standpoint, that is to say, a standpoint that *encompasses* culture, language, economy and community, then the issue for state authorities is how to turn around the current use of destinations and communities to create sustainable tourism destinations, to the use of tourism in order to support, protect and help to sustain communities.

Sharpley's (2000) argument that true sustainable development must take place simultaneously on a global, mass-market scale, addressing issues of power, inequality, marginalisation and globalisation is one that impacts on the role of local authorities involved in tourism development. Inevitably, local development issues and priorities are influenced by both the state at the local or regional level, and international forces that remain outside the control of local or community level actors. Furthering this argument, Potts and Harrill (1998) suggest that unless international and national forces can agree upon, and adhere to, sustainable 'life-styles', sustainable tourism development will remain a local, ultimately non-sustainable phenomenon.

Nonetheless, despite a recent upsurge in the range and depth of sustainable development and sustainable tourism strategies emitting from national and international state, and other, bodies (e.g. Department for Culture, Media & Sport, 1999; English Tourism Council, 1992, 2001; Tourism Concern, 1996; World Sustainable Tourism Conference, 1995), which have the capacity to impact directly on local and regional state governed tourism strategy development, a *simultaneous* adoption of sustainable initiatives has not been forthcoming. Although theoretically desirable, the idea of a simultaneous acceptance and implementation of sustainable tourism initiatives on a global, or even national level, is implausible. Taking Britain as an example, the differing levels of tourism activity, strategy and priorities that exist at local, regional and national state level within the separate countries of England, Scotland, Wales and Northern Ireland reveal the inadequacies of imposing a pan-Britain sustainable tourism ideal.

It is essential not to see tourism as an isolated phenomenon, but to place it in the social context within which it is enacted, and it is because of this that sustainable tourism development must be owned and managed by community-led initiatives that are able to link together to form a wider sustainable tourism network. As Leslie (1999) asserts, for harmony to exist between the visitor, the destination and the host it is necessary for communities to be involved at the planning, development and management stages of any development or initiative. In adhering to this necessary consultative and collaborative approach, there follows an inevitable shift of power from centralised state authorities, be they local, regional or national, to the empowerment of community-level discourse and decision making that could lead to a truly sustainable approach to tourism development.

A Shift of Power: Rural Community Participation

On the surface, the definition of 'rural tourism' may well be accepted as visits to rural areas. However, as Lane (1993) explains, definitional problems surround the very nature of rural areas themselves, as their functions change within the global economy. In addition, rural tourism is multifaceted, including everything from nature-based activities, sports and activity holidays to 'ecotourism' and cultural tourism. The very nature, and more often than not the very attraction of rural tourism destinations is that the sector is extremely fragmented and dominated by small, generally family-run, enterprises. As Ioannides (2001) remarks, as far as tourism development, sustainability and quality issues are concerned, this often results in a short-term perspective caused by the shifting nature of tourism operators and the resultant shift in the nature of community value systems. In addition, rural communities in particular increasingly focus on tourism as a means of economic growth in response to failure in attracting new industry and as a result of the decline of resource-based industries (Reid *et al.*, 2000). It is this diversity of socio-cultural ideals inherent in any community that makes an *integrated* approach to tourism development so important.

Community-based sustainable tourism development is in itself paradoxical. Communities are not homogenous entities and neither are they necessarily geographically contained. They may be communities of interest, politics, geography, culture and so forth. This diversity of the very nature of communities leads us to argue, alongside Hunter (1997), that to be effective, sustainable tourism has to be understood as an adaptive concept in as much as it can take varying forms in different places. In essence, in order to succeed, sustainable tourism development needs to be defined within the community itself in relation to the internally perceived needs of that community and the needs of the tourist to that community.

Hunter further argues (1997: 859–63) that the process of sustainable tourism could be visualised as occurring along a continuum. At one end of the continuum would exist those communities with a 'tourism imperative', or an agreement that some community resources may be sacrificed in order to generate tourism income, while at the other end would exist those communities actively discouraging tourism in order to preserve the environment, culture and/or sociality. In agreeing with Hunter's theories, however, we would argue that in order to be successful, each stage of community planning and development of sustainable tourism initiatives needs to be carried out in conjunction with the support and input of both local and regional state bodies and interest groups, without whom the degree of integrated cooperation, be it financial, managerial or otherwise, may well be limited.

However, integrated or otherwise, sustainable tourism is not a short cut to economic prosperity and the usual quest for the maximisation of tourist numbers should give way to the aim of maximising tourist expenditure. It is this search for expenditure maximisation that leads both theorists and policy-makers towards developing tourism quality initiatives aimed at increasing the experiential value of the visit for both guest and host. This context of developing quality tourism destinations and enterprises in a sustainable and integrated manner has led to the development of IQM as a potential means of bridging the gap between theory and practice in sustainable tourism.

An integrated Approach to Quality Management

All operators within the tourism industry are aware that they operate in an increasingly competitive marketplace, and therefore, as Go and Govers (2000) explain, tourism destinations are increasingly reliant on the provision of quality services, products and experiences. Consequently, the measurement of customer perceptions of quality have become ever more important to state tourism policy-makers, and have resulted, in most instances, in an emphasis being placed on the introduction and take up by tourism businesses of nationally recognised quality accreditation schemes. As a result, the number of accredited tourism businesses in a destination is often the only measurable indication of quality provision.

Integrated quality management (IQM), however, is not only concerned with the tangible aspects of quality provision. The European Commission defines IQM as:

> ... an approach to managing a tourism destination which focuses on an ongoing process of improving visitor satisfaction, while seeking to improve the local economy, the environment and the quality of life of the local community. (European Commission, 1999b: 11)

It is this definition that has been the underlying principle of this research, and has been accepted by both local and regional state tourism authorities in the research area as a means of increasing competitiveness and quality within tourism businesses and destinations, while simultaneously addressing local needs. As such, IQM can be understood as a quest for both internal and external quality within a destination, where the internal quality can be defined as the quality and value visitors experience from initial information prior to departure through to 'after sales service', and where external quality can be understood as the development of a sustainable form of tourism through a rational use of services, environment, heritage and culture. It is this need to develop and manage both the internal and external quality of destinations that lies at the heart of IQM policies, whose key elements focus on:

- improving the quality of provision for visitors, thereby satisfying their needs and exceeding expectations, encouraging maximum spend, repeat visits and recommendations; and
- the involvement of local communities and tourism enterprises in the planning, development and management of the destination.

The principles of IQM take into account the whole of a destination's tourism system (see Figure 13.1). It is an initiative that relies heavily on community involvement and participation, from both tourism-receptive and tourism-hostile perspectives, and allows a form of integrated dialogue to develop among visitors, tourism operators, interest groups and other stakeholders, which in turn drives sustainable development initiatives.

The introduction of an IQM approach to sustainable tourism development will, in theory, help to close the gaps between quality provision and expectations/perceptions of quality for both the provider and the visitor (see Figure 13.2) through a range of actions, including:

- an integrated, partnership approach;
- ongoing monitoring and evaluation of customer satisfaction;
- ongoing involvement from both community and tourism stakeholders;
- market realism;
- customer orientation;
- accurate communication both internally and externally;
- improved marketing and branding opportunities; and
- attention to detail.

However, despite the rhetoric of sustainable tourism policies, they remain as policy documents that often have no clear methodology for implementation. This research shows that the introduction of IQM principles at both a micro (enterprise and community) and a macro (state authority) level can beneficially influence the ways in which sustainable, quality, tourism initiatives are developed and implemented.

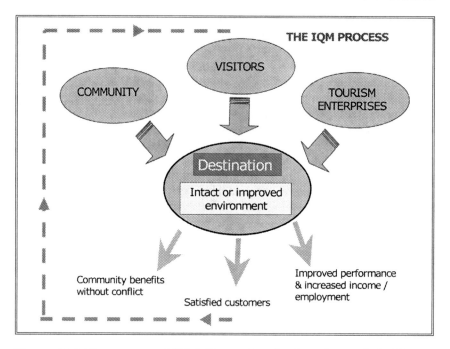

Figure 13.1 The process of IQM, illustrating the three key stakeholders – community, visitors, and tourism enterprises – and the beneficial outcomes of the process – community benefits without conflict, satisfied customers, improved performance, and increased income/employment (*Source*: European Commission (1999b))

Tourism in Ceredigion

The county of Ceredigion is a rural tourism destination in the west of Wales, with a coastline fronting Cardigan Bay and a spine comprised of the Cambrian Mountains and the Teifi Valley. With a population of approximately 70,000, the principal industries are agriculture and tourism, the latter accounting for 25% of total employment in the county. In 2000, tourism spend in Ceredigion amounted to approximately £117 million, of which 84% was contributed by holiday visitors and the remainder by business or other visitors. Some 5568 actual jobs, or 4054 full-time equivalent (FTE) jobs are supported either directly or indirectly through tourism, where the total workforce in the county is approximately 22,000 (Geoff Broom Associates, 2003: 40).

Although Ceredigion, with its coastline and rural hinterland, offers the visitor an attractive holiday destination, it suffers, like many other

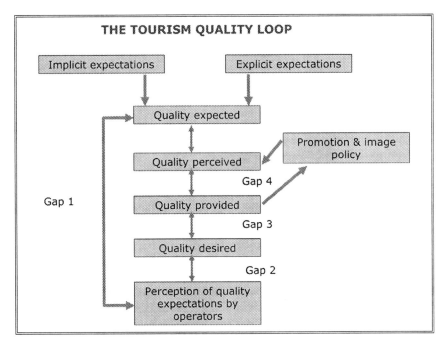

THE TOURISM QUALITY LOOP

Figure 13.2 Illustrating the dynamic and symbiotic relationship between provider and visitor, and the perceived, and often very real, gaps between implicit and explicit expectations of quality provision in tourism destinations (*Source*: European Commission (1999c))

geographically marginal regions, from a number of problems in terms of tourism development:

- Tourist activity remains highly seasonal, with 49% of activity in June, July and August (Geoff Broom Associates, 2003: 34).
- Caravan and camping accommodation make up 79% of the total accommodation stock, at the expense of high-quality serviced accommodation. Within this 79%, 80% of static caravans are privately owned, limiting the number available for letting purposes (Ceredigion County Council, personal communication).
- Access points to the county remain limited, and within certain parts of the area tourism infrastructure is underdeveloped.

As with all unitary authorities within Wales, the county council is under no statutory obligation to deliver a tourism service. On a national basis, Ceredigion is situated within the recently established Wales Tourist Board (WTB) designated Tourism Partnership – Mid Wales region, and as such works towards the targets and goals set out in the tourism strategy for mid Wales, *Mid Wales – Naturally Different* (Mid Wales Partnership, 1999). Although currently under review, this strategy sets out in no uncertain terms the need for Ceredigion to both increase its market share of emerging tourist segments and to halt the decline in traditional markets, recognising (Mid Wales Partnership, 1999):

- UK long holidays – the study area has been losing modest levels of revenue market share;
- UK short breaks – the study area has been losing revenue market share over recent years; and
- overseas visitors – the study area has been losing revenue market share.

The recognised need for Ceredigion to gain market share in all UK visitor markets, except that of 'main holiday', is illustrated by the targets to which tourism managers in the county are working (Table 13.1).

Ceredigion is an extremely rural area where the largest town (Aberystwyth) contains less than 15,000 residents, the majority of the county's inhabitants being dispersed over more than 150 small towns, villages and rural settlements. Community regeneration, combating the effects of continued decline in the agricultural sector and subsequent out-migration are very real issues within Ceredigion. The challenge, however, of helping to create, or enhance, sustainable communities through the use of tourism is one that has been embraced by state tourism managers within the county.

Already a European Objective 1 area, in 2001 Ceredigion was designated a regional Tourism Growth Area (TGA) by the Wales Tourist Board, a designation that brings with it potential grant aid of £1 mn (c. €1.5 mn) over five years to be used in match funding against private sector capital investment in tourism. In addition, Ceredigion commissioned a five-year implementation plan for the development of tourism in a sustainable manner across the county (Institute of Rural Studies, 2002), which carries at its heart a commitment to the introduction of and adherence to the principles of IQM.

The SWOT analysis contained within the implementation plan saw Ceredigion tourism managers identifying as a very real threat:

A general danger of the development of tourism being perceived by the community at large as an end in itself – to the benefit of the visitor – rather than as a means to an end, that of creating additional wealth and employment for residents of Ceredigion. (Institute of Rural Studies, 2002: 37)

Despite this perception, tourism initiatives and development in Ceredigion, in terms of community collaboration, participation and integration, are already far ahead of many of their competitors. In line with Local

Table 13.1 Ceredigion tourism growth targets

Mid Wales tourism strategic targets – implications for Ceredigion			
	1995–1997 average Ceredigion	*2003 Ceredigion targets*	*Difference*
Long holiday– main			
• Earnings	£43.13 mn	£39.68 mn	−£3.45 mn
• Nights	1.52 mn	1.44 mn	−80,000
• Trips	0.21 mn	0.22 mn	+10,000
Additional holidays			
• Earnings	£11.95 mn	£15.36 mn	+£3.41 mn
• Nights	0.57 mn	0.69 mn	+120,000
• Trips	0.09 mn	0.11 mn	+20,000
Short breaks			
• Earnings	£11.54 mn	£14.87 mn	+£9.3 mn
• Nights	0.37 mn	0.48 mn	+110,000
• Trips	0.17 mn	0.23 mn	+60,000
Visiting friends/relations			
• Earnings	£1.61	£2.50	+£0.89 mn
• Nights	0.15 mn	0.24 mn	+90,000
• Trips	0.05 mn	0.08 mn	+30,000
Business visits			
• Earnings	£3.56	£4.85	+£1.29 mn
• Nights	0.07 mn	0.11 mn	+40,000
• Trips	0.03 mn	0.04 mn	+10,000
UK visitors – total			
• Earnings	£72.87	£76.74	+£3.87 mn
• Nights	2.71 mn	3.11 mn	+400,000
• Trips	0.56 mn	0.70 mn	+140,000
Overseas tourists			
• Earnings	£9.22 mn	£12.68 mn	+£3.46 mn
• Nights	0.25 mn	0.30 mn	+50,000
• Trips	0.04 mn	0.05 mn	+10,000

Source: Institute of Rural Studies (2002: 18)

Agenda 21 and the Ceredigion Local Action Plan (LAP) (Ceredigion County Council, 2000), tourism managers within the county have initiated a Ceredigion Tourism Working Group (CerTWG) (Ceredigion County Council, 2001), with representation from all community groups in the county, tourism stakeholders and community development groups. They have adopted as their priority Action 42 of the national tourism strategy:

> [to] encourage the development of community tourism partnerships and integrated action plans which seek to balance the needs of residents and tourists through careful quality control, management and planning. (Wales Tourist Board, 2000: 82)

CerTWG is now the driving force behind strategic tourism policy and development issues within the county, and serves to illustrate that community discourse and participation within the decision-making process of tourism, while recognising the inherent difficulties surrounding *true* community representation, is nonetheless a very large step towards achieving a tourism business environment that is more sustainable than that which was current. Ceredigion has not only succeeded in involving local communities in the decision-making process, but has also been able to establish an integrated vision for the whole county, thereby overcoming what Ioannides (1995: 583) sees as two of the major obstacles towards realising sustainable development.

Integrated Quality Management in Practice

Despite the general move towards community collaboration within Ceredigion, there still remains the need to strengthen the processes of integration and participation. It was recognised at the outset of this research that the common sense principles of IQM already exist to varying degrees in many tourism destinations and individual businesses. However, it is also recognised that a large number of elements have an impact upon the tourist's perceptions of, and expectations from, a destination and the subsequent level of satisfaction derived. The research aimed towards establishing whether the introduction of IQM principles in an holistic sense, that is, as a process through which tourism development and business is approached and implemented, is a valid way in which to encourage sustainable, quality, community-led, tourism initiatives.

The basic tenets of the IQM process seek to focus on improving visitor satisfaction, while simultaneously seeking to improve the local economy, environment and the quality of life of the local community. The project set out to achieve these goals through encouraging more local awareness of tourism across local residents and across all sectors, better integration

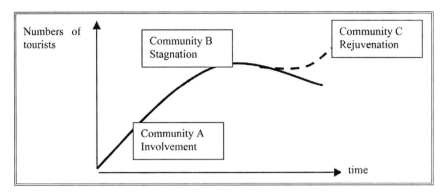

Figure 13.3 IQM Research Project Communities as situated on the destination life-cycle (*Source*: authors' research, after Butler (1980))

between local tourism enterprises, greater involvement for communities in the management and marketing of the destination, creating an improved image of the destination that is not based on false expectations, and encouraging a greater awareness of the impacts of tourism.

The research concentrates on three community development areas within Ceredigion, identified through an open bidding process. Each area is distinct in the way that tourism has evolved and each has, in the past, attracted different market segments and has had differing levels of tourist activity. At the beginning of the project each area was identified, using available data, as being situated at differing stages on the 'destination lifecycle', as defined by Butler (1980) (Figure 13.3).

Community A

Established within the last year, the development group within Community A has an identified aim of improving tourist provision and activity in the area, while encouraging the sustainability of local economies and community. The group enjoys representation from all aspects of the communities for whom it advocates, including those who are more tourism hostile than others. As is generally the case with all new 'activist' groupings, Community A is imbued with dynamism and commitment from both the core development group and the community at large. It is too early in the lifespan of the group to establish whether this commitment can be sustained over time.

Strong links have been forged by the group with the County Council, CerTWG, Forest Enterprise (a major employer in the area), the Countryside Council for Wales (CCW) and the Welsh Development Agency (WDA), all of whom are key players in tourism development for the area. Identified as being situated at the 'involvement' stage on the destination life-cycle, Community A has been found to be very receptive to new initiatives and ideas and quick to involve itself in the implementation of IQM processes. The fact that the community development group has been established relatively recently serves in some measure to explain the receptiveness of the community in general to such initiatives as IQM. Nonetheless, there is a wide recognition within the group that working through IQM towards sustainable tourism is not an overnight 'fix', but a dynamic process that must be incorporated into everyday actions.

Finding new methodologies for communicating tourism initiatives and strategic aims to the wider community has been an important goal for Community A. A series of presentations and workshops was organised in order to both discuss and introduce IQM principles and processes and to allow communication channels to be opened between the local state tourism authorities and individuals within Community A. In addition, a vision statement, SWOT analysis and destination tourism strategy have been produced, which complement the Ceredigion TGA strategy, and a series of tourism training programmes organised. An integrated events programme has been developed with the specific aim of extending the season past the shoulder periods and a programme of integrated walking and cycle ways with supporting multilingual literature and marketing is being developed.

A group of business operators, including accommodation, shops and attractions, is working towards a 'green accreditation' scheme, with the aim, not only of improving their environmental practices, but of increasing their market appeal by being so accredited. Increased interpretation of the locality is being introduced for both the visitor and local people alike in the form of local history, culture and environment information, accessible on carefully sited boards, but also available electronically for schools and libraries. A commitment to ongoing monitoring of visitor satisfaction and numbers has been demonstrated in the form of community asset surveys, visitor satisfaction surveys and the collection of visitor statistics. This will prove particularly useful in future years by providing baseline data for monitoring visitor perception and behaviour in conjunction with an expected increase in the provision of a quality tourism product.

Despite the short nature of this research, it is apparent that for Community A, the introduction of IQM into tourism initiatives and development has had beneficial results for the community at large. The process of developing a sustainable tourism destination has begun through the recognition that a product-centric push for quick economic gain does not have long-term viability. Increased communication, monitoring, training opportunities, access to the countryside, access to local knowledge and history has resulted in an increased understanding by all members of the communities within the geographic boundary of Community A of the benefits of developing a destination that can meet and perhaps exceed the expectation of visitors. The challenge now is for Community A to continue to progress along Hunter's (1997) sustainable tourism continuum to the benefit of both hosts and guests alike.

Community B

Although geographically adjoining the southern edge of Community A, tourism in Community B has been developing in a very different manner despite aiming to attract the same target market as its neighbours. Recreational and events-based tourism is a very important aspect of the economy in the area and, situated as it is on the eastern borders of Ceredigion, Community B is in a prime position to capitalise on the local, regional and national focus on walking and cycling holidays.

There has been a long-term development group in Community B, but despite having representation on CerTWG and having strong working links with national bodies such as WDA and CCW, it has had, nonetheless, a very nominal community input into decision-making and development issues. Although local community councils are represented on the Board of the group, and despite their influential status within the community they represent, it remains unclear as to how much influence they are able to bring to bear within the development group on behalf of the communities for whom they are elected to advocate.

In the initial stages of this research, in order to further the understanding of and participation in IQM and sustainable tourism issues, open community workshops and presentations were organised within each area. These proved to be a very successful way of introducing the aims and principles of the project and answering concerns and queries that individuals raised. Consultation exercises were carried out in Communities A and C within the first month of the research, using the development groups as a conduit for wider community communications and participation. It proved difficult in the case of Community B to gain the confidence of the development group executive and thereby gain access to community members, and it was not until the final quarter of the research project that a community consultation exercise was initiated.

As stated previously, communities are by their very nature disparate entities, composed of social, political and cultural values that differ from individual to individual. It had been recognised at the outset of this research that each area would react in different ways to the project, and despite having applied to become a part of the research, the social politics surrounding Community B is perhaps the cause of the active non-participation in the project. Despite having been in existence for approximately 10 years, and having had many successes during this time (a strong events strategy, a strong community regeneration strategy and good working relationships with CCW and WDA), there is no evidence of a truly integrated, inclusive, or sustainable approach to tourism development.

It became apparent within this research that Community B has suffered in recent years from a downturn in traditional tourism markets and a subsequent collapse in tourism trade. This has resulted in a marked suspicion, even distrust, of the perceived hegemony of state tourism authorities at both a local and national level, resulting in a reluctance to participate in state-sanctioned activities, be they marketing, promotion or quality initiatives. This suspicion is due, in part, to a lack of communication in the past by both the development group itself *and* the tourism authorities on a local and regional level, to the tourism businesses and the wider community, concerning changing market trends and tourist expectations. This has resulted in a lack of understanding concerning the decline in tourism numbers and the various policies aimed at addressing this.

Nonetheless, this project has recognised that IQM is not achievable overnight, and despite interest expressed from community members, Community B seems unable to embrace the principles of IQM in any meaningful way. It is certainly not, however, without the means and methods to do so. Indeed, in recent times the communication between tourism stakeholders in the area has greatly improved, and an interest has been expressed in addressing and targeting local and regional tourism objectives within the community as a whole. It remains to be seen, however, whether IQM can become, over time, an integral part in the quest for stability and sustainability in tourism terms within Community B. It would appear that the community as a whole has become more receptive to new initiatives, and has begun to engage in a true community-led approach to communication, discussion and decision making for the area. It is this new approach to development that will enable the process of sustainable tourism initiatives to become embedded in community actions.

Community C

Situated on the coast of Ceredigion and dominated by the caravan and camping sector, Community C has traditionally been a long-stay, family holiday destination. The previously illustrated downturn in these traditional markets has left Community C in a similar position in tourism terms to Community B, including a very marked community and business malaise. However, the development group based in Community C enjoys strong community participation in a variety of project-based enterprises and has strong working links with the county council, WDA and CCW. The introduction of ongoing community participation and consultation exercises has resulted in community members taking ownership of tourism development issues in the area and strong tourism projects aimed at community sustainability are starting to emerge.

The inclusive nature of Community C, with its programme of communication and collaboration, has achieved a surprising turnaround in community attitude in a short space of time. A series of workshops and presentations by tourism policy-makers, as well as the introduction to the community of the IQM project and the principles by which it works, have served as a means of increasing interest and enthusiasm from tourism providers. In addition, a new understanding has been reached concerning new market trends, opportunities available, and the subsequent need for rejuvenation and quality initiatives.

The use of an IQM approach within the area has allowed for an understanding of the nature of tourism and, in particular, sustainable tourism issues to emerge. Community C has developed an approach that not only includes the communities within its own geographical boundary, but provides integration, communication and collaboration with other communities in Ceredigion. This approach has achieved the agreement of an integrated series of themed walks across the area, with associated marketing and branding opportunities and accompanying multilingual literature and interpretation boards. In addition to these physical projects, Community C, in a similar fashion to Community A, has an ongoing programme of monitoring and evaluation of visitor needs, expectations, satisfaction and numbers.

Community cohesion and understanding concerning sustainable tourism issues has been increased and the creation of a quality tourism destination that will meet the expectation of tourists, while not foregoing the needs of residents, is being progressed through applying IQM principles to tourism development and businesses in the area.

Can IQM Assist in Developing Sustainable Rural Tourism Businesses?

Preliminary analysis of the results of Ceredigion visitor satisfaction surveys undertaken in 2002 and 2003 as part of the IQM project reveals significant increases in levels of visitor satisfaction across a range of variables, including satisfaction with service received, quality of accommodation used and quality of attractions visited. Visitors were asked to rate perceived quality on a scale of 1 to 5, with 5 being the highest and 1 the lowest rating (see Figure 13.4).

While it is difficult, and perhaps dangerous, to attribute these increases in visitor satisfaction levels solely to the establishment of IQM principles, there is little doubt that the introduction of IQM can, at the very least, have the result of establishing increased communication and understanding

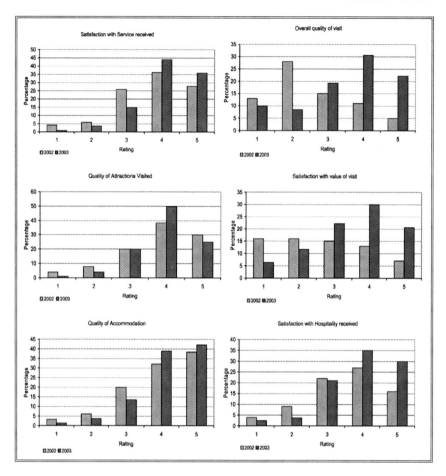

Figure 13.4 Visitor satisfaction levels in Ceredigion 2002–2003 (*Source*: authors' research)

of sustainable, quality, tourism development within rural tourism businesses and destination communities. Future years will reveal whether the research areas have been able to sustain or increase visitor satisfaction levels as a result of incorporating IQM principles into sustainable rural tourism development.

What has become apparent during the course of this research is that adopting IQM principles in rural destinations has provided a welcome *focus* for enterprise and tourism business development. In many areas, applications for Wales Tourist Board capital funding grants have increased significantly. In addition, the collaborative nature of IQM has provided often remote and isolated tourism businesses with a sense of community and willingness to cooperate with other sectors of the rural tourism industry. Even at this early stage of the research process, it is clear that rural tourism businesses are likely to be most effective when operating under the 'umbrella' of an integrated tourism initiative such as IQM, rather than working in isolation, given the benefits of collaborative effort.

Conclusion

It has been argued previously that the creation of sustainable rural tourism destinations from a community-led perspective is very much a dynamic process, and as such it is too soon to say whether the introduction of IQM principles and practice into the three communities discussed will increase the propensity of their becoming sustainable in the long term.

While this research project has only been able to assess a snapshot of the benefits of IQM methodologies, several issues have emerged that inform the introduction and implementation of IQM initiatives in rural tourism destinations. While it is implicit in any community-based project that it is virtually impossible to encompass all players within that community, owing to competing claims and ideologies inherent in any grouping, the three research areas within the project have demonstrated that inclusion of those individuals who wish to participate is vital to a truly integrated approach that addresses community issues and concerns.

Sustainable rural tourism development at community level is a negotiated process and recognition should be given to the resultant relative nature of socially constructed sustainability within a community. Initiating an IQM approach to sustainability allows a form of integrated negotiation to occur between local, regional and national stakeholders that takes into account the socio-political dynamics inherent within any community. Despite this, as Community B illustrates, in the short term IQM in itself may not be enough to overcome any perceived negativity of state tourism policy and its relevance in a local context.

Taken, however, in its true sense of an ongoing, dynamic process, the introduction of IQM into rural tourism destinations should, through an approach that encompasses both vertical and horizontal forms of integration and communication (Grant, 2000: 45), allow a linkage to become established between both local projects and wider sustainable tourism ventures, and simultaneously between state and other stakeholder bodies. Allowing such a linkage to develop in an unhurried, or 'organic' way rather than being perceived as a dictat from state, or other, authority, benefits both community and tourism enterprises as such a linkage is likely to be inclusive and consistent.

Although limited in its scope to three geographical areas within Ceredigion, this project clearly illustrates that the receptiveness to, and uptake of, IQM principles within rural tourism destinations is defined by the position of those destinations upon the 'destination life-cycle'. Indicative findings reveal that Communities A and C, at the involvement and rejuvenation stages, have embraced IQM in all aspects of tourism and community development, albeit at differing speeds. This receptiveness to new initiatives has allowed for a truly inclusive and collaborative environment to prevail and has resulted in both areas moving forward with new marketing initiatives aimed at identified target segments, development aimed at target market needs and improvement in quality provision aimed at meeting visitor expectations. Significantly in these areas, both the tourism community and the wider community are, in the main, now committed to these developments and have been able to ensure that both the visitor and resident will benefit by their introduction into the destination.

Ceredigion tourism managers remain committed to community-led, sustainable tourism initiatives, and by forming an integrated vision for the entire region, in the form of the TGA Implementation Strategy, have removed a major obstacle from the path towards sustainable tourism development in the area. However, it remains to be evaluated over the coming years in Ceredigion whether such a methodology as IQM is able to effectively close, and keep closed, those gaps as illustrated on the tourism quality loop (Figure 13.2). It would seem, nonetheless, that however elusive true sustainable tourism development remains, the introduction of IQM into rural tourism destinations develops a workable community *and* state approach to sustainability issues that is both resident- and visitor-focused, and progresses towards exceeding visitor expectations and the growth of the economic, environmental, cultural and social viability of communities.

References

Aronsson, L. (2000) *The Development of Sustainable Tourism*. London: Continuum.

Butler, R.W. (1980) The concept of a tourist area cycle of evolution: implications for the management of resources. *Canadian Geographer* 24 (1), 5–12.

Ceredigion County Council (2000) *Ceredigion Local Action Plan*. Aberaeron: Ceredigion County Council.

Ceredigion County Council (2001) *CerTWG Action Plan*. Aberaeron: Ceredigion County Council.

Department for Culture, Media and Sport (DCMS) (1999) *Tomorrow's Tourism*. London: DCMS.

English Tourism Council (ETC) (1992) *The Green Light: A Guide to Sustainable Tourism.* London: ETC.

English Tourism Council (ETC) (2001) *Time for Action: A Strategy for Sustainable Tourism in England.* London: ETC.

European Commission (EC) (1999a) *Towards Quality Coastal Tourism: Integrated Quality Management of Coastal Tourism Destinations.* Brussels: European Commission.

European Commission (EC) (1999b) *Towards Quality Rural Tourism: Integrated Quality Management of Rural Tourism Destinations.* Brussels: European Commission.

European Commission (EC) (1999c) *Towards Quality Urban Tourism: Integrated Quality Management of Urban Tourism Destinations.* Brussels: European Commission.

Garrod, B. and Fyall, A. (1998) Beyond the rhetoric of sustainable tourism? *Tourism Management* 19 (3), 199–212.

Geoff Broom Associates (2003) Ceredigion Tourism: Local Area Tourism Model Final Report. Unpublished report, Ceredigion County Council.

Go, F.M. and Govers, R. (2000) Integrated quality management for tourist destinations: a European perspective on achieving competitiveness. *Tourism Management* 21 (1), 79–88.

Grant, M. (2000) PACE: Guiding rural tourism development in a fragile area. In F. Brown and D. Hall (eds) *Tourism in Peripheral Areas* (pp. 39–57). Clevedon: Channel View.

Hunter, C. (1997) Sustainable tourism as an adaptive paradigm. *Annals of Tourism Research* 24 (4), 850–67.

Hunter, C. and Green, H. (1995) *Tourism and the Environment. A Sustainable Relationship?* London: Routledge.

Institute of Rural Studies (2002) *Ceredigion Tourism Growth Area (TGA) Implementation Plan.* Aberystwyth: University of Wales.

Ioannides, D. (1995) A flawed implementation of sustainable tourism: the experience of Akamas, Cyprus. *Tourism Management* 19 (8), 583–92.

Ioannides, D. (2001) Sustainable development and the shifting attitudes of tourism stakeholders: toward a dynamic framework. In S.F. McCool and R.N. Moisey (eds) *Tourism, Recreation and Sustainability* (pp. 55–76). Wallingford: CAB International.

Jurowski, C. (2002) BEST think tanks and the development of curriculum models for teaching sustainability principles. *Journal of Sustainable Tourism* 10 (6), 536–45.

Krippendorf, J. (1989) *The Holiday Makers.* Oxford: Butterworth-Heinemann.

Lane, B. (1993) Sustainable rural tourism strategies: a tool for development and conservation. In B. Bramwell and B. Lane (eds) *Rural Tourism and Sustainable Tourism Development* (pp. 102–11). Galway: University

College Galway, Proceedings of the Second International School on Rural Development, 28 June–9 July.

Leslie, D. (1999) Sustainable tourism – or more a matter of sustainable societies? In M. Foley, D. McGillivray and G. McPherson (eds) *Leisure, Tourism and Environmental Policies* (pp. 173–93). Eastbourne: Leisure Studies Association.

Mid Wales Partnership (1999) *Mid Wales – Naturally Different, a Tourism Strategy for Mid Wales 1999–2008.* Newtown, Powys: Mid Wales Partnership.

Potts, T. and Harrill, R. (1998) Enhancing communities for sustainability: a travel ecology approach. *Tourism Analysis* 3, 133–42.

Reid, D.G., Mair, H. and Taylor, J. (2000) Community participation in rural tourism development. *World Leisure Journal* 42 (2), 20–27.

Robinson, M. (1999) Collaboration and cultural consent: refocusing sustainable tourism. *Journal of Sustainable Tourism* 7 (3/4), 379–97.

Sharpley, R. (2000) Tourism and sustainable development: exploring the theoretical divide. *Journal of Sustainable Tourism* 8 (1), 1–19.

Tourism Concern (1996) *Sustainable Tourism Moving from Theory to Practice: A Report.* London: WWF-UK.

Turner, R.K. (1992) *Speculations of Weak and Strong Sustainability.* London: Centre for Social and Economic Research on the Global Environment (CSERGE).

Wales Tourist Board (2000) *Achieving Our Potential – A Tourism Strategy for Wales.* Cardiff: Wales Tourist Board.

Wall, G. (1997) Sustainable tourism – unsustainable development. In S. Wahab and J. Pigram (eds) *Tourism, Development and Growth: The Challenge of Sustainability* (pp. 33–49). London: Routledge.

World Commission on Culture and Development (1995) *Our Creative Diversity. Report of the World Commission.* Paris: UNESCO.

World Sustainable Tourism Conference (1995) *The Sustainable Tourism Plan of Action.* Lanzarote: World Sustainable Tourism Conference.

Youell, R. (2003) Integrated quality management in rural tourism. In D. Hall, L. Roberts and M. Mitchell (eds) *New Directions in Rural Tourism* (pp. 169–82). Aldershot: Ashgate.

Chapter 14

Rural Tourism Businesses and Environmental Management Systems

DAVID LESLIE

Introduction

The mid- to late-1980s witnessed a significant increase in international attention to issues arising from economic development and environmental degradation. Collective recognition of this was clearly signposted at the United Nation's Stockholm Congress of 1987 and most manifest at The Earth Summit of 1992. Tourism, as one of the most globally manifest sectors of economic activity, and dependent for successful development on the quality of the environment, not surprisingly came under further scrutiny. This led to a host of international initiatives promoting 'best practice', including attention to the use of resources in the delivery of tourism products and services. Thus, the operational practices – the environmental performance and environmental management systems – of tourism businesses became an area of attention. It is this area that is the focus and subject of this chapter.

The environmental performance of tourism businesses is germaine to the development of tourism throughout the globe, and collectively their use of resources is of international significance and impact. However, in order to explore this particular aspect in a meaningful way beyond general theory and practices, and to establish whether the aims of initiatives alluded to above and related developments are evidencing success, it is necessary to investigate the actual businesses. This is the objective of this chapter.

While many examples could be chosen from across the world, it would be invaluable and more informative to identify a suitable locality from which a comprehensive sample of tourism businesses could be obtained. Secondly, it is important to establish that connections such as development and promotion between these initiatives and the businesses involved are in evidence. To progress these aims, the UK was chosen given its manifest support for the outcomes of the Stockholm and Earth Summit Congresses. This led to identifying the Lake District National Park as a particularly suitable locality for scrutiny. The reasons for this are as follows. It is a rural area of international renown. Secondly, as a National Park there is a clearly defined requirement for maintaining the quality of the environment. Thirdly, it is generally considered to be the most popular rural visitor destination in the UK. Finally, it has a history of attention paid to the impacts of tourism development dating back at least to the mid-19th century (see Leslie, 1986).

The attractiveness, and indeed popularity, of rural destinations – the countryside and its environment – is the result of centuries of development. This development has been shaped by prevailing socio-economic factors and the physical geography of the local environment. The key to maintaining rural localities, to conserve rural landscapes – the real raw material of tourism itself – lies in support for those traditional practices, the local economy and community that help shape them. This must encompass effective responses to change and the need to maintain investment. However, no rural destination is safe from rash assault (to paraphrase Wordsworth's sonnet) nor an 'island', immune to the influences of wider economic and societal forces or from global issues such as pollution. In effect, rural destinations are facing the challenge of maintaining, and not just in the short term, '. . . an acceptable standard of living for all people, while conserving or restoring the viability of the natural environment and hence, the very basis of human life' (Welford, 1995: 25). This is a complex challenge involving pressing problems that require major shifts in attitudes on the part of business, consumers and the public sector (DETR, 2000). Therefore there is a need for the adoption of the principles of sustainable development and major objectives of (DETR, 1999: 1):

- social progress, which recognises the needs of everyone;
- effective protection of the environment;
- prudent use of natural resources; and
- maintenance of high and stable levels of economic growth and employment.

The route to sustainability lies in recognising, promoting and developing the linkages of economic, social and environmental objectives in balance. Clearly, the tourism sector is no less susceptible than any other sector of the economy to the impacts of the growing environmental agenda and the need for attention to the environmental performance of the businesses involved. This is especially so in rural areas, where tourism is often seen as essential to their economies (see DCMS, 2002b). In effect, this is to adopt contemporary environmentalism, which, most simply expressed, means 'going green': an approach which reflects much greater awareness of the interconnectedness of the economic, physical and social dimensions of the environment rather than just the physical or natural, for example, pollution and damage. Recognition of this is increasingly evident in the promotion of tourism, a factor that reflects changing public attitudes and the potential to influence their choice of destination on the basis of environmental performance (see Moore *et al.*, 2003). In other words, there is a need for tourism businesses not to be treated solely in terms of their products/services but in the wider context of their external environment; an approach recognised by the EU (EC, 2003). Through the processes involved in the provision of products and services these businesses generate pollution and waste, thereby placing additional burdens on the locality, the infrastructure and wider environment to handle these byproducts. As tourism demand and supply increase so too does the pressure on local resources. If tourism and the locality are to be sustained it is therefore necessary to use resources more efficiently and effectively and reduce wastes, thereby reducing environmental impacts, with the objective of achieving a balance between exploitation and utilisation (Wallis & Woodward, 1997).

This was officially recognised in the UK as a key issue in leisure and tourism in the mid-1990s (DoE, 1996: 6). Essentially, tourism businesses need to operate within the natural capacity of the destination. The environmental performance – the adoption of environmental management systems (EMS) – of tourism businesses therefore is very much a part of today's agenda.

Attention to the environmental impacts of the operations of tourism businesses emerged at the end of the 1980s, primarily catalysed by the Bruntland Report and the advocacy of sustainable development. This was exemplified by a key action point of the UK government's latest tourism strategy, which is described as: '... a blueprint for the sustainable development of tourism to safeguard our countryside, heritage and culture for future generations' (DCMS, 1999: 4) and explicitly encompasses the stated objectives of sustainable development (DCMS, 2000: 50). Significantly, government agencies directly or indirectly involved in tourism have been promoting attention to environmental performance and aspects of EMS since the late 1980s (e.g. Countryside Commission, 1993a; DoE, 1990b; RDC, 1996; RDC *et al.*, 1989). Also, and notably, various professional associations and bodies have been promoting aspects of environmental management practices. Additionally some local authorities have developed award schemes designed to promote such practices. It is these areas that are explored first in this chapter, commencing with an overview of the main UK government initiatives. In total, these policies and initiatives cover all the actions and practices involved in an EMS, the implementation of which could lead to a more balanced and sustainable approach to tourism development within any area. The question thus arises as to whether these businesses have introduced such systems and/or related practices. This is addressed through discussion of key findings from an extensive investigation into the environmental performance of rural tourism businesses.

Overview of the Main Government Initiatives

Closely following the outcomes of the Stockholm Congress was the publication of *Tourism in National Parks: A Guide to Good Practice*, (RDC *et al.*, 1989) coupled with the *Shades of Green* conference in York in 1989. These events heralded the first clear indicators of government attention being paid to the environmental performance of tourism businesses – the 'greening' of tourism. Notably, these two initiatives also demonstrated partnerships and agreements between the key government agencies involved. The *Tourism in National Parks* report established a number of key principles for tourism. In particular, attention was given to the use of local skills and market needs; building linkages within the local community; the encouragement of visitors to contribute to conservation initiatives; and the provision of information to influence visitor behaviour.

In 1990 the Government set up a tourism task force with the remit of identifying ways through which the negative impacts of visitors could be minimised and to produce a *Green Charter* for sensitive locations. The terms of reference for the Task Force are significant, that is 'to draw up guidance on how the tourism industry and other agencies might ensure that their present activities and policies as well as future tourism developments are in harmony with the need to conserve and preserve the environment, and to serve the well being of host communities' (ETB & EDG, 1991: 5). Particularly conspicuous is that 'the environment' was interpreted as being 'the place' (i.e. the destination *per se*), which clearly indicates wider connotations than 'the environment', a term which is often taken as referring to just the physical locality.

The involvement of the community in supporting sustainability was also reinforced in the early 1990s (Countryside Commission, 1993b). One of the key principles established was the recognition that in the long term there is a need now for attention to managing the tourism/ environment interrelationship (Countryside Commission, 1993b). For tourism to be more sustainable necessitates examining tourism supply in terms of three key elements – local economy, local people, and local environment. In other words a balance must be achieved between the three, as recently reaffirmed by the government (DEFRA, 2003a) and seen to be particularly applicable to National Parks (DEFRA, 2003b). A major weakness was the omission of attention to the environmental performance of the enterprises and organisations involved. This was addressed in the subsequent report *The Green Light* (RDC *et al.*, 1991).

In other words, managers should address and take positive action to improve the environmental performance of their businesses. Furthermore, they should also contribute to the conservation and enhancement of their environment, a factor identified by the Countryside Commission (now Countryside Agency) and considered to be one of the critical areas to the future well-being of the countryside (Countryside Commission, 1993a). Subsequent initiatives since the early 1990s contribute further detail and examples of best practice, notably the launch of the *Green Audit Kit* in 1996, 'a do-it-yourself guide (basically an environmental audit) to "greening" tourism businesses' (RDC, 1996: 1), which was revised and relaunched in 2000.

In terms of business generally, the UK government has also been promoting EMS and environmental auditing, which essentially involves the comprehensive evaluation of the environmental performance of an enterprise. This is seen by Goodall (1994: 658) as '... an integral management tool of a tourism firm with a proactive commitment to environmentally responsible tourism'. In essence, an EMS requires a business to ensure: '... their products or services are produced, delivered and disposed of in an environmentally friendly manner, minimising any adverse effects on the environment...' (PRC, 1998: 103). The systems promoted mainly are:

- BS7750 – a formalised method of demonstrating how an enterprise complies with environmental legislation and regulations;
- the Eco-Management and Audit Scheme (EMAS) – a national and international environmental benchmarking system for smaller firms; and
- ISO 14001 Environmental Management System – designed to develop an environmental management quality standard in the work place.

One of the main benefits and perhaps the most appealing aspect of this standard is that it can be promoted to gain a competitive advantage (BSI, 1993). However, these systems are not necessarily appropriate to small/ micro-businesses due to their scope and potential costs, particularly for independent verification.

While there have been other developments in the UK policy arena, they tend to reiterate and consolidate what is already encompassed in the foregoing reports, as evident in the Government's latest tourism policy (DCMS, 1999), which aimed to inform the development of: 'A wise growth strategy for tourism ... which integrates the economic, social and environmental implications of tourism and which spreads the benefits throughout society as widely as possible' (DCMS, 1999: 48). This message was subsequently reinforced by *Time for Action* (ETC, 2001), which reiterated that tourism should be founded on sustainable development and was further supported by other initiatives such as the Countryside Agency's *Eat the View* campaign, which seeks to encourage visitors to consume by preference locally produced food and drink, and the *Sustainable Farming and Food* initiative (DEFRA, 2002), which pays attention to encouraging production for local markets.

A substantive outcome of the 'Earth Summit' was Agenda 21 – a framework of action for the 21st century. This has been recognised and adopted by the UK Government (House of Lords, 1994) and, in the wider context, the EU (EC, 2003). The majority of initiatives and actions required to progress towards sustainable development, manifest in Agenda 21, must take place at the local level, a fact clearly articulated in Chapter 28 of the Agenda, which enlarges on this and calls for each local authority to develop (originally by 1996) a 'Local Agenda 21' plan (LA21). The presence of this is now a performance indicator for local government leisure and cultural services (ILAM, 2000). The importance of these plans to encompass explicitly tourism planning and development is now widely recognised (EC, 2003; ETC, 2001; UNEP, 2003). A key factor of LA21 planning is the explicit criterion of promoting awareness of LA21 to all sectors of the community and seeking their participation in the formulation of such plans (Leslie & Hughes, 1997). This is particularly apposite given that the majority of rural tourism businesses are small/ micro businesses that are owned and managed by local residents. Indeed, it has been argued that if people are not only given guidance on what they should do but are also enabled in practice, then they are more likely to take responsive action (Countryside Commission, 1993b), and therefore influence their business practices.

Additionally, schemes designed to promote EMS have been developed by area tourist organisations and local authorities invariably in liaison with tourism businesses – for example, VisitScotland's Green Business Scheme, the *Little Acorns LA21 Tourism Kit* developed by the New Forest District Council, and Lancashire County Council's *The Green Lantern* (for further discussion see Font & Tribe, 2001; Leslie, 2001). Overarching all such schemes is the publication of extensive and detailed guidance on how to develop tourism in a more sustainable way (ETC & TMI, 2003).

Tourism Sector Based Initiatives

The aim of this section is to highlight key initiatives and schemes. While there are many of these identifiable today (Font & Buckley, 2001), they tend to be variations on a limited number of themes. What is evident from the literature of the professional organisations representing tourism interests is just how little attention they have paid and continue to give to EMS, with the exception of international associations such as the World Travel and Tourism Council (WTTC). The adoption of EMS by an enterprise is substantially influenced by company policy as evidenced, for example, by Intercontinental Hotels. However, in comparative terms, this applies to very few tourism operations because of the high number of small, privately owned businesses, which notably predominate in rural areas. Therefore the perceptions and attitudes of the owners of these businesses are key in stimulating the introduction of EMS, as are levels of awareness and knowledge of such practices. This factor is clearly recognised in the UK Government's tourism strategy (DCMS, 1999).

Thus, attention given to environmental matters by the professional associations of which they may be members and the professional press in the tourism sector is important. For example, the Hotel, Catering and International Management Association (HCIMA) (1993) produced a technical brief for their members on environmental issues within which it was argued that all hospitality businesses should produce an environmental policy statement. More recently, environmental briefings have included the aptly titled *Energy: an issue we can no longer ignore* (Forte, 2000: 18). Significantly, environmental audits were being advocated by the WTTC in 1991 and in 1994, which established Green Globe as a means to promote and provide guidance to businesses wishing to develop 'environmental practices' within their organisation (see Hawkins, 1995). In recognition of the implications of Agenda 21, the WTTC and other organisations (1996) prepared their *Agenda 21 for the Travel and Tourism Industry*. This was the first sector based response to the issues presented at the Earth Summit, and pointed to the fact that the cost of inaction would far outweigh those of action. Further echoing the policies of government agencies and particularly the Countryside Commission (1993) is the WTTC's view that tourism has a role to play in contributing to enhancing the sustainability of local communities (WTTC *et al.*, 1996).

Of those environmental management initiatives specifically designed to promote EMS practices (in other words the 'greening' of tourism businesses), the most renowned is the *International Hotels Environment Initiative* (IHEI) established in 1993 (Black, 1995). This has been extensively promoted, gaining financial aid from the EU to further its aims of awareness raising and the adoption of environmental management practices, particularly among the managers of smaller businesses.

The start of this century witnessed further initiatives, the most comprehensive collection of which is encompassed in the report on the progress of tourism towards sustainable development (UNEP, 2002). Further, there continues to be an ever-growing range of initiatives, literature and advice, most of which is non-sectoral specific and thus of general application. For example, *Finding Hidden Profit* (DoTI/DoE, 1996), BRESCU's (1997) *Awareness Campaign* and the Energy Saving Trust *Lightswitch* initiative were designed to promote the use of energy-efficient lighting by small businesses. The schemes discussed, and other similar developments, in encouraging more responsible operational practices and more efficient use of resources are all seen as positive steps forward, but what progress has been made?

Adoption of Environmental Management Systems

Given these initiatives it might be anticipated that many tourism businesses have and are addressing the environmental performance of their operations and have introduced EMS and related practices. However, as attested by the findings of a major study designed to investigate the environmental performance of tourism businesses in the English Lake District National Park (LDNP), this is not the case (Leslie, 2001). The question that therefore arises is how aware are the owners/managers of these businesses of government initiatives and/or related activities by professional associations in the tourism sector? While it is not possible to present most of the outcomes of the project here, the aim is to present those key findings that provide insights into the levels of awareness of the owners/managers of the businesses of a range of initiatives promoted in the reports noted above. Recognising that awareness of the need for attention to environmental performance and related management practices would not necessarily be solely due to government agencies and professional associations, the potential influence of 'green' organisations was also considered (Table 14.1).

The Project

The overall objective of the project was to assess the environmental performance, including sustainability, of the tourism sector in the Lake District National Park. The LDNP is a part of Cumbria, a rural area in north-west England with a population of 440,000 people, and comprises less than half of the area of the county. Approximately 10% of Cumbria's population live in the LDNP. The volume and value of tourism to the area is shown in Table 14.2, and visitor spend by sector is presented in Table 14.3. The significance of these figures is manifest in the estimated number of jobs supported by tourism in Cumbria, which have been cited as approximately 10% of the population at 42,000 (Collier, 2000), 50% of which are located in the LDNP, compared to about 6% nationally (Leslie, 2001).

Clearly, the LDNP has a substantial tourism economy and therefore as a destination it is an appropriate area for a study seeking to investigate progress in addressing the environmental performance of tourism businesses. This has been recognised by the Cumbria Tourist Board (CTB) in its attention to the promotion of 'sustainable tourism'. Thus, the extent to which policies advocating 'the greening of tourism' and related initiatives have been realised was encompassed in the project's

Table 14.1 Awareness of range of 'Green' initiatives

Factor	*Aware (%)*					
	S-A	*R*	*I*	*A*	*C*	*SC*
BS 7750	19[#]	8	19	23	9	14
Ecolabelling	18	8	22	14	18	18
Tomorrow's Tourism	10[#]	8	22	14	18	11
ISO14001	10[#]	0	15	14	0	11
The Green Audit Kit	7[*]	0	3	23	9	11
Green Globe	7[*]	8	3	9	9	18
British Airways Environment Awards	7	8	7	9	9	11
Local Agenda 21	10	25	11	41	18	18
International Hotels Environment Initiative (IHEI)	2	0	3	9	9	4
Made in Cumbria	68	66	63	91	64	57
Tourism & Conservation Partnership	28	34	19	50	36	39
Involved in the Tourism & Conservation Partnership	12	8	19	32	9	18

Notes:
1. The table also includes attention to localised initiatives, the aims of which are encompassed in the above noted reports, i.e. Made in Cumbria, which promotes local products and produce and the Tourism and Conservation partnership, which promote participation in visitor conservation schemes.
2. The figures for the categories other than serviced accommodation may appear comparatively substantially higher; to some extent this is a factor of the comparatively small numbers of enterprises involved.

S-A = serviced accommodation; R = restaurants; I = inns; A = attractions; C = caravan and camping sites; SC = self-catering operations.
[#]More likely to be members of the HCIMA (Hotel and Catering International Management Association).
[*]All are members of the Cumbria Tourist Board (represents 10% of membership in survey) and also probably members of HCIMA.

aims, to identify and evaluate the level of awareness, attitudes and perceptions of green issues, and associated practices, of owners/managers of tourism enterprises. The methodology formulated involved the design of a primary survey for serviced accommodation, which was subsequently amended for surveying other categories of tourism businesses (see Table 14.4). More detailed investigations, in effect environmental audits based on an extensive set of sustainability indicators

Table 14.2 Volume and value of tourism to Cumbria

Category	UK residents	Overseas residents
Trips (mn) • Holiday • VFR • Business	2.9 77% 8% 11%	0.29 69% 19% 7%
Nights (mn)	11.5	1.4
Spending (£mn)	380	49
Accommodation • hotel, guesthouse	28	70
Day visits • Trips (mn) • Spending (£mn)	9 107	

Notes:
1. The majority of UK residents (24%) are from North West England and Merseyside.
2. Revenues: short breaks account for 9%; holidays 38%.
3. 'No activity' is undertaken by 30%; 44% cite hiking/walking.
4. Day visitors account for 73% of all trips and 20% of total visitor spend.
Source: Leslie (2001)

(Bell & Morse, 2000; Ceron & Dubois, 2003), specifically derived for the study, were then undertaken to establish the approach and actual practices of owners/managers of tourism businesses. Further, the surveys sought to establish key influential factors that either help or hinder the

Table 14.3 Lake District National Park: Percentage visitor spend by sector

Sector	Day visitors	Domestic tourists
Accommodation	–	37
Retail	12	11
Catering	60	26
Attraction	13	5
Travel	16	20
Total	100	100

Note: Minor differences in summation reflect rounding errors.
Source: Leslie (2001)

Table 14.4 Lake District National Park: Surveys and returns

Category	*Database*	*Responses*	*Responses (%)*
Phase I: Serviced accommodation			
• Hotels	303	36	28
• Inns	23	17	74
• Guests houses	266	93	34
• B&B	261	84	32
Total	853	230	27
Phase II: Other sectors			
• Restaurants (other than those in hotels and inns)	28	12	43
• Inns	129	27	21
• Attractions	36	22	61
• Self-catering	120	28	23
• Caravan & camping sites	36	11	31
Total	349	100	29

adoption of such practices. Details of the categories and responses to the surveys are presented in Table 14.4.

Awareness of 'Green Initiatives'

The levels of awareness of respondents drawn from the survey of the various indicators are presented in Table 14.1. The fact that only one respondent noted an additional initiative to those cited when presented with the opportunity to comment, reinforces the comprehensive nature of the lists presented. Clearly, very few enterprise owners/managers are familiar with a range of the factors identified. The very limited awareness of the *Green Audit Kit* is especially notable given that this was actively promoted by the Cumbrian Tourist Board in the late 1990s (CTB, 1998: para. 66).

While there is little evidence of awareness of national and international initiatives, there appears to be a comparatively substantial level of awareness both of 'Made in Cumbria' (a joint initiative of Cumbria Council and local councils to promote Cumbrian produce and products) and of the Tourism & Conservation Partnership (TCP). This is not surprising given that these two initiatives are localised and widely disseminated and promoted to the tourism sector. Even so, the fact is that approximately 1 in 3 and 7 out of 10 persons respectively are not aware of these initiatives. In contrast, given this may also be seen as a localised initiative, there is a marked lack of awareness of LA21. This is significant given that so many businesses are owner-managed and are also the homes of the owners and thus embedded in the local community. The entrepreneurs should be aware of LA21 irrespective of their involvement in tourism and thus be aware of the need to address the environmental performance of their operations. For example, the first page of 'South Lakeland's Local Agenda 21 in Action Plan' highlights efficient use of resources and minimising waste. Knowledge of their local authority LA21 plan could therefore stimulate greater awareness of 'good housekeeping practice' and thus potentially influence the environmental performance of their businesses.

Following on from the enquiries into awareness, the surveys sought to investigate the extent to which businesses may be involved in 'green' initiatives. The findings revealed that there are very low levels of involvement, indicating that while awareness is a factor it is not necessarily an indicator of involvement or appropriate responsive action. The limited involvement in directly supporting the TCP is especially pertinent (see Table 14.1) as support for this sort of activity has been advocated for much of the 1990s, the TCP itself being an oft-cited example.

Potential Influences on Awareness

Of two areas identified as possibly influencing awareness, the first is membership of professional associations and conservation organisations (see Table 14.5). The most commonly held membership, and substantially greater than any other organisation, is that of the CTB. This is undoubtedly due to the perceived benefits of the enterprise being registered with the Board. The high level of membership certainly brings into question the effectiveness of the CTB in promoting attention to environmental performance and the adoption of 'environmentally friendly' practices. It was also identified that few interviewees had attended seminars on 'Going Green'. A number of reasons were offered as to why such seminars had not been attended, such as lack of time, and cost. This finding further helps to explain the general levels of lack of awareness.

The second area identified here is that of the attitudes and perceptions of the owners/managers with regard to the impact of their sector on the environment and related aspects of 'Going Green'. To investigate their views and perceptions, the surveys invited respondents to grade a number of statements, as presented in Table 14.6, on the basis '1 = strongly disagree' to '5 = strongly agree'. Evidently, there is a high degree of ambivalence across the range of statements, suggesting a lack of concern in general. One category that stands out is that of caravan and camping sites, the managers of which clearly consider that their activities do have an impact on the environment and that it is also possible

Table 14.5 Lake District National Park: Membership of a range of organisations

| | Aware (%) | | | | | |
Organisation	S-A	R	I	A	C	SC
Cumbria Tourist Board	72	33	52	60	44	61
The National Trust	34	17	33	14	22	39
Royal Society for Prevention of Cruelty to Birds	12	8	7	0	22	18
Hotel, Catering and International Management Assocaition	13	0	22	0	0	0
World Wide Fund for Nature	7	8	0	5	11	18
The Tourism Society	6	8	0	9	11	0
Licensed Victuallers Association	2	8	29	0	0	4
Friends of the Earth	1	8	0	0	0	14
Greenpeace	4	17	0	5	0	11
Council for the Protection of Rural England	1	8	0	0	0	11
Local Agenda 21 Group	<1	0	0	5	0	0

S-A = serviced accommodation; R = restaurants; I = inns; A = attractions; C = caravan and camping sites; SC = self-catering operations.

to be profitable and be environmentally friendly. One explanation for this small divergence compared to the other categories is that the physical environment of these sites is recognised more readily as an important element of their operation.

Conclusion

The foregoing discussion principally sought to establish to what extent tourism businesses are addressing their environmental performance. In pursuit of this objective, a background as to why tourism businesses should be aware of and address their environmental performance was established. In the process, the connection between, and the development and promotion of initiatives relating to, the outcomes of international concerns over environmental degradation were identified in the context of the UK. The focus then turned to the environmental performance and EMS of tourism businesses. To investigate what progress these businesses have made in adopting EMS, the internationally renowned Lake District

Table 14.6 Perceptions of the sector's impact and related aspects

Question	Mean					
	S-A	*R*	*C*	*SC*	*I*	*A*
The * sector has an impact on the environment.	3.77	3.75	4.10	3.23	3.26	3.85
The * sector's impact on the environment is significantly less than the manufacturing sector.	3.58	2.92	3.60	3.46	3.81	3.60
Operators who claim to be 'green' are using it as a marketing ploy.	3.58	3.83	2.60	3.50	3.11	3.00
Most owners/managers do not have time to worry about the environment.	3.11	3.67	2.60	2.96	3.07	2.60
Customers are not interested in whether an operation is environmentally friendly.	3.13	3.33	2.90	2.88	3.07	2.60
It is not possible to be profitable and be environmentally friendly.	2.42	2.75	1.90	2.04	2.78	2.00

Mean: Based on scale of 1 = 'Strongly disagree'; 5 = 'Strongly agree'.
*The appropriate category was stated in each of the surveys.
S-A = serviced accommodation; R = restaurants; I = inns; A = attractions;
C = caravan and camping sites; SC = self-catering operations.

National Park, which encompasses a large number and diverse range of tourism businesses in a relatively small area, was chosen. However, as the outcomes of the investigation demonstrated, not only are many tourism businesses not addressing their environmental performance, but also many owners/managers evidence little awareness of initiatives designed to promote such action. This finding is of major concern now and even more so to the ongoing development of tourism.

The 21st century will see continuing growth in demand and worldwide expansion of tourism. As demand and supply expand, so does the consumption of resources and production of waste. We will also see a growing awareness and rising concerns over the environment and a gradual shift in attitudes and practices towards more sustainable forms of developments. These factors will further bring into question the development of tourism and particularly an increased emphasis on the value of tourism to destination localities and more equitable distribution of the related benefits to host communities. Tourism businesses must respond effectively and efficiently to meet these twin challenges of worldwide competition and the environmental agenda. It is therefore essential for all businesses and those organisations involved in tourism – as well as the visitors themselves – to address these issues of resource usage, consumption and waste. The introduction of EMS by tourism businesses therefore is very much a part of today's agenda. In effect, this means addressing environmental performance and the adoption of what are perceived as 'environmentally friendly' management and operational practices. This 'greening' of the tourism sector may be seen as a matter of sound economic and environmental good sense. Most of the practices that can be adopted are, in effect, often no more than 'good housekeeping'.

As the major study on which this paper is based found, and the indicative results presented here attest, the awareness specifically of leading government policy on tourism in general, and promotion of 'green' initiatives and EMS is very low. Further, membership of 'green' organisations and professional associations, through which owners/managers might have gained knowledge of these areas, was also low. Indicative of this is the lack of awareness of, and adoption of the principles and practices contained within the *Green Audit Kit*, despite its promotion by the main agencies and national/regional tourism organisations since the mid-1990s. Furthermore, it was found that 'being aware' is not a strong indicator of subsequent positive action; as the even lower levels of involvement in a range of initiatives/activities demonstrated.

Overall, the substantial lack of awareness is perhaps not to be unexpected given the findings of earlier studies. That more progress has not been made serves to reinforce the view that the availability of literature and/or advice is not in itself sufficient to assume awareness and to engender positive action. As the DETR (2000: 10 para. 41) noted, there is limited awareness of the problems and need for long-term solutions. Further support for this view is not hard to find, as the findings from the attitudinal questions indicate. The results across all the sectors were similar, evidencing a degree of cynicism and a large amount of ambivalence. As such they are the least likely to go out of their way to get information, yet are possibly the managers who most need environmental advice. In other words, it is the attitudes and values of the individual – in this case, predominantly business owners – which, combined with their knowledge and understanding of environmental issues and related practices, are the key influence. Clearly, obvious and more direct encouragement and promotion is needed. As the Countryside Agency has recognised, ways must be developed to address this problem (Countryside Agency, 2000; ETC/Countryside Agency, 2000).

Evidently, government, both central and local, has been largely ineffective given that the former has been advocating the 'greening of tourism' since the start of the 1990s, a position taken up by the network of national and regional tourist boards. This outcome is not altogether unexpected and effectively demonstrates that the policies presented by the leading bodies involved are often little more than rhetoric. This is not surprising given that such organisations are not part of the actual business sectors they seek to influence (to which one might add – and who do not 'practise what they preach'). This factor not only brings into question their value, approaches to dissemination and implementation, but also poses the very question, just who are such policies designed to serve? However, attention and promotion continues, witness recent initiatives (DCMS, 2002a; EC, 2003; ETC/TMI, 2003), increasingly supported by the role of English regional development agencies in furthering the objectives of sustainable development.

A factor that will certainly play a part in the wider adoption of EMS is the possibility of regulation, perhaps legislation, which directly targets energy consumption and waste, and the influence of consumer pressure groups, which is already evident in some areas, such as the imposition of a landfill tax, the reuse of building aggregates, and a tax on energy usage. This leads to speculation that, in time, environmental auditing of a tourism business will become as much a part of an enterprise as the auditing of its accounts. Essentially this is no more than the positioning of the sector to respond to the emerging environmental challenge that will be a key issue of the 21st century.

References

Bell, S. and Morse, S. (2000) *Sustainability Indicators: Measuring the Immeasurable*. London: Earthscan.

Black, C.W. (1995) The Inter-Continental Hotels Group and its Environmental Awareness Programme. In D. Leslie (ed.) *Promoting Environmental Awareness and Action in Hospitality, Tourism and Leisure* (pp. 31–46). Glasgow: Environment Papers Series No. 1, Glasgow Caledonian University.

BRESCU (1997) *Running an Awareness Campaign*. Watford: Building Research Establishment.

BSI (British Standards Institute) (1993) *Draft British Standard: Revision of BS7750: 1992 – Specification for Environmental Management Systems*. Milton Keynes: BSI.

Ceron, J.-P. and Dubois, G. (2003) Tourism and Sustainable Development indicators: the gap between theoretical demands and practical achievements. *Current Issues in Tourism* 6 (1), 54–75.

Cockerell, N. (1994) The changing role of international travel and tourism organisations. *Travel and Tourism Analyst* 5, 69–83.

Collier, C. (2000) *Presentation by Chief Executive, Cumbria Tourist Board at Fifth Meeting of the Rural Forum for the North West of England*. Kendal: Lake District National Park Authority.

Countryside Agency (2000) *Tomorrow's Countryside – 2020 Vision*. Cheltenham: Countryside Agency.

Countryside Commission (1993a) *Sustainability and the English Countryside – Position Statement*. Cheltenham: Countryside Commission.

Countryside Commission (1993b) *Wise Growth; The Actions Collectively of Micro-Businesses Will Affect Most Other Businesses in Tourism*. Cheltenham: Countryside Commission.

CTB (Cumbria Tourist Board) (1998) *The Regional Tourism Strategy for Cumbria*. Carlisle: CTB.

DCMS (Department of Culture, Media and Sport) (1999) *Tomorrow's Tourism: A Growth Industry for the New Millennium*. London: DCMS.

DCMS (Department of Culture, Media and Sport) (2000) *The Tourism Summit: 1 March 2000: Report on the Conclusions*. London: DCMS.

DCMS (Department of Culture, Media and Sport) (2002a) *Minutes of the 4th Tourism Summit held on 26 November*. London: DCMS.

DCMS (Department of Culture, Media and Sport) (2002b) *Measuring Sustainable Tourism at the Local Level: An Introduction and Background*. London: DCMS.

DEFRA (Department of the Environment, Food and Rural Affairs) (2002) *Strategy for Sustainable Farming and Food*. London: DEFRA.

DEFRA (Department of the Environment, Food and Rural Affairs) (2003a) *Changing Patterns: UK Government Framework for Sustainable Consumption and Production*. London: DEFRA.

DEFRA (Department of the Environment, Food and Rural Affairs) (2003b) *Conservation is Not Enough – Minister Sets Out Living*. London: DEFRA.

DETR (Department of Environment, Transport and the Regions) (1999) *The UK Government's Strategy for Sustainable Development: A Better Quality of Life*. London: DETR.

DETR (Department of Environment, Transport and the Regions) (2000) *Indicators of Sustainable Development, UK Round Table on Sustainable Development*. London: DETR.

DNH (Department of National Heritage), RDC (Rural Development Commisison), ETC (English Tourism Council) and Countryside Commission (1995) *Principles of Sustainable Rural Tourism: Opportunities for Local Action*. Cheltenham: DNH/RDC/ETC.

DoE (Department of the Environment) (1990a) *This Common Inheritance*. London: HMSO.

DoE (Department of the Environment) (1990b) *Tourism and the Environment – Into the 1990s*. London: HMSO.

DoE (Department of the Environment) (1996) *Indicators of Sustainable Development for the United Kingdom.* London: HMSO.

DoTI (Deparment of Trade and Industry) & DoE (Department of the Environment) (1996) *Finding Hidden Profit.* London: DoTI/DoE.

EC (European Commission) (2003) *Basic Orientations for the Sustainability of European Tourism.* Brussels: Enterprise Directorate-General, EC.

ETB (English Tourist Board) & EDG (Employment Department Group) (1991) *Tourism and the Environment: Maintaining the Balance.* London: ETB & EDG.

ETC (English Tourism Council) & Countryside Agency (2000) *Rural Tourism: Working for the Countyside: A Consultation Paper by the English Tourism Council and The Countryside Agency.* London: ETC.

ETC (English Tourism Council) (2001) *Time for Action.* London: ETC.

ETC (English Tourism Council) and TMI (Tourism Management Institute) (2003) *Destination Management Handbook – A Sustainable Approach.* London: ETC/TMI.

Font, X. and Buckley, R.C. (eds) (2001) *Tourism Ecolabelling: Certification and Promotion of Sustainable Management.* Wallingford: CAB International.

Font, X. and Tribe, J. (2001) Promoting green tourism: the future of environmental awards. *International Journal of Tourism Research* 3, 9–21.

Forte, J. (2000) Energy: an issue we can no longer ignore. *Hospitality* February, 18–19.

Goodall (1994) Environmental auditing: current best practice (with special reference to British tourism firms). In A. Seaton (ed.) *Tourism: The State of the Art* (pp. 655–74). Chichester: John Wiley & Sons.

Hawkins, R. (1995) The Green Globe Programme: Developing a Greener Future for Travel and Tourism. *Journal of Sustainable Tourism* 3 (1).

HCIMA (Hotel & Catering International Management Association) (1993) *Managing Your Business in Harmony with the Environment.* London: HCIMA.

House of Lords (1994) *Report From the Select Committee on Sustainable Development Volume 1.* London: HMSO.

ILAM (Institute of Leisure and Amenity Management) (2000) *Performance Indicators for Leisure and Cultural Services 2000/2001,* Fact Sheet 00/05. Reading: ILAM.

Leslie, D. (1986) Tourism and conservation in national parks. *Tourism Management* 7 (1), 52–56.

Leslie, D. (1995) Promoting environmentally friendly management and practices. In D. Leslie (ed.) *Promoting Environmental Awareness and Action in Hospitality, Tourism and Leisure* (pp. 11–30). Glasgow: Glasgow Caledonian University.

Leslie, D. (2001) *An Environmental Audit of the Tourism Industry in the Lake District National Park.* Glasgow: Report for Friends of the Lake District and the Council for the Protection of Rural England.

Leslie, D. and Hughes, G. (1997) Local Authorities and Tourism in the UK. *International Journal of Managing Leisure* 2 (3), 143–54.

Moore, S.A., Smith, A.J. and Newsome, D.N. (2003) Environmental performance reporting for natural area tourism: contributions by visual impact management frameworks and their indicators. *Journal of Sustainable Tourism* 11 (4), 348–75.

PRC (Policy and Resources Committee, Jersey) (1998) *Jersey in the New Millenium: A Sustainable Future Framework Consultation Document.* St. Helier: PRC.

RDC (Rural Development Commission), Countryside Commission, ETB (English Tourist Board), WTB (Wales Tourism Board) and CCW (Countryside Commission Wales) (1989) *Tourism in National Parks: A Guide to Good Practice.* Cheltenham: RDC, CC, ETB, WTB and CCW.

RDC (Rural Development Commission), ETB (English Tourist Board), Countryside Commission (1991) *The Green Light: A Guide to Sustainable Tourism.* Cheltenham: RDC, ETB and CC.

RDC (Rural Development Commission) (1996) *Green Audit Kit: The DIY Guide to Greening Your Business.* Cheltenham: RDC.

UNEP (United Nations Environment Programme) (2002) *Industry as a Partner for Sustainable Development: Tourism.* Paris: UNEP.

UNEP (United National Environment Programme) (2003) *Tourism and Local Agenda 21 – The Role of Local Authorities in Sustainable Tourism.* Paris: UNEP.

Wallis, J. and Woodward, S. (1997) Improving the environmental performance of Scotland's Hospitality Sector. *International Journal of Hospitality Management* 2 (2), 94–109.

Welford, R. (1995) *Environmental Strategy and Sustainable Development – The Corporate Challenge for the 21st Century.* London: Routledge.

WTTC (World Travel and Tourism Council), WTO (World Tourism Organisation) and Earth Council Report (1996) *Agenda 21 For the Travel and Tourism Industry: Towards Environmentally Sustainable Development.* Madrid: WTTC.

Chapter 15

Researching the Links Between Environmental Quality Kite Marks and Local Tourism Business Performance: A Discourse Analysis of the Welsh Rural Beach Quality 'Green Coast Award'

DAVID BOTTERILL and CLIFF NELSON

Introduction

The 'Beach' is an important national asset in Wales for a number of significant reasons. First, it provides a public leisure resource that supports a broad range of recreational experiences: informal and formal, active and passive, thereby contributing significantly to the quality of life in Wales. Secondly, the beach provides an important component in the Welsh tourism product. The beach is an integral subsystem of the coastal zone that is a significant driver of UK domestic tourism activity. Coastal tourism is essential to the Welsh economy (Botterill *et al.*, 2000) generating in excess of 45% of all tourist trips in Wales (WTB, 2003a). Total tourism spend in 1997 was estimated to be £1.9 bn (c. €3 bn), a 7% contribution to the gross domestic product of Wales (WTB, 2003b). Expectations of growth in tourism's contribution to the economy have been the subject of debate within the Welsh Assembly Government (WAG), and by 2006, the end of the Objective 1 funding in Wales, a target contribution of around 10% has been mooted. The tourism industry in Wales is, however, under a number of serious threats to its long-stay holiday markets from an increasing seasonal migration of British people to international holiday destinations (Wavelength, 1999) and a struggle to define itself as an international destination for tourists (Foster, 1999). In response to these conditions the most recent strategic directive for the industry in Wales, *Achieving our Potential*, highlights four key factors that should underpin future developments in Wales – sustainability,

268

quality, competitiveness, and partnership (WTB, 2000). The natural and cultural resources of Wales are recognised to be important assets in countering a decline in traditional markets and securing growth in tourism's contribution to GDP.

The seaside resorts of Wales have seen a marked decline in popularity for long-stay holidays as a result of extensive competition from Mediterranean short-haul summer sun destinations. Demand in domestic tourism is indicating a steady shift into the growth markets of short-stay holiday breaks where a resort's environmental quality rather than its entertainment assets are principal motivating factors. There has been, therefore, an increased recent emphasis on improving and measuring environmental quality through beach award schemes and highlighting these achievements in beach resort promotion. The 'signing' of the Welsh coast as being of high environmental quality is in part achieved through a range of statutory and non-statutory designations. Wales has both European and national recognition for a wide range of designations for natural beauty situated along its 1248 km of intricate coastline. Over 70% of the Welsh coast lies under protective or indicative designations. For example, there are 14 designations of Heritage Coast (covering 496 km of coastline), the aims of which are to preserve conservation and natural beauty of the coast and inshore waters while promoting sustainable development (Countryside Council for Wales, 1998). In addition, the coastline of Pembrokeshire is part of the only coastal national park in the UK. Wales also hosts 942 Sites of Special Scientific Interest (SSSIs), covering 220,759 ha that define sites of special flora, fauna, geological or physicographical features. In addition, five Areas of Outstanding Natural Beauty (AONB) have been designated, covering 83,200 ha, with the purpose of preserving natural beauty and public enjoyment (Countryside Council for Wales, 1998). Even though the designation of SSSIs and AONBs is not specific to the coast, major Welsh sites lie within coastal boundaries, such as the AONB on the Gower Peninsula. In a European context a number of candidate Marine Special Areas of Conservation have been identified for Wales under the Habitat and Species Directive, including the Severn Estuary (Countryside Council for Wales, 1999).

Beach Award Schemes

In recent years the beach award scheme has become the highest profile measure of beach quality. Disjointed arrays of beach (management) award schemes are currently in operation, spanning local, regional, national and supranational echelons. It is their common aim to provide a basis upon which to protect the natural environment while promoting tourism and recreation. For a discussion of the full range of beach award schemes currently available see Nelson *et al.* (2000). Beach award schemes have a dual purpose, first as a tool to aid beach managers, and secondly to instil confidence in the consumer that the beach provides a quality environment. They are therefore important to both the problems of the beach as a managed leisure resource and by implication, the fortunes of the Welsh tourism industry (Nelson, Botterill & Williams, 2000).

The most notable beach award scheme of relevance to Wales' beaches is the Blue Flag, designed and implemented by the Foundation for Environmental Education in Europe (FEEE) and administered in the UK by the Tidy Britain Group (TBG) (TBG, 1999a). FEEE have widened their remit to cover countries outside the European Community, including the Caribbean, for example, and consequently dropped 'Europe' from their title, becoming instead the Federation for Environmental Education (FEE). The Blue Flag is directed at resort beaches capable of offering tourist amenities such as toilets and shops. In all, 27 criteria detail the Blue Flag, all of which must be complied with for a beach to be successful in application. The dominant criterion in the award of the Blue Flag is the assessment of the ability of the beach to attain the highest standard of recreational water quality, the Guideline parameter, defined by the European Directive on the Quality of Bathing Waters (CEC, 1976). The TBG also runs its own schemes (TBG, 1999b) in conjunction with its European counterpart, which incorporate beaches that only conform to the less stringent bathing water quality Mandatory Standard (CEC, 1976). The TBG argues that the shore-side parameters of a beach may be of significant value even though the water quality only barely passes minimum standards. Paradoxically, even though the TBG tried to simplify the system it has only succeeded in further confusing the public by introducing more classification schemes (TBG, 2000).

Beach Award Schemes and the Tourism Industry

The explicit emphasis within beach award schemes is very much upon measures of environmental quality. Implicitly a link is presumed, however, between the award schemes and the fortunes of the tourism industry who depend on the quality of the beach as a part of the tourism product offering. Evidence of this presumed link is found in the documents that surround beach awards. For example, publicity in respect of the European Blue Flag identifies First Choice Holidays & Flights Ltd., a large UK tour operator, as a sponsoring partner. The FEE points out that, 'The company is an important partner for the Blue Flag Campaign involving a sponsorship contribution, promotion of the Blue Flag beaches in destination brochures and an active co-operation on environmental issues' (FEE, 2003a). Furthermore the 'link' to tourism is displayed in the composition of the European Blue Flags International

Jury where representatives of the World Tourism Organisation (WTO) sit alongside appointees from the United Nations Environment Programme (UNEP), European Union for Coastal Conservation (EUCC), the Environmental Committee of the European Parliament, and the Foundation for Environmental Education (FEE) (FEE, 2003d). 'WTO is a very important partner to FEE in informing the public about ecotourism with the Blue Flag as example and extending the principles of the Campaign to non-European regions. With the support of WTO, FEE was able to start the implementation of the Blue Flag Campaign in the Caribbean and South East Asia' (FEE, 2003b). As the interest in beach awards develops outside Europe it is often at the instigation of the ministry of tourism, as is the case in Mexico, or of the tourism trade organisation, as in the case of the Caribbean (FEE, 2003c).

The 'link' in the case study Green Coast Award (GCA) can be detected in the way the main sponsoring agency, *Keep Wales Tidy*, positions the award in its portfolio. On its Website, details of the GCA are found under a tourism heading:

> Keep Wales Tidy recognises the importance to tourism of well managed natural and built environments. We aim to support the work of the Wales Tourist Board and local tourism managers in raising the quality of local environments with particular concern to our beach and coastal work. Not only do we recognise good beach management through Blue Flag and Seaside Awards but we have also developed the innovative Green Coast Award for rural beaches of the highest environmental quality. (Keep Wales Tidy, 2003)

Opening the 'black box' of the presumed link between beach flag awards and the tourism industry is the main focus of the research reported in this chapter.

The Green Coast Award

The GCA was first mooted during the later stages of the Green Seas Initiative (GSI), itself driven off the back of a £650 mn (€1 bn) investment into new sewage treatment works around Welsh coastal waters between 1993 and 1998. The GCA was seen to be a part of a broader objective 'to publicise this effort and its achievements for the benefits of communities, tourism, the Welsh economy and the public's enjoyment of these environments' (Welsh Water, 1997: 3). This early statement of achievement opens the issue of the assumed link between improvements in environmental management, in this case wastewater treatment, and several broader social and economic objectives. In an earlier statement the partners of the Green Seas Initiative had set themselves the target of achieving 50 Blue Flag beaches in Wales. This proved to be an unwise objective to set given the 'rural' setting of so many of Wales' beaches and the scale of beach infrastructure expected to be present at Blue Flag beaches. To some extent the creation of a Green Coast Award was proposed as a more meaningful way of utilising the environmental kite mark of a beach award in the context of Wales. It is also the case that the GCA served to deflect from the non-achievement of the original, and unsound, objective relating to Blue Flags. Specifically proposed by Keep Wales Tidy and supported by the Wales Tourist Board, it was initially seen as an accreditation scheme for small rural beaches that do not qualify for resort status because of their limited tourist facilities (WTB, 1996).

The GCA programme is designed to cater for rural beaches that have reached Guideline water quality standards – in effect a rural version of the Blue Flag (Hyder, 1999), but substituting the measures of shore-side facilities with environmentally sensitive management practices. Definitive statements on the criteria used for the Green Coast Award are compounded by the evolutionary status of the award. The list of criteria used in making a GCA is shown in Table 15.1.

Research Aims

The research reported in this chapter is drawn from a larger study utilising the GCA as a case study that was designed to provide answers to two main research questions:

(1) To what extent do consumers understand the meaning of beach award schemes and incorporate them within both their beach choice decision making and evaluation of their beach experience?
(2) To test the presumed link between beach award schemes and the performance of tourism businesses.

This chapter specifically discusses the findings of a qualitative study addressing the second of these, but in its conclusion it briefly draws upon the results of a consumer survey undertaken to inform the first research aim.

Operationalising Research Aim 2

We have described above how a presumed link is made between beach awards and the tourism industry. There is little research-based evidence in the literature to support the link beyond its assertion and the involvement of both environmental and tourism interest groups in the promotion and implementation of award schemes. To our knowledge this link has never been tested empirically in any location where beach award schemes have been used.

The main difficulty in operationalising the research aim was to find a way to measure the 'performance of tourism businesses' variable.

Table 15.1 Criteria for the awarding of a Green Coast Award

(1) The beach must comply with the Mandatory and Guideline water quality standard of the bathing water Directive 76/160/EC. The water quality of the current and previous years must be displayed at a central information point and updated on a weekly basis.
(2) It must be shown that the managing body has established a beach management committee where all the statutory bodies and other relevant organisations associated with beach management have been consulted; any issues raised must be addressed.
(3) Each Green Coast Award beach must have a beach management plan in place produced by the beach management committee to ensure the protection of any environmentally sensitive areas of the beach.
(4) There should be no industrial or sewage discharges affecting the beach area. Keep Wales Tidy should be notified of any discharge points within one mile of the beach.
(5) There should be no gross pollution by sewage-related debris or other waste including oil, glass and litter either on the beach or the surrounding area.
(6) Manual removal of litter only, leaving all naturally occurring debris such as seaweed and driftwood, unless it becomes contaminated with a material or substance such as oil that is hazardous to public health.
(7) Where appropriate, the provision of properly secured and covered litter bins in adequate numbers must be made available for litter and dog faeces. These would be of suitable character and appearance and sited where appropriate to the surroundings.
(8) Dog and horse owners should be encouraged, by the provision of suitable facilities and literature at a central access point, to clean up after their animals when using the beach.
(9) Public access to the beach area must be safe and well maintained; this is to include the enclosure or removal of hazardous or derelict buildings to prevent public access.
(10) The beach, under normal conditions, should be considered locally as being relatively safe for bathing. A risk assessment should have been conducted and appropriate control measures, such as hazard warning signs, safety equipment and emergency planning, identified within the assessment, should be in place.

(*continued*)

Table 15.1 *Continued*

(11) Information on locally organised environmental activities and events should be made readily available to the public.
(12) Information should be in place to encourage visitors to consider the sensitivity of the local flora and fauna and their habitats.
(13) Each Green Coast Award beach must have a guardianship scheme in place.
(14) An information point with advice about nearest telephone and emergency services, local hazards, latest water quality results, previous three years (at least) water quality standards, local authority and KWT address and a map of Award area showing location of facilities, water sampling points and safety information should be present.

Source: Keep Wales Tidy (2003)

The tourism industry in the rural case study location comprises many micro-businesses and typifies the disjointed structure of the tourism SME economy (Jones *et al.*, 2004). Previous experience of researching micro-business performance indicates an unwillingness of respondents to disclose financial or other performance data. We were not particularly minded to collect quantitative data as we saw considerable difficulty in attempting to test the relationship by segregating out the effect of a beach award on income or other business volume or firm efficiency measures. Instead we looked to find a way in which the implied link between a beach award and business performance could be evidenced in discourse (Howarth, 2000).

The literature on small businesses indicates that networks and network analysis offer ways into understanding 'business relations, industrial organisation, regional agglomeration, strategic management, and the culturally induced outlooks and behaviour of small firms' (Lynch, 2000: 95). Research into tourism micro-business networks reported in the literature has demonstrated that micro-business performance is linked to the operator's engagement with support networks (see, for review, Lynch, 2000; Lynch *et al.*, 2000). We decided therefore to explore with micro-business respondents the extent to which they networked around their business operation. Our argument was that because networks are important to small business performance then evidence of a shared interest in environmental quality through the active networks would provide evidence of a *direct* link between business performance and environmental kite marks. To test for the presence of a *direct* link from the environmental kite mark end of our model we sought evidence of the consideration of tourism business performance in the environmental and provider/intermediary samples.

In all interviews we asked a series of questions that moved from the general to the specific. At a general first level we began with an exploration of the nature of networks the respondent was involved in, followed by an exploration of the frequency of interactions within the networks and the substance of the conversations – the lines of discourse. The questions posed at the second level became more specific to the research aim. For the micro-businesses we asked about the extent to which matters relating to the environment featured as a topic of conversation within the networks and whether the link between the businesses performance and the environment was considered. For the environmental stakeholders we asked about the extent to which the condition of the economy and particularly the tourism economy featured in conversation before exploring whether the link between the agencies' work and tourism businesses ever featured. Finally we asked the micro-business operators about beach award schemes and the GCA in particular. Consequently the judgements we have made in our analysis of discourses have tested the extent to which the beach award scheme has contributed to tourism business performance by:

(1) the extent and nature of environmental discourse that had entered the micro-business networks; and
(2) the extent and nature of business performance discourse that had entered the environmental networks.

In the cases of interviews with provider/intermediary stakeholders it was sometimes necessary to run these questions through from both angles.

Qualitative Study Methodology

Initially a sampling frame was constructed of potential interview respondents structured by stakeholder group, subsequently by organisation and, finally, by named individual. Our priority was to interview micro-businesses from the attractions, activity operators, and accommodation sectors. In order to identify potential respondents we contacted the managing director of the appropriate regional tourism company, explained the purposes of the research and asked them to suggest local members who might be interested in our work. The key environmental agencies were identified and specific individuals were approached to participate in the study. Lastly, major public and non-profit providers and intermediaries (e.g. economic development agencies and local authorities) were identified and advice was sought from informed tourism professionals as to whom would be most appropriate to include in the study. In most cases interviews were arranged well in advance, although in the case of micro-businesses we often found that too long a period between arranging the interview and conducting it was counterproductive.

All interviews followed the same pattern of questions and most were conducted by both researchers. In a small number of cases the interview was held with more than one respondent, although this was avoided wherever possible. An opening statement described our research interests and a schedule of questions, supplemented by relevant follow-up questions, enabled respondents to develop their answers. The interviews, therefore, took the form of semi-structured conversations. In total we conducted 20 interviews involving 25 respondents over two periods of fieldwork: approximately one week in Anglesey and ten days in Pembrokeshire. In 2000 the GCA was only available in these two counties; however, by 2003, 48 beaches in seven counties had been awarded a GCA. In the summer of 2000 eleven interviews were conducted with micro-businesses (six accommodation providers, two attractions, and four activity holiday operators), four with environmental agencies and five with provider/intermediary agencies (two local authority officers, two economic development agency officers, and one national park officer).

Interviews ranged from 35 to 120 minutes, with most being completed within an hour. All respondents gave permission to record the interviews and full transcriptions were made during the winter of 2000/2001. Data were analysed using the constant comparison technique (Lincoln & Guba, 1985).

Results and Discussion: Stakeholder Groups, Individual Voices, and Different Discourses

What follows in this section is the identification of the dominant discourses around the GCA that have emerged from the analysis of interview transcripts using the constant comparison method. We call these discourses 'innocent irrelevance', 'myopic commitment' and 'quiet indifference' (Figure 15.1). Each of these is closely associated with one of the three stakeholder groups in our sample. For example, the discourse of commitment is largely to be heard in the environmental agencies. To some extent, then, the sampling structure shapes where one might expect to find evidence of these discourses, and our analysis began with constant comparison of the transcripts of interviews undertaken *within* stakeholder groups.

As the analysis progressed, however, we became aware of the influence of the individuals we spoke to, who each, regardless of their organisational context, might speak within one or more of the three dominant discourses. For example, because a national park authority owns considerable stretches of coastline it is considered part of a 'provider' stakeholder sample, but the individual interviewee may reflect a strong

Figure 15.1 One kitemark, three discourses

environmental discourse in their comments about GCA. Similarly certain micro-business interviewees would clearly be identified as a part of the tourism micro-business stakeholder group, but they may equally contribute to the environmental discourse because they are personally committed to environmentalism. They might also frame their commentary within the provider discourse because they see themselves as having some collective responsibility beyond their business interest.

The analysis of the interviews then attempts to cut across the somewhat simplistic stakeholder structure of the sample. An implication of this development in the analysis was that our method became less mechanistic as prescribed by the constant comparison technique and more instinctive. This approach is consistent with the lead author's exploration of critical realist studies of tourism (Botterill, 2001, 2003). The tendency was to move towards transcending the reported accounts to produce what Bhaskar (1978) calls an analysis of the 'real' as opposed to an analysis of the 'actual' social reality.

A discourse of innocent irrelevance

The discourse of innocent irrelevance is largely constructed around tourism SME operators' perceptions of consumer demands and their satisfaction in order to achieve short-term business advantage. Informal networks of tourism operators enable consumer demands to be met through information brokerage about the attractions or accommodation available and the onward referral of consumers to known tourism operators. Operators, therefore, use informal networks as vital ways to deliver satisfying holiday experiences that will be beneficial to individual businesses but also to the destination as a whole. More formal networks offer support on operational matters such as short-term equipment supply problems or marketing consortia solutions among same-sector operators. Within sectors competition mitigates against the flow of business performance information in local networks. More geographically distant sector networks combat the local competitiveness quotient, and in these 'safer' networks there is more open discussion of business bookings and volume patterns, advertising effectiveness, and ICT exploitation.

Local cross-sector tourism networks exist in both Anglesey and Pembrokeshire but within these, as in the formal sector networks and the local informal networks that deliver on consumer demands, the environmental discourse was very weak. Respondents from the self-catering accommodation businesses recognised that their consumers are increasingly environmentally conscious, but construed such interest as beyond the concern of the individual business.

In Pembrokeshire, for example, it seems that an official designation such as the National Park is assumed by micro-businesses to convey to consumers, through this 'official kite mark', that they are buying into environmental quality. Beyond this background to consumer choice, businesses construe that consumers are more interested in the quality of the tangible product being purchased (the hotel, cottage, or activity holiday) than any other kite mark of a destination's attributes such as beaches that they may or may not visit.

In Anglesey, where no such 'official' designation exists, micro-businesses recognised the growing importance given by consumers to environmental attributes, but seemed unwilling to take on the collective task of communicating the environmental quality of the island. It was as if these qualities of Anglesey as a destination were outside the micro-business domain, even where in one case the nature of the attraction was very directly related to aquatic life, and where 'new' product developments depended on environmental quality. The environmental qualities in which operators reported consumers to be interested were predominantly land-based and visibly strong, related to landscapes, ecosystems and the flora and fauna, and coastscapes. In Pembrokeshire these attributes of the destination were perceived to be encompassed by the official National Park designation and in Anglesey they were recognised as being under-exploited in destination marketing. In either location these 'qualities' were construed as being outside of the micro-business domain – an indication of 'indifference'.

Where environmental quality was discussed in formal micro-business networks then the reported discourse stressed the perceived consumer preoccupations with immediate experience of the managed environment: toilets, dog bans, and litter. The exception to this was in activity holiday sector networks specific to Pembrokeshire, where micro-businesses demonstrated an acute awareness of the importance of the quality of the environment for business performance. This was particularly the case for water-based activities where water quality was a consumer concern, and these micro-businesses showed interest in, but very little knowledge of, the GCA. However, the over-riding emphasis within the micro-business discourse was that water or beach quality was very seldom if at all mentioned as a concern of consumers. As one Pembrokeshire self-catering operator commented: 'In 37 years I can't remember any interrogation from customers on water quality'. The telesales staff at the same agency confirmed that very few consumers enquired about water quality and consumer questions about beaches referred mainly to dog restrictions. This is clearly important to our analysis as the GCA and other beach awards foreground water quality as a principal if not pivotal criterion in the award. The innocent indifference discourse we encountered persistently reinforced that the consumer perception of this criterion was virtually insignificant to their purchasing behaviour, and this finding clearly undermines, from the micro-business perspective, the claim of a link between beach award schemes and tourism business performance.

A discourse of myopic commitment

The myopic commitment discourse is undoubtedly the strongest discourse that emerged in our analysis of the GCA. This was largely but not exclusively heard in the environmental stakeholder sample. Its discursive arguments were most explicitly concerned to use the award to drive up the standards of beach environment management, and exercised a deeply utilitarian, bordering upon manipulative, attitude towards the contribution of the GCA to tourism business performance. The award was undoubtedly seen as a means to an end rather than being valued in its own right. Precisely because beach awards generally have become associated with claims that the end result is an improved tourism business performance, the environmental discourse unashamedly exploited the GCA to justify increased resources for the environmentalist community and environmental improvements. We differentiate between environmentalist community and environmental improvement deliberately. The GCA project resulted in the creation of a small number of jobs for the environmentalist community and was clearly being used by one respondent as a career progression route. Our evaluation was undertaken in the second year of the GCA and early indicators of its success, according to its architects, were provided by its year-on-year expansion (eight in 1999, 25 in 2000, 23 in 2001, 28 in 2002, and 48 in 2003).

Here we note the somewhat contradictory strands found within the myopic commitment discourse that are best evidenced in the annual negotiations over the number and purpose of any expansion in the GCA. Such negotiations take place within a largely environmentalist/provider stakeholder network that meets on approximately four occasions a year to review progress on the GCA. Part of the environmentalist discourse displayed a suspicion about the awarding of a kite mark to any proposed beach because it was unclear as to the effect of the kite mark on consumer behaviour. Such suspicion rested on the potential of a kite mark to cause material changes to the beach environment through either additional built facility (signs, litter bins, access structures) or through increased usage and negative environmental impacts, and consequently these voices sought to limit the expansion of the GCA. In contrast, the interest of others within the environmental stakeholder group, particularly the scheme's architects, who saw jobs, budgets and career aspirations as being fulfilled by the GCA, deliberately sought to expand the scheme. One respondent reported how sometimes this debate centred on whether the mechanism of the GCA should be used to attack difficult beaches where environmental improvements to water quality would be expensive and difficult to achieve; or whether granting a GCA to a beach that had *de facto* reached the threshold criteria might expand the scheme more effectively. This difference of point of view was ultimately accommodated in modest growth in the number of beach awards made because both parties knew in the end that the award did lever additional funding for environmental improvement. There was plenty of evidence within the environmental discourse that the award was viewed as a positive influence on increased resource allocation, and this, we argue, created a form of myopia in the discourse.

It was also the case that consensus about the meaning of the award was constructed in the myopic commitment discourse in a number of ways. It was seen as a way of introducing greater stewardship of the beach environment, a stronger sense of local ownership, a more structured management approach through written-down plans, and greater effectiveness in raising environmental standards through a multi-agency approach. Thus the discourse was almost entirely inclusive of the hegemony of localised bottom-up environmental improvement captured in the 'think globally act locally maxim' of the environmental movement because it contains both an appeal to recognise the value of the beach environment and a 'localised' response to managing the beach environment. When respondents were challenged to provide evidence of the implied relationship between the award and improving tourism business performance, the full impact of the power of this discourse 'to close down' on the meaning and purpose of the GCA was seen: tourism businesses' voices were silenced in the discourse by the exclusion of such business interests from the discussion. The networks in which the environmental discourse was constructed seldom included any tourism micro-business interest, and communications between the tourism stakeholders and the environmental stakeholders was extremely rare. A *direct* link was not found: there was little evidence in the environmental discourse that the GCA award had anything to do with improved tourism business performance, except in the sense that it was politically expedient not to challenge this assumption. It was also suggested that the forging of such links was either part of the future work of the project or the work of other agencies. It was difficult not to see this as anything other than a rather lame excuse, given the thrust of the award and its main sponsors (WTB, 1997).

A discourse of quiet indifference

In contrast to the vigorous commitment shown within the myopic commitment discourse to construct a particular meaning for the GCA, the quiet indifference discourse was something of a pale shadow. The indifference is expressed in varying intensities dependent upon the social and political context in which these mainly local authority and economic development officers work. It means that the GCA is in some cases an irrelevance to mainstream discourses on rural development, or tourism marketing, or micro-business development. Consequently little is actually known about the award. However, even where the GCA is part of a provider/intermediary's domain, the discourse that surrounded it stressed the utilitarian strand found among environmental stakeholders – the resource leverage characteristic, the multi-agency approach, the paper-driven quality system – but without the conviction of the environmental voice. Additionally, the quiet indifference discourse explicitly constructed the GCA as a low-cost, added-value marketing icon for the tourism product. The fragmented nature of the tourism industry in rural North and West Wales is well understood, and as we have commented is typical of the tourism SME economy. The quiet indifference discourse we accessed contained a 'corporate' view of this fragmented industrial structure, a kind of 'tour operator' presence in the tourism destination but without the advantage of direct ownership.

The intermediary and to a lesser extent provider agencies we spoke to depended on building constituency networks of micro-businesses and providing them with a range of interventions in training, marketing and business development. In one case the agency operated as an incoming tour operator. It might be assumed therefore that these agencies could speak for the micro-businesses in some way and much of what they constructed was a view of the priorities of the industry. Although they were able to evidence an interest in and recognition of the environment in the agendas of their networks, these were constructed as subservient to the short-term business case thinking that dominates; the exception being where environmental disaster caused immediate impacts (e.g. tanker oil spills). In most cases the networks eschewed explicit discussion of the broader environmental matters even though the quiet indifference discourse consistently argued that these businesses were acutely aware of the importance of environment/business relations. Success in achieving engagement by the business community with environmental quality was reported in the area of 'business greening', where uptake on training had been popular. Even here the quiet indifference discourse construed such interest as most likely to be based on the social interactions afforded by such training and the contribution such training made to satisfying the well-documented 'life-style' motivations of micro-business operators. There was little evidence that the GCA had featured in any of these training interventions. In some cases the dominance of land-based rural redevelopment discourse foreclosed on coastal matters, and development agency aspiration was driven towards an over-arching kite mark, such as the Green Globe, that would kite mark the destination rather than its constituent attractions or micro-businesses.

The economic development agencies and in particular the local authorities were by the nature of their work closely connected to local residents' political agendas. Where beach award schemes did feature, a further factor that shaped the quiet indifference discourse emerged. In several reported cases the beach award is constructed to sit between tourism business interests and the interests of residents who see it as introducing constraints on their freedoms and counter to the interest of their communities. It was noted that on occasions the awarding of a GCA to a beach could become the site of mild anti-tourism protest by local residents. Faced with this dilemma the quiet indifference discourse contains what appear to be highly selective messages that sit uncomfortably together and contribute to what we describe as 'indifference'. In the face of local resident pressure, the producer/intermediary falls back onto the environmental discourse and argues that the award drives up environmental standards that result in improved beach facilities for local resident leisure use. Furthermore, it is mistaken of the residents to construe the beach award as a 'tourism' award. This is somewhat of a contradictory position, because at the same time the producer/intermediary is seeking to satisfy another set of political interests that insists upon ever-increasing 'boosterism' for the tourism industry through the corporate marketing of the destination area. The producer/intermediary agencies, therefore, find themselves Janus-faced on the subject of beach awards. Having convinced the local resident of the value of the award using the environmental discourse, the award to a specific beach is used to satisfy the tourism business community through its incorporation into the tourism promotion literature as an added-value quality icon. The conflicting political interests facing the producer/intermediary stakeholders are partially responsible for the quiet indifference discourse.

Conclusion: One Kite Mark, Separate Discourses

This chapter has attempted to test the often presumed relationship between beach award schemes and the performance of tourism businesses through the case of the nascent GCA. We operationalised this research aim through a discourse approach. Specifically we were interested in the extent to which an environmental discourse had entered the tourism micro-business networks, and, vice versa, a business discourse had entered environmental networks. A visual depiction of our findings is shown in Figure 15.1. The analysis of the innocent irrelevance discourse we encountered showed some awareness of broader environmental interest among the individual operators. However, we also uncovered a disparity between the operators' understanding of environmental quality in certain macro-markets and the perception of the actual importance given to environmental matters by individual consumers in making their buying choices. Consequently, we found a discourse dominated by short-term business performance concerns, defined by the consumer's expectations, and little evidence of a broader environmental discourse in micro-business networks (an understandable innocence).

Our challenges on the identification of the broader environmental issues that might have entered the micro-business networks were persistently answered by reference to two factors. First, operators had full confidence in the power of the National Park designation to kite mark Pembrokeshire as an environmentally high quality destination. In Anglesey operators had no such political institution for consumers to refer to, and individuals recognised a void in any attempt to kite mark the environmental qualities of the island, but seemed unwilling or unable to take collective action to rectify this situation. Secondly, the immediate, but short-lived, impact of the *Sea Empress* oil tanker disaster on the agenda of business networks in Pembrokeshire and the devastating impact of the 2001 foot and mouth epidemic on Anglesey galvanised operators to take environmental concerns seriously. Any expressed concern over the water quality or beach quality was rare in the micro-business discourse except where consumers had demonstrated to operators through their questions that they were sufficiently informed of the importance of these indicators (e.g. water sports enthusiasts). In contrast to the position taken by tour operators in respect of the FEE Blue Flag, micro-businesses in rural Wales saw little business advantage in using a GCA designation to promote beach quality.

Furthermore, we were interested in the extent to which business performance discourse had entered the environmental networks. As we report above, the environmental networks, while being absolutely vital to achieving real improvements in beach management, eschewed tourism business performance as a legitimate part of their discourse.

The quiet indifference discourse displays the complexity of such approaches to research. The full influence of the political and cultural context of the quiet indifference discourse reminds us of the power of institutions to frame legitimate discourse. We were particularly struck by the land use based preoccupations of economic development agencies and the extent of influence of 'local' resident interests on local authority beach managers. This resulted in an almost 'whispering' promotion of the GCA.

What can we draw from this analysis for a formative evaluation of the GCA? In this element of our research we have, in essence, produced a supply-side view of the GCA. Where we have explored the influence of consumer demand we have done so only in as far as it is mediated by supply-side stakeholders. We have reported the results of the survey of consumers' views elsewhere (Nelson & Botterill, 2002), and intend to combine the separate investigations into a prescriptive model in a future paper. The results of the consumer survey indicate an expected low level of awareness of the GCA by tourist consumers that were using the award beaches, a finding that confirms the low levels of consumer knowledge and understanding of beach award schemes generally (Nelson *et al.*, 1999).

There are some encouraging trends, however, in respect of a growing environmental consciousness in 'new' consumer markets. What is of more interest is that when asked to detail the attributes of beaches that lead to a consumer perception of good beach quality, consumers indicated almost exactly the likely outcomes when criteria that are used to designate a GCA are implemented. This finding opens up the 'black box' of the links between beach quality awards and tourism business performance. We suggest that the process of achieving an environmental kite mark and the incumbent improvements in environmental quality are better understood as a link *directly* to improved levels of consumer satisfaction. The contribution of the GCA to consumer satisfaction and *indirectly* to tourism business performance through increased incidence of repeat visitation and new business through 'word of mouth' marketing may be the essence of the 'link'. Poor levels of understanding of the 'real' nature of the presumed link in all stakeholder groups needs to be countered by an effective public relations campaign particularly aimed at tourism micro-businesses and consumers of rural beaches in Wales.

References

Bhaskar, R. (1978) *A Realist Theory of Science*. Brighton: Harvester.

Botterill, D. (2001) The epistemology of a set of studies of tourism. *Leisure Studies* 20 (3), 199–214.

Botterill, D. (2003) An autoethnographic narrative on tourism research epistemologies. *Society and Leisure* 26 (1), 97–110.

Botterill, D., Owen, R.E., Emanuel, L., Foster, N., Gale, T., Nelson, C. and Selby, M. (2000) Perceptions from the periphery; the experience of Wales. In F. Brown and D. Hall (eds) *Aspects of Tourism: Tourism in Peripheral Areas* (pp. 7–38). Clevedon: Channel View.

CEC (1976) *Council Directive of 8 December 1975 Concerning the Quality of Bathing Water (76/160/EEC)*. Strasbourg: Journal of the European Communities.

Countryside Council for Wales (1998) *Annual Report 1997–98, Volume II, Digest of Statistics*. Bangor: Countryside Council for Wales.

Countryside Council for Wales (1999) *Annual Report 1998–99, Volume II, Digest of Statistics*. Bangor: Countryside Council for Wales.

FEE (Foundation for Environmental Education) (2003a) *Blue Flag Sponsors*. On WWW at http://www.blueflag.org/Sponsors.asp. Accessed 12.01.04.

FEE (Foundation for Environmental Education) (2003b) *Links*. On WWW at http://www.blueflag.org/Links.asp. Accessed 12.01.04.

FEE (Foundation for Environmental Education) (2003c) *New Caribbean Countries Starting the Blue Flag Implementation*. On WWW at http://www.blueflag.org/NewsArchive.asp. Accessed 12.01.04.

FEE (Foundation for Environmental Education) (2003d) *The Blue Flag Campaign 2003*. On WWW at http://www.blueflag.org/NewsArchive. asp. Accessed 12.01.04.

Foster, N. (1999) Representing Wales: Congruence and Dissonance in Tourism Imagery. Unpublished doctoral dissertation, Open University.

Howarth, D. (2000) *Discourse*. Buckingham: Open University Press.

Hyder (1999). *Green Sea Update*. Treharris: Dwr Cymru Public Information.

Jones, E., Botterill, D., Lynch, P. and Thomas, R. (2004) United Kingdom. In A. Morrison and R. Thomas (eds) *SMEs in Tourism: An International Review*. Arnhem: ATLAS.

Keep Wales Tidy (2003) *Green Coast Award Guidance Notes*. On WWW at http://www.keepwalestidy.co.uk/english/default.asp?Category=Tourism &NewsID = 17&Menu = 0. 26.12.61. Accessed 12.01.04.

Keep Wales Tidy (2003) *Tourism.* On WWW at http://www.keepwalesti dy.co.uk/english/default.asp?Category=Tourism&NewsID=9&Menu =0.26.12. Accessed 12.01.04.

Lincoln, Y. and Guba, E. (1985) *Naturalistic Inquiry.* Beverly Hills: Sage.

Lynch, P.A. (2000) Networking in the homestay sector. *Services Industry Journal* 20 (3), 95–116.

Lynch, P., Halcro, K., Johns, N., Buick, I. and Gilham, M. (2000) Networks and networking a strategic tool for small hotel survival and success. In A. Williams (ed.) *Proceedings of the 9th Annual CHME Hospitality Research Conference* (pp. 114–24) 26–27 April, 2000.

Nelson C. and Botterill, D. (2002) Evaluating the contribution of Beach Quality Awards to the local tourism industry in Wales – The Green Coast Award. *Journal of Ocean and Coastal Management* 45, 157–70.

Nelson, C., Botterill, D. and Williams, A. (2000) The beach as a leisure resource: measuring user perceptions of beach debris pollution. *Journal of World Leisure and Recreation Association* 42 (1), 37–43.

Nelson, C., Morgan, R., Williams, A.T. and Woods, J. (2000) Beach awards and management. *Ocean and Coastal Management* 43 (1), 87–98.

Nelson, C., Williams, A.T. and Bin, H. (1999) Award schemes and beach selection by tourists – a Welsh (UK) perspective. *Coastal Engineering* 2, 156–68.

TBG (Tidy Britain Group) (1999a) *European Blue Flag and Seaside Award.* Wigan: The Tidy Britain Group.

TBG (Tidy Britain Group) (1999b) *Green Coast Award.* Wigan: The Tidy Britain Group.

TBG (Tidy Britain Group) (2000) *The 2000 Seaside Awards.* Wigan: The Tidy Britain Group.

Wavelength (1999) The news letter of the National Coastal Fora in the UK. Issue 4, Autumn.

Welsh Water (1997) *The Green Sea Initiative.* Treharris: Dwr Cymru Welsh Water.

WTB (Wales Tourist Board) (1996) *Green Seas Directory.* Cardiff: Wales Tourist Board.

WTB (Wales Tourist Board) (1997) *Green Sea News, Issue 2, June 1997.* Cardiff: Wales Tourist Board.

WTB (Wales Tourist Board) (2000) *Achieving Our Potential.* Cardiff: Wales Tourist Board.

WTB (Wales Tourist Board) (2003a) *Domestic (UK) Tourism to Wales 2002. Research Note.* On WWW at http://www.wtbonline.gov.uk. Accessed 12.01.04.

WTB (Wales Tourist Board) (2003b) *Volume and Value of Tourism to Wales. Research Note.* On WWW at http://www.wtbonline.gov.uk. Accessed 12.01.04.

Chapter 16

Entrepreneurial Personality Traits in Managing Rural Tourism and Sustainable Business

WALTER SCHIEBEL

Introduction

Austrian agriculture has been going through a period of necessary structural change, prompted in particular by the country's membership of the EU. This change is challenging producers to become more entrepreneurial both with regard to agricultural marketing and cooperation and to diversification activities that can appeal to differentiated foreign markets.

This not only requires appropriate quality and quantity in terms of supply, but also that farmers think and act like entrepreneurs. Direct marketing, farm holidays, producer groups and strategic alliances need committed entrepreneurial personalities. As one response to this requirement, the Federal Ministry of Agriculture, Forestry, Environment and Water Management (BMLFUW) commissioned a national survey of those personal characteristics of farmers relevant to entrepreneurship.

The research on such personality traits as 'locus of control of reinforcement', problem-solving activities and social initiative is based on psychology-oriented decision research. This research on empirical success factors allows us to define five different types of personality: the self-responsible, the powerless, the helpless, the socially-active, and the indifferent. The existence of a large number of self-responsible personality types is decisive when building efficient systems of cooperation. The scales measuring locus of control of reinforcement were combined with the four scales measuring social initiative and the result expressed as entrepreneurial type. The research described in this chapter found that 10% of the sample corresponded to those success factors required for entrepreneurs. This figure bodes ill for male and female farmers, who should take an increasingly (even totally) entrepreneurial approach to future cooperation ventures.

These results are being applied within the extension initiative 'farming families as entrepreneurs' to support the work of the BMLFUW's extension department and youth training programmes. The focus of this application relates to the general lack of self-responsibility and self-confidence identified in the empirical research. An 'objective-driven behaviour and action' training programme for farmers designed to strengthen their locus of control and their ability to cope with anxiety has been one successful outcome.

Theoretical Principles

The German language psychology literature reveals that, apart from a few publications by Heckhausen (e.g. 1977), no studies have been undertaken that are directly concerned with starting a business or with entrepreneurs themselves.

There are disproportionally more publications relating to this subject in the English language literature, particularly in that originating from the United States (Luthans *et al.*, 1995). In terms of results-oriented research, there have been a relatively large number of US studies on the person or character of the entrepreneur. Key subjects for practice-oriented research are the education of entrepreneurs and the development of successful strategies for founding businesses. Discussions also centre on how the state, local government and universities can encourage and support the creation of new businesses.

Essentially, two research approaches have emerged, both of which seek to explain the character or nature of the process of starting a new business. The first and older approach includes the work done in the field of entrepreneurship research. This approach seeks to identify the personality traits, characteristics and behavioural patterns of those setting up a business and then to compare these with those of non-entrepreneurs, at the same time taking account of the context within which this entrepreneurial activity takes place. The second approach draws on biological concepts and works within an evolutionary–ecological framework. This approach seeks to explain differences in the rate of business start-ups within a population of organizations (such as a particular branch of industry, such as agriculture) in terms of the relevant operating environment – social, economic and political factors – and across a relatively long period of time.

The ecological perspective is a promising approach allowing us to tackle entrepreneurial research from a new angle. Nevertheless, it is still in early development and a number of relevant issues still need to be resolved, as evidenced in the range of criticisms that have been levelled at this new approach.

The academic literature underpinning the empirical parts of the study presented here is dominated by English-speaking, predominately US, research. This material has been supplemented more recently by a range of German-language empirical studies that have concentrated almost exclusively on aspects of the business foundation act itself.

The core thesis of the German-language research is that entrepreneurs are much more convinced of their ability to influence those outcomes that are important to them than are the general population. Entrepreneurs are also much more likely to have a father who was himself self-employed.

The work by Klandt (1984) is worth noting in this context, particularly the following observations:

- *Dynamic aspects*: entrepreneurs are more ambitious than other people, are more prepared to take risks, have a clear tendency to seek independence, but are average in terms of the desire to wield power (a politician is a typical example of a power-oriented individual).
- *Personality traits*: entrepreneurs show social initiative, are easily enthused, are flexible and distinctly individualistic, show a clear desire to dominate, are less cunning and more spontaneous.
- *Skills and abilities*: entrepreneurs tend to be complex, uncertain and obscure personalities, with a network of personal contacts; these characteristics do not reflect the dimensions normally measured in intelligence tests and similar. Klandt (1984) therefore recommends using the approaches taken in more recent psychological research when measuring an individual's problem-solving skills in the context of a complex and unclear task.

The current position regarding psychology-oriented decision research

Locus of control of reinforcement

In a semi-scientific sense, there are numerous dimensions that could be used to describe the human character. It would seem sensible to systematically reduce this number to a small group of important and more useful dimensions. This need has been addressed in research on the fundamental psychology of personality, through approaches based on factor analysis. Cattell's (1973) 16 PF personality inventory is an example of the factor analysis approach. This 16 personality factor questionnaire is a self-report assessment instrument that measures the 16 normal adult personality dimensions discovered by R.B. Cattell in his landmark research over 40 years ago. Also exemplified below is the 'Locus of Control of Reinforcement' construct (which has much in common with McClelland's (1975) achievement motive approach). Such work was unable to find any significant correlation between the intensity of the achievement motive and the attitude to control of later supported reinforcement by Shapero and

Sokol's (1982) supposition that the control of reinforcement is a better indicator of character.

- *The 16 PF approach*: the empirical work undertaken by Klandt (1984) and Szyperski and Klandt (1988) confirms the importance of factors Dominance (Submissiveness: deferential, cooperative, avoids conflict, submissive, humble, obedient, easily led, docile, accomodating vs. Dominance: dominant, forceful, assertive, aggressive, competitive, stubborn, bossy), Liveliness (Desurgency: serious, restrained, prudent, taciturn, introspective, silent vs. Surgency: spontaneous, enthusiastic, happy-go-lucky, cheerful, expressive, impulsive), Social Boldness (Threctia: shy, threat-sensitive, timid, hesitant, intimidated vs. Parmia: socially bold, venturesome, thick-skinned, uninhibited, can take stress) and Abstractedness (Praxernia: grounded, practical, prosaic, solution-oriented, steady, conventional vs. Autia: abstracted, imaginative, absent-minded, impractical, absorbed in ideas). Entrepreneurs score above average for Dominance, Liveliness, Social Boldness and Abstractedness.
- *The 'Locus of Control of Reinforcement' construct*: the Austrian study carried out in 1975 by Zoihsl (the first and only European study of locus of control, until the research by Schiebel (1988)) showed that entrepreneurs were much more convinced of their ability to control events than were the control group.

Differentiation of the construct

As indicated in the research carried out by Krampen *et al.* (1987), it would seem to make sense to differentiate between an individual's locus of control for activities and situations where problems need to be solved ('farm holidays'), and his or her more generalised locus of control.

The variability of the locus of control

Hofmann and Preiser (1987) have verified that the extent of the internal locus of control rises until early adolescence, after which it remains more or less constant. The external locus of control can intensify in adulthood. They carried out research on individuals that were induced experimentally to reflect on the causes and potential of their own actions when pursuing and achieving personal objectives (in the sense of specific practical experience). This reflective process was predominately induced through appropriate help and enforced self-responsibility. The research showed that these individuals achieve more personal control of their working lives, irrespective of the way in which this internal awareness is created.

People experience successful and unsuccessful attempts to exert control as they pursue objective-driven action. Different action-related cognitive and emotional states develop or change as a result of these experiences. Examples include expectations of competence, locus of control, expectations of success and fear of failure. These kinds of cognitive and emotional states act as variables moderating action and behaviour; that is, they modify the relationships between objectives (and their evaluation) and the extent or expression of personal, objective-driven activities (Pfrang & Schenk, 1986).

Those environmental conditions whose effects are felt in the long term influence the development and change of the awareness of control. This conclusion can be drawn from Rotter's (1966) underlying social learning theory and was identified in different forms by Schneewind (1985). Hofmann and Preiser (1987) showed in addition that relatively short-term, new experiences in the context of some specific sphere of activity can also lead to a change in the awareness of control (see the discussion of the 'objective-driven behaviour or action' training programme below).

Strategies for coping with anxiety

In 1964, Berelson and Steiner described one of the central theses of communications research, namely that the selection of information is controlled by existing predispositions. In this context, Vitouch (1989) highlighted the importance of the ability of the recipient to process information and, following a comprehensive review of the literature, concluded that anxiety (in the form of the strategy for coping with anxiety) was the dominant factor in this information process.

Epstein (1976) talks of three different strategies for coping with anxiety: non-depressive, depressive–repressive, and depressive–sensitized. Krohne (1971) points out that those individuals following an 'avoidance' strategy not only seek out less information than those taking a 'non-defensive' strategy, but they may also seek out different information content. The 'sensitiser' consumes mainly anxiety-provoking stimuli, thereby raising his or her state of activation. This means that sudden and unexpected anxiety stimuli can then no longer lead to an uncomfortable rise in this state of activation. This kind of recipient deliberately looks for information about uncontrollable events, about 'the bad things going on in the world'. The 'repressor', on the other hand, avoids any kind of information that might cause anxiety (anxiety-inducing inputs). He or she certainly does not watch, read or listen to the news, political/economic/medical commentaries or situation reports.

The success factors

A number of conclusions can be drawn from the publications and studies dealing with success factor research. These publications cover research from European research groups, particularly those of Szyperski *et al.* (1983) and Klandt (Klandt, 1984; Szyperski & Klandt, 1988); from the Anglo-American world (in particular the work of the research group around McClelland, Rotter and Cattell), and also the current author's own work (Schiebel, 1988).

Successful entrepreneurs differ in terms of three personality traits (success factors):

(1)   locus of control of reinforcement;
(2)   problem-solving abilities; and
(3)   social initiative.

'Belief in the ability to control events' is understood in terms of a person's general expectations, where we can differentiate between:

- those people who believe that they can have a strong influence on the events going on around them ('Internality');
- those who believe that the events going on around them are strongly influenced by other people ('Powerful Others'); and
- those who believe that the events going on around them are determined by luck or chance ('Chance Control').

'Problem-solving ability' is an expectation specific to a particular field of action and relates to possible future forms of cooperation. 'Social initiative' is expressed through a person's dominance, liveliness, social boldness and abstractedness. The construct is a measure of the socialisation process undergone by a male or female farmer, and acts as a second estimate of control of reinforcement.

Comparable international results

There are no comparable international research results available that deal with the measurement of entrepreneurial personality traits in the agricultural sector. However, there are some research studies that deal with rural entrepreneurship and entrepreneurial traits more generally. A detailed study of West German entrepreneurs was published by Klandt in 1984. The Senate for Economy and Employment in Berlin commissioned a review of the situation for women regarding business start-ups (Assig *et al.*, 1985). This study also included the first overview of global empirical research into female entrepreneurs. Only two of the reviewed studies (one from Belgium, one from England) mentioned the individual, her characteristics or her performance, factors which also, of course, contribute to business success. The results from the two studies that did mention these issues are somewhat meagre: women plan for the short term and do not have enough self-confidence.

Results from comparable professions in Austria

A few surveys have dealt with the public image of entrepreneurs. Other surveys were conceived as detailed studies of specific issues, such as stress or expectations (Austrian Chamber of Commerce, 1984, 1985; Fessel & GfK, 1983).

Schiebel (1988) studied the dynamics and decision-making strengths of 4320 female entrepreneurs in Austria, in research commissioned by the Austrian Chamber of Commerce (Table 16.1). The proportion of women classified as 'self-responsible' was twice that for the sample of men and women as a whole. To overcome perceptions of helplessness, Austrian women have since demanded that the organisations that represent their interests establish appropriate encounter groups.

Describing the personalities of entrepreneurs

The insights gained through empirical success factor research allow us to define the following typology, based on the different expression of expectations (see also Krampen, 1981):

- *Type A*: characterised as self-responsible;
- *Type B*: powerless;
- *Type C*: helpless;
- *Type D*: socially active;
- *Type E*: indifferent.

These five different types of personality are described in more detail below.

The self-responsible entrepreneur (Type A)

This type is socially active and emotionally stable. They tend to be capable of self-actualisation, are less aggressive or dogmatic, and learn quickly and easily. They are not easy to influence. Indeed, they are able to successfully influence others through the use of argument. They can tolerate a high level of stress, are willing to take on more strenuous tasks and tend to form their own independent opinion. They prefer a participatory management style, use more cognitive control strategies and are less likely to call for professional help (and then only at a

Table 16.1 Categorisation of Austrian farmers' personality factors

Category	All (%)	Women only (%)
Self-responsible	21.5	53.3
Powerless	9.6	4.5
Helpless	17.3	9.3
Politically or socially inactive	10.7	12.6
Indifferent	40.8	20.3
	100.0	

Sources: Schiebel (1988); author's survey

relatively late stage in the proceedings). They are more willing to take risks and suffer less from stress, since they tend to view stressful events positively. In social situations, they seek out other people sharing these same characteristics (self-responsibility).

The powerless entrepreneur (Type B)

This type is more conformist when making judgements. They tend to change their own attitudes if the social status of the partner they are cooperating with is high. They are more susceptible to stress, and are easier to convince, talk round or control. They do not influence other people through the use of argument, but through compulsion or the threat of punishment. They are more risk averse and spend more time looking for (and selecting) information.

The helpless entrepreneur (Type C)

The behaviour of the helpless entrepreneur is based on the expectation (itself based on experience), that their own behaviour has no influence, and that what they perceive to be important events in their own specific environment cannot be controlled. Helplessness is expressed, for example, through a weak will, fear, passivity, a reduced learning capacity, and an inability to change expectations in response to changes in marginal conditions.

The socially-active entrepreneur (Type D)

This type is characterised by social commitment and involvement. These characteristics arise from a combination of self-responsibility and a feeling of subjugation through free-market majorities. These entrepreneurs are what Witte (1972) would call 'helpers', rather than 'doers'. Their personality is influenced by an above-average (even far above-average) internal and external locus of control of reinforcement, which makes it difficult for them to act or behave in a steady and purposeful way. The little empirical evidence available gives no indication of any relationship between the dynamic characteristic 'gregariousness' and entrepreneurial activities. Klandt's research also found no significant correlation between the two.

The indifferent entrepreneur (Type E)

This personality type has no particular leanings in any one direction – they represent the 'average'.

The existence of a large number of self-responsible personality types is decisive when building efficient systems of cooperation. This means that the general and cooperation-specific expectations of male and female farmers must be such that they believe they can have a strong influence on the events taking place around them.

The BMLFUW's development plan for cooperation partners (the 'farming family as entrepreneur' extension focus) will help support the development of these personality types to the benefit of future (efficient) producer organisations and strategic alliances.

The hypothesis

It can, therefore, be expected that efficient producer organisations and strategic alliances will feature a higher proportion of self-responsible (Type A) farmers (both male and female). If there is a relatively high proportion of helpless and/or indifferent personality types, then we need to ask whether this is related to particular psychographic, job-related, or microeconomic features.

The implicit basis of the model is the assumption of population homogeneity, that is, the assumption that there are no real differences in the contributions made by individual organisations to competition and the legitimisation of the system (Wiedenmayer *et al.*, 1995). In reality, the potential influence of an organisation varies considerably with size; large organisations often control a much larger proportion of the resource base than do a multitude of smaller organisations. The dynamics of competition in a population made up of organisations of a similar size may be very different to those in a population featuring a few large organisations and many small ones.

Since we are looking at personality characteristics relating to the entrepreneurs themselves, enterprise size (as a determining variable within the framework of the socialisation process (the 'microsocial surroundings') is recorded, but not accorded special attention.

The study should also test the hypothesis that the proportion of female farmers falling into the category 'self-responsible' is the same as the equivalent proportion of male farmers. After all, it is generally the female farmers who are responsible for applying business skills to the management of 'direct marketing' or 'farm holiday' ventures.

Method

As specified in the project design given in the research contract, a questionnaire based on Schiebel (1988) was developed by the project leader and used in a representative national survey carried out by IFES, the Institute for Empirical Social Research, Vienna in 1996.

Research participants

The IFES survey used a boosted sample size and returned $n = 881$ completed questionnaires. The raw data set was tested for completeness and plausibility by the Department of Agricultural Marketing, and declared valid for $n = 881$.

Material

Locus of control of reinforcement was evaluated using the IPC questionnaire (24 questions) and problem-solving ability evaluated using Krampen's IPC-PL questionnaire (also 24 questions). The social initiative of farmers of both sexes was measured using values for Factor 'Dominance' (submissiveness vs. dominance, 12 questions), Factor 'Liveliness' (desurgency vs. surgency, 12 questions), Factor 'Social Boldness' (threctia vs. parmia, 12 questions) and Factor 'Abstractedness' (praxernia vs. autia, 12 questions), in accordance with the 16 PF test developed by Schneewind *et al.* (1984).

Implementation and evaluation

The hypothesis was tested using the data collected in standardised questionnaire interviews. Socio-demographic and micro-economic information about the respondents was recorded for use in further analyses.

The project leader and his co-workers were responsible for the design of the research, questionnaire design, data evaluation and analysis, and overall project management. The questionnaire survey was carried out by the Institute for Empirical Social Research (Vienna).

Typology

Respondents were categorised using stanine values ('stanine' is a recognised abbreviated form for 'standard nine': stanine scores range from a low of 1 to a high of 9) and in accordance with the procedures stated by Krampen (1981).

'Stanine' values – 'standard nine' scores – combine the understandability of percentages with the properties of the normal curve of probability. A scale is created with nine intervals, each interval representing half of a stand deviation. The 5th stanine straddles the midpoint of the distribution, covering the middle 20% of scores. Given the range of the raw values, they were grouped into three classes (below average, average and above average) for each of the three scales, I, P and C, and then combined (Krampen, 1981) into the five character types: self-responsible (internality above average), powerless (powerful others above average), helpless (chance control above average), politically or socially active (internality and powerful others above average including internality, powerful others and chance control above average), and indifferent (no scale above average).

According to Krampen *et al.* (1987) and Preiser (1989), dominance, liveliness and abstractedness are predominately the result of family-based socialisation processes (family life on the farm), while social boldness is predominantly socialised in non-family environments (e.g. school). Generalised expectations with regard to the locus of control are primarily regarded as the result of those socialisation processes that take place outside the family environment; helpless personality types therefore lack self-confidence.

Entrepreneurial personality

The success factors recorded for each potential cooperation partner were assigned a value of one (self-responsibility and social initiative) or zero, reflecting their value for an efficient cooperation system. An entrepreneurial personality is defined as someone with a points total greater than, or equal to, four.

The four dimensions of personality ('dominance', 'liveliness', 'social boldness' and 'abstractedness') were measured with the help of the appropriate 16 PF scales; that is, the raw data from the item batteries were converted to stanine values, and stanine values greater than 7.5 (i.e. those values outside the standard deviation) were then used for determining an entrepreneurial personality.

Results

The data

The following variables were recorded and analysed for the purpose of characterising the sample; location (state), size of district, age group (as defined in Krampen (1981) and Schneewind *et al.*'s (1984) test manuals), gender, education, income from agriculture and forestry, number of dependents and enterprise classification. The sample was made up of a total of 881 respondents. Of these, 64.4% are less than 50 years old, 35.6% are 50 or older, 47.3% of respondents live in districts with a population under 2000 and 63.6% are male, 44.1% are full-time farmers, 46.9% part-time farmers, 72.6% describe their enterprise as a mixed farm, while 34.4% have three to four dependents.

IPC-typology, social initiative and entrepreneurial personality

IPC-typology

The methodological approaches described earlier were used to calculate each respondent's locus of control of reinforcement, both in the general (IPC, questionnaire part B) and problem-specific (IPC-PL, questionnaire part d) sense. The results were then grouped into types. The underlying sample values used were weighted for gender (50 : 50) and age (quota given by ÖSTAT, the Austrian Statistical Office). The following comments relate to the weighted results.

In terms of their general locus of control of reinforcement, Austria's farmers can be categorised as in Table 16.1. The results are almost identical for the problem-related locus of control of reinforcement. The only meaningful changes are in the proportion of politically or socially active personalities (just 6.9%) and the proportion of indifferent personalities

(43.6%). Powerless and helpless personalities are in danger of being 'left out'; the following strategies would help to integrate them more into society:

(1) Strengthen the farm family (as the basis for the development of social initiative).
(2) Strengthen the internal locus of control of reinforcement, through:
     (a) intervention strategies, such as a school training programme;
     (b) establishment of encounter groups;
     (c) creation of networks of small initiatives and cooperative ventures.

Social initiative

The results (weighted for gender and age) for dominance, liveliness, social boldness and abstractedness are:

- 33.9/30.4%: Dominance ('Dominance')
- 25.3/29.6%: Surgency ('Liveliness')
- 0.2/0.2%: Parmia ('Social Boldness')
- 49.0/53.5%: Autia ('Abstractedness')

Continuing extension efforts would seem necessary, given the very low degree of social boldness. The separation of stanine values by age and gender produces some interesting results; surgency increases with age, and female farmers have a higher degree of dominance than their male equivalents.

Entrepreneurial personality

The two scales measuring locus of control of reinforcement were combined with the four scales measuring social initiative and the results expressed as entrepreneurial types (in accordance with the methodological procedure described earlier in this chapter).

Eighty-five respondents were found to have a combination of personality traits that corresponded to those required for entrepreneurs, that is, about 10% of the sample. This figure would be acceptable for the population as a whole, but bodes ill for a group that should take an increasingly (even totally) entrepreneurial approach within future cooperative ventures.

The hypothesis that the same proportion of entrepreneurial types can be found in both male and female farmers can be confirmed using the chi-squared test. Both sexes are therefore in the same initial position.

Further training and education

In the questionnaire survey, male and female farmers were asked about their training and education activities, and also about their potential interest in particular extension initiatives. The results showed that 55% of farmers attend seminars and lectures, around 50% keep themselves informed through newspapers, 40% visit relevant fairs and exhibitions, and 39% attach importance to farm visits. Each year, about 38% of farmers spend up to five days on this kind of education and training. Some 28% of farmers 'sacrifice' between six and ten days for such purposes.

Most interest was expressed in extension activities relating to:

- direct marketing (39%);
- sales support (32%);
- marketing (26%);
- cooperative ventures (17%); and
- communication skills (10%).

Topics relevant to improving income are given top priority, although individualism (as a direct marketer) is preferred to the exploitation of synergistic effects through cooperative ventures. Only one in every ten farmers attaches importance to the development of communication skills, a poor attitude when you consider that direct marketing is based on sales talks. Conversational and communications skills need the *parmia* personality characteristic, which is more or less non-existent in this population. It would seem that farmers are over-estimating themselves; in nine out of ten cases, their own self-image does not match the image that others have of them.

These results can be used to identify the most promising focus for further education and training activities. This focus relates of course to the general lack of self-responsibility and self-confidence identified in the empirical research. The identified deficiencies can be ameliorated or eliminated through some of the approaches discussed in the next section, which are based on Preiser's (1989) training model. Training in communication skills should also be made a fixed part of farm extension activities and should also be taught in the curriculum of agricultural and forestry schools.

A solution-oriented approach: 'objective-driven behaviour or action'

The information processing that male and female farmers (henceforth referred to as decision makers) need to undertake to manage agricultural marketing tasks are determined to a large extent by their strategy for dealing with anxiety and their locus of control of reinforcement. The latter characteristic is an individual's state of expectation in terms of their perception of events (e.g. those resulting from particular decisions) as being controlled:

(1) predominately by the individual him- or herself,
(2) predominately by other individuals, or
(3) predominately through chance or luck.

Those individuals falling into the first group are referred to as 'internally controlled', those falling into the second group as 'externally controlled', and those falling into the third group as 'fatalists'. The development of a farmer's personality should be oriented toward the development of an internally-controlled decision maker. The other two personality types are undesirable because such individuals are much less willing to look for and absorb information, and are less interested in innovating; they perform much worse than their internally-controlled colleagues when faced with complex and poorly structured decision-making problems in agricultural marketing.

An individual's strategy for dealing with anxiety is the second key personality trait 'controlling' the processing of information by this individual. So-called 'normal' anxiety (e.g. when faced by something new or a risky decision), where an individual copes with anxiety in a non-defensive way, does not need to be addressed in personal development.

Defensive strategies for coping with anxiety do, however, need to be tackled through personal development. These strategies find two different types of expression (the 'sensitiser' and the 'repressor'), both of which reduce the decision-making or processing efficiency of male and female farmers. The 'sensitiser' attempts to gather 'all' information relevant to a decision (in the belief that this reduces the risk associated with the decision), and thereby delays the actual decision-making process. The 'repressor' tries to avoid any risk- or anxiety-inducing information, and thereby reduces the complexity of the problem in an arbitrary and non-causal manner.

The amount and type of information considered relevant for a decision-making process in agricultural marketing is to a large extent determined by these two features of personality, and has a huge impact on the quality of the subsequent decision made, through:

(1) the subjective risk preferences of the farmer, and
(2) the information resources demanded by the farmer in the context of this decision-making process.

Psychologically oriented decision research has developed a training programme designed to strengthen the locus of control and the ability to cope with anxiety. The programme consists of eight modules and teaches decision makers 'objective-driven behaviour and action'. The course helps strengthen the internal locus of control of reinforcement (i.e. it increases self-responsibility) and encourages the development of more non-defensive strategies for coping with anxiety. A range of reliable testing instruments is available for recording personality traits and measuring the locus of control of reinforcement, anxiety and strategies for coping with anxiety. These tools can be used separately, in order to determine initial personalities as part of, for example, some kind of school programme for entrepreneurs, or they can be applied before and after an appropriate training programme.

The training programme is suitable both for small groups (ca. 20 participants) and for coaching individuals. The eight modules are 'developed' in collaboration with the trainer. A two-day follow-up programme one year later is recommended. The programme draws on the theory-based approach to behaviour and action developed by Krampen (1981) and Preiser (1989). The diagnosis of personality is undertaken with the help of Krampen's (1991) FKK (Competence and Control Orientations Scale), Taylor's (1953) Manifest Anxiety Scale and the Repression–Sensitization Scale developed by Byrne (1961) and Krohne (1974). The state of mind of the decision makers is measured before and after each training unit using the Zerssen scale (1976). The Zerssen method is always used for evaluating the impacts of the training programme, but the use of any other diagnostic instrument must be agreed separately with course participants.

Outlook for the teaching programme

The 'objective-driven behaviour and action' training programme for farmers' personal development is based on the latest results of empirical decision research. The programme encourages self-responsibility and non-defensive approaches to the management of anxiety, both of which form the basis for a non-arbitrary reduction in complexity in the context of personal information processing and information retrieval processes. The use of various diagnostic instruments for determining personality allows differences in the state of development of decision makers to be identified, in turn allowing the training programme to be better targeted to needs. This diagnosis and training programme supports the qualitative personal development of farmers to the benefit of their decision-making and information-processing behaviour.

Summary and Conclusions

Validated tests in the form of batteries of questions were used to measure success factors (and thereby to identify entrepreneurial personalities) in a nationally representative sample of male and female farmers. The 'entrepreneurial typology' derived from the results allows us to describe the current situation with regard to those personality traits of farmers related to entrepreneurship. It also allows us to make available targeted measures in the context of the BMLFUW's extension focus on the 'farm family as entrepreneur'. The results of this research project have therefore contributed to an improvement in the willingness of farmers to cooperate with each other via special training programmes designed to strengthen their locus of control and their ability to cope with anxiety (to become more self-responsible). They thus support the development of the producer organisations and strategic alliances needed in the rural restructuring process demanded by the challenges of the internal EU market for agricultural products.

The suggested training programme has already been used successfully by Preiser in Germany and by the current author, both of whom have used the programme in teaching and practice. The 'objective-driven behaviour and action' training programme for farmers' personal development has been successfully managed:

(1) in several postgraduate management courses at the University of Natural Resources and Applied Life Sciences, Vienna, with 120 participants; and

(2) as part of a short course on regional development carried out in Styria and Waldviertel (Austria) with 45 participants.

A test comparison (before and after) has shown that the control conviction and the self-assessment of the self-responsibility of the participants has increased. 'How to become an Entrepreneur?' is now introduced to all Viennese students and also to the agricultural and tourism students and graduates of the Free University Bolzano, Italy. Possible adoption is being sought for testing and training farmers within research centres at the universities of Guelph (Canada), Zagreb (Croatia), Nizhni Novgorod (Russia) and the Technical University Zurich (Switzerland). The programme cannot produce successful entrepreneurs (in the sense of business success), but can improve the chances of such success by changing personality traits.

Acknowledgements

The author would like to thank Dr Oliver Meixner of the Institute for Marketing and Innovation, BOKU Vienna, for undertaking the programming work required for the study.

References

Assig, D., Gather, C. and Hübner, S. (1985) *Voraussetzungen, Schwierigkeiten und Barrieren bei Existenzgründungen von Frauen, Untersuchungsbericht für den Senator für Wirtschaft und Arbeit*. Berlin: unpublished paper.

Austrian Chamber of Commerce (ed.) (1984) *Belastung und Erwartungshaltung von UnternehmerInnen in Österreich*. Vienna: Austrian Chamber of Commerce.

Austrian Chamber of Commerce (ed.) (1985) *Belastung und Erwartungshaltung von UnternehmerInnen in Österreich*. Vienna: Austrian Chamber of Commerce.

Berelson, B. and Steiner, G.A. (1964) *Human Behaviour. An Inventory of Scientific Findings*. New York: Harcourt, Brace & World.

Byrne, D. (1961) The Repression-Sensitization-Scale: rationale, reliability and validity. _Journal of Personality_ 29, 334–49.

Cattell, R.B. (1973) _Die empirische Erforschung der Persönlichkeit._ Basel: Weinheim.

Epstein, S. (1976) Anxiety, arousal and the self-concept. In I.G. Sorason and C.D. Spielberger (eds) _Stress and Anxiety_ (Vol. 3, pp. 185–224). Washington: Hemisphere.

Fessel & GfK (1983) _Das Image österreichischer Unternehmerinnen und Mitunternehmerinnen._ Wien: unpublished paper.

Heckhausen, H. (1977) Achievement motivation and its constructs: a cognitive model. In H. Heckhausen (ed.) _Motivation and Emotion_ (Vol. 1, pp. 283–329). New York: Plenum.

Hofmann, J.M. and Preiser, S. (1987) _Veränderungen von Kontrollüberzeugungen während des Lehramtspraktikums._ Frankfurt and Main: Institutsberichte 1987 des Instituts für Pädagogische Psychologie der J.W. Goethe-Universität Frankfurt/Main.

Klandt, H. (1984) _Aktivität und Erfolg des Unternehmensgründers, Eine empirische Analyse unter Einbeziehung des mikrosozialen Umfeldes._ Bergisch Gladbach: Eul.

Krampen, G. (1981) _IPC-Fragebogen zu Kontrollüberzeugungen._ Göttingen: Hogrefe.

Krampen, G., von Eye, A. and Brandstädter, J. (1987) Konfigurationstypen generalisierter Kontrollüberzeugungen. _Zeitschrift für Differentielle und Diagnostische Psychologie_ 8 (2), 111–19.

Krampen, G. (1991) _Fragebogen zu Kompetenz- und Kontrollüberzeugungen (FKK)._ Göttingen: Hogrefe.

Krohne, H.W. (1971) _Der Einfluß von Umweltkomplexität, Angstabwehr und konzeptionellem Niveau auf die Informationsverarbeitung._ Marburg: unpublished doctoral thesis, Phillips-University.

Krohne, H.W. (1974). Untersuchungen mit einer deutschen Form der Repression-Sensitization-Skala. _Zeitschrift für Klinische Psychologie_ 3, 238–60.

Luthans, F., Enwick, B.R. and Anderson, R.D. (1995) A proposed idiographic approach to the study of entrepreneurs. _Academy of Entrepreneurship Journal_ 1 (1), 1–18.

McClelland, D.C. (1975) _The Achievement Motive._ New York: Irvington.

Pfrang, H. and Schenk, J. (1986) Kontrollüberzeugungen als Moderator des Zusammenhangs zwischen Verstärkungswert und Verhalten. _Zeitschrift für Sozialpsychologie_ 17, 99–108.

Preiser, S. (1989) _Zielorientiertes Handeln._ Heidelberg: Asanger.

Rotter, J.B. (1966) Generalised expectancies for internal versus external control of reinforcement. _Psychological Monographs: General and Applied_ 80 (1), 1–28.

Schiebel, W. (1988) *Dynamik und Entscheidungsstärke der österreichischen Untenehmerinnen und Mitunternehmerinnen.* Vienna: Austrian Chamber of Commerce.

Schneewind, K.A., Schröder, G. and Cattell, R.B. (1984) *Der 16-Persönlichkeits-Faktoren-Test (16PF).* Bern: Huber.

Schneewind, K.A. (1985) Entwicklung personaler Kontrolle im Kontext der Familie. In W.F. Kugemann, S. Preiser and K.A. Schneewind (eds) *Psychologie und komplexe Lebenswirklichkeit* (pp. 203–23). Göttingen: Hogrefe.

Shapero, A. and Sokol, L. (1982) The social dimensions of entrepreneurship. In C.A. Kent, D.L. Sexton and K.H. Vesper (eds) *Encyclopedia of Entrepreneurship* (pp. 72–90). New Jersey: Prentice-Hall.

Szyperski, N., Darscheid, K., Kirschbaum, G. and Naujoks, W. (eds) (1983) *Unternehmensgründung und Innovation.* Göttingen: Hogrefe.

Szyperski, N. and Klandt, H. (1988) New concepts in entrepreneurial testing. In A.B. Kirchhoff, W.A. Long, W.E. McMullan, K.H. Vesper and W.E. Wetzler (eds) *Frontiers of Entrepreneurship Research 1988* (pp. 66–69). MA, USA: Wellesley-Cambridge Press.

Taylor, J.A. (1953) A personality scale of manifest anxiety. *Journal of Abnormal and Social Psychology* 48, 285–90.

Vitouch, P. (1989) *Der Einfluß von Angstabwehr und Umweltkomplexität auf die Informationsverarbeitung.* Wien: Österreichisches Institut für Bildungsforschung.

Wiedenmayer, G., Aldrich, H.E. and Staber, U. (1995) Von Gründungspersonen zu Gründungsraten. *Die Betriebswirtschaft* 55 (2), 221–36.

Witte, E. (1972) *Organisation für Innovationsentscheidungen. Das Promotorenmodell.* Göttingen: Hogrefe.

Zerssen, D.V. (1976) *Depressivitäts-Skala (D-S).* Weinheim: Beltz.

Zoihsl, V. (1975) *Der Gründungsprozeß technischer Unternehmungen, Analyse und Lösungsansätze.* Graz: unpublished doctoral thesis, Karl-Franzens-University.

Chapter 17

Business Development, Rural Tourism, and the Implications of Milieu

FIONA WILLIAMS and ANDREW COPUS

Introduction

Recognition of the role and growth of tourism in rural areas has taken place within the broader context of rural development. A review of rural development literature informs us of the historical perspective that has helped to shape contemporary 'rural tourism' and also introduces a number of ideas pertaining to the 'differential economic performance' of rural areas. It is suggested here that the economic vitality of an area (and the relative performance of its tourism industry) is determined by a variety of local environmental characteristics, so-called 'soft factors' or 'milieu'. Such characteristics include the nature of local business networks, governance and 'institutional thickness', and social capacity. Drawing upon exploratory research, an analysis of key aspects of the 'local milieu' in contrasting areas of Scotland is undertaken. Given that the findings of this research have important policy implications regarding the development of rural regions and, within this framework, the viability of rural tourism in areas displaying less dynamic characteristics, this chapter concludes with insights to form the basis of more appropriate forms of policy intervention.

Rural Change

Rural areas are implicated in global processes in that circumstances and situations that occur far beyond the locality or nation state will ultimately impact upon the development of its rural areas. The mobility of many factors of production, such as financial and capital flows, skilled labour and information (Bryden & Dawe, 1998), and exogenous factors such as technological innovation, transnational corporations and economic restructuring, have changed market conditions and orientations for traditional products. Consequently, the development of non-agricultural activities such as tourism and consumer services has been central to change.

Change has coincided with a commodification of 'the rural', 'the image of the countryside becoming an ever more attractive object of the tourist gaze' (Urry, 1990: 96). Embedded in rural localities are local identities that form the 'culture' or 'essence' of an area and effectively provide further resources for development by local actors (Ray, 1999). These resources are inextricably linked with the local territory and can be strategically used to add value to local products and services, and to create positive images that motivate people to visit. Territorial marginality can be embodied as cultural difference or distinctiveness in a range of goods (such as speciality foods) and services. At its most extreme, we are witnessing a commodification of the less tangible aspects of an area through the social and cultural re-evaluation of rural and peripheral attributes (Gomez Martin & Lopez Palomeque, 2001).

The political and economic climate has encouraged rural areas to market themselves just as urban areas have done in the past. 'The importance of the image of rural areas has only recently been appreciated, and major efforts have been made in a variety of settings to deliberately improve, establish and change the allure of rural areas through the creation and recreation of specific images' (Butler *et al.*, 1998: 14). While the overall image of rural areas in the developed world tends to be a very positive one, these images may not always be authentic, but they are powerful enough to create demand for access to, and in some cases acquisition of, parts of the rural landscape.

In short, all of these economic, social, cultural, political and technological developments have led to the restructuring of rural areas. The transition from an industrial economy towards a service economy presents new opportunities for tourism sector growth, particularly in rural and peripheral areas where returns from the traditional primary industries (farming, fishing and extractive industries) are limited or fluctuating (Ravenscroft, 1994). It is widely acknowledged (e.g. Bryden & Bollman, 2000; Wanhill, 2000), that the tourism sector, through capitalising on the natural environment, is one of few development opportunities open to rural areas, as they undergo a significant restructuring and diversification process. Underdevelopment has favoured the preservation of unique landscapes, environmental features, culture and tradition, which are being re-valued in post-modern society (Cloke, 1993) at the same time as reduced travel time and cost has deconstructed spatial notions of distance (Burns, 1999: 50). It would appear therefore that recreation and tourism demands on rural areas look set to increase.

Differential Economic Performance

Whereas it is now accepted that these various (more contemporary) influences, characterised by uneven changes in population, economy and life-styles, affect rural areas in different ways, this was not always the case (Hall & Jenkins, 1998a). Previous explanations of diversity tended to focus upon hard factors such as resource availability and location. More recently, however, there has been a shift away from exogenous and sectoral approaches to rural development towards 'a more endogenous approach favouring local control and direction and more integrated strategies based on combined and sustainable economic, social and environmental development' (Bryden & Dawe, 1998: 5). Within this context a considerable body of literature has emerged that emphasises '... the critical role of regional institutional arrangements, social structures and cultures in successfully negotiating relationships between the region and the globalising economy ...' (Hudson *et al.*, 1997: 365).

Conventional thinking assumes that the implications of globalisation serve to further disadvantage remote rural areas. Bryden and Dawe (1998) characterise this view as one where increased globalisation serves to intensify the competition between public and private economic actors, in addition to that between territorial entities. But with so many regions looking to tourism as a development opportunity, to what extent can they compete in a finite market where there is an ever-growing number of products from which to choose (Hall & Jenkins, 1998b)? In a differentiated market, places have been forced to sell themselves, with the result of '... the production of "recursive" and "serial" monotony, as places are cast in existing moulds to produce virtually identical attractions in different locations' (Hudson & Townsend, 1992: 65). While this may paint a gloomy picture for the future of tourism in remote rural areas, it would be too pessimistic to assume that this is wholly the case.

> Seemingly hopeless rural economies either remain hopeless, despite the best efforts of developmental actors, or suddenly show quite unexpected signs of health and vitality, signs that defy interpretation by even the most experienced observers. (Murdoch, 2000: 407)

There is evidence to suggest that some areas appear to be embracing change and maximising the opportunities presented by globalisation. Copus *et al.* (2001) note that new forms of production and organisation have flourished in some regions though not in others, and that the explanation does not lie entirely in conventional competitive or comparative advantage, but rather in certain imperfectly understood and difficult to quantify (socio-cultural) environmental characteristics known as 'regional milieu'.

Aspects of milieu that have received particular attention in the literature include:

- 'social capital', and 'local capacity', stressing the educational, cultural and attitudinal characteristics of a region's population (Bennett & McCoshan, 1993; Tzamarias & Copus, 1997);
- the role of 'institutional thickness' (Amin & Thrift, 1995) and the 'associational economy' (Cooke & Morgan, 1998), both concepts stressing the importance of the quality of agencies and organisations involved in regional development, and the interaction between them; and
- 'untraded interdependencies': the network of links between firms, development agencies, educational institutions and research establishments, which, if well developed, facilitate the rapid diffusion of information (Storper, 1995) in 'learning regions' (Morgan, 1997).

Despite the burgeoning literature on the above, Copus *et al.* (2000a, 2000b) found that much of the existing work takes the form of conceptual or theoretical debate, and empirical analysis is relatively rare. They also noted that rural or peripheral areas receive relatively little attention in the literature. If such factors are acknowledged at all in this context, there is a tendency to assume that their influence is invariably negative. However, some peripheral areas exhibit positive trends that at least partially compensate for locational disadvantage.

To discuss these issues further, the Scottish results of a recent research project, a one-year study known as 'MILIEUX' (funded by the EU Northern Periphery Programme), are presented. The project sought to investigate why some rural areas display many dynamic economic and social characteristics, while others, possessing (in conventional economic terms) broadly similar resources and potential, tend to lag behind, are less innovative, and have a less entrepreneurial culture (Williams *et al.*, 2000).

The Case Study Areas: Mainland Orkney and South-East Caithness

The two areas studied in Scotland were Caithness, the most northerly area of mainland Scotland, and the Orkney Islands, lying ten miles (16 km) north east of the Scottish mainland (Figure 17.1).

The Caithness landscape varies from relatively fertile arable land along the North Sea coast, to barren moorland culminating in some of the highest cliffs in Europe, facing Orkney across the Pentland Firth, and to extensive areas of blanket peat bog (much of it recently afforested) known as the 'Flow Country'. The climate is harsh by UK standards,

Figure 17.1 Location of Caithness and Orkney (*Source*: Author's compilation)

with a high annual rainfall, frequent high winds, and a short growing season.

There are some 70 Orkney islands, the 15 largest of which are inhabited. The MILIEUX project focused on the largest island 'Mainland', together with Burray and South Ronaldsay, which are connected by a causeway. Most of Orkney has a rolling treeless landscape, higher hills being found only in the centre of Mainland, and on the island of Hoy. Much of the land is relatively fertile compared with other parts of the Highlands and Islands, and is mainly used for rearing beef cattle. The highly indented coastline and the sheltered natural harbour of Scapa Flow has given the islands a rich maritime and naval history, and more recently, has resulted in the construction of a major oil storage terminal at Flotta.

As noted in Table 17.1, Caithness has a population of almost 26,000, of which 11,000 live in East Caithness. During the 1980s the population declined by almost 15%. In the 1990s the rate of loss slowed, to only 3.6% during the first seven years. Orkney has a smaller population, at

Table 17.1 Some socio-economic indicators for Caithness and Orkney

Descriptors	Caithness	Orkney	Sources
Population 1998 (,000)	25.8 (11.1)	19.6 (16.5)	(a) + (b)
Population change 1981–1991	−14.6% (−14.8%)	+4.0% (+7.6%)	(c)
Population change 1991–1997	−3.6%	−0.1%	(a)
Primary employment %	10.9%	22.0%	(c)
Manufacturing employment %	11.9%	6.3%	(c)
Service employment %	77.2%	71.8%	(c)
Firms employing <10 persons (%)	84.8%	84.0%	(d)
Business start-ups per 1000 population	4.4	5.5	(b)
GDP per capita (EU15 = 100) 1996	64	77	(e)
Unemployment rate 1999	6.3% (8.0%)	3.0%	(f)
% Unemployed >6 months Feb 1999	46.6% (48.6%)	42.3%	(f)

Note: Figures in brackets are for East Caithness and Mainland Orkney, respectively.
Sources: (a) General Register Office Scotland (annual); (b) HIE (2004); (c) National Statistics (1981, 1991); (d) National Statistics (1998); (e) Copus *et al.* (2000b); (f) National Statistics (Annual)

around 20,000. Over 80% of the islands' population lives on Mainland and the linked islands, and half live in the two major towns of Kirkwall and Stromness. During the 1980s (in contrast to Caithness) the islands' population grew by 4%, and there was also a tendency for population to drift from the outer islands towards Mainland, where the growth rate was almost 8%. During the 1990s numbers were stable.

The Caithness economy was traditionally dependent upon farming and fishing. Both of these have declined steadily for several decades. Farming – mixed arable and stock rearing on the east coast, mainly extensive sheep rearing elsewhere – has been heavily dependent upon subsidies, while fishing is severely constrained by the Common Fisheries Policy. Since the 1950s the economy of West Caithness has been dominated by the Dounreay experimental nuclear reactor and waste reprocessing plant. In its heyday this boosted employment, both directly and indirectly, through stimulating the growth of associated engineering companies. Thus in 1991 the manufacturing sector accounted for almost 12% of the workforce, slightly above the average for the Highlands and Islands. Recently, direct employment has declined as the site has been wound down, although the engineering legacy seems set to survive independently of it, and there has been some inward investment by high technology firms. Tourism, together with the associated craft and food processing industries, are also increasingly significant economic activities in Caithness.

The Caithness area falls within the remit of the Highlands of Scotland Tourist Board. Specific tourism figures for the Caithness study area are unavailable, although some indication can be gleaned from data detailing visits to the tourist information centres (TICs) in the area. In 1998, Thurso TIC received 19,493 visitors, with Wick and John O' Groats TICs receiving 26,275 and 28,390 respectively. All of these figures show a downward trend on previous years (6–35% reduction). Tourism in Caithness has been developing under the auspices of the area strategy *Wider Horizons* (Caithness Tourism Development Group, 1997). The strategy has four main aims: to increase the volume and value of tourism to the area; to generate additional holiday and business tourism; to develop in a sustainable manner; and help to develop the skills of tourism operators. Approximately 80% of the measures detailed in the strategy have been achieved, although tourism in the area cannot currently be described as buoyant.

The Orkney economy was similarly dominated by farming and fishing, indeed agriculture still accounts for almost a fifth of employment. Fishing has declined somewhat, specialising recently in shellfish, and employing around 400 people in total. Fish farming (salmon) employs a further 90. The Flotta oil terminal provided most employment during its construction phase, its main impact on the economy today is through a levy on throughput collected by the Islands Council. This provides significant sums for local economic development. In recent years tourism has become a key sector in the Islands.

A survey of visitors to Orkney was carried out between May and October 2000. This study was to provide a comprehensive overview of the visitor market and to update and extend previous visitor surveys undertaken in 1989/1990 and 1996. The number of visitors to Orkney for the 2000 season was estimated at 92,000, a decrease of 10,000 on 1996 figures. However, the value of tourism to Orkney increased, with £16.5 mn (€25 mn) expenditure by these visitors (Sandison, 2000). The visitor market can be segmented according to origin as follows: Scotland (30%), elsewhere in the UK (38%), and overseas (32%).

Orkney's heritage and natural attributes are prime factors in attracting actual and potential visitors (Orkney Tourist Board, 1999). Closely associated with tourism are the thriving arts and crafts (especially jewellery) and food processing industries. Both of these benefit from the romantic and wholesome image of the islands.

Caithness and Orkney, like most of the Highlands and Islands, are characterised by large numbers of small firms, over 80% employing fewer than ten people. The rate of new business start-ups is lower in Caithness than in Orkney, at 4.4 and 5.5 per thousand head of population respectively. The Caithness rate is the second lowest in the Highlands and Islands.

Productivity is also relatively low in Caithness. The area generates less than two-thirds of the EU average GDP per capita. The equivalent figure for Orkney is 77%, which is above the average for the Highlands and Islands. Unemployment in Caithness is relatively high (8%) in the east (Wick travel to work area (TTWA)), but relatively low (4.9%) in the west (Thurso TTWA). The rate for Orkney is even lower, at 3%. In February 2000 almost half the unemployed of Caithness had not worked for over 6 months. In Orkney the proportion was 42%.

Methodology

The 'MILIEUX' project methodology comprised three elements. First, a multidisciplinary literature review, statistical mapping and pilot survey work was undertaken to establish the choice of study regions. Secondly, survey work was carried out with key personnel in local government and development agencies and with a sample of local entrepreneurs. The third and final phase constituted analysis, review (through the use of focus groups), and reporting.

The entrepreneur survey targeted regional production and manufacturing sectors. In Orkney, these sectors were jewellery, crafts, food and drink, and in Caithness they comprised the crafts, food and drink, and engineering sectors. No tourism specific, retail or service enterprises were approached, but the craft sectors and food and drink sectors in each area were closely associated with tourism. A total of 22, face-to-face, semi-structured interviews (supplemented with a self-completion questionnaire) among small-scale/micro-enterprises were carried out in each study area. Statistical information not included in this paper is available from the authors, as are the unpublished papers cited in the references at the end of this chapter.

Elements of the Local Milieux

Of the surveyed businesses, in both areas, indigenous start-ups were common and business management tended to be the responsibility of the owner. Retaining control of the business was an issue for many owners for both business development and life-style reasons. Businesses tended to be younger in Orkney (less than 20 years), although of those surveyed business turnover was greater, relative to the Caithness sample (where nearly two-thirds of businesses had a turnover of less than £150,000 (€220,000)). There was evidence of a greater rate and frequency of innovations among the Orcadian firms and only isolated examples of successful innovative practice among the surveyed Caithness firms.

The institutional environment

Important themes pertaining to the institutional environment in the literature are the 'associational economy' or third way (Cooke & Morgan, 1998), and 'institutional thickness' (Amin & Thrift, 1995). The former stresses the need for an effective network of institutional actors, including central and local government, regional development agencies, public sector bodies (universities, research institutes), 'intermediate' institutions (trade associations, chambers of commerce), and even individual firms. 'Institutional thickness' refers both to the number of institutions present within a region, and to the strength of the relationships between them (not only in terms of the frequency of interaction, but also in terms of structures of power and coalition, and the development of a common agenda). The survey evidence suggested that economic vitality was influenced by the quality and density of the linkages between local development agencies, supporting institutions and business networks.

There was less density in terms of Caithness firm–organisation linkages than in Orkney. The frequency of firm–agency contact was much higher in the Orkney sample and when seeking assistance there was a greater likelihood that the business and organisation would have already established contact on another, previous occasion or project. In Caithness, contact with the agencies for assistance was usually a new experience. Agency contact in Caithness was less frequent, fewer businesses were assisted financially, and advice was sought from a wider range of sources.

The partnership approach and individual effectiveness of the main economic development agencies in Orkney were recognised to be very important to business development. An effective institutional network was seen to assist several business clusters on Orkney. The presence of specialist education/training schemes, such as industry-specific, vocational qualifications, and the availability of financial assistance for some specialist recruitment, were examples of the supportive activity tailored to sector requirements.

Firms on Orkney had more experience of working with a number of organisations, such as economic development agencies, local authorities, industry associations and training and research institutes, on various projects. This complexity appeared to be managed effectively as interaction between the various organisations was considered to be effective by the entrepreneurs. In addition, there was consensus of cooperation among the Orkney entrepreneurs, particularly where the outcome was considered beneficial to all participants.

For example, agencies and businesses involved in marketing Orkney were developing a core image through 'Orkney the Brand'. The concept had already gained considerable currency through the efforts of Orkney Quality Food and Drink (OQFD) and also the Orkney craft sector. The values on which these sectors promoted their products were similar to those targeted by the tourism industry and at the time of study attempts were being made to 'merge' the sectoral images and brands (Orkney Tourist Board, 1999).

Business linkages and networks

In the literature dealing with the various types of relationships between firms, and between firms and institutions, one way to organise the various schools of thought is via two main questions. First, is the strength of the relationships between firms seen predominantly in terms of rivalry or in terms of cooperative behaviour? Secondly, are those relationships mainly physical/formal business transactions, or are informal links and the sharing of knowledge/information more important?

A number of studies focus on the nature of the linkages binding business networks together. Again these seem to divide fairly neatly into those stressing the importance of formal or physical business transactions, and those that argue that informal and less tangible social contacts or information flows are the key. Michael Storper has championed the latter view, coining the generic term 'untraded interdependencies' to encompass all forms of extra-transactional contacts between firms (Storper, 1995).

The existence and potential benefit of business clusters was investigated in the two study areas along with the extent to which 'competitive rivalry' at the local and regional scales was an effective stimulus to economic vitality. The diffusion of various kinds of information within the business community through business networks was examined.

The significance of rivalry is in its potential impact in intensifying attention to market requirements. Pricing becomes aggressive to gain or maintain market share, product variety is greater, and product development innovations are stimulated. In Orkney, firms were clearly much more focused on new product development than in Caithness. Market saturation occurs earlier under these conditions, and pressures to internationalise increase. Again, much more evidence of internationalisation of the customer base was apparent among firms in Orkney than in Caithness. Vigorous domestic demand can enhance foreign demand by building a strong national or regional image for the industry, as has again occurred with the Orkney jewellery sector.

Firms in both areas emphasised the importance of physical and formal transactions, particularly their relationships with customers, suppliers and the labour market. The availability of labour, while important to both areas as a factor of business success, was considered to be a more critical factor among the Orkney sample. This was attributed to the competitive rivalry apparent among the jewellery sector on the island, where the top three companies vie for available skilled labour. Domestic rivalry also creates other important benefits, in particular stimulating new rivals through spin-offs; creating and attracting factors; upgrading and expanding home demand; encouraging and upgrading related and supporting industries; and channelling government policy in more effective directions. All these effects would appear to be present in Orkney, but were less evident in the Caithness area.

Orkney is the more innovative of the two areas, yet the existence of strong local networking and interaction between the 'business cluster' in Orkney led to links with other groups involved in the industry being described as mainly local. Malecki (1997) suggests that economic vitality is higher in areas where the local network of enterprises has effective links with markets and sources of information outside the area, and economic vitality is lower where the networks have a more local focus.

In practice, information on the geographical 'range' of links (local, regional, national, or global) proved difficult to interpret. This is partly due to definitional variations (distinguishing local from regional is for instance much easier on Orkney than in Caithness), and partly because range varies according to the type of interaction involved. The range of input–output transactions varies (as one might expect) according to sector, the geography of input availability, and customers for intermediate outputs.

However, if geographical markets targeted by firms are taken as the main indicator of the presence of effective links with markets and sources of information outside the area, then the survey findings would appear to support arguments in the literature. In Orkney, tourism played a key role in the development of some overseas markets (most notably among the larger businesses in the crafts and jewellery sectors), in that it put firms in direct contact with consumers. The Orcadian craft producers were much more active in markets outside Scotland than those of Caithness.

Without doubt, networks and linkages between firms and organisations were stronger and more positive in Orkney than in Caithness, and the Orkney firms attributed greater importance to a range of benefits associated with the impact of these linkages on the business environment. However, there was broad agreement in both study areas regarding the most widely appreciated benefits, namely increased viability of business services, the exemplar effect and opportunities for cooperative marketing.

Innovative activity in the two areas was influenced by the role of non-physical resources. Orkney had relatively dense and active informal networks facilitating the diffusion of various kinds of information within the business community, factors that were much less apparent within the Caithness sample. Dynamic competition leading to continuous change was apparent among the Orcadian businesses. Knowledge accumulation, its application, and the resulting incremental, yet competitive, development, was evident in a number of sectors. It is suggested therefore, that the presence of formal and informal networks facilitated the diffusion of information and contributed to higher levels of economic vitality.

Aspects of social capital

Social capital refers to 'certain features of economic and social organisation – which facilitate effective collective action for mutual benefit' (Commins, 2001: 1). Contemporary conceptualisations of social capital fall into three different approaches, advocated by Bourdieu, Coleman and Putnam. Bourdieu (1986) uses the term to refer to human activity primarily aimed at accumulating and controlling different types of capital and the advantages (or disadvantages) that accrue through membership of certain communities (Commins, 2001). Coleman (1988) on the other hand perceives social capital to be a resource or public good that emerges from the social ties of individuals. Putnam (1993), possibly the most recognised academic in this field, describes social capital as features of social organisation (trust, norms and networks) that can improve the efficiency of society by facilitating coordinated actions (Bryden & Dawe, 1998). It is anticipated that an area rich in social capital is more likely to demonstrate evidence of innovative and entrepreneurial activity.

Social capital is considered an outcome of longer-term processes and this makes it particularly problematic to develop or build in an area in which it is weak or dysfunctional. However, local capacity building, described by Mannion (1996: 3) as '... the strengthening of knowledge, skills and attitudes of people – their capacity – for establishing and sustaining development within an area' is now a key theme in the policy arena.

With reference to entrepreneurial activity in the two areas, a number of factors support the argument that Orkney is the more entrepreneurial in character. The presence of features that can support an entrepreneurial tradition were evident among the Orkney sample. Agglomerative advantages were present in terms of shared commercial support services, specialised education, training and research in some sectors (e.g. Orkney jewellery), and the accumulation of skills and tacit knowledge in the workforce.

Elements of the above were also present in the Caithness sample and acknowledged as benefits of business clusters. However, overall networks were less cohesive, development agencies were considered to be less supportive, and the role of tacit knowledge in the innovation process was sparse. Much of the entrepreneurial activity acknowledged in the region was attributed to incomers to the area.

There was greater unity in behaviour patterns among the Orkney sample both in terms of actions and perceptions. Entrepreneurs in Orkney considered 'entrepreneurship' to be more the norm than was the case in Caithness. Firms in both areas agreed that the success of local entrepreneurs was an encouragement to others, but strength of agreement was greater (and disagreement less) in Orkney than in Caithness. The survey findings were consistent with the claim that there is a relationship between economic vitality and the local development of an 'entrepreneurial culture'.

It may be that Orkney has achieved a 'critical mass' of entrepreneurs in a relatively small radius and this has enabled the development of business linkages and networks. While there is evidence of some networking in Caithness, this is less dynamic and cohesive in comparison.

The Implications for Rural Tourism Business: Discussion and Conclusion

Regional milieux are elusive phenomena, very difficult to identify in an objective way, and almost impossible to quantify using conventional data sources. To a large extent they are intangible, common perceptions, or social constructs. However, despite its relatively modest scale and resources, the project reported here succeeded in showing that both entrepreneurs and regional/local development agency staff recognise the role of 'soft factors' in determining the state of health, and innovativeness of local economies.

Rural areas are undergoing significant change that presents both opportunities and challenges for the development of tourism in those areas. Characteristics of the rural tourism sector can include remote locations, a large number of relatively organised small businesses, resource constraints and often a lack of management skills (Dolli & Pinfold, 1997). Wanhill (1997: 51) has highlighted a number of weaknesses that occur in tourism SMEs that can act as barriers to tourism development. Some of these weaknesses can be attributed to lack of agglomerative advantage, such as '... transactions and information costs taken as major barriers to obtaining knowledge', and supply dominated by family businesses with limited business skills.

Tourism is vulnerable to fashion, economic fluctuations, and political change. With access to fewer markets than core tourist regions, peripheral areas can be more prone to industry volatility. However, there are challenges to this mode of thinking. Some of the influences behind rural restructuring and change have resulted in the economic potential of all regions becoming less closely related to location and increasingly influenced by a variety of aspatial characteristics, some aspects of which have been highlighted in this chapter.

One of the most valued aspects of the local business environment is the aggregate skills and knowledge base of the local labour force, though much of this 'human capital' is associated with 'tacit knowledge', practical skills and experience, rather than formal education. An influential feature of the market environment for tourism has been the structural decline in traditional industry, with diversification into tourism presenting a need for retraining and skills acquisition (Williams & Brannigan, 2000). To the extent that the 'human capital' resource is a product of the area's economic history, policy interventions cannot modify it. However, the research showed a clear 'training deficit' between dynamic and lagging areas.

Successful development of a destination area necessitates a coordinated and planned approach. Individually, SMEs experience difficulties in achieving an appropriate scale to overcome deficiencies in market structure. Cooperation and partnership are obvious means of doing this, but some sectors are more amenable than others; market conditions and an acceptance by SMEs of the need to change are critical factors.

Development agencies in peripheral areas should seek to assist local entrepreneurs in the development of both local networks and effective links with distant sources of technical and marketing information. In the case of the former, it will be necessary to find imaginative ways and resources to overcome the barriers imposed by sparseness. Initiatives such as 'enterprise clubs', which are already fairly common in core industrial areas, need to be adapted to facilitate the development of local fora with sufficient 'critical mass' to allow effective networking and interactive learning. In relation to the enhancement of external linkages, it will be more important to assist entrepreneurs to sharpen more formal skills associated with tapping standardised information sources on a global basis.

Development agencies should not view themselves as a reactive branch of the public sector or local government. Their role should be as a proactive element of a local innovation system, or network, working alongside local firms, and a variety of other actors, including their distant suppliers/customers, national government and agencies. The implications of this are manifold, relating to:

- the variety of services offered – with a strong emphasis on provision of both technical and marketing information, reflecting a process of interactive learning rather than compensatory local subsidy;
- the frequency of contact – following a systematic programme rather than waiting for firms to make the first move; and
- the relationships between agencies – where better coordination is required.

To conclude, local and regional development policies should address the needs of their area in a holistic way, taking account of all aspects of the local situation, not only those that are easily measured by conventional indicators, but also the 'softer' aspects that are not. While the project highlighted the difficulties of researching soft factors in rural development, it provided further evidence that they are important, especially if considered as part of an ensemble of causal processes that include traditional location factors. The study also demonstrated the feasibility of quantitative analysis, using primary and secondary data, allowing the relative importance of soft and hard factors to be assessed.

Further research is required to develop a set of assessment tools capable of 'benchmarking' institutional thickness and the associational economy, human and social capital, and the functionality of local business networks. An EU Fifth Framework project (of three years duration, 2001–2004) entitled 'Aspatial Peripherality, Innovation and the Rural Economy' (AsPIRE) provides the opportunity to address some of the issues raised. The rationale behind 'AsPIRE' seeks to bridge the widening gap between theory and practice in relation to the issues surrounding 'milieux'. Under the auspices of 'AsPIRE' (Copus, 2004), key 'soft factors' are investigated under the headings of information technology, social capital, business networks, governance and tourism. Attempts will be made to develop new indicators and an efficient standard methodology to allow regional agencies to generate comparable assessments of these 'soft' factors in their regions.

References

Amin, A. and Thrift, N. (1995) Globalisation, institutional thickness and the local economy. In P. Healy, S. Cameron, S. Davoudi, S. Graham, and A. Madani-Pour (eds) *Managing Cities: The New Urban Context* (pp. 92–108). Chichester: John Wiley & Sons.

Bennett, R.J. and McCoshan, A. (1993) *Enterprise and Human Resource Development – Local Capacity Building*. London: Paul Chapman.

Bourdieu, P. (1986) The forms of capital. In J.G. Richardson (ed.) *Handbook of Theory and Research for the Sociology of Education* (pp. 241–58). New York: Greenwood Press.

Bryden, J. and Bollman, R. (2000) Rural employment in industrialised countries. *Agricultural Economics* 22 (2), 185–97.

Bryden, J. and Dawe, S.P. (1998) Development strategies for remote rural regions: what do we know so far?' Albarracin, Spain: paper presented at the OECD International Conference on Remote Rural Areas – Developing through Natural and Cultural Assets, 5–6 November.

Burns, P.M. (1999) *An Introduction to Tourism and Anthropology*. London: Routledge.

Butler, R., Hall, C.M. and Jenkins, J. (1998) Introduction. In R. Butler, C.M. Hall and J. Jenkins (eds) *Tourism and Recreation in Rural Areas* (pp. 3–16). Chichester: John Wiley & Sons.

Caithness Tourism Development Group (1997) *Wider Horizons, Caithness Tourism – Towards 2000 and Beyond*. Thurso: Caithness Tourism Development Group.

Cloke, P. (1993) The countryside as commodity: new rural spaces for leisure. In S. Glyptis (ed.) *Leisure and the Environment* (pp. 53–67). London: Belhaven.

Coleman, J.S. (1988) Social capital in the creation of human capital. *American Journal of Sociology* 94, S95–S120.

Commins, P. (2001) *Introductory Ideas: WP5 Social Capital*. Dingwall, Scotland: Working Paper presented at AsPIRE (QLK5-2000-00783) co-ordination meeting, 3–6 March.

Cooke, P. and Morgan, M. (1998) *The Associational Economy – Firms, Regions, and Innovation*. Oxford: Oxford University Press.

Copus, A. (ed.) (2004) *Final Report of the AsPIRE Fifth Framework Project*. Aberdeen: Scottish Agricultural College. On WWW at http://www.sac.ac.uk/AsPIRE. Accessed 06.03.04.

Copus, A.K., Gourlay, D. and Williams, F. (2000a) Holding down the global: regional milieux, innovation, and economic vitality in the periphery. Aberdeen: Paper presented at the International Conference: European Rural Policy at the Crossroads, Arkleton Centre, University of Aberdeen, 29 June–1 July.

Copus A.K., Hanell, T. and Petrie, S. (2000b) Mapping patterns of economic vitality in the northern periphery area. Aberdeen: Scottish Agricultural College, Working Paper of MILIEUX Northern Periphery Programme Project. On WWW at http://www.nordregio.se/Stats/milieux/stat_map_report.PDF. Accessed 06.03.04.

Copus, A., Kahila, P., Jansson, B. and Mariussen, A. (2001) *The Role of Regional Milieux in Rural Economic Development: Final Report*. Aberdeen: Scottish Agricultural College, Northern Periphery Programme, 3107982/15.

Dolli, I.N. and Pinfold, J.F. (1997) Managing rural tourism businesses: financing, development and marketing issues. In S. Page and D. Getz (eds) *The Business of Rural Tourism*. London: International Thomson Business Press.

General Register Office Scotland (Annual) *Annual Population Estimates*. Edinburgh: General Register Office Scotland. On WWW at http://www.gro-scotland.gov.uk/grosweb/grosweb.nsf/pages/popest. Last accessed 11.03.04.

Gomez Martin, B. and Lopez Palomeque, F. (2001) Tourism, territory and marginality: principles and case studies. Stockholm: paper presented at the Annual Conference of the IGU Commission on Evolving Issues of

Geographic Marginality in the Early 21st Century World, 25 June–1 July.

Hall, C.M. and Jenkins, J.M. (1998a) The policy dimensions of rural tourism and recreation. In R. Butler, C.M. Hall and J. Jenkins (eds) *Tourism and Recreation in Rural Areas* (pp. 19–42). Chichester: John Wiley & Sons.

Hall, C.M. and Jenkins, J.M. (1998b) The restructuring of rural economies: rural tourism and recreation as a government response. In R. Butler, C.M. Hall and J. Jenkins (eds) *Tourism and Recreation in Rural Areas* (pp. 43–67). Chichester: John Wiley & Sons.

HIE (Highlands and Islands Enterprise) (2004) *Area Economic Profiles.* Inverness: HIE. On WWW at http://www.hie.co.uk/LEC-area-profiles.htm. Last accessed 11.03.04.

Hudson, R., Dunford, M., Hamilton, D. and Kotter, R. (1997) Developing regional strategies for economic success: lessons from Europe's economically successful regions? *European Urban and Regional Studies* 4 (4), 365–73.

Hudson, R. and Townsend, A. (1992) Tourism employment and policy choices for local government. In P. Johnson and B. Thomas (eds) *Perspectives on Tourism Policy* (pp. 49–68). London: Mansell.

Malecki, E.J. (1997) *Technology and Economic Development. The Dynamics of Local, Regional and National Competitiveness* (2nd edn). Harlow: Longman.

Mannion, J. (1996) Strategies for local development in rural areas – the 'bottom up' approach. Cork: paper presented at the European Conference on Rural Development, 7–9 November.

Morgan K. (1997) The learning region: institutions, innovation and regional renewal. *Regional Studies* 31 (5), 491–503.

Murdoch, J. (2000) Networks – a new paradigm of rural development? *Journal of Rural Studies* 16, 407–19.

National Statistics (1981) *Census of Population.* Newcastle-upon-Tyne: National Statistics. On WWW at http://www.nomisweb.co.uk. Last accessed 11.03.04.

National Statistics (1991) *Census of Population.* Newcastle-upon-Tyne: National Statistics. On WWW at http://www.nomisweb.co.uk. Last accessed 11.03.04.

National Statistics (1998) *Annual Employment Survey.* Newcastle-upon-Tyne: National Statistics. On WWW at http://www.nomisweb.co.uk. Last accessed 11.03.04.

National Statistics (Annual) *Claimant Unemployment Rates.* Newcastle-upon-Tyne: National Statistics. On WWW at http://www.nomisweb.co.uk. Last accessed 11.03.04.

Orkney Tourist Board (1999) *Orkney Tourism Strategy.* Kirkwall: Orkney Tourist Board.

Putnam, R.D. (1993) *Making Democracy Work: Civic Traditions in Modern Italy.* Princeton, NJ: Princeton University Press.

Ravenscroft, N. (1994) Leisure policy in the new Europe: The UK Department of National Heritage as a model of development and integration. *European Urban and Regional Studies* 1 (2), 131–42.

Ray, C. (1999) Endogenous development in the era of reflexive modernity. *Journal of Rural Studies* 15 (3), 257–67.

Sandison, I. (2000) *Orkney Visitor Survey 2000 Final Report.* Kirkwall: Orkney Tourist Board.

Storper, M. (1995) The resurgence of regional economies. *European Urban and Regional Studies* 2, 191–219.

Tzamarias, N. and Copus, A.K. (1997) The role of local capacity building in rural development. Chania, Crete: paper presented at the XVII of the European Society for Rural Sociology, 25–29 August.

Urry, J. (1990) *The Tourist Gaze.* London: Sage.

Wanhill, S. (1997) Peripheral area tourism: a European perspective. *Progress in Tourism and Hospitality Research* 3, 47–70.

Wanhill, S. (2000) Creative innovations in attraction development. Bornholm, Denmark: paper presented at the 9th Nordic Tourism Research Conference, 3–6 October.

Williams, F. and Brannigan, J. (2000) Rural tourism: quality, imagery and the development of competitive advantage. Brighton: RGS-IBG Annual Conference, University of Sussex, 4–7 January.

Williams, F., Copus, A. and Petrie, S. (2000) *The Role of Regional Milieux in Rural Economic Development: Entrepreneur Survey – Scotland.* Aberdeen: Scottish Agricultural College, Northern Periphery Programme, 3107982/15.

Chapter 18

Sustainable Rural Tourism Business Practice: Progress and Policy in South East Cornwall

JON VERNON, STEPHEN ESSEX and KAJA CURRY

Introduction

Rural tourism is especially dependent upon the quality of its environment for its economic viability and is, therefore, a sector that has a fundamental interest in the sustainable development approach (Lane, 1994). Resource depletion and environmental degradation affecting a range of 'free' environmental and cultural resources upon which rural tourism is based can threaten the long-term viability of the sector and individual businesses. Sustainable tourism attempts to promote a collective responsibility amongst all stakeholders as a basis for modified behaviour to reduce the detrimental impacts on the environment and to contribute to environmental protection and resource conservation (MacLellan, 1997; Wanhill, 1997). The former English Tourism Council defined sustainable tourism in its strategy for rural tourism as tourism 'which benefits the economy in tourism destinations, protects and enhances the built and natural environment, and meets the social and cultural needs of people' (Countryside Agency and English Tourism Council, 2001: 11). Sustainable tourism is no longer regarded as an optional extra, but fundamental to safeguarding the long-term competitiveness of the industry (DCMS, 1999).

The widespread adoption of sustainable tourism will not be achieved, however, unless it is embraced fully by the small business community (Middleton, 1999). Research evidence suggests that tourism businesses are proving remarkably resistant to calls to operate more sustainably. While there are studies that offer generalised explanations of the reluctance to change, few have investigated the factors that lie behind businesses' reticence and laggardness in detail. Such insights are essential if appropriate policies are to be framed that are capable of encouraging businesses to embed sustainable practices within their operations.

323

This chapter examines the way that rural tourism businesses have responded to environmental sustainability based on a study conducted in the Caradon district of Cornwall, UK. The research was initiated and part-funded by Caradon District Council for the purpose of informing a strategy for sustainable tourism, but was also supported by the University of Plymouth, Caradon Area LEADER II (an EU-funded initiative for rural development), and South West Tourism (the regional tourist board for southwest England). The study had four key aims. The first was to investigate the extent and manner in which tourism-related businesses within the district had responded to the concept of environmental sustainability through the adoption of sustainable practices, and thus, to gauge their awareness, understanding and potential to adopt additional practices in the future. Secondly, the main issues that had constrained the adoption of sustainable practices by tourism-related businesses within the district were to be identified. Thirdly, an assessment of the efficacy of relevant policy interventions to reduce the identified barriers and encourage the adoption of further environmentally sustainable business practices was to be undertaken. The final aim of the study was to develop an actionable strategy, based upon the results of the research, which the District Council could implement to encourage sustainable business practices within the local industry. The results of this research have policy implications beyond the study area.

Progress in Rural Sustainable Tourism

Although the implementation of sustainable tourism is in the interests of the industry, most tourism businesses have been remarkably slow to respond (Berry & Ladkin, 1997; Donovan & McElligott, 2000; Hobson & Essex, 2001; Stabler & Goodall, 1997). Tourism encompasses a wide range of diverse sectors, which have little in common other than they share a proportion of each others' customers. The industry is complex, fragmented and heterogeneous, and, therefore, difficult to influence through policy initiatives. The predominance of small businesses in the sector limits the capacity of the industry to innovate. Small private operators have been shown to be generally reluctant to participate in initiatives for environmental sustainability as a result of confusion about the meaning and relevance of the concept and the practical constraints of limited available resources, knowledge and expertise. Many small tourism businesses have been established for non-financial reasons, such as life-style or retirement decisions (Clegg & Essex, 2000; Shaw & Williams, 1998; Thomas *et al.*, 2000). Consequently, business owners may have little interest in developing their business (Margerison, 1998). Small operators typically operate on the margins of commercial viability and are more concerned about day-to-day survival rather than making long-term plans for environmental conservation. Economic and commercial criteria usually dominate the decision making of such small businesses (Carlsen *et al.*, 2001). The portrayal of tourism businesses as largely reluctant adopters of sustainable practices is a rational response to limited environmental regulation in the industry and a lack of confidence in the market for sustainable tourism.

Goodall's work in Guernsey identified four distinct responses to environmental sustainability among tourism accommodation businesses, distinguished by their perceived environmental performance in relation to their overall technical performance (Goodall, 1995). Almost half of the hospitality businesses were 'under-performers', with low technical and environmental ability, and only surviving through the provision of a low-cost service. Approximately 20% were categorised as 'conventionals': businesses providing a traditional hospitality service and adopting few sustainable practices other than for economic reasons. About 30% were described as 'worthies': businesses that had reviewed their environmental performance and had made changes as a consequence. Only 5% were categorised as 'green champions': businesses that regularly reviewed their environmental and technical performance and continuously made improvements as a consequence. A key challenge to policy-makers is to encourage movement through these notional groups by providing appropriate support and signals to small businesses.

In the last ten years, little has changed in the manner by which businesses have been encouraged to adopt sustainable practices. In 1991, the English Tourist Board urged tourism-related businesses to 'go green' by undertaking an environmental audit to recognise the financial benefits of adopting sustainable business practices (English Tourist Board *et al.*, 1991). In 2001, the English Tourism Council encouraged businesses to participate in 'environmental management schemes', such as the Green Audit Kit, 'to improve their environmental performance and raise awareness of the issues among their customers' (ETC, 2001b: 7; ETC, 2000). The ETC intends to measure business commitment to sustainable tourism through recorded participation in such schemes (ETC, 2001a, 2001b).

The established approaches to encouraging adoption of sustainable practices vary in the level of support provided (in terms of the depth and personalisation of available information and advice), and the business motives targeted (i.e. the extent to which schemes promoted the commercial and environmental benefits of adopting environmental innovations) (see Figure 18.1). A large proportion of the schemes are in the form of stand-alone self-help guides, such as the Green Audit Kit (see group A in Figure 18.1), with little additional support. A minority have been established as inspection and certification schemes offering site visits and personal assistance from professional advisers (e.g. the

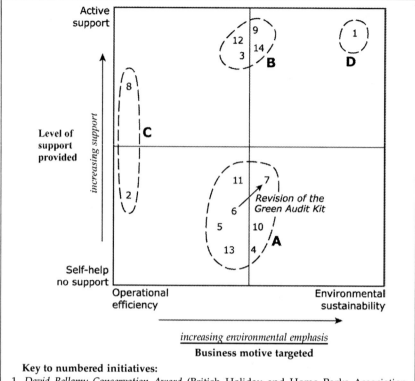

Figure 18.1 Initiatives to encourage the adoption of sustainable practices amongst small tourism-related businesses

Green Tourism Business Scheme, promoted by the Scottish Tourist Board) (see groups B and D). Accordingly, the costs of participation also vary greatly, from £10 (€15) for the Green Audit Kit (ETC, 2000) to almost £200 (€300) for membership of the Green Tourism Business Scheme. Most schemes have targeted commercial motives for adopting sustainable practices (see groups A, B and C), primarily through a reduction in costs. The wider environmental or social benefits of adoption are also highlighted, but are secondary to the main commercial motive. Significantly, the revised edition of the Green Audit Kit (2000) has moved away from targeting financial motives explicitly to stress the more holistic and shared benefits of conserving local tourism resources and the sector's long-term viability, which reflects changing policy within the ETC. The David Bellamy Conservation Award is distinct, both in its approach and the motives that it targets (see group D). Within the award scheme, camping and caravan parks are advised and assessed by conservation professionals on the basis of their contribution to wildlife habitats and biodiversity. Of the initiatives highlighted in Figure 18.1, arguably, this scheme is the only one that considers tourism from the perspective of the environment rather than the industry.

Considered together, the schemes reflect very different assumptions about the nature of business behaviour and the most appropriate manner in which principles of sustainability can be introduced to private operators. The range of approaches indicates not only the variety of stakeholder interests in tourism, but also a lack of consultation between schemes, and the absence of publicly available research into the effectiveness of each (Goodall, 1995). The purpose of the research outlined in this chapter was partly to fill this gap.

Study Area: South East Cornwall

Caradon is one of six Cornish districts and is located in the south east corner of the county (see Figure 18.2). Its main attraction for tourists lies in its high-quality countryside and coast, which is recognised by the designation of Areas of Outstanding Natural Beauty and Heritage Coast. Parts of Caradon have a reputation as 'Cornwall's forgotten corner' (Carne, 1985). In 2001, the South West Regional Research Group estimated that the district accounted for only 12.1% of visits to the county, making it the second least popular destination area after Kerrier (11.1%) (South West Regional Research Group, 2003). These low visitor volumes might partly be attributed to the small nature of its resorts and the less recognised value of its countryside. Tourists pass through the district en route to other destinations in Cornwall or on their way home at the end of their holiday. Nevertheless, over the period 1971 to 1994, growth

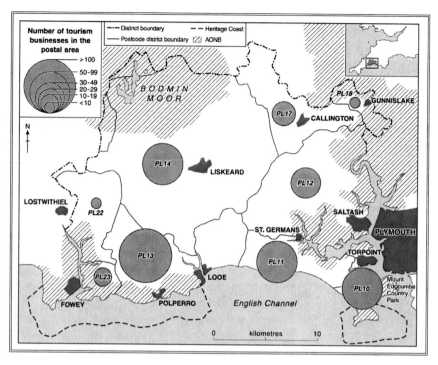

Figure 18.2 Geography of Caradon District, South East Cornwall

in visitors to Caradon (38%) outperformed the county as a whole (24%) (Atlantic Consultants, 2001).

The sector supports 4510 jobs in the district, which equates to 12% of the working population (WCTB, 1997). For the purposes of this research, a total of 451 tourism-related businesses were identified as operating within Caradon in April 2000. Accommodation businesses (serviced and unserviced) represent 86% of all tourism-related businesses. Three-quarters of such establishments catered primarily for small groups and families (i.e. self-catering accommodation, guesthouses, farm B&Bs/self-catering), reflecting the nature of demand within Caradon. Only four hotels in the district offered more than 50 bed spaces (Caradon District Council, 1999). A total of 35 tourist attractions are located in the district, ranging from theme parks to retail factory outlets, country houses and gardens, zoos, and museums, although only one (Mount Edgcumbe Country Park, which, in any case, lies within easy reach of the region's largest city, Plymouth) featured in the list of top ten most popular attractions in Cornwall (Cornwall County Council, 2001).

Given that the principal tourism assets in Caradon relate to features of its natural, cultural and built environment, the conservation and protection of these resources are essential to ensuring the continued viability of its main industry. The principles of sustainable tourism, by instilling greater environmental responsibility throughout the industry, represent perhaps the main means by which environmental resources can be maintained and impact on the environment can be minimised. In this way, the future sustainability of the tourism industry can be ensured. The approach also has the potential to create niche markets, which would assist the district in reducing its dependence on peak season family holidays and removing the perception of the district as a transit region.

Since the early 1990s, Caradon District Council has gained a reputation as a leading exponent of sustainable tourism within the UK through a number of initiatives it has taken (Atlantic Consultants, 2001). Between 1991 and 1996, the Council operated Project Explore, which attempted to enhance visitor management in the area and to develop and promote tourism based on the area's beauty, culture and wildlife. A long-term legacy of the project has been the establishment of the South East Cornwall Discovery Centre in Looe, which has facilitated the exploration of the local countryside, heritage and culture by visitors (Department of National Heritage *et al.*, 1995). Between 1996 and 1998, the District Council established SUSTAIN (the SUStainable Tourism, Audit and Implementation Network) as a local tourism business organisation with the objective of encouraging operators in the district to adopt more sustainable business practices based upon guidance within the Green Audit Kit. The network was supported for a year by a dedicated project officer (employed to recruit new members and encourage participants to adopt sustainable practices), and thereafter by a team of four 'ambassadors' (unpaid local operators who had joined the network, and were experienced in implementing measures from the Green Audit Kit. These 'ambassadors' were trained to provide advice and guidance to other members). Despite initiating some successful projects, such as the introduction of a 'Hoppa Bus' service between Looe and tourism businesses in the surrounding area, the network folded in 1998 after attracting only 16 members. The Council recognised that, in order to extend sustainability within local tourism, they needed to understand the barriers perceived by businesses concerning the adoption of sustainable practices and obtain a clearer grasp on the type of support that businesses might be expecting. This 'implementation gap' was one of the motivations for this study.

The Research Project

In December, 1998, Caradon District Council established a joint research project with the University of Plymouth, with support from

South West Tourism and the European Regional Development Fund (ERDF) through Caradon Area LEADER II, to obtain a more detailed understanding of the issues and barriers that tourism enterprises face in implementing sustainable business practices. The project ran from December 1998 to November 2001 and its objectives were to gauge in detail the potential of tourism-related businesses to adopt environmentally sustainable practices; to identify the barriers to the adoption of sustainable practices; and to inform the development of an actionable strategy to help overcome the identified barriers. In order to reduce the effects of possible bias and to establish a consensus of views, methodologically the research was designed in three phases, each informing the next: focus groups (involving 25 businesses, May–September, 1999), a district-wide questionnaire survey of tourism businesses (including 197 businesses [45%], April–September 2000), and in-depth face-to-face interviews (involving 22 businesses, January–April 2001). To support the project, a Small Grants and Innovation Scheme, funded by the ERDF through Caradon Area LEADER II, was established by the partners to fund innovative actions by businesses that sought to overcome identified barriers to sustainability (2000–2001). The main outputs of the research were therefore the research results, which informed the strategy to be implemented 2001–2006, and demonstration projects, funded by the Small Grants and Innovation Scheme (Vernon *et al.*, 2003). This chapter reviews some of the main results of this study, with the main emphasis being placed on the results of the questionnaire survey, although findings from the other aspects of the research are included where relevant.

Results of Survey

Business characteristics

All businesses in the district were invited to participate in the questionnaire survey, and the final sample, after two reminders and incentives (garden centre vouchers), was based on a 45% response rate (197 businesses). The characteristics of the businesses included in the sample were typical of the total population, but obviously self-selecting. The sample of businesses comprised mostly accommodation businesses (80%), particularly self-catering and bed and breakfast accommodation, with a small number of attractions (11%), and campsites and holiday parks (9%). Most (90%) were micro-businesses (with less than 10 employees). Almost half of respondents (49%) had over ten years' industry experience and 39% had run their own businesses during that time. The sample also reflected the attraction of running a tourism business as a life-style or retirement choice. More than half of the respondents (55%) were aged over 50 and only a small minority (13%) had commenced business to maximise their income. Fewer still (10%) expected dramatic growth from their business. For most, the aim was to maintain a comfortable standard of living (35%) or to establish a viable enterprise, with or without growth (50%). In terms of entrepreneurship, therefore, most businesses could be described as 'satisfiers' rather than 'maximisers'.

Attitudes towards the environment

While four-fifths of respondents (81%) were concerned about the state of the local environment, reflecting their dependence upon the environment as the main attraction for visitors to the area, progressively smaller proportions considered the role of tourism (60%) and their own business in particular (29%) in contributing to these environmental impacts. Owners were largely unaware of the ways in which their activities impacted upon the environment. It is significant that when this issue was discussed in the focus groups, the awareness was limited and focused on the impacts of visitors (waste, traffic congestion, crowds). With further prompting, however, the wider dimensions of the potential environmental and resource implications of tourism were gradually acknowledged, such as the relevance of energy use, water pollution, impact on flora and fauna, and purchasing strategies. These findings suggest that owners are not especially environmentally conscious in the operation of their business. Indeed, many owners in both the questionnaire and focus group surveys pointed out that such concerns were the responsibility of regulatory authorities or utility companies. Participants in the focus group discussions considered it acceptable commercial practice to test the willingness of planners to apply the regulations rather than the businesses taking any responsibility for their proposals and actions. It would also appear that the signals from the tourism market itself concerning the appeal of environmental sustainability are weak. While nearly half of owners (47%) detected an interest in environmental issues among their customers, only 9% judged that their customers would be willing to pay a premium for environmental quality. In fact, only a quarter of respondents (26%) informed visitors of their environmental work, suggesting that attempts to gain competitive advantage or to raise customer awareness were not significant motives for adoption. Market research by the English Tourism Council (2002) suggests that these perceptions may be erroneous: 65% of customers were willing to pay extra to stay with an accommodation provider who was committed to good environmental practices (ETC, 2002).

Adoption of sustainable practices

Great diversity in the adoption of sustainable practices was apparent within the sector. The frequency distribution of the number of practices adopted by businesses revealed an almost normal distribution centred about an average of about ten practices (median 9.2). Two-thirds of the sample had adopted 6–13 practices (high and low majority adopters), while 17% of businesses had adopted more than 13 practices, and might be termed 'high adopters', and 17% had adopted fewer than six practices, and could be described as 'low adopters'. On further analysis, each of these adopter categories appeared to have distinct characteristics (see Table 18.1). Half of the sample accounted for more than two-thirds (69%) of the practices that had been adopted.

While many businesses had adopted established and conventional activities, the number of more substantive practices was relatively limited (see Table 18.2). Over 70% of the businesses in the sample had adopted practices that required little commitment, expertise or capital, such as simply publicising specifically local events, purchasing local produce and using recycled paper. Between 25 and 65% of the sample had adopted well-established practices of environmental management, such as waste management, energy conservation and water conservation. Less than 25% of the sample had adopted practices requiring more specialist expertise and/or financial outlay, such as installation of an alternative energy supply or condensing boiler. Given that the sample was self-selecting and potentially biased towards those with an existing interest or commitment to the environment and sustainability, the results indicate a strikingly low level of proactive innovation.

Analysis of the types of applications received for the Small Grants Scheme indicated a similar pattern of generally undemanding ideas and relatively unsophisticated interpretations of sustainability. Large numbers of applications were received for projects involving visitor interpretation (29%), improved facilities (20%) and landscaping (11%), rather than for projects with potentially greater environmental benefits, such as energy conservation (15%), recycling (13%), water conservation (7%), and public transport initiatives (2%).

By carefully monitoring the combination and sequence in which businesses had adopted sustainable practices, it was possible to gain an additional insight into the decision-making processes that had been involved in the Caradon case. Key practices where adoption was instrumental in developing a longer-term commitment to sustainability could thereby be identified. Significant associations emerged between different combinations of adopted practices, suggesting that many were implemented as groups or clusters of innovations. The strongest clustering related to the disposal of business waste. Each waste-related practice was strongly associated with every other, together with local purchasing and activities that encouraged environmentally friendly tourism (e.g. communicating environmental improvements to customers). A further discrete clustering was detected between projects that sought to improve local sustainability through collaborative effort. Such practices were distinct from waste-related activities by appealing to social or

Table 18.1 Distinguishing features of adopter categories

High adopter	High majority	Low majority	Low adopter
Conducted an environmental review	←———	Not conducted an environmental review	———→
Less than 2 yrs or 6–10 yrs experience running business	←———	3–5 yrs or more than 10 yrs	———→
Member of a tourism organisation	←———	Not a member of a tourism organisation	———→
			Main market: families
	Established as a sole trader	Established as a partnership	
Motivated by a personal concern for the environment			
←———	Recognise the impact of tourism on the environment	———→	
Concerned about the impact of own business on the environment	←———	Not concerned about the impact of own business on the environment	
←———	Prepared to take time to improve environmental performance	———→	

Source: Vernon (2002)

Table 18.2 Types of sustainable practices adopted by tourism businesses in sample ($n = 197$)

Sustainable practices	Percentage of sample adopted practices
Low sustainability: little commitment, expertise and capital	
Provided details of local events to customers	90.9
Provided details of walking and cycling routes	86.3
Actively purchase local goods	85.8
Recycled paper	70.1
Accepted areas of environmental management	
Recycled bottles	64.5
Fitted low-energy light bulbs	59.4
Encouraged customers to use public transport	64.5
Actively purchased environmentally friendly products	52.8
Created wildlife areas	50.8
Composted garden and kitchen waste	49.2
Reduced toilet flush capacities	44.7
Actively purchased goods with minimum packaging	44.2
Recycled tins	33.0
Provided facilities for customers to recycle waste	32.5
Organised tourism event with local community	27.9
Communicated environmental improvements to customers	26.3
Conducted an environmental review	25.8
Innovative: expertise and investment	
Worked with community on environmental project	16.8
Installed a condensing boiler	12.7
Installed an alternative energy supply	3.6

Source: Vernon (2002)

community-orientated motives and required very different policy interventions to encourage participation. Not surprisingly, all types of discriminatory purchasing behaviour were closely related. In contrast, practices that reduced businesses' consumption of resources (e.g. installing low-energy light bulbs), which might appeal to financial motives, showed little clustering. Such activities were viewed and adopted largely in isolation to fulfil specific objectives.

There were also statistically significant differences in the order in which clustered practices were adopted. Most notably, the adoption of certain 'core' practices tended to precede and lead to the adoption of the other 'dependent' practices (Figure 18.3 summarises the direction of significant rank order relationships). Within the main cluster of sustainable practices, composting was usually adopted first, and represented the initial step towards the implementation of other sustainable waste-related practices. Other 'early' practices included the creation of wildlife areas, providing details of walking and cycling routes, and actively purchasing local products. It may be argued that policy interventions that target 'core'

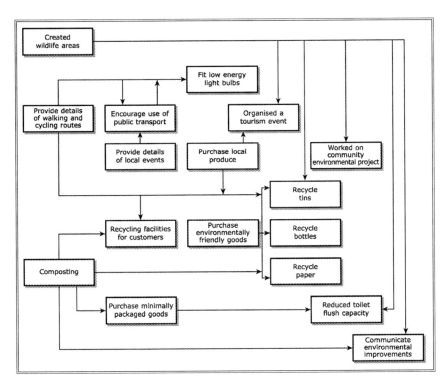

Figure 18.3 Direction of rank order relationships between activities (*Source*: Vernon (2002))

practices within key clusters of activity are likely to establish a sound basis for encouraging other related practices. Significant patterns in the diffusion of individual practices suggest that tactical solutions should be sought whereby core practices within the main clusters of activity (e.g. waste-reducing practices, local purchasing) are targeted as a means to support the diffusion of innovations that have yet to gain wide acceptance (e.g. installing a condensing boiler). However, variances in the number of practices adopted by tourism-related businesses also suggest that more strategic interventions will be required to encourage iterative responses from all sections of the industry (e.g. through targeted information and advice).

Factors influencing adoption

Perhaps surprisingly, a much higher proportion of businesses stated personal concern as the main motivation for introducing sustainable practices. Over one-third of the sample stated personal concern (38%) as their main motivation, whereas about one-fifth (21%) suggested financial reasons. A further 16% of respondents stated that both personal concern and financial gain were factors in their decision making, while a desire to reduce waste motivated a further 10% of businesses. The adoption of sustainable practices appears to have appealed more to the personal values of business owners rather than their estimation of the commercial needs of businesses, which was well illustrated in the in-depth interviews. Within the smallest businesses, owners did not distinguish between their business and personal lives. The business was viewed as an extension of the home and reflected the same personal attitudes. A low adopter explained:

> My problem is that I do not think of us as being business people. We are simply people who have cottages where people come. It is just what we do. I think living on the site, as we do, it is simply an extension of the way we live.

Within larger businesses, however, owners were able or were required to distance themselves from their home values and adopted a more hard-headed approach to decision making. The importance of personal values in the decision-making process of businesses was an unexpected finding of the research and one that is not currently recognised in strategies to promote sustainable tourism. It might be that future support for businesses could focus on personal values about the environment as a trigger for innovation, rather than relying on the commercial benefits of cost savings and creating a competitive market edge.

Barriers to adoption

Encouragingly, nearly two-thirds of owners (62%) were prepared to improve the environmental performance of their business in the future, but action was often constrained by real or perceived barriers. Significantly, while two-thirds of respondents (68%) indicated barriers to future adoption, less than one-third (29%) of existing adopters reported past problems. This finding may, of course, reflect issues of respondent recall, but it might also indicate a search for reasons to justify inaction. Consequently, publicity highlighting the practicalities of innovations, as well as the benefits, may go some of the way in reducing perceived barriers.

The most frequently cited problems related to refuse recycling, which were mentioned by almost half (48%) of existing adopters in the sample. The issue here is that waste from tourism businesses is classed as trade waste, and therefore its collection is subject to a charge. Trade waste cannot be disposed through public facilities. The absence of a kerbside collection scheme or accessible bring-banks for businesses meant that the segregation and disposal of recyclate materials was considered to be messy and time-consuming. A respondent in the in-depth interviews explained:

> It is not a problem, but a fag. You have to collect all our stuff in our garage so that you can hardly get the car in, take a massive trip up [to the recycling point], and then we come back smelling of beer. Implementing recycling is quite an awkward and messy business really. (High adopter)

Recycling problems were most acute during the main season when the volume of waste was greatest, owners were at their busiest, and traffic congestion in towns impeded access to bring-banks. In lieu of a business collection system, business owners had developed their own recycling processes, including the expedient (but illegal) use of public recycling facilities. Of the businesses that recycled their waste, more than three-quarters (87%) disposed of it through public bring-banks. Although waste regulations presented a statutory barrier to adoption, most businesses were either unaware of them or chose to ignore them. They considered that the volume and type of waste produced was no different from that of a large household. As one business explained:

> It needs to be clear what our responsibilities are as businesses. Caradon's policy [on waste regulations] needs to be clarified and those barriers to people doing it need to be removed, and their perception of barriers, because they are not necessarily there. (High adopter)

While infrastructural shortcomings were the main frustration for those who had already adopted sustainable practices, it was the economic realities of adoption that was a greater issue for those contemplating further adoption. By far the most frequently mentioned barriers to further adoption were the perceived costs (50%) and time and effort (30%) to implement environmental improvements (see Table 18.3). The interviews confirmed that businesses reached a financial and practical limit to adoption, beyond which they felt unable to invest in sustainable practices:

> We are always looking for more efficient things to do, but again it comes down to practicalities and finance, which is horrible to say, but it does come down to that in the end. (Low adopter)

Among low adopters, this point of financial and practical limits was soon reached, bounded by low awareness and interest. For such businesses, time and money represented absolute barriers to adoption. Among higher adopters, the same issues were treated as variables against which financial and non-financial benefits might be balanced. Shortages of time and money were less likely to prevent the adoption of day-to-day maintenance practices (e.g. recycling, local purchasing), which required little financial outlay and could be accommodated within normal routines, but were more often mentioned as barriers to the adoption of capital improvements. One owner explained:

> Finance would be the barrier to stop me doing more . . . I would like to get rid of the gas appliances and electric appliances and have it all done by solar panels, but it is out of financial reach. We use recycled paper and energy-saving bulbs, things like that, which are within my financial range. (High majority adopter)

Businesses that believe that they are already fully committed to sustainability will require financial and practical support to increase adoption.

A lack of guidance and support for sustainable practices in the district was highlighted as a problem by 19% of respondents and as a barrier to future adoption by 19%. Over half of all respondents (54%) were either uncertain or confused about sustainable practices. Although this proportion was lower amongst high and high majority adopters (45%), even these 'innovators' admitted to an incomplete understanding of the practical implementation of sustainable development:

> We try to practise environmentally, but there is a hell of a lot that we do not know. We are ignorant about a lot of things. (High majority adopter)

While most businesses (71%) had consulted one or more sources of information or advice about sustainable practices, there was no

Table 18.3 Barriers to adoption

Issues	Past problems		Barriers to future adoption	
	No.	% businesses[†]	No.	% businesses[†]
Lack of recycling collection/facilities	13	48.1	16	12.0
Costs of implementation	8	29.6	66	49.6
Lack of help and support	5	18.5	25	18.8
Time and effort	3	11.1	40	30.1
Lack of customer cooperation	2	7.4	5	3.8
Available space	1	3.7	10	7.5
Too small to make a difference	–	–	6	4.5
Lack of public transport	–	–	5	3.8
Other	4	14.8	21	15.8
Number of respondents	34/117* (29.1%) of which 27 specified problems		133/197 (67.5%)	

*Not answered = 80.
[†]Percentages expressed as a proportion of businesses who specified problems. Percentages add up to more than 100 as respondents could provide more than one answer.
Source: Vernon (2002)

recognised single point of contact within the district. A total of 31 different sources of information had been used by the sample. The District Council (13%) and the Green Audit Kit (10%) were the most widely referenced sources, but had only been used by a minority of businesses. Only one respondent had consulted a professional advisor. Not surprisingly, few lower adopters (7%) had consulted more than one source of information, compared to almost half (48%) of high adopters. In view of the large proportion of owners who were either confused or uncertain about investing in sustainable practices, the absence of a recognised point of contact for assistance represents a significant barrier to adoption.

Only a minority of respondents had experienced resistance (7%) or expected resistance (4%) from customers to the implementation of environmental improvements. However, as one owner explained in the in-depth interviews:

> You cannot go telling people 'don't flush the loo, don't wash or don't shower'. You have got to restrict the amount of restrictions you put on people really. (Low adopter)

In this respect, businesses require reassurance that sustainable practices will add value and not detract from the perceived quality of the tourism product, particularly in relation to energy and water conservation. Nevertheless, the analysis detected more fundamental barriers relating to the nature of visitor demand in the district. Less than 10% of businesses felt that their clientele would be willing to pay a premium for a more sustainable holiday experience. Significantly, high adopters noted greater interest (71%) and willingness to pay (26%) among their clientele, suggesting that, for some, sustainable tourism was a recognised business opportunity. Most business owners, however, were more sceptical and required hard evidence of a profitable customer demand, which now appears to exist (ETC, 2002).

Policy interventions to encourage adoption

Business views on the interventions necessary to reduce the barriers to adoption were examined. Not surprisingly, the list of suggested measures reflected the main issues that respondents believed had constrained their response to sustainability: the availability of time and money; a lack of support for recycling; and weaknesses in information support networks (see Table 18.4).

Financial incentives

Financial incentives were the most popular form of policy intervention. Unprompted, more than half (53%) of respondents suggested a range of financial measures, including grants, soft loans, product discounts and reductions in business rates (see Table 18.4). When prompted, more than three-quarters (76%) considered financial support to be of 'significant' or 'substantial help'. To some extent, financial incentives were also likely to overcome business owner reticence to invest time in sustainable practices. It may not, therefore, be necessary to target the constraints of time and money separately. Financial measures were particularly important to high adopters – almost all of whom considered them to be of 'significant' or 'substantial help' – compared to only half of low adopters:

> There are larger things that I would like to do here. I would like to do more environmental activities and maybe more environmental activity weekends for guests ... but in order to do that we would need a grant. (High adopter)

For low adopters, financial incentives were required to stimulate an initial interest in sustainable practices. In contrast, high adopters, who had

Table 18.4 Suggested policy interventions

	Suggested initiative	*No.*	*% businesses mentioned*
Financial measures	Financial support	47	34.1
	Reduction in costs	14	10.1
	Tax incentives	9	6.5
	Reduction in business rates	3	2.2
	Subtotal	73	52.9
Infrastructure measures	Collection of waste for recycling	27	19.6
	Local recycling facilities	17	12.3
	Council support	8	5.8
	Separate bins for recycling	3	2.2
	'Legalise' recycling	3	2.2
	Fines for non-implementation	2	1.4
	Better water pressure	2	1.4
	Remove planning restrictions	1	0.7
	Subtotal	63	45.7
Information & advice	More information	15	10.9
	Relevant advice	15	10.9
	Proven cost-effectiveness	5	4.7
	Reliable alternatives	2	1.4
	Subtotal	37	26.8
Time-saving measures	More time	6	4.3
	Time-saving initiatives	5	3.6
	More staff	2	1.4
	Subtotal	13	9.4
Local measures	Safe paths & cycleways	3	2.2
	More bins for dog waste	1	0.7
	Limit the use of HGVs	1	0.7
	Subtotal	5	3.6

(continued)

Table 18.4 *Continued*

	Suggested initiative	*No.*	*% businesses mentioned*
Other	Don't know	4	2.9
	Nothing	3	2.2
	Already environmentally friendly	3	2.2
	Other	2	1.4
	Subtotal	12	8.7
Total responses = 138		203	–

Not answered = 59
Source: Vernon (2002)

already adopted a wide range of sustainable practices, sought financial support to implement more innovative capital improvements.

The interviews highlighted a number of potential pitfalls in relation to financial measures. First, adoption decisions that are dependent upon financial subsidies may prompt only short-term changes in behaviour, which can be quickly reversed when funding ceases. Financial support needed to be carefully targeted to build long-term capacity. The potential dangers were highlighted by one respondent in the in-depth interviews:

> [I would be interested in grants] because that would save money. In the fishing [industry] we used to go for things we could get a grant on, not because you wanted it. (Low adopter)

Secondly, the disproportionate interest of high adopters in financial measures raises questions of additionality in supporting activities that would have been undertaken regardless. A number of discrete interventions may be required to target high and low adopters separately (e.g. by offering 'first-time buyer' discounts, but also capital grant schemes for more innovative projects). Thirdly, the bureaucracy attached to grant funding may itself act as a barrier to adoption, which may be counterproductive, as the following comments suggest:

> [I have] never applied [for any grants], but would like to. But I have always got the impression that they were very long-winded, very difficult to get hold of ... lots of conditions. (Low adopter)

Support for recycling

Almost half (46%) of the sample suggested that infrastructural improvements would encourage adoption (see Table 18.4), most of which (79%) related to recycling. Although recycling was well established in the district, this activity reflected the personal commitment of business owners rather than District Council support. Without additional support, further adoption is unlikely. Additionally, a stricter application of the waste regulations (which preclude businesses from using public recycling facilities) could lead to the collapse of existing recycling activity. To date, the District Council has tended to overlook 'illegal' recycling practices that have contributed to household recycling figures (now subject to statutory Best Value Performance Indicator targets). Such was the perceived importance of recycling that, if this activity continues to be overlooked, the number of tourism businesses practicing the principles of sustainable tourism is unlikely to increase.

Information and advice

Measures that provided information and advice about sustainable practices were suggested by more than a quarter (27%) of respondents (see Table 18.4). When prompted, three-quarters agreed that information about the environmental (70%) and financial (79%) benefits of adoption, and personal advice on sustainable practices (77%) would be of at least 'moderate help'. Businesses required access to reliable information and advice at all stages of the adoption process to improve the quality of decision making. A number of features of business behaviour indicated that a range of interventions would be required to inform such decisions, based on the information needs of individual businesses, the preferred means of communication and dissemination, and the stage in the business life-cycle. Key points in the business life-cycle, such as at start-up, refurbishment and expansion, represented opportunities to introduce sustainable options to influence decisions about operational procedures and capital asset purchases.

Information needs varied greatly according to the circumstances, priorities and motives of individual businesses. Most businesses were interested in the relative merits and practicalities of adoption, but the level of required detail varied considerably. The range of views, even among higher adopters, is illustrated by the following comments:

> I would like to know what actually happens to the wool I put in such and such a woollen bank, or the cans or whatever. And whether it is costing them more to recycle than it would to extract the raw materials from a third world country in which it was also providing jobs for people, who would not be having those jobs if we were recycling here, and so on and so forth . . . (High adopter)

Not too detailed or complicated, basic points and bullets of how you can cut your energy costs, that sort of thing. The moment you make it too long-winded, if it is anybody like me, they just haven't got time to read all the small print. You just want something that says 'for further information contact this number'. (High majority adopter)

Where personal advice was preferred, high adopters, with wide experience of sustainable practices, typically required advice on complex or site-specific issues (e.g. building materials that are not harmful to wildlife or the installation of solar panels):

I'm sure we do things that we are not aware of that are actually damaging the bird populations. We have barn owls here and trying to find out ... We had to go off our own backs to the Barn Owl Trust and get nesting boxes put in because there was no local information. (High majority adopter)

In contrast, lower adopters were less confident and had more basic needs, such as understanding the general merits of sustainable practices and how to compost green waste. Although such information was available, low adopters felt that they had neither the time nor motivation to search for it. The lowest adopters typically required face-to-face persuasion to adopt even the most basic sustainable practices, as indicated in the following comments:

We probably, most likely, don't know enough about it, do we? We're ignorant, aren't we? ... what we could possibly be doing ... I think you take it in more if somebody is telling you, than you do reading it? (Low adopter)

There were also wide differences in the preferred manner in which information should be communicated. No single method of disseminating information appealed to all businesses. While most high adopters considered training seminars (67%) and meetings with other businesses (83.3%) to be of at least 'moderate help', they were of limited interest to low adopters (23% and 39.3%, respectively). Mechanisms that require a substantial time commitment were considered inappropriate for targeting businesses without strong environmental values. Case study examples of best practice were more popular with support from all adopter categories, although it was important that the examples were transferable to small operators. Interestingly, the provision of information on CD-ROM or through the Internet was of limited appeal. A total of 46% and 52% of respondents, respectively, considered such methods to be of 'no' or 'minimal' help. Communication channels that rely upon new technologies may reinforce, but cannot yet replace the main communication channels (i.e. written and face-to-face). A strong consensus within the group was that the distribution of such information should occur in the off-season, when the businesses were more able to take time to read the material.

During the interviews, the provision of advice as part of an inspection and rating scheme was not popular, reflecting scepticism about the commercial relevance of sustainable tourism and perceptions that sustainable practices were often not consistent with customer care. Owners, who were already members of rating schemes, were averse to the inclusion of additional performance criteria, while non-members would not contemplate joining any scheme because of the perceived bureaucracy, costs and limited value to their business. Willingness to participate in a separate scheme was dependent upon critical mass so that the achievement of an award gained meaningful recognition.

The interviews confirmed that needs and preferences changed during the life of a business. At 'start-up', the financial pressures to generate income meant that only practices that required little financial outlay could be adopted (e.g. composting, recycling, local purchasing). More substantial innovations might be possible at refurbishment and expansion. The survey indicated that the seventh year of a business often was a time when owners were making investment decisions. Advice on the installation of environmentally friendly capital equipment was more relevant towards the end of an asset's life or when wholesale changes were contemplated (e.g. refurbishment or expansion), which was often only considered after a period of financial consolidation. One owner stated:

> When people are doing major refurbishments or extensions, or what have you. I would like to see that if somebody is refurbishing or building an extension, that that environmental advisor could come out and say 'right, this is what you could do to conserve energy, these are the best sort of materials to use'. That guidance and support, not mandatory, but that people should be making sure that they are using the best available materials. (High majority adopter)

Directories were the most popular methods of disseminating information about such 'maintenance practices' (e.g. local recycling facilities, suppliers of 'green' goods and services). Personal advice was only appropriate where substantial changes were contemplated before trading commenced. Factsheets were preferred for communicating detailed information on capital improvements; however, opinion was divided as to whether they should be available electronically or on paper.

Discussion and Conclusion

Although situated within the District of Caradon, the results of this study potentially have important implications at all levels of policy formulation. Most small rural tourism businesses require outside direction to progress sustainability issues. However, the level and nature of necessary support varies greatly depending upon business commitment to sustainability, their stage in the business life-cycle, and the personal preferences of individual owners. Consequently, there is a mismatch between the single policy solutions that have so far characterised public sector responses to sustainability and the diverse needs and preferences of the industry. Interventions to date have assumed a homogenous industry motivated by commercial opportunity and have offered single solutions, such as the Green Audit Kit and accreditation schemes.

The results from Caradon reveal a remarkable mismatch between existing policy interventions and the behaviour, needs and preferences of small tourism businesses in a number of respects. First, policy interventions do not currently recognise the strong altruistic motives for adopting sustainable practices, which were relevant to all adopter categories. Consequently, most businesses are not being encouraged to make environmental improvements in the most appropriate manner. Secondly, present support mechanisms do not reflect the very different needs of low, medium and high adopters, or the changing requirements of a business through a typical life-cycle, particularly at 'start-up', expansion and refurbishment. Thirdly, the continued promotion of even semi-formal tools of environmental management is at odds with the manner in which businesses have adopted sustainable practices. Businesses require less formal and more flexible support that encourages the adoption of new practices over time. Fourthly, policy interventions have yet to address the main barriers to adoption, particularly financial constraints and a lack of infrastructural support, which have limited the capacity of tourism businesses to make environmental improvements. Arguably, the infrastructural barriers, which relate to the context within which adoption decisions are made, are the most pressing for policy-makers. It is likely, therefore, that a range of sensitive and flexible policy interventions will be required to support the changing needs, priorities and preferences of a diverse population of businesses throughout the adoption process.

The main policy implications of this research were used to formulate Caradon District Council's own 'Strategy for Greening the Tourism Industry: 2001–2006', which might have relevance to policies being formulated in other rural areas. The priorities focused on mainstreaming sustainability so that it is considered integral to tourism as opposed to an optional extra. In order to achieve this, the first priority was to establish a much better infrastructure for recycling by businesses in the district. Failure to address this issue, which was the business owners' primary environmental concern, could potentially undermine the credibility of other elements of the plan. This action was regarded as a basis for encouraging other sustainable practices.

A second measure was to increase the dissemination of information about the practicalities, opportunities and benefits of adopting sustainable practices. The lack of business awareness of sustainable practices represented a barrier that could be easily removed to facilitate more informed decision making. The strategy proposed a range of communication messages and media (e.g. newsletters, factsheets, directories) to reflect the diversity of needs and preferences within the industry. It was recognised that greater attention needed to be given to the format and distribution of such material. Potentially greater impacts might be achieved if such material was distributed in a printed form (rather than being made available on Websites) and circulated in the off-season.

A third priority was to increase access to advice on sustainable practices. The provision of face-to-face advice would provide the necessary flexibility to vary the level of assistance and encouragement in response to business needs and reduce some of the barriers of time and effort. The plan suggested that such support might be best achieved by the appointment of a dedicated officer, either based in the public sector or business organisation. A tactical measure to introduce both information and advice to businesses was to encourage 'environmental audits' within the industry. Audits were proposed, not as a formal evaluation of environmental performance, but integrated within guidance on general business matters, particularly at the key business life-stages of 'start-up', refurbishment, and expansion. With financial cost being the most frequently mentioned barrier to adoption, a further policy initiative was to explore financial support as a means of encouraging adoption. Financial incentives might be targeted at popular clusters of activities to broaden the participation in sustainable development, or the more innovative and isolated practices to extend the range of activities.

The results of this research also suggest broader challenges to the successful implementation of sustainable tourism. To address the infrastructural barriers to adoption, the District Council will need to target policy inconsistencies within its own departments (e.g. in relation to planning, economic development, waste collection) and to develop a corporate response to environmental sustainability within the constraints of its statutory duties and roles. Indeed, the District Council is arguably the largest and most influential tourism-related organisation in the district and, through its interface with the private sector, offers great potential to act as a powerful example of good practice to local operators. Additionally, the absence of a coherent policy would undermine the credibility of a

Council strategy to encourage environmental improvements within the industry. The Council also needs to address other infrastructural weaknesses that are beyond its direct control, such as deficiencies in public transport and the availability of environmentally friendly products in the district. To achieve this objective, the District Council will need to work in partnership with a range of private sector stakeholders both within and outside the area. Such infrastructural barriers will not be addressed overnight, but by commencing a dialogue with stakeholders, the scope for adjustment in policy and the commercial opportunities for new services can be examined. The extent to which commonality about the implementation of sustainable tourism exists between relevant groups, the ways in which constructive partnership working can be established, and the effectiveness of outcomes from this approach represents an area of future research.

References

Anderson Associates (1995) *Holiday Caravan Parks, Caring for the Environment: A Guide to Good Practice.* London: English Tourist Board.

Atlantic Consultants (2001) *South East Cornwall Tourism Partnership: Caradon Tourism Strategy (Draft Strategy).* Truro: Atlantic Consultants.

Berry, S. and Ladkin, A. (1997) Sustainable tourism: a regional perspective. *Tourism Management* 18 (7), 433–40.

British Holiday and Home Parks Association (BHHPA) (2000) *The David Bellamy Conservation Award: Guidance for Park Owners and Managers.* Gloucester: BHHPA.

British Research Establishment (1996) *Energy Efficient Refurbishment of Hotels and Guesthouses: Best Practice Guide.* London: Department of the Environment.

Caradon District Council (1999) *South East Cornwall Accommodation Register, 1999.* Liskeard: Caradon District Council.

Carlsen, J., Getz, D. and Ali-Knight, J. (2001) The environmental attitudes and practices of family businesses in rural tourism and hospitality sectors. *Journal of Sustainable Tourism* 9 (4), 281–97.

Carne, T. (1985) *Cornwall's Forgotten Corner.* Plymouth: Lodenek.

Clegg, A. and Essex, S. (2000) Restructuring in tourism: the accommodation sector in a major coastal resort (Torbay). *International Journal of Tourism Research* 2 (2), 77–95.

Cornwall County Council (2001) *Impact of Tourism in Cornwall 1996.* On WWW at http://www.cornwall.gov.uk/Facts/tour12.htm. Accessed on 19.03.01.

Countryside Agency and English Tourism Council (2000) *Green Audit Kit.* Cheltenham: Countryside Agency.

Countryside Agency and English Tourism Council (2001) *Working for the Countryside: A Strategy for Rural England, 2001–2005.* Cheltenham: Countryside Agency.

Department of National Heritage, Rural Development Commission, English Tourist Board and Countryside Commission (1995) *Principles of Sustainable Rural Tourism: Opportunities for Local Action.* Cheltenham: Countryside Agency.

DCMS (Department of Culture, Media and Sport) (1999) *Tomorrow's Tourism.* London: DCMS.

Donovan, T. and McElligott, B. (2000) Environmental management in the Irish hotel sector: policy and practice. In M. Robinson, J. Swabrooke, N. Evans, P. Long and R. Sharpley (eds) *Environmental Management and Pathways to Sustainable Tourism* (pp. 55–79). Sunderland: The Centre for Travel and Tourism.

English Tourist Board (ETB), Countryside Commission and Rural Development Commission (1991) *The Green Light: A Guide to Sustainable Tourism.* London: ETB.

ETC (English Tourism Council) (2000) *Green Audit Kit.* London: ETC.

ETC (English Tourism Council) (2001a) *Time for Action: A Strategy for Sustainable Tourism in England.* London: ETC.

ETC (English Tourism Council) (2001b) *National Sustainable Tourism Indicators: Monitoring Progress Towards Sustainable Tourism in England.* London: ETC.

ETC (English Tourism Council) (2002) *Visitor Attitudes to Sustainable Tourism.* London: ETC.

Goodall, B. (1995) Environmental auditing: a tool for assessing the environmental performance of tourism firms. *Geographical Journal* 161 (1), 21–28.

Green Globe (2001) *What We Do.* Canberra: Green Globe. On WWW at http://www.greenglobe21.com/index_cp.html. Accessed 19.03.01.

Hobson, K. and Essex, S.J. (2001) Sustainable tourism: a view from accommodation businesses. *Service Industries Journal* 21 (4), 133–46.

Hotel and Catering International Management Association and Building Research Establishment (2000) *Hospitable Climates.* London: Hotel and Catering International Management Association and Building Research Establishment.

International Hotels Environment Initiative (1993) *Environmental Management for Hotels: The Industry Guide to Best Practice.* Oxford: Butterworth-Heinemann.

Lane, B. (1994) What is rural tourism? *Journal of Sustainable Tourism* 2 (1–2), 7–21.

MacLellan, L.R. (1997) The tourism and the environment debate: from idealism to cynicism. In M. Foley, J. Lennon and G. Maxwell (eds) *Hospitality, Tourism and Leisure Management: Issues in Strategy and Culture* (pp. 177–94). London: Cassell.

Margerison, J. (1998) Business planning. In R. Thomas (ed.) *The Management of Small Tourism and Hospitality Firms* (pp. 101–16). London: Cassell.

Middleton, V. (1999) More sustainable tourism: a marketing perspective. *Insights* May, A16–A22.

Payback (2000) *The Green Compass*. Plymouth: Payback.

Rural Development Commission (1996) *Green Audit Kit*. Salisbury: Rural Development Commission.

Scottish Tourist Board (1998) *The Green Tourism Business Scheme*. Inverness: Scottish Tourist Board.

Shaw, G. and Williams, A. (1998) Entrepreneurship, small business culture and tourism development. In D. Ioannides, and K.G. Debbage (eds) *The Economic Geography of the Tourism Industry: A Supply-Side Analysis* (pp. 235–55). London: Routledge.

Solway Rural Initiative (1999) *The Solway Green Award Scheme: Audit Kit*. Aspatria: Solway Rural Initiative.

South West Regional Research Group (2003) *The Value of Tourism to the South West Economy in 2001*. Exeter: South West Tourism.

Stabler, M.J. and Goodall, B. (1997) Environmental awareness, action and performance in the Guernsey hospitality sector. *Tourism Management* 18 (1), 19–33.

Sustainable Somerset Group (1999) *The Somerset Green Audit Checklist*. Taunton: Somerset County Council.

Thomas, R., Lashley, C., Rowson, B., Xie, G., Jameson, S., Eaglen, A., Lincoln, G. and Parsons, D. (2000) *The National Survey of Small Tourism and Hospitality Firms: 2000 – Skills Demand and Training Practices*. Leeds: Leeds Metropolitan University Centre for the Study of Small Tourism and Hospitality Firms.

Tourism and the Environment Initiative (1997) *Going Green: A Handbook for Managers of Tourism Businesses*. Edinburgh: Tourism and the Environment Initiative.

Vernon, J. (2002) *Barriers to Sustainability Among Tourism-Related Businesses: Identification and Reduction*. Plymouth: unpublished PhD thesis, Department of Geographical Sciences, University of Plymouth.

Vernon, J., Essex, S., Pinder, D. and Curry, K. (2003) The 'greening' of tourism micro-businesses: outcomes of focus group investigations in South East Cornwall. *Business Strategy and the Environment* 12, 49–69.

Wanhill, S. (1997) Introduction: tourism development and sustainability. In C. Cooper and S. Wanhill (eds) *Tourism Development: Environmental and Community Issues* (pp. xi–xii). Chichester: John Wiley & Sons.

WCTB (West Country Tourist Board) (1997) *A Strategy for Tourism in the South West, 1999–2003: Consultation Draft*. Exeter: WCTB.

Part 5
Conclusion

Chapter 19

Rural Tourism Business as Sustained and Sustainable Development?

DEREK HALL and MORAG MITCHELL

The title of this volume was self-consciously provocative, being comprised of four contestable terms: rural, tourism, sustainable and business. As such, questions concerning the priority of, and relationships between, sustaining business, sustaining tourism and/or sustaining the environmental, social and cultural context of rural tourism, have been subject to the emphasis, interpretation and experience of the individual contributors to this volume, albeit within editorial parameters.

The book's origins resided in the framework of providing a critique of 'sustainability' for rural tourism business, with objectives that included the exemplification, often through case study analysis, of rural tourism policy and practice; the identification of areas of policy and practice that might be informed by research; an exploration of likely future developments in rural tourism theory and practice; and the identification of key contemporary research issues within a framework emphasising relationships between the local and the global.

Five further chapters were commissioned specifically to complement those based on the original concept of the book, to broaden and consolidate the national and cultural environments within which the experience of rural tourism business is examined, including North America, the Caribbean and Taiwan. The long-running theme of the continuing policy implementation gap between the debates, claims and declarations surrounding 'sustainable development', and what actually happens on the ground in reality, has permeated several of the chapters in this volume.

This final chapter aims to reflect a convergence of the book's overall aims and the varied research presented by the authors in this volume, highlighting key issues and relating them to the sustainability of rural tourism business.

Change and Diversity in Rural Tourism

Tourism is now considered as having the potential for bringing considerable economic and social benefit to rural areas through income enhancement and infrastructure upgrading, particularly for marginal and less economically developed regions. But while rural tourism and recreation industries support economic and social restructuring, they tend to be most successful in rural economies that are already healthy (Roberts & Hall, 2001). This clearly has implications for new business development. The role of collaborative partnerships is now considered essential for business survival in many areas. The sustainability of rural tourism business and its contribution to the sustainability of rural development is rendered more likely by inclusion in development plans and policies that integrate across both regions and sectors and emphasise partnership, collaboration and inclusiveness (see Chapter 2).

However, while the potential roles of rural tourism business in rural and regional development processes may be well understood in principle, the ways in which they might be achieved in practice depend a great deal on local circumstance (Roberts & Hall, 2001). The restructuring of agriculture, the emergence of rural development policies, and changes in rural consumption for leisure purposes all contribute to significant rural change. The varying degrees of recognition and acknowledgement between countries of these important changes, as they interact with rural tourism business development, reflect a range of policy attitudes – including perceptions of 'sustainability' – and relationships that remain largely unquantified and poorly evaluated in the existing literature.

Rural resources – 'countryside capital' – are of course an essential ingredient. They provide a backdrop within which 'pure' forms of rural tourism (Lane, 1994, 1999) can take place, and act as a vehicle for 'contemporary' or 'new' tourism and recreational activities that often have little to do with either rural characteristics or values (Butler, 1998: 215). It seems to be widely accepted that these 'new' forms are changing the nature – the sustainability? – of the industries that contribute to rural tourism (Roberts & Hall, 2001: 224), and certainly they are influencing the way in which 'the rural' is being socially constructed by potential consumers. Increasing visitor numbers and the changing nature of consumption have combined to bring significant changes to the scope and scale of rural tourism and recreation and to its role as an agent of rural development (e.g. Sharpley, 2001).

This permits a brief comparative evaluation and reassessment of the definitional components employed by Lane (1994), Page and Getz (1997) and Roberts and Hall (2001) when discussing 'rural tourism' (Table 19.1).

Table 19.1 Comparative evaluation of the definitional components of 'rural tourism'

Components	Lane (1994)	Page & Getz (1997)	Roberts & Hall (2001)	Current editors' observations
(1) Scope	Located in 'rural areas'	Add remote areas and wilderness – there is a spectrum	Useful 3-fold categorisation (sparsely populated, rural core areas, rural areas near towns), for practical purposes, within a recognised spectrum	The 3-fold categorisation has a strong practical application; 'wilderness' has a range of culturally-based interpretations and social constructions
(2) Function	'Functionally rural'	Need to allow for specialist (mass) resorts	Recognition of the functional and scale differences between 'rural tourism' and 'tourism in rural areas'	We need to appreciate that 'rural tourism' and recreation can involve mass activity while 'tourism in rural areas' can have a niche dimension – e.g. rural conference centres, corporate incentive and hospitality activities
(3) Scale	'Small in scale'	Enterprises need to be sufficiently large to be viable	Importance of collaboration and networks to help overcome smallness and fragmentation	The predominance of micro-businesses in rural tourism renders collaboration and networks essential – scale and external economies can be gained through spatial and functional clusters

(continued)

Table 19.1 *Continued*

Components	Lane (1994)	Page & Getz (1997)	Roberts & Hall (2001)	Current editors' observations
(4) Provenance	Traditional, growing organically, locally based	It is not always practical to have all these attributes	*Embeddedness* in local economy and society is an important attribute for success, e.g. for rural food tourism	Local provenance and embeddedness can assist the complementary development of e.g. *trails* and customer-oriented networks
(5) Form	Enterprises should be diverse	This reflects the *complexity* of the rural environment	Diversity and *complementarity* are important	Rural business structure and morphology may not be complex compared to their urban counterparts, but complementarity again emphasises the importance of collaboration

Sources: Hall & Page, 1999; Lane, 1994; Nylander, 2001; Page & Getz, 1997; Roberts & Hall, 2001.

Content Summary

The five sections of this volume have provided broad themes within which particular, often case study focused chapters, have been placed. Comprising the first, introductory section, Chapter 1 established parameters for examining rural tourism as sustainable business. It raised critical questions and indicated the key dimensions and issues to be addressed in the ensuing chapters:

- *competition*: particularly the need to be aware of and respond to ever-changing markets, and the ability to embrace characteristics that enhance competitiveness;
- *marketing*: often a weak link, reflecting knowledge, or lack of it, relating to competition, market structure and demand, information technology, sector networks and promotion strategies;
- *cooperation and networking*: arguably the essence of rural tourism business is local cooperation and community involvement through appropriate forms of networking; and
- *globalisation*: as a driver of market development and demand, network development, information (and) technology diffusion, this amorphous phenomenon or series of phenomena, demands constant attention because of the potential positive and negative impacts that it might exert at a number of different levels.

Five perspective chapters comprised the book's second section, 'strategic considerations'. As a generic term, 'policy' for rural tourism within a European context was discussed in Chapter 2 with particular reference to the appropriateness of an explicit rural tourism policy, and its contribution to wider tourism and rural development processes, not least in relation to the 'new Europe'. A not unfamiliar conclusion was the continuing apparent fragmentation of policy – perhaps reflecting the nature of rural tourism business itself – and the need for further research in this area.

In Chapter 3, Dallen Timothy provided a usefully comprehensive North American overview that incorporated US and Canadian experience, drawing parallels and contrasts to that of Europe. Rarely evaluated in detail in the tourism literature, legislative and regulatory frameworks within which rural tourism can develop were the focus of Chapter 4, drawing on specific studies from Spanish experience. In this chapter, Gerda Priestley and colleagues highlighted the potential for much empirical work to illuminate the theoretical approaches taken to legal and regulatory dimensions of rural tourism and rural business development.

Chapter 5 offered a practical approach to effective marketing for rural tourism business from one of the UK's leading analysts. In a practical approach, Jackie Clarke assessed the issues influencing marketing for rural tourism, and provided a checklist of propositions or questions to guide those responsible for rural tourism towards the more effective use of marketing. The crucial role and take up of, and attitudes towards, information and communications technology (ICT) by rural tourism entrepreneurs was the focus of Chapter 6. With particular reference to research undertaken in the Spanish region of Aragon, Graeme Evans and Paola Parravicini argued that while ICT and e-commerce present technical opportunities, micro-enterprises still require physical clusters and other spatial networks in order to compete and innovate. They suggested that such an admission is unlikely to be found in the ICT literature.

Section 3 of the book – 'Networking, partnerships and community support' – was opened by Chapter 7, where Catherine Gorman examined, through specific example, cooperative marketing structures in Ireland. She argued that the benefits of cooperation could be seen to contribute considerably to the rural tourism sector's development in Ireland. This was despite a number of issues and problems highlighted that surround the cooperative structure.

Regional cooperation in rural theme trail development in Austria comprised the focus of Chapter 8, where Kim Meyer-Cech analysed the organisational structure of theme trails. With some 70 such trails in Austria, often located in economically weak rural areas, the chapter examined the qualities of and difficulties encountered in partnership relations, which were seen often as responsible for the success or failure of a theme trail. This was neatly complemented in Chapter 9 by Michael Hall's focus on rural wine and food tourism cluster and network development in New Zealand. He reinforced the argument that the establishment of communicative relationships between partners is fundamental to such network development. For rural regions, he suggested that the greatest benefits in the establishment of networks were not to be found within the tourism sector *per se*, but through encouraging the development of intersectoral linkages and networks between firms that had previously seen themselves as having little in common.

Community power in the context of rural tourism was related to processes of globalisation in Chapter 10, in which Heather Mair and colleagues provided a Canadian perspective. They offered a detailed case study of a local community that was determined to take a proactive approach to addressing economic downturn. As such, this community may not have been typical, but was nonetheless able to use its power in employing tourism development in a positive way for its local area.

Chapter 11 particularly focused on the community problems of developing distinctive rural cultural tourism in Jamaica. In this chapter, Donna Chambers pointed to the trade-off between the integration of a minority cultural group within Jamaican society and the reinforcement of that group's distinctiveness in order to sustain identity and economic endeavour. By contrast, Chapter 12 focused on farm tourism cooperation through the development of 'pick-your-own' (PYO) farm establishments and associations in Taiwan. Within a framework emphasising farmers' livelihood strategies, Ming-Huang Lee assessed the policies, institutions and processes involved in the development of agricultural tourism enterprises there, emphasising the important role of PYO associations in shaping policy and influencing financial success.

Part 4 of the volume, 'Quality sustainable business', had a strong UK emphasis. It opened with an evaluation of quality as a key driver in sustainable rural tourism business through integrated quality management (IQM) frameworks (Chapter 13). In this chapter, Ray Youell and Roz Wornell argued that the 'implementation gap' could be bridged, at least in part, by the adoption of IQM principles at both the micro (enterprise and community) and macro (national) levels. They suggested that individual rural tourism businesses were most likely to prosper if located within a destination that has adopted IQM, rather than working in isolation.

Chapter 14, drawing on experience from the English Lake District, examined the environmental management systems available to rural tourism business. In it, David Leslie specifically sought to establish the extent to which rural tourism businesses were addressing their environmental performance. He rather pessimistically concluded that not only were many tourism businesses not addressing their environmental performance, but that many owners/managers revealed little awareness of initiatives available in their area designed to promote such action. Chapter 15, looking to Welsh experience, focused on the relationship between environmental quality kite marks and local tourism business performance with particular reference to the rural beach quality 'Green Coast' award. David Botterill and Cliff Nelson employed this award to explore the actual and perceived, direct and indirect dimensions of environmental quality – business performance relationships and discourses.

Chapter 16 broke the UK monopoly of Part 4 by evaluating the methods for examining and understanding entrepreneurial personality traits in managing rural tourism and sustainable business in Austria. Walter Schiebel indicated that such methods had wide application and held important implications for the training of rural entrepreneurs, particularly for farmers entering the tourism industry.

In Chapter 17, Fiona Williams and Andrew Copus provided an examination of the 'soft' factors relating to business development and rural tourism through the implications of *milieu,* with particular reference to northern Scotland and the Orkney Islands. They argued that 'soft' factors in rural development are difficult to research, and emphasised the need for local and regional development policy-makers to endeavour with greater vigour to account for them as part of a more holistic appraisal of rural areas' capacities and needs. The final chapter in this section, Chapter 18, looked to sustainable rural tourism business practice in Cornwall. Focusing on a local district council, Jon Vernon and colleagues highlighted a number of challenges to the successful implementation of 'sustainable' tourism. These included infrastructural weaknesses, the insufficiency of the availability of environmentally friendly products, limited partnership development, and, turning full circle back to the themes of Chapter 2, policy inconsistencies and shortcomings.

Constraints and Opportunities

Two themes emerge from the preceding chapters. First is the diversity of rural tourism products and environments within which business may be sustained, where such diversification may be seen to be healthy, stimulating and indeed, vital for a dynamic sector. But such diversity also often renders generalisation and the promotion of widely adoptable principles difficult. Further, the influence on development of both endogenous local and exogenous global forces and the balance between them will vary considerably from place to place. Each rural area has its own natural environmental, cultural, economic and social conditions establishing the supports and constraints for development. Secondly, the sector's fragmentation and the intangibility of many of its characteristics represent both its essence and its challenges. They go some way towards explaining its lack of clear presence in the rural development and policy arenas. As such, for potential new rural tourism businesses, they provide both constraints – in, for example, trying to gain a clear picture of market conditions – and opportunities – such as for niche product development. This volume has sought to debate and exemplify these issues.

The economic performance of rural areas often falls short of entrepreneurial expectations, perhaps because of economic structure, infrastructures and/or spatial peripherality. But rural sustainability problems may also be attributed, not necessarily to the intrinsic features of rural areas themselves, but to the ways in which the complex sets of national and global forces influence their development. Market failure may result.

In relation to rural tourism business, market failure can result from any one or all of the issues discussed in this volume: poor economic evaluation of negative externalities, a perpetual lack of necessary business and marketing skills including those of being able to work cooperatively, the diversity, dispersion and fragmentation that make it difficult to define sectors, identify their characteristics and needs, and develop coordinating structures to support development, and the resource inefficiencies and inadequate returns on capital that a sector characterised by a predominance of family-run businesses contends with (see also Clarke, 1999; Hjalager, 1996; McKercher & Robbins, 1998; Roberts & Hall, 2001: 205).

For most rural tourism businesses, and arguably for the conservation of the majority of rural areas, visitor management programmes, which focus visitor activity at a limited number of 'honey-pot' destinations, may be efficient in terms of generating critical mass economies of scale in any one place, and limiting physical impacts outside of the honey-pot areas. However, within such honey-pot destination areas, congestion, overcrowding, littering, erosion and other concentrated physical impacts require imaginative and effective conservation and enhancement programmes (e.g. Osborn & Crake, 2001). For this to be a reality we need to know much more about rural visitors' motives and needs, and about the ways in which these can be addressed and interpreted in a sustainable way. In other words, what does rural visiting mean to both suppliers and consumers, and how much (and what kinds of) change will stakeholders be prepared to accept in pursuit of its development?

In Europe, EU enlargement into Central and Eastern Europe and the Eastern Mediterranean raises and emphasises issues of the changing and varied nature of niche and mass markets, cultural diversity and social construction, marketing and promotion. Both domestic and international demand for recreational use of the countryside continues to increase. Despite inconsistent and incomplete data, an emerging pattern internationally shows that visitors are already the largest contributors to many rural economies, a fact not always palatable to political interests responding to the perceived needs of the farming lobby.

This brief concluding chapter has summarised the foregoing chapters and the key issues surrounding the relationships between rural tourism and recreation development and the sustainability of business responding to rural tourism and recreation markets. The extent to which rural tourism and recreation industries can contribute to the sustainability of integrated rural policy partly depends on the nature of research and the extent to which its findings can inform policy development and support good practice, for example, in areas such as developing market knowledge and awareness, training, and quality benchmarking. Rural tourism researchers need to communicate their work to help understand, inform and evaluate the complexities of policy-making and strategy development (Hall, 2000). Equally, practitioners, whether individually or through collaborative ventures, should not be reticent in approaching the research community for collaboration and support in such tasks as strategy and business development. Only through such synergies and convergences of interest among stakeholders can tourism and recreation business begin to approach sustainability ideals for rural development. At any level, 'sustainability' depends on a convergence of mutual understanding (social capital). It requires management of an environment that embraces people as well as landscapes and reflects the needs of both.

References

Bethemont, J. (ed.) (1994) *L'Avenir des Paysages Ruraux Européens*. Lyon: Laboratoire de Géographie Rhodanienne.

Butler, R. (1998) Rural recreation and tourism. In B. Ilbery (ed.) *The Geography of Rural Change* (pp. 211–32). Harlow, UK: Addison Wesley Longman.

Butler, R. and Hall, C. (1998) Conclusion: the sustainability of tourism and recreation in rural areas. In R. Butler, C.M. Hall and J. Jenkins (eds) *Tourism and Recreation in Rural Areas* (pp. 249–58). Chichester and New York: John Wiley & Sons.

Clarke, J. (1999) Marketing structures for farm tourism: beyond the individual provider of rural tourism. *Journal of Sustainable Tourism* 7 (1), 26–47.

Edgell, D.L. (2002) *Best Practice Guidebook for International Tourism Development for Rural Communities*. Provo, UT: Brigham Young University.

ETC/CA (English Tourism Council with the Countryside Agency) (2001) *Working for the Countryside. A Strategy for Rural Tourism in England 2001–2005*. London: English Tourism Council.

Featherstone, M. (1991) *Consumer Culture and Postmodernism*. London: Sage.

Hall, C.M. and Page, S.J. (1999) *The Geography of Tourism and Recreation*. London and New York: Routledge.

Hall, D. (2000) Rural Tourism Management: Sustainable Options conference. *International Journal of Tourism Research* 2, 295–99.

Hjalager, A.-M. (1996) Agricultural diversification into tourism. *Tourism Management* 17, 103–11.

Lane, B. (1994) What is rural tourism? *Journal of Sustainable Tourism* 2, 7–22.

Lane, B. (1999) What is Rural Tourism? Its Role in Sustainable Rural Development. Kongsvinger, Norway: Paper presented at Nordisk Bygdeturism Nätverk Conference.

Macleod, D. (2003) Ecotourism for rural development in the Canary Islands and the Caribbean. In D. Hall, L. Roberts and M. Mitchell (eds) *New Directions in Rural Tourism* (pp. 194–204). Aldershot, UK and Burlington, VT: Ashgate.

McKercher, B. and Robbins, B. (1998) Business development issues affecting nature-based tourism operators in Australia. *Journal of Sustainable Tourism* 6, 173–88.

Mormont, M. (1987) Tourism and rural change. In M. Bouquet and M. Winter (eds) *Who From Their Labours Rest? Conflict and Practice in Rural Tourism* (pp. 35–44). Aldershot, UK: Avebury.

Nylander, M. (2001) National policy for 'rural tourism': the case of Finland. In L. Roberts and D. Hall (2001) *Rural Tourism and Recreation: Principles to Practice* (pp. 77–81). Wallingford, UK: CAB International.

Osborn, D. and Crake, P. (2001) What is the countryside for? A radical review of land use in the UK. In *What is the Countryside For? Paper 1*.

London: The Royal Society of Arts. On WWW at http://www.thersa. org/projects/project_closeup.asp/[what-is-the-countryside-for[1].pdf. Accessed 23.11.03.

Page, S.J. and Getz, D. (1997) *The Business of Rural Tourism: International Perspectives*. London: International Thomson Business Press.

Pine, B. and Gilmore, J. (1998) Welcome to the experience economy. *Harvard Business Review* July–August, 97–105.

Priestley, G.K., Edwards, J.A. and Coccosis, H. (eds) (1996) *Sustainable Tourism? European Experiences*. Wallingford, UK: CAB International.

Roberts, L. and Hall, D. (2001) *Rural Tourism and Recreation: Principles to Practice*. Wallingford, UK: CAB International.

Sharpley, R. (2001) Sustainable rural tourism development: ideal or idyll? In L. Roberts and D. Hall (eds) *Rural Tourism and Recreation: Principles to Practice* (pp. 57–58). Wallingford, UK: CAB International.

Swarbrooke, J. (1999) *Sustainable Tourism Management*. Wallingford, UK: CAB International.

Thomas, M.J. (1996) Consumer market research: does it still have validity? Some postmodern thoughts. *Marketing Intelligence and Planning* 15, 54–59.

Index

Printed in the United Kingdom
by Lightning Source UK Ltd.
128518UK00001B/25-51/A